THE POLITICS OF REPRESENTATION

The POLITICS
of
REPRESENTATION
Continuities in Theory and Research

Heinz Eulau and John C. Wahlke

with

Alan Abramowitz
William Buchanan
LeRoy C. Ferguson
Paul D. Karps
Samuel C. Patterson
Kenneth Prewitt

 SAGE PUBLICATIONS   Beverly Hills   London

For information address:

SAGE PUBLICATIONS, INC.
275 South Beverly Drive
Beverly Hills, California 90212

SAGE PUBLICATIONS LTD
28 Banner Street
London EC1Y 8QE

Printed in the United States of America

CI AUG. 1 4 1979

Library of Congress Cataloging in Publication Data

Eulau, Heinz, 1915-
    The politics of representation.

    Bibliography: p. 291
    Includes index.
    1. Legislative bodies—Addresses, essays, lectures. 2. Representative government and representation—Addresses, essays, lectures. I. Wahlke, John C., joint author. II. Title.
JF511.E9   328′.07′2   78-17128
ISBN 0-8039-1013-4
ISBN 0-8039-1014-2 pbk.

FIRST PRINTING

PAIS
Core

CONTENTS

To

Warren E. Miller

*Architect of the Inter-University Consortium
for Political and Social Research*

ACKNOWLEDGMENTS

Chapter 1, "The Problem of a Legislative Model," is excerpted from "The Theory of Legislatures: A Summary of Working Papers and Reflections from the State Legislative Research Project," presented to the Committee on Political Behavior, Social Science Research Council, 1958, pp. 8-16.

Chapter 2, "Changing Views of Representation," is reprinted, with permission of the publisher, from Ithiel de Sola Pool, ed., *Contemporary Political Science: Toward Empirical Theory* (New York: McGraw-Hill, 1967), pp. 53-85.

Chapter 3, "The Puzzle of Representation: Specifying Components of Responsiveness," is coauthored by Paul D. Karps and reprinted, with permission of the publisher, from *Legislative Studies Quarterly* 2 (August 1977): 233-254.

Chapter 4, "Policy Demands and System Support: the Role of the Represented," is reprinted, with permission of the publisher, from *British Journal of Political Science* 1 (1971): 271-290.

Chapter 5, "Polarity in Representational Federalism: A Neglected Theme of Political Theory," is reprinted, with permission of the publisher, from *Publius: The Journal of Federalism* 3 (Fall 1973): 153-172.

Chapter 6, "The Role of the Representative: Some Empirical Observations on the Theory of Edmund Burke," is coauthored by William Buchanan and LeRoy C. Ferguson and reprinted, with permission of the publisher, from *American Political Science Review* 53 (September 1959): 742-756.

Chapter 7, "Political Matrix and Political Representation: Prolegomenon to a New Departure from an Old Problem" is coauthored by Kenneth Prewitt and reprinted, with permission of the publisher, from *American Political Science Review* 63 (June 1969): 427-441.

Chapter 8, "Policy Determinants and Legislative Decisions," is reprinted from S. Sidney Ulmer, ed., *Political Decision-Making* (© 1970 by Litton Educational Publishing, Inc.), pp. 76-120. Reprinted by permission of Van Nostrand Reinhold Company.

Chapter 9, "Policy-Making in American Cities: Comparisons in a Quasi-longitudinal, Quasi-experimental Design," is reprinted, with permission of the publisher, from J.A. Laponce and Paul Smoker, eds., *Experimentation and Simulation in Political Science* (Toronto: University of Toronto Press, 1972), pp. 59-93.

Chapter 10, "Policy Representation as an Emergent: Toward a Situational Analysis," is coauthored by Paul D. Karps and excerpted from a paper presented at the American Political Science Association's annual meeting in Washington, D.C., September 1977.

Chapter 11, "Contemporary Perspectives on Legislatures," is reprinted from Samuel C. Patterson, Ronald D. Hedlund and G. Robert Boynton, *Representatives and Represented: Bases of Public Support for the American Legislatures* (copyright © 1975 by John Wiley and Sons, Inc.), pp. 1-20. Reprinted by permission of John Wiley and Sons, Inc.

Chapter 12, "Recent Research on Congress in a Democratic Perspective," is coauthored by Alan Abramowitz and reprinted, with permission of the publisher, from *The Political Science Reviewer* 2 (Fall 1972): 1-38.

Chapter 13, "Trends and Prospects in Legislative Behavior Research," is coauthored by Samuel C. Patterson and reprinted, with permission of the publisher, from Samuel C. Patterson and John C. Wahlke, eds., *Comparative Legislative Behavior: Frontiers of Research* (New York: Wiley-Interscience, 1972), pp. 289-303.

PREFACE

This volume is only partial evidence of a collaboration begun in 1955 when, to-gether, with William Buchanan and LeRoy Ferguson, we were associated in the State Legislative Research Project, a cooperative study of legislative behavior and institutions in four American states conducted under the auspices of the Social Science Research Council's Committee on Political Behavior. The origin, structure and purpose of the project have been described elsewhere (see Wahlke et al., 1961), as has its quest for genuine comparative analysis (see Eulau, 1962). The Project's major publication, *The Legislative System: Explorations in Legislative Behavior* (Wahlke et al., 1962) has had, we can modestly claim, some influence on the development and shape of comparative legislative research in the United States and abroad. We were also federated in editing the first comprehensive collection of modern legislative studies (see Wahlke and Eulau, 1959), an exercise that permitted us to take a long look at the field of legislative behavior, processes and institutions as a whole.

Although our direct collaboration ceased with the completion of SLRP, the common experience we had during the project's seven-year existence left its mark on our thinking and approach. This should be quite evident in the chapters of this book. Although independently authored, or in some cases coauthored with new collaborators, a coherent theme runs through all the chapters: legislative research is necessarily collaborative because it must be comparative.

We are fortunate to have found, in the years since publication of *The Legislative System*, colleagues who introduced us to new ideas and helped us to develop our own ideas in fresh ways. At Stanford University, the City Council Research Project under the joint direction of Eulau and Kenneth Prewitt (1973), made possible by grants from the National Science Foundation, was a direct descendant of SLRP (see Eulau, 1971) but underwent critical changes in design and analysis as a result of new enthusiasms brought into the project by Gordon Black, Thomas E. Cronin, Robert Eyestone, Katherine A. Hinckley, Ronald O. Loveridge, Peter Lupsha, Kenneth Prewitt, Betty H. Zisk, and others. At a later time, Alan Abramowitz and Paul D. Karps, both coauthors of chapters in this volume, joined the Stanford menage. At the University of Iowa, Wahlke has the good fortune of being associated with the Comparative Legislative Research Center and its active cadre of legislative scholars including Joel D. Barkan, G. Robert Boynton, Chong Lim Kim, Gerhard Loewenberg, Samuel C. Patterson and others. We are indebted to all of these colleagues for making our work possible.

January 1, 1978   *Heinz Eulau*
                                                                John C. Wahlke

INTRODUCTION
The Best Is Yet. . . .

Legislative research is eminently collaborative because it must be comparative. The centrality of collaborative effort in the study of legislatures is critical in the specification of the data needed for comparative analysis and their collection. We can best warrant this centrality by reference to *The Legislative System,* the product of a relatively inexpensive cooperative effort undertaken by four individual scholars from different universities. The design of that study called for interviews with interactive, institutional elites in four American state legislatures and comparison of their responses concerning attitudes, perceptions, role orientations and behavior across institutional settings. This design could be readily and cheaply applied to other legislatures at any level of government—national, state, local—and was so applied in numerous studies following SLRP's inception in 1955. In fact, even prior to publication of *The Legislative System* in 1962, some individual scholars had come to adopt the strategy of studying a single assembly at a time, often striving for genuine and systematic comparison by replicating or revising and extending the questionnaire items developed in the four-state study. As a result of the research strategy developed in SLRP, then, there was a flowering of primary legislative research in the sixties and seventies as younger scholars, paper and pencil in hand, descended on legislative bodies both domestic and foreign.

The "invisible college" of legislative researchers thus is a distinctly *producer* community: getting one's own data by doing field research and observing legislative bodies in action is the mark of the well-trained legislative scholar. As a producer community the legislative researchers are highly cooperative: the early exchange of research designs, questionnaire items, working papers and field experiences is commonplace. Although theoretical orientations may differ a great deal, the "institution-as-universe" design remains the basic approach in original legislative studies, even those which involve more than one legislature or as many as the eighty-two city councils reported on in *Labyrinths of Democracy* (Eulau and Prewitt, 1973).

Given the collaborative and producer-oriented nature of the legislative research community, it should not surprise that we have learned a great deal from those who, through the years, followed up on some of the leads that we had suggested in prior work. But we must also note that our work was partial and preliminary, limited partly by the state of the legislative field at the time, partly by the then available research technology and partly by the decision not to explore everything worthy of exploration. Although more careful and detailed appraisal of research in the wake of *The Legislative System* is to be undertaken on another occasion, we should allude here to two matters which, it seems to us, require much more thoughtful attention than they have been given. One of these pertains to the assumptions underlying, and to certain operational aspects of, what is called "role analysis"; the other pertains to the meaning and use of the word "represent."

One of the criticisms made of role analysis as practiced in *The Legislative System* is that the "roles" or "role orientations" elaborated there do not predict "behavior." Meant by behavior is usually the legislator's vote on roll calls, as if he or she did not *do* anything else in the course of *acting* as a legislator. A number of things should be said in this connection. First, we have never assumed that role definitions in response to interview questions would yield anything more than definitions; and definitons certainly do not predict behavior (granting, for the moment, that "prediction," especially in the sense of forecasting historical events, is the iron test of a concept's scientific viability, something we do not believe). What we may assume is that legislators' own definitions of various legislative roles are acceptable as surrogate indicators of what one might find, somewhat less than distally, if one had the resources for a full-fledged inquiry into legislative roles. An empirically fully constructed role requires evidence not simply of self's own definition of a role but of self's expectations concerning other's definition of self's role as well as self's expectations of other's role in a particular interpersonal relationship. If all this necessary evidence were available, it would be possible to construct a role as a culturally and normatively defined specification of the relationship that it presumably expresses and that, all other things being equal, might serve as at least one predictor of behavior. It is clear that legislative research has not even come close to such operational closure. It is altogether inappropriate, therefore, to impose on legislators' own definitions of a role or on their role orientations a predictive burden that the relevant role concepts cannot possibly carry and are not meant to carry.

But, second, even if one had all of the information needed to construct a person's role in a particular interpersonal situation properly, it would still be inappropriate to use the construct as a variable to predict all kinds of behavior. A role concept can only be used to estimate probabilities of behavior germane to the particular relationship, that is, the person's actings and doings that are in performance of a given role and that derive their meaning and significance from the relationship expressed in the roles of player and counterplayer. This is so because there is no *social* behavior that is not enmeshed in role relationships and that is not dependent for interpretation on the role conceptions that self and other bring into the interpersonal situation. If everything that one would want to know about social or political behavior were known—how persons actually behave and what expectations they entertain about their own roles and the roles of others—the resultant knowledge would be tautological. Role analysis in its fullest sense is a means of interpreting the meanings that people give to their behavior; it can be "predictive" of behavior only in a cultural sense (because there are rewards for conducting oneself as expected and sanctions for misconduct) but not in a scientific sense.

The error of positing a mistaken premise about the predictive power of role analysis, especially if truncated as it is in most research, is confounded when the behavior in question is as limited in options as roll call voting necessarily is. This is our third point: no generic role construct, whether derived from ideally full evidence or from surrogate information, can possibly predict whether a legislator will say "yea" or "nay" (or abstain from either) in a particular choice situation whose prior complexities are, at this critical juncture, not accessible to observation. This is of course precisely the reason why, in *The Legislative System,* we made no effort to relate legislators' role conceptions to their roll call votes (which we could have easily obtained). We did not do so because *we had no theoretical reason or justification* for doing so! The argument or discovery that role orientations articulated by legislators in response to interview questions are poor predictors of roll call voting on public issues is a case of misplaced concreteness.

It is relatively easy to say what role analysis is not, what it cannot do and should not be expected to do, or what the authors of *The Legislative System* did not intend to do in explicating legislators' role orientations; it is more difficult to say just what they envisaged. Actually, when stripped of pretensions, their objective was very simple: they wanted to find out how a legislature functions. It seemed, at the time, that one way of finding out was to discover how legislators see themselves and others as participants in a "system" whose boundaries are clearly wider than the legislative institution as such. The research was "exploratory," as the book's subtitle indicates; it means that the authors were not covering the whole terrain but were exploring some parts of it that either seemed theoretically interesting to them or simply opened themselves up to exploration as they designed the study and prepared the research instruments. The primary task was one of description and, by way of comparison, of generalization. The notion that discovering roles might be a first and convenient way of proceeding recommended itself because it seemed to permit, by specifying those significant others—constituents, lobbyists, party leaders and so on—with whom legislators interact, a determination of the "legislative system's" boundaries and a formulation of relevant interview questions. It was assumed that if role orientations "hang together" (i.e., correlate) in a theoretically plausible way, the resultant matrix could be accepted as a surrogate construction of the legislature and its interpersonal context.

Our purpose here is not to justify or defend what we did in *The Legislative System* but to clarify. Readers and users of that work and of the present volume should recognize that role analysis does not, any more than any other mode, exhaust the wide range of concerns that make research on legislative behavior and politics, and the further development of relevant theorizing about them, an ever-continuing enterprise. We should make it clear that we did not then, or since, presume otherwise. By the same token, we should disclaim reponsibility for intentions or formulations attributed to us but not of our own making.

TO BE (PRESENT) AND NOT TO BE

Of the role orientations explicated in *The Legislative System* two sets had more impact in legislative study than any others—the set called "representational roles" and the complementary set called "areal roles." The original report in which we presented a reformulation of the Burkean theory of representation and our empirical findings is reproduced in this volume (Chapter 6). There have been innumerable replications, revisions, extensions, uses and criticisms of the typology—trustee, politico, delegate. In fact, so prominent and popular has this typology been that it sometimes seems as if it were either the only set of role orientations that matters or the only significant set of the SLRP study as a whole. Needless to say, we do not share this view. But it does reveal the enormous interest in representation as a crucial property of all political systems. It is therefore all the more necessary to guard against mistaken interpretations of the representational role typology and of what it seeks to capture in political reality.

Unfortunately, mistaken interpretations are rampant. This is evidently due to the fact that there are several major descriptive and normative theories which, if not clearly distinguished, make for ambiguity and confusion. What is surprising, however, is that ambiguity and confusion are treated rather intolerantly despite the publication, now some ten years ago, of Hanna Pitkin's great work, *The Concept of Representation* (1967). One might expect empirical researchers to pay the closest attention to this important book and what it has to teach. What one finds, instead, are ritualistic citations and out-of-context quotations that suit the investigator's bias, with the major drift of Pitkin's arguments ignored. As Pitkin made clear, "representation" is not the name of an empirically stable entity but a construct used by different users in different ways. The criterion for evaluating any given use of it, therefore, is not whether it matches some (nonexistent) clear meaning, but whether it is clearly defined and consistently employed in each case:

> [R]epresentation, taken generally, means the making present *in some sense* of something which is nevertheless *not* present literally or in fact. Now, to say that something is simultaneously both present and not present is to utter a paradox, and thus a fundamental dualism is built into the meaning of representation (Pitkin, 1967: 8-9).

Misunderstanding of "representation" in general inevitably leads to misunderstanding of the representational role typology derived from Burke. One example must suffice. The notion circulates that, counter to assumption, the delegate is "more representative" of his district's views or demands or interests than is the trustee. When research finds that trustees are more aware of, concerned with or responsive to the views, demands, needs or interests of constituents than delegates are, the finding is thought to be anomalous, and the typology is judged to be theoretically useless and normatively inappropriate. Alas, there are several false premises in this conclusion.

First, the representational role typology makes no assumptions whatever about degree of representation, and it certainly makes no assumption to the effect that a delegate is necessarily "more representative" of his district than is a trustee. This is precisely the reason why we introduced the notion of "focus of representation" as conceptually and possibly empirically distinct from "style of representation." The delegate is prepared to take instructions, the trustee is not; and style of representation is mute on the question from whom a delegate receives instructions. A trustee may be highly "district-oriented," while a delegate need not be because he may seek and receive instructions from clients other than his local constituents. The representational typology specifies the legislator's stance and style as he relates himself to the job of being a representative, not to the focus of his attention or activity. The assumption that delegates are "more representative" than are trustees was not made by the authors of *The Legislative System* but is the invention of those who find it flawed.

Second, one may ask how such misunderstanding comes about. It stems, we believe, from the mistaken notion that "representation" and "representativeness" are interchangeable concepts. Representativeness presumably refers to a correspondence between characteristics of representative and represented. The most naive version of this view has it that if only representatives were facsimiles of their constituents' demographic characteristics (age, sex, race, residence and so on), they would be "more representative" than if they possessed noncorresponding traits. It is further assumed, by implication, that those who look alike also think alike and that, therefore, maximal representativeness assures maximal representation. A more creditable version of the correspondence theory has it that if policy attitudes or views of representatives are similar to those of their constituents, representation can be said to occur. This conception has had much sway in recent years and is referred to as "issue congruence" (Miller and Stokes, 1963) or "policy concurrence" (Verba and Nie, 1975). We are dealing critically with this view, and especially with its vulgarization, elsewhere in this volume. But adoption of this conception explains how it comes about that when trustees are found to be more in agreement with the policy views of their areal constituents as measured by some criterion of central tendency, they are also "found" to be "more representative" than delegates are.

This curious logic is clearly an artifact of a false integration of the representational role typology, thoroughly misunderstood, with a simplified version of the policy congruence or concurrence model of representation. But, as we mentioned, the representational typology in no way posits the trustee to be any more or less "in tune" with his electoral constituents than the delegate. On the contrary, if the representational typology were porperly interpreted in this connection, one would expect the delegate to be indeed "less representative" of his areal constituency's modal views on matters of public policy precisely because his style makes him available for instructions from all kinds of clienteles, including special interests or political segments in his district. By way of contrast, the trustee, seeking freedom of choice and trying to resist pressures, should be in a much better position than the delegate to take a broad view of his district's interests and needs. The findings, therefore, that trustees are "more representative" of their district's views than are delegates are not counter to any assumptions made about the representational role typology. The typology is altogether mute on the sources of the representative's cues in legislating or other dealings.

Finally, most of these arguments and counterarguments are not really to the point, which, it seems to us, revolves around the meaning of representation not as it may be found in the books, but as it can be constructed from observations in the present-day real world in which those called representatives go about their business of representing. In an age in which there is a premium on participation on the part of the represented, in spite of the many difficulties in the way of such participation (treated especially in Chapters 4 and 8), there is much to be said for Pitkin's (1967: 221-222) notion that representation "is primarily a public, institutionalized arrangement involving many people and groups, and operating in the complex ways of large-scale social arrangements. What makes it representation is not any single action by any one participant, but the overall structure and functioning of the system, the patterns emerging from the multiple activities of many people." Pitkin's influence on our own work is most evident in Chapters 7 and 10, but that research on legislatures as representative institutions responsive to the needs and interests of people must bridge the gap between individual-level and macrolevel construction is evident throughout.

We close this volume with three chapters that, as we were forced to do twenty years ago, take a long look at what has been recently accomplished in legislative research and what is still promises. And these lines from Robert Browning's "Rabbi Ben Ezra" strike us as especially appropriate on this occasion:

> Grow old along with me!
> The best is yet to be,
> The last of life, for which the first was made.

PART I.
Theory

INTRODUCTORY NOTE

A sense of intellectual excitement accompanied the emergence of contemporary legislative research. The best evidence and testimony are not the publications of the period, circa 1955, but the informal working memoranda that circulated among the very few scholars who gradually came to constitute the first "invisible college" of legislative researchers. From among these memoranda, Wahlke's "The Problem of a Legislative Model" (Chapter 1) has not lost its glow. A summary of the working papers and reflections from the State Legislative Research Project, it is a document of the times that was intended to be a document for the future. As one reflects on it twenty years later, what impresses is the rudimentary state of theorizing in the legislative field but also in political science more generally. Given the rudimentary state of theory, Wahlke and his associates evidently returned to fundamentals—not the image of the legislator as a rational actor, so postulated in theories of substantive and methodological individualism, or as a creature of habits or drives, so proposed in "conservative" theories from Burke to Jung, but as a person who responds to an interpersonal situation that is defined in terms of cognitive orientations to action. Thus anticipating the revival of the phenomenological viewpoint, on the one hand, and the course of cognitive psychology, on the other hand, Wahlke's essay remains a characteristic expression of the "new" behavioralist's search for viable assumptions about "human nature" that could serve his research interests as a *political* scientist and not as a political *psychologist* or political *sociologist*.

This is not to say that the developing theory of legislative role behavior and of the legislature as a structure of roles is particularly elegant. But it is economical. By concentrating on legislators' self-definitions of the roles they might take in response to their perceptions of interpersonal situations, the model of the legislative system as a network of role relationships is able to bridge the gap, at least in theorizing, between individual behavior and the resultant informal interpersonal patterns that, along with formal arrangements, constitute the legislature as an institution. It would be desirable, of course, to have empirical evidence of the legislative role definitions held by significant counterplayers in the legislative relation-

ship, such as constituents, party functionaries or lobbyists, or to have direct observations of actual legislative conduct, but the resouces needed for this more ambitious research objective, much thought and talked about, are most often unavail-
able. But it is noteworthy that Wahlke's essay anticipates the "cue-taking model"
of the legislative actor formulated more fully much later by Matthews and Stimson
(1975) in their study of "normal decision-making" in the U.S. House of Representatives—one of the few congressional studies concerned with the generic properties of legislative behavior. Indeed, as one compares Wahlke's essay as an effort
in theory construction with most later efforts, one will recognize both its originality
and its unfulfilled promises.

The intellectual effervescence in the study of legislative behavior and institution,
so pronounded in the fifties, gradually abated. Not that a decade later one could
speak of intellectual disenchantment. The period from, roughly, 1955 to 1966 was
one of extraordinary expansion in research in the legislative field. But, paradoxically, the more the new generation of scholars learned, by way of empirical inquiry, about the dynamics of legislative behavior and the functioning of legislative processes, the less happy they came to be with the theoretical underpinnings
of their work. In retrospect, it seems, Wahlke underestimates the difficulty of
integrating the behavioral approaches in empirical research with those segments
of inherited political theory that are most germane to legislative study. For instance, although some investigators sought to link their work to one or another
tradition in theorizing about representation, the (long-prevailing) gap between
political theory and political research remains a professional malaise. Taking a
long look in the middle sixties at what had been accomplished by way of theoretical
development of the study of legislatures as representational institutions, Eulau in
"Changing Views of Representation" (Chapter 2) concludes that, insofar as empirical research had shown anything, it was that "we have come to know what
representation is not." No viable theory of representation had come out of "these
years of travail." Common conceptions of representation, he asserts, "are obsolete.
We have representative institutions, but like the Greeks we do not know what they
are about."

This despondent view, at the very time when empirical research seemed to be
flowering, was rooted in a number of theoretical dilemmas that, by the middle
sixties, had forced themselves on scholarly attention. Some of these dilemmas are
summarized and assessed, in a fresh perspective made possible by yet another
decade of development, in Eulau and Karps' "The Puzzle of Representation:
Specifying Components of Responsiveness" (Chapter 3). As they try to make clear,
whether conducted in the tradition of the model proposed by Wahlke and associates (1962) or of the model employed by Miller and Stokes (1963), most research accepted the normative assumption that, in a representative democracy,
the relationship between representative and represented should be only a one-way
street, with influence flowing from the represented to the representative. It is this
view that Eulau challenged in "Changing Views" when he suggests that research
should proceed from the structural assumption of a built-in status difference
between representative and represented, and when he argues that representational

theory must therefore deal with the tensions arising out of status differentiation rather than ignore or deny their existence.

Interestingly but not surprisingly, Wahlke comes to a similar conclusion about the representational relationship but with different implications for research in "Policy Demands and System Support: The Role of the Represented" (Chapter 4). He also has difficulty with the normative assumptions traditionally made by democratic theorists about citizen behavior. On the most careful examination of the role of the represented in the representional relationship, he finds that empirical evidence does not justify treating citizens as significant sources of policy views that are somehow directly "represented" in the policy-making process. Citizens simply lack the necessary information for effective policy choices to be communicated to their representatives, even if they were to make the effort to communicate. This being the case, Wahlke concludes that the "simple demand-input model" of representation is not sufficient to explain policy-making in a representative democracy. He therefore suggests that a "support-input model" might be more appropriate—a suggestion which he exposes to empirical testing in "Policy Determinants and Legislative Decisions" (Chapter 8).

It is clear, in retrospect, that in the middle sixties legislative researchers were practicing normal science. The accent in normal science is on replication, refinement, revision and extension of dominant models. If Eulau and Wahlke, at the time working separately, sensed the anomalies created for theory by the empirical findings, their immersion in research did not permit the broad perspective that a political philosopher would bring to the situation. As Eulau and Karps acknowledge, it is impossible to write about the transition in thinking about representation without giving the closest attention to Pitkin's (1967) masterly analysis of the concept of representation. One of the few contemporary political theorists to take some cognizance of empirical work, Pitkin had significant influence on both empirical theorizing and research in the decade following publication of her book. On the side of research, her suggestion, that representation is not just an interpersonal relationship but can and perhaps must be treated as a systemic property of the political order that may or may not emerge at the level of the collectivity, had an almost immediate and profound effect on the work of Prewitt and Eulau (1969; see Chapter 7) but also of others. More problematic remains her definition of political representation as "acting in the interest of the represented in a manner responsive to them" (1967: 209). For, as Eulau and Karps point out in their critique of responsiveness as "congruence" or "concurrence," the concept can refer to several aspects of the representational relationship which may or may not emerge at the same time—a condition that makes evaluation of effective legislative representation hazardous at any one point in time.

The conception of representation as an emergent property of the political system would seen to be particularly applicable to the functioning of federal arrangements in a representative democracy. Eulau, in "Polarity in Representational Federalism: A Neglected Theme of Political Theory" (Chapter 5), suggests that the American constitution-makers were eminently sensitive to the consequences of federalism for representative government and that, indeed, the synthesis of representational and federalistic structures in the American system is one of the great political inventions in the modern era. Yet, he notes, because of the long-held dualistic conception of the country's federal constitution, representation has been empirically studied only at one or another level of the federal system—national, state or local—but not in terms of a set of linkages among the levels. As a result, neither the fungibility nor the plasticity of representation in a federal system, and the implications of these system properties for the emergence of representation at one or another level, have been properly treated in a theoretical perspective. He suggests a research design for the study of legislative representation in a federalistic theoretical perspective that might come to grips with some of the very difficult operational aspects of relevant investigations.

Chapter 1

THE PROBLEM OF A
LEGISLATIVE MODEL

JOHN C. WAHLKE

If there were a satisfactory general theory of politics, it would include hypotheses about the determinants of legislators' and other political actors' behavior. One difficulty with most available theories of political behavior—individualistic, group, class, and other theories—is their too-great generality: we are interested primarily in the peculiar and unique contributions of legislative actions to the process of governance. But the available theories usually discuss supposedly universal determinants of behavior which affect legislators and other actors alike. Each of these theories would require considerable modification and extension before it could help answer the kinds of questions we think legislative research should answer, questions which concern the functioning of a political system. This is not to say that we may not find significant hypotheses and major propositions in any or all of these theories, but that, on purely logical grounds, we can expect any of them to be inadequate for our purposes.

RATIONALITY, PERCEPTION AND BEHAVIOR:
THE QUESTION OF A MODEL POLITICAL MAN

Any conception of a legislature pictures it to begin with as a collection of individuals engaging in various actions. No theory or explanation of why a legislature does what it does, therefore, can altogether dispense with a conception of why individuals do what they do. Some theory or model of individual behavior must underlie every model or theory of legislative behavior.

In the ideal-type scientific situation, the behaviorist political scientist would have merely to adopt the substantially validated theory of psychologists concerning human behavior and apply it to his political curiosities. Unfortunately there is not a substantiated theory of behavior; there are fragments of theory, bound up in two loose bundles known respectively as "individual" and "social psychology," not to mention the fact of competing theories within these bundles. Nevertheless, there are certain basic concepts and broad base-line propositions reasonably wide-spread throughout all the fragments and competing theories of psychology and sociology which can be used in constructing a crude but serviceable model of the political actor as a human being.

Perhaps the weakest point of political theories to date has been their frequent acceptance of an unserviceable model of the political actor which has been called the *rational-man model.* The coldly calculating Benthamite robot, painstakingly guiding each physical jerk by the mental arithmetic of pain and pleasure has been sufficiently belabored to dismiss him from discussion summarily. But it should be recognized that the political actors of Plato, Aquinas, Aristotle and other long-dead theorists, as well as the actors of Rousseau and many later theorists are basically as rationalistic as that of Bentham and other disciples of Hobbes. In every case mentioned, the political actor is pictured as a man who somehow or other (writers disagree on how) is apprised of an end and takes action as a means to that end. Even though there may be the utmost disagreement about proper ends for actors to pursue, there is remarkably little disagreement that action will be moti-vated by pursuit of the perceived end. Whether the action will in fact produce the desired result is irrelevant to this discussion; the important thing is that action is seen as motivated by the perception of ends and the selection of means (actions) to attain them.

The model of Hume and Burke, which envisions a man engaging in many ac-tions through sheer force of habit, without rational consideration of the ends-means relationship, is in many respects more realistic; but the psychological-theory details of the mechanism of habit is so incomplete as to require considerable supple-menting for any analytical use. Besides, for certain crucial purposes, the rational man was allowed to maintain his sway even in these conservative theories.

Following the suggestive remarks of Wallas and Merriam, some theorists, notably those of the school of Harold Lasswell, sought consciously to adapt the *psychoanalytical* model first made familiar by Freud. More common, if less sub-stantial in the long run, are adaptations of the notions of Jung and other non-Freudians which often resembled or amounted to substantially the same thing as the ancient rational-man model, with something called "power" postulated as an end consciously pursued by political actors.

The models previously mentioned concern themselves primarily with the *motivational* aspects of the individuals' actions, and constitute, in fact, so many competing theories of individual motivation. A more useful focus would seem to be what might be called the *perceptual* aspects. The guiding ideas of such an ap-proach are essentially those suggested by George Herbert Mead and utilized for political analysis first and most notably by Walter Lippmann. Borrowing from the rationalistic conception, we picture any actor acting politically only in a certain *situation,* which, from the actor's standpoint, is an objective set of things and persons influenced by his actions and acting with effects on him. Borrowing from the phenomenological viewpoint in psychology, and explicitly modifying the rationalistic conception, we postulate that the actor's view of this situation is a construct and not an exact picture or replica of the "real" situation. Whether we have in mind the actor's view of something called the total situation or his view of some "object" constituting a component part of this situation, his perception presents two distinct aspects—a cognitive aspect, which has to do with his recognition of the object, person, or situation, and an affective aspect, which has to do with his emotional posture or preferences toward it. Without pursuing further the psychological theory of the interaction between these two aspects, it can be stated that we accept as one of our base-line propositions that what the situation "is" for any actor is his perceptions comprising these elements. Where the situation is one involving a number of actors (as any political situation is, by definition), it must be assumed that however similar they may be in some respects, the various actors' perceptions of the situation differ in many other respects. But the more important theoretical assumption is that action will always be related to these perceptions, and not to what is sometimes thought of as the "real" or "objective" situation. (It should be obvious, of course, that this "real" or "objective" situation is nothing more than a perception by the theorist or commentator ascribing objectivity to it.)

Perception thus becomes (at least for purposes of political analysis) an intervening variable between motivation in the general sense (instinct, drive, purpose) and action. The significant feature of such a concept (again for purposes of political analysis) is that it spans all the models of the individual actor previously described. Whether he is motivated by rational pursuit of an end, subconscious, sublimated, displaced, or projected drives and instincts, or otherwise, insofar as his actions impinge on other persons or objects in a situation, these actions will be in some discoverable relationship to the actor's perception of the objects, persons, and events making up the situation for him. By fastening upon the intervening variable of perception, the political scientist is able to avoid needless commitment to a particular psychological school—"needless" being any commitment which limits his range of choice more narrowly still than his original philosophical and behavioral assumptions. Such generality and freedom of choice is justified by the fact that the aim of legislative research is not to explain the idiosyncratic behavior of any individual legislator or to contribute directly to theories of individual behavior in general. It is rather to explain the constellations of individual actions which constitute legislative behavior and to explain their relation to the political system. Our legislative researcher is assumed to be a political scientist, not a psychologist or sociologist, however much he can profit by intellectual collaboration with sociologists and psychologists.

THE CONCEPT OF ROLE

An important corollary of the perceptual outlook leads us, at last, to a notion which can serve us better than any other as an organizing concept. This corollary asserts that an important part of the perceptual apparatus of any actor is his perception of himself, his *self-concept,* which comprises the same cognitive and affective aspects as any other perception. To a large degree, the person sees himself not as a mere isolated and unique "thing" in a universe of unique things, but as standing in certain relationships to other things and persons. The word which refers to his perceptions of his relationships to the things and persons in the universe around him is "*role.*" A person in any situation perceives not merely himself and an "objective" situation; he perceives himself in a series of roles, which he defines to himself in terms of actions and attitudes toward other persons and things. To put it another way, the situation "is," to any actor, largely the roles he thinks himself and others do or should play.

The concept of role is a concept relating to social rather than individual psychology. It refers not to the actions, even regular and uniform actions, of a single individual but to the actions of an individual with reference to others. It refers, that is, to *relationships* among people. It is a normative concept in that it refers not to unique, particular actions of individuals but to uniformities and regularities of an individual's actions (behavior) over time. It is a normative concept also in that it refers to expected and preferred actions, to imperatives of behavior, as well as to description of observed statistical regularities.[1]

The behavior of any individual—A, B, C, . . . or N—comprises a finite but almost infinite sum of actions—a, b, c . . . n. A social (interpersonal) situation consists of acting individuals, which we can represent (taking the simple case of two persons) as follows:

$$A(a, b, c, \ldots n) : B(d, e, f, \ldots o)$$

The concept of role predicates that significant actions of an individual in such a situation will be "cued" by the observed actions of other individuals. Thus, whenever A sees B, he may engage in actions b, c, e, g (along with many other actions occurring uniquely at the time of each encounter). If these four actions always accompany A's sight of B, we can suspect we are dealing with a role of A. Likewise, if B, upon seeing A do actions b, c, e, g, always responds with actions h, l, m, q, we can be pretty sure we are dealing with a role of B. Putting the two together, we have a role-relationship between A and B:

$$A(b, c, e, g)—R—B(h, l, m, q)$$

Two facets of this relationship deserve special notice. First, from the fact that certain cues always produce certain actions by each individual, we can postulate that there is some notion of propriety or legitimacy surrounding the perceptions of each actor by the other. However unconsciously or subconsciously, A can be presumed to feel that he *ought* to do actions b, c, e, g, under certain circumstances, just as B can be presumed to feel obligated in some fashion to actions h, l, m, q. Second, we can postulate further that each has certain expectations with respect to the actions of the other. In the simplest case, A can perform actions b, c, e, g, *expecting* B to respond with actions h, l, m, q, or *vice versa.* It follows that the role relationship comprises not only the manifest actions and not only the perceptions or feelings of legitimacy concerning those actions on the part of each actor for himself, but also the expectations of each toward the other.

There arise from this conception of the role-relationship three possible situations which differ from the generic role-relationship previously described. In two of them, a given actor has conflicting notions of the actions appropriate for him in a given situation (i.e., in response to given cues). He may be uncertain about the responses appropriate for him to a clear and unambiguous cue, by virtue of entertaining two (or more) conceptions of appropriate actions. Symbolically, he cannot choose between the alternatives represented:

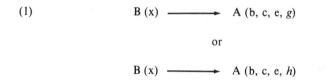

(1)   B (x) ⟶ A (b, c, e, g)

                              or

                       B (x) ⟶ A (b, c, e, h)

Another possibility is that simultaneous cues suggest to A closely related but yet not identical sets of appropriate responses:

(2)   B (x) ⟶ A (b, c, e,g)
                       B (y) ⟶ A (b, c, e, h)

                              but

                       B (x, y) ⟶ A (b, c, e, ?)

                              or

                       B (x) ⟶ A (b, c, e, g)
                       C (y) ⟶ A (b, c, e, h)

                              but

                       B (x)⎫ ⟶ A (b, c, e, ?)
                       C(y) ⎭

In either of these two cases A experiences role-conflict. It makes little difference at this point whether we choose to look upon this as conflict about how one particular role should be played or as conflict about which of two roles he should play in the given situation. Which interpretation should be preferred depends upon the system actually being investigated and its actual, i.e., empirically demonstrable, character. There is no theoretical reason to think that one or the other type of conflict is more important in controlling the behavior of the system.

The third case to be considered is one where there is no role-conflict for any of the actors of the two sorts just described. But its importance for system-analysis is equally great. This is the case where the occupants of a role-relationship have clear but incompatible or at least different conceptions of their respective roles. Divergent conceptions of a given role may be entertained by two persons linked in a given role-relationship or they may be entertained by two persons with respect to a common role they play toward a third person:

(3)

$$\text{It appears to A that B (x)}$$
$$\longrightarrow \text{A } (b, c, e, g)$$
$$\text{It appears to B that B (x)}$$
$$\longrightarrow \text{A } (b, e, e, h)$$

or

$$\text{It appears to A}_1 \text{ that B (x)}$$
$$\longrightarrow \text{A } (b, c, e, g)$$
$$\text{It appears to A}_2 \text{ that B (x)}$$
$$\longrightarrow \text{A } (b, c, e, h)$$

In general it can be postulated that a system can subsist only if there is a minimum occurrence of all three of the above types of role-conflict. Role-theory further postulates (though we need not pursue the matter further here) that there are mechanisms operating in any system to bring all role-concepts (self's concept of self and others' concepts of him, self's concepts of others and others, concepts of themselves) into congruence and to maintain them in congruence. It is sufficient here to point out that explication of any role-system must include all such instances of incongruence found or suspected.

The character of the role-relationship is significant at this point in demonstrating the connection between that behavioral approach which concentrates exclusively on uniformities of observed, concrete behavior (actions) and that which incorporates a perceptual focus. For one thing, if roles are the normative sort of thing we have suggested, we can elicit (by questionnaire, e.g.) from any actor his perceptions of the actions he considers appropriate toward any given person in any given situation. We thus elicit action (verbal responses) of the kind the strict behaviorist demands. For another thing, we now have a logical (theoretical) framework which enables us to establish theoretical relationships, working through perceptions, among two or more observed uniformities. We have also a concept so defined that we can always establish empirically, for any desired case, the correspondence between a role-relationship defined by the perceptions of the role-takers and the same relationship defined by an outside observer. In other words, we can dispense with one troublesome theoretical and methodological problem which has at times plagued behavioral researchers. We can be "loose constructionists" with respect to the types of admissible data for empirical research without sacrificing the empirical rigor demanded by strict behaviorists.

There remains but one more comment concerning the general role-concept. We have so far talked as if role-relationships exist only between particular individuals, as if they were particularized for innumerable face-to-face sets of persons. This restriction is by no means necessary. It is, in fact, undesirable. Social psychologists have long talked about the "generalized other," just as political scientists have long talked about "the public." There is good grounds for assuming that an individual will see certain actions as appropriate for himself in the light of what he perceives as "public" expectations. So long as we can specify the cues which lead A to think it proper for him to undertake actions b, c, e, g, even if there is no particular person B toward whom he sees himself acting, we can define his role-concept exactly as if we were dealing with a two-person, A to B, relationship. No new theoretical problems are raised.

ROLE THEORY AND POLITICAL THEORY

The word "model" has been used during the preceding discussion deliberately to point up the degree of theoretical commitment involved in acceptance of role theory as a guide to legislative research. In taking it for a guide we are doing no more than accepting a model of individual behavior in terms of which we can describe and classify the political behavior of legislators. We acquire, by assuming role theory as a basis, a primitive organizing concept and a limited number of categories for organizing data, but we acquire no hypotheses about relationships among the data. In short, we take on an explicit conceptual framework but not yet a theory. The enormous theoretical power of the concept of role for political analysis stems from the fact that it entails no commitment to or rejection of any existing body of political theory but enables us to incorporate significant contributions from all of them, by interpreting these theories themselves (class, group, etc.) in role terms and thereby relating them to each other.

For example, the concept of role is particularly fruitful for incorporating insights from so-called "group-approaches" to the study of political behavior and institutions. It is compatible with the basic premise of group-based theories: that institutionalized governmental groups (e.g., Congress, the Supreme Court, the Democratic National Committee, etc.) are generically comparable and commensurate with all other groups of persons. It goes beyond this, however, to suggest that what differentiates one from the other type of group is to be found in the role-concepts of the various group-members and the role-concepts of others in their relationships with group-members. A given citizen plays a role as Chamber-of-Commerce member; he plays a role too as member-of-the-political-community. For him, legislative decisions constitute a significant class of cue-giving actions; for him, the legislature is a "generalized other" toward whom he must play roles. Comparison of his role-concepts respecting legislatures with his role-concepts respecting the Chamber of Commerce and of his with others' role-concepts will go far toward explaining for us the character and functions of the political system in society.

An important concept in the literature of groups and institutions is that of "organization." It should by now be fairly obvious how organization-theory can be translated into role-theory terms. Indeed, the very concept of role began with the attempt to describe and explain something called social "*structure.*" Briefly, organization approached in this way becomes an abstracted system of roles which can be described independently of the particular persons playing those roles at any particular time. An organization can be described in terms of the roles which *any* person occupying certain *statuses* empirically found to constitute the organization will play if they assume those statuses. This brings us back to the conception of institutional groups as sets of *offices* which specify roles for all incumbents of those offices.

In short, we can conceive *any* subsystem of the social system as a system of roles. We can describe the principal roles (or statuses, if they are fully abstracted) which make up the subsystem. We can do the same thing for more than one subsystem. We can therefore explore the linkages (through relevant role-relationships) between subsystems. The concept of role is therefore strategically located whether we wish to move from legislative decisions forward towards explaining "end-variables" of political inquiry or move backward towards explaining why a given system of roles exists in some political subsystem or why individuals occupying cetain statuses in that system hold the kinds of role-concepts which produce the role-system we find.

Finally, use of the role concept helps to eliminate some spurious argumentation between "institutionalists" and "behaviorists." The concept of institutions is meaningless if divorced from the behavior of people. The usual way of defining institutions is to call them regularized ways of doing things, which immediately says that institutions are visible only as uniform classes of activity by people. Whatever else they are, institutions are uniformities of behavior. This alone, even without the notion of roles, suggests the futility of dichotomizing behavioral and institutional study into mutually exclusive approaches. This implication is frequently overlooked because many "institutional" studies concentrate upon the functional or what-is-accomplished aspect of the behavioral uniformities called institutions. Use of the role-concept to conceptualize behavior does not require abandoning all concern with functional questions of this sort; on the contrary, we arrived at this organizing concept because we started with just such a concern.

NOTE

1. The conceptual framework which follows is adapted largely from Nadel, 1957.

Chapter 2

CHANGING VIEWS OF REPRESENTATION

HEINZ EULAU

My theme is the invention of institutions, the role that ideas play in their survival, and the obsolescence of political theories. My target is the problem of representation, because, it seems to me, the development of structurally discrete and functionally specific agencies of government was predicated, historically, on the invention or discovery of the technique of representation; and because government, whatever its constitutional form, remains based on representative institutions.

At the outset, let me simply say that our common conceptions of representation are obsolete! Please note that I am not saying that representation is obsolete, but only that our common conceptions of it are. This, at least, is the conclusion I draw from all the studies of representation which in recent years have finally subjected our ordinary notions of representation to the crucial test of empirical validation. Regardless of whether the empirical attack has come from the study of representatives, as in my own work and the work of many others (see Wahlke et al., 1962; Sorauf, 1963), or from the study of the represented, as in the work of that extraordinary team of researchers assembled at Michigan's Survey Research Center (see Miller and Stokes, 1963; Stokes and Miller, 1962; Miller, 1964), we can finally say with some confidence what representation is not. But, in spite of many centuries of theoretical effort, we cannot say what representation is.

This state of affairs in the theory of representation confronts us as a scientific challenge. Thirty years ago, when I was a student, there was much talk about the "crisis" of representation. From today's perspective, I think that those who spoke of crisis mistook their particular conceptions of what representation should be with representation as an institutional requisite of any political system larger than an ideal-type polis. Because representative institutions did not work as preferred models of representation said they should work, the institutions were blamed rather than the models. It is an indication of the profound transformation in our approach to political phenomena that we have overcome the normative fallacy. As propositions derived from normative doctrines of representation have been exposed to empirical scrutiny, their obsolescence has become evident.

If there is a crisis, then, it is a crisis in the theory of representation and not in the institution of representation. I find it enormously interesting that the recent literature on the politics of the developing nations only very rarely uses the concept of representation as an explicitly analytical tool. This does not mean that representation is not a problem in the new nations; on the contrary, it is a central problem of nation building. But, apparently, our colleagues in the field of comparative politics do not deal with it in the familiar terms because they do not find our inherited formulations of representation particularly germane to the real-world problems with which the new nation builders must deal.[1]

The obsolescence of theories of representation, evident in the crucible of modern empirical research and evident in the crucible of modern nation building, makes my assignment quite tantalizing. For, I had to ask myself in preparing this chapter, can a look at history really help us as practicing political scientists? Can it fruitfully aid us in better explicating the problems with which a modern and as yet unborn theory of representation should concern itself? I am still not sure whether such an exercise can and will have the payoffs that the investment of time and effort would lead one to hope for. For I fear that of all the muses, Clio, the Muse of History, is the most treacherous. I could not proceed without coming to grips with History.

THE USES OF HISTORY

Because any attempt to link modern developments in the study of politics with older forms of theorizing about things political necessarily involves historical reconstruction, it is likely to encounter the danger of misconstruction. In general, sciencing, the activity in which the scientist is engaged, proceeds without being unduly hampered by the history of Science, with a capital S. It is therefore less prone to be victimized by Clio than is the study of the arts and letters. But only scientists altogether barbarian in outlook would be oblivious to or deliberately ignore the historical rootedness of their enterprise. And, precisely because any scientific enterprise has historical roots which, in many ways, define its outlook and commitments, no scientist can ultimately avoid doing battle with History.

The alienation of the study of political theory from the rest of political science, which began at the turn of the present century, is a well-known story (Easton, 1952). And it has become fashionable to deplore it. But the story is more complicated than it appears to be. Indeed, I believe that the separation of the history of political theory from the empirical concerns of political science has not been completely dysfunctional. For as long as the study of political theory involved the regurgitation and exegesis of the classical texts, it could only be an obstacle to scientific development. Galileo's enemy was Aristotle. In freeing himself from the dead hand of Aristotle, Galileo liberated modern physical science (Lewin, 1935). In rejecting many of our inherited political ideas, empirical political science opened up new vistas for scientific inquiry. It could come to deal with problems that historicist and legal-positivist political science had failed to recognize—and these problems were almost everything that was interesting in contemporary politics: modern mass movements, charismatic leadership, popular apathy, problems of nation building and development, the growth of bureaucracy, political bargaining, the articulation of social interests, political pathology, and so on.

But, perhaps, the pendulum has swung too far, and the time has come to assess the reciprocal contribution which traditional political theory can make to empirical political science and which empirical political science can make to political theory. This is not to say that Clio, the Muse, is a faithful leader on the road ahead. Although we sometimes speak of "historical method" as if it were a straightforward and unambiguous guide to understanding, nothing could be further from what in fact is the case. Indeed, it was the mistaken identification of chronological description with history that, for so long, put the study of political theory in the bind it was in. The simple assumption that meticulous attention to historical detail and faithful reconstruction of "exactly what happened and what was said" are sufficient to make history serviceable can no longer be entertained (Ranke, 1877: vii). The analysis of what Aristotle or Hobbes "really meant," or the minute, sequential tracing of particular concepts through time, so widely practiced by the historians of political thought, hardly meets the requirements of empirical political science. Whatever broadly humanistic purposes this method may serve, it fails to tell the scientist just what he most wants to know, namely, what concepts are viable, what theoretical formulations are valid, or what propositions have withstood the test of falsification.

But I also find it impossible to accept the alternative of using history to explain "how things have come to be what they are" (Teggart, 1960). The evolutionary bias implicit in this formulation of the historical method is not the sole reason why I find it unpalatable. Although this approach implies a frank recognition that the historian's look at history is inevitably colored by his contemporary circumstances,[2] it introduces a level of uncertainty into historical writing which empirical science, though itself now accustomed to think in probabilities rather than in certainties, cannot possibly accept with any degree of confidence.

Quite recently, an enterprising political scientist has attempted to make the classics of political theory relevant to our contemporary concerns by juxtaposing some ancients and some moderns, not for the purpose of implying causal relationships or of tracing influences, but for the purpose of noting "significant similarities and differences" (Bluhm, 1965: 14). I find this effort intellectually stimulating for the teacher and student, but I very much doubt its utility for the modern researcher. The problems of the researcher, as he approaches the history of political theories, are somewhat different. If, as researchers, we go to history at all, we must ask of the history of political theory what we are asking of empirical political science. And this is something other than noting similarities or differences between theoretical formulations.

What we are asking of empirical science is that it help us solve problems in the real world. The dilemma we face in empirical research often is, of course, that the real-life problems we wish to solve are not the problems which are theoretically interesting. Therefore, the first task of the scientist invariably is to translate real-life problems—what John Dewey once called "problematic situations"—into scientific problems (Dewey, 1938, in Northrop, 1947: 12-13). Formulations of problematic situations and formulations of scientific problems are not identical. It is well to remember that however much we get immersed in purely scientific problems, some real-life problem or problematic situation lurks in the background of our scientific endeavors. The older political science, inordinately preoccupied with practical problems of governmental reform, tended to minimize the distinction between the practical and the scientific. The newer political science, it seems to me, all too often loses touch with reality in its preoccupation with scientifically interesting problems. But just as a practical political science is inevitably predicated on some scientific assumptions, no matter how inarticulate, so a theoretical political science is inevitably rooted in real-life problematic situations.

All of this is relevant to our strategy of looking at the history of political theories. When I say, therefore, that we should ask of that history what we are asking of empirical political science, I mean that we should study the political theories of the past in a double perspective: first, in the perspective of the real-life problems to which the theorists addressed themselves; and second, in the perspective of how these real-life problems were "solved," that is, translated into theoretical terms. Otherwise, it seems to me, the history of political thought becomes what it has so often been—either textual exegesis, or ideological handmaiden, or merely intellectual game.

Needless to say, perhaps, I do not subscribe to the attitude of those who promise themselves from the study of political theories in history some novel and unexpected revelations. I think they are thoroughly mistaken, for we go to the history of political thought not only to learn, but also to unlearn. If I read the history of science correctly, and admitting that one may read the history in different ways, it seems to me that, along with learning from his predecessors, the creative scientist is particularly successful in unlearning. Copernicus had to unlearn Ptolemaic astronomy; Galileo had to unlearn Aristotelian physics; and a scientist like Darwin was fortunate in that his immediate predecessors had already unlearned the dogma of creation. In general, not the proposition that is true, but the proposition that is false is the beginning of scientific discovery. Only if we know what is false are we motivated to continue the search for what may be true.

In spite of much historical scholarship on the theory and history of representation (De Grazia, 1951), and in spite of all the contemporary research on the representational process, we do not know what representation "is like," at least not under the conditions of political life that characterize our own time. Hence our efforts to recover from the shock of recognition that our "normal science" is in transition.

But I think we are troubled by something else as well. Put as a question, we are increasingly asking: "Just what contribution has our knowledge, whatever the state of this knowledge, made to the art of government?" This question may come as a shock to those among us who are practicing "normal science." In asking the question, I am not assuming that the practical application of scientific knowledge is the sole or ultimate justification of scientific activity. I would argue that even if empirical political science had no practical payoffs at all, it would still be worthwhile to pursue it. It would probably have survival difficulties, but survive it would, for no other reason than that men have been, are, and will continue to be curious about the world they live in. Nevertheless, asking about practical payoffs is appropriate, for empirical inquiry is, in fact, evaluated in these terms.

We often shrink away from payoffs as a standard for appraising our work as political scientists because it invariably leads to invidious comparisons between the physical and the social sciences. But these comparisons become invidious only if we ignore what I think is a profound difference between the study of man and his works and the study of nature.[3] The difference does not lie, as is sometimes said, in the logics or methods of the natural and the social sciences; these, I believe, are generic to all the sciences. Rather, the difference lies in the "raw materials" with which the natural and social sciences deal.[4]

What is this difference in raw materials? The raw materials of the natural sciences are given by nature as they are in nature; they are, indeed, "raw" as the word implies. By way of contrast, the materials with which the social sciences deal are, in most respects, already fashioned by human intervention even before the social scientist comes to deal with them. They are not raw, but they are invariably artifacts of human endeavor. Even the simplest phenomena with which the social sciences deal—say the mother's care of her child, or primitive economic exchange—are creations of man and not creations of nature.

The differences between the natural and the social sciences, then, lie in the character of the objects with which they deal—"natural facts" in the case of the former, "artifacts" in the case of the latter. My only point in making the distinction is that man has established a great deal of control over his social environment without the benefit of an empirical social science, whereas his control over the physical environment has often had to await the prior discoveries of physical science. Of course, man has also made inventions for the control of nature without the benefit of science, and science has sometimes had to catch up by way of post-facto theories or experiments. But the difference in the degree to which this occurs in the two types of science is still considerable. For almost all the things that we study in the social sciences have been largely inventions unencumbered by prior scientific investigations, often going back to times immemorial. Correspondingly, we should not try to measure the payoffs of empirical social science on the same scale as that used in measuring the payoffs of physical science.

In dealing with representation as an invention or a discovery that preceded theoretical or scientific analysis,[5] as an artificial rather than as a natural phenomenon, we are not only forced to journey into history, but we are also put in a better position to explain its relationship, at a particular moment in time, to some of the other functional problems which any political system is likely to face in the course of its development—notably the problem of interest articulation, the problem of integration, the problem of authorization, and the problem of legitimization. Not all historical or contemporary discussions of representation were or are concerned with all four of these problems. In fact, preoccupation with one or another has not infrequently obfuscated understanding of the representational aspects involved. Because representation is then treated as ancillary or auxiliary to other problems—in democratic representation, say, those of equality in voting or political responsibility—the tendency has been to substitute "real" definitions as obiter dicta of low or no explanatory power for genuine analysis.[6] Actually, the juxta- or counterpositioning of definitions in lieu of relating representational to other functional problems may be scientifically harmful, because it gives an impression of theoretical closure where there is none (see Gosnell, 1948: 124-142).

Finally, if representation refers to the structure of the relationship between representative and represented, and to the functions which this structure performs for the political system, it precludes self-fulfilling usages that are empirically nondemonstrable and therefore nonfalsifiable. I have in mind the metaphysics of Prof. Eric Voegelin (1952: 1) who, in making representation "the central problem of a theory of politics," sees in it "the form by which a political society gains existence for action in history," and who seeks to explore "the symbols by which political societies interpret themselves as representatives of a transcendent truth."[7]

I shall, in the remainder of this chapter, deal with three historical "cases" which are instructive from the perspective developed so far. I shall first review the failure of the Greek philosophers to understand representation, a failure that points up the importance of theory, even if it is post-facto theory, for the survival of political systems. I shall then jump the centuries and discuss the efforts of medieval theorists, notably the conciliarists, to come to grips with representation and some of its functional implications. My third case will be Edmund Burke's now classical treatment of representation which has had a more profound impact on our own thinking than that of any other theorist. I shall not deal with the populist treatment of representation, and especially the problem of responsibility that looms so large in democratic theory, because I think it is only a special case of the more generic problem with which Burke was concerned. In conclusion, I shall make a few remarks about the consequences of contemporary empirical research for a modern theory of representation. In fact, I shall conclude that our contemporary real-life problems are such that none of the traditional formulations of representation are relevant to the solution of the representational problems which the modern polity faces.

GREEK AND MEDIEVAL PHILOSOPHY

If we approach an institutional artifact, like representation, as a problem of invention or discovery, the case of the Greeks—their failure to comprehend what they were practicing—is especially instructive. We are then in a better position to advance empirical theory and relevant research than when we treat representation as a matter of definitions. That the Greeks, and later the Romans, did in fact conduct a good deal of public business through representative instititions has been reasonably well established by contemporary historical scholarship (see Larsen, 1955). This is not to say that the Greek system of representation was highly de-

veloped or that it was properly appreciated as a technique of governance. Moreover, it would be a grievous mistake to read into what representative institutions
there were meaning that the Greeks could not possibly have entertained. On the
contrary, as a technical invention, representation seemed to have been designed
for the purpose of limiting rather than extending the participation of citizens in
government. Yet even this use of representation as an instrument of power escaped
theoretical understanding. Aristotle (1943: 264), for instance, discusses the situation in Mantinea where the people,

> although they do not all share in the appointment of offices, except through repre-
> sentatives elected in turn out of the whole people, as at Mantinea;—yet, if they have
> the power of deliberating, the many are contented.

He interprets this case as follows: "Even this form of government may be regarded
as a democracy, and was such at Mantinea." In interpreting this interpretation,
one must keep in mind that by "democracy" Aristotle did not mean "representative
democracy," but what we think of as "direct democracy." Although the *boule* or
council finally became the only institution of the Greek polis that mattered, it was
not and probably could not be perceived as a representative institution in the
sense that it was a council of individuals who represented the community as a
whole (see Ehrenberg, 1957: 44-48). The representative institution could not be
visualized as an instrument of power because the aristocratism of Greek democracy was effectively camouflaged by the ideology that every citizen directly and
personally participated in the government of the polis. Both Plato and Aristotle
were deceived by the prevailing myth, and their approach to knowledge prevented
them from penetrating to reality.

So strong was this myth that even after the federalistic experiments of the
various Hellenic confederacies—which, as J.A.O. Larsen has conclusively shown,
provided for representative assemblies based on population, though they were
insufficiently empowered to make collective decisions—the principle of representation was not understood. Even Polybius, Larsen notes (1955: 104),

> gives us no theory of representative government. The reason seems to be that Greek
> formal political theory was so dominated by the city state that even a laudation of a
> federal government took the form of the claim that it was almost a polis.

The price which the Greeks paid for this theoretical failure to understand their
own governmental inventions has often been commented upon. As Professor
Friedrich (1946: 267) has pointed out,

> necessity for personal participation became fatal whenever such a city reached larger
> proportions. The attempts at solving this problem through a federal organization
> foundered upon the inability of the ancients to work out a representative scheme.

The failure of practice, then, was partly predicated on a failure of theory. The
Greek case is of interest, therefore, precisely because it emphasizes the role of

political theory in practical governance.[8] Whether the Greek city-state or the Greek confederacies could have survived the Macedonian and Roman onslaughts if they had been successful in solving the problem of representation is a matter of speculation of no relevance here. Of interest is the question of just why the rudimentary representative institutions that they did have could not be properly conceived for what they were.

Political theory failed the Greeks in their most fateful hours because it was based on an epistemology that obscured political reality. This is not the place to belabor all the points often made about Aristotle's approach to knowledge. But they do help us understand, I think, why even Aristotle could not see representation as an important discovery of the Greek city builders. In the first place, what stood in the way of a theory of representation was the practice of essentialist definitions which were presumed to identify both the essence and the meaning of a phenomenon (Popper, 1945, II: 12-13). In the Aristotelian universe of definitions concerning the forms of the polis and the processes of politics, there was no place for the kind of behavior that the existence of representative modes of governance entailed. Second, "knowledge" for Aristotle meant the compilation of the definitions of essences, a sort of encyclopedia of names, together with their defining formulas, which becomes an "authority." But knowledge does not grow by way of authoritative definitions, but by way of challenging hypotheses, such as that the earth is not flat. Finally, though Aristotle was less inclined than Plato to hold that knowledge is a matter of intellectual intuition, we should not overestimate, as is sometimes done, the empirical temper of his thinking about politics. It is true that Aristotle collected over 150 constitutions; but this was done, it seems, not for the purpose of empirical inference, but rather for more or less illustrative purposes *after* the foundations of his political theory had already been formulated. Observation, then, does not function to verify or falsify propositions, but rather to stimulate the mind in its task to comprehend universal essences.

Let me reemphasize that it is not my intention to beat a dead dog from the vantage point of modern scientific epistemology. My emphasis is on what happens when in our quest for knowledge we depart too far from the real-life problems that are at the base of inquiry. Benjamin Farrington (1963: 141), in an illuminating book on Greek science, concerns himself with just this aspect of knowledge making. He writes:

> In the earlier period of Greek thought, when the sciences were not distinguished from the techniques, science was plainly a way of *doing* something. With Plato it became a way of knowing, which, in the absence of any practical test, meant only talking consistently. . . . The kind of science they [i.e., Plato and Aristotle] aimed at creating was a science for citizens who would not directly engage in the operational control of the physical environment. Their modes of explanation necessarily excluded ideas derived from the techniques.

The tragedy of Greek political theory was that it served as an ideology of defense of the master-slave system that, by Plato's time, had become dominant. In this apologia, there was no room for interest in techniques, including techniques of government, even though they were practiced. Representation as a technique could not be accommodated in a teleological thought system that, in assuming men to be born as either masters or slaves, sought to help nature realize its intentions. Farrington (1963: 302) sums up this "real paralysis of science":

> During four hundred years there had been, as we have seen, many extensions of knowledge, much reorganization of the body of knowledge, fresh acquisitions of skill in exposition. But there was no great forward drive, no general application of science to life. Science had ceased to be, or had failed to become, a real force in the life of society. Instead there had arisen a conception of science as a cycle of liberal studies for a privileged minority. Science had become a relaxation, an adornment, a subject of contemplation. It had ceased to be a means of transforming the conditions of life.

If the writers of antiquity did not lay even the barest foundations of a theory of political representation, those of the Middle Ages got it off to a wrong start. Representation was discovered, or rather rediscovered, as an instrument of power wielded by medieval monarchs to facilitate the conservation of peace, the administration of lucrative justice, and the replenishment of royal treasuries (Beard and Lewis, 1932). Although, later, representation was also seen as a technique to limit the power of the ruler, the universalistic, sacerdotal, and traditional outlook on society—that strange melange of Aristotelian and Christian ideas which had been fused by St. Thomas into a grand design of order—could not conceive of representation in other than hierarchical terms. As a result, and as long as the medieval order was relatively undisturbed by the later controversies over rulership, representational theory was a theory of impersonation that legitimized the power of the ruler. The king or prince represented in his person the realm as a whole, just as the Pope impersonated the whole of Christendom.

As a theory of personification, representational theory could not cope with the important functional problem of integration that was as basic to the medieval order as it later became to the modern order and as it is today in the developing nations. Given the controversies of the later Middle Ages—between emperor and Pope, between king and estates, between bishops and cathedral chaplains, between the old monastic orders and the self-governing new ones, and finally between the papacy in Avignon and the conciliar movement—one wonders how the problem of integration in state or church would have been solved if representational theory had not been transformed in such a way that it could at least take cognizance of the changes in relationships between the effective political forces of the time. Clearly, a theory which only asked, "*Who* represents the *whole*?" however the whole was defined, could not possibly break out of tautological polemics. For the claim to authority by one would-be representative was as good as the claim by another. Indeed, most of the arguments, even many of those made at a relatively late date by some conciliar theorists, led nowhere because they were legitimizing rather than analytical propositions. History being what it is, we cannot say what might have happened in the real world if theoretical development had failed to transcend the medieval paradigm of a hierarchical social structure in which the parts were both unequal and subordinate to each other. For this paradigm, if it ever corresponded to reality, was increasingly in conflict with it. All we can say is that the problem of integration was solved, and that a new conception of representation, along with other theoretical developments, played a role in its solution.

A theory of representation that would take account of the relationship between representative and represented had to be based on a view of politics that was sensitive to the interplay of diverse interests—whether of persons, groups, or territories. Such a view could not emerge as long as political thought was in the Aristotelian bondage of definitional essentialism, with its emphasis on a primary classification of politics and its fascination with universal categories. Nominalism, in rejecting "real" definitions and starting with the individual phenomenon rather with the whole as its unit of analysis, was an epistemological revolution. It not only produced a new paradigm for the comprehension of all social formations, but was also of critical importance for the emergence of a rudimentary theory of representation as delegation. It thus enabled theorists to catch up with the custom of the "imperative mandate" that was practiced in early representative government (Holden, 1930). Moreover, once the superiority, by definition, of the whole over the parts, or of the general over the specific, was questioned, the theoretical door was opened for seeing politics as an arena of conflicting interests. And finally, the legitimacy of all claimants to be represented in collective decision making was recognized. Though such writers as Marsilius of Padua, William of Ockham, or Nicholas of Cusa took different stands in the struggles between emperor and Pope and in the controversies within the Church, the focus of theoretical attention shifted to the represented as significant parties to the representational relationship.

This is not to say that nominalism alone was responsible for the breakthrough in thinking about representation. Any adequate appreciation of the new view of representation as delegation rather than impersonation cannot ignore the confluence of all those factors that laid the foundations for constitutional government in the late Middle Ages, notably the rejuvenation of Roman law and the pervasiveness of the German Law of Corporations. Moreover, the budding medieval constitutional thought was strongly supported by the Christian conception of equality. So Roman legal notions of agency and consent were combined with the Christian idea of all being equal before God. In secular terms, all were conceded the equal right of being heard and represented in law making. And Aristotle's concept of the right of citizens to participate in all decisions affecting the polis, which previously had purely rhetorical meaning, reduced the tension between the built-in radicalism of the Christian concept of equality and the conservative view of social structure. Note how Marsilius presents the solution (Gewirth, 1956: 45):

> Let us say, then, in accordance with the truth and the counsel of Aristotle in the
> *Politics,* Book III, Chapter 6, that the legislator, or the primary and proper cause of
> the law, is the people or the whole body of citizens, or the weightier part thereof,
> through its election or will expressed by words in the general assembly of the citizens,

commanding or determining that something be done or omitted with regard to human civil acts, under a temporal pain or punishment. The aforesaid whole body of citizens or the weightier part thereof is the legislator regardless of whether it makes the law directly by itself or entrusts the making of it to some person or persons, who are not and cannot be the legislator in the absolute sense, but only in a relative sense and for a particular time and in accordance with the authority of the primary legislator.

Once limitations on rulership—something the Greeks had failed to work out—had been accepted as legitimate, representation could be conceived as the effective technique to limit political power, provided that the representative institution took cognizance of diverse claims. But all the theoretical creativity involved in this new synthesis of partly inherited, partly novel notions of politics would have been impossible, it seems to me, without the decisive metamorphosis in the *ways* of thinking about the world which the new approach of the nominalists made possible.

But, again, we must guard against reading modern democratic notions into the evolving view of the representational process. Men like Marsilius of Padua or William of Ockham were not advocates of what later came to be called "individualism." That the representative stood for the many was clearly recognized, but the many themselves still constituted largely indivisible wholes—be it an undivided church, or the people as a whole, or the estates as wholes. As Professor Sabine (1937: 310) pointed out, "certainly, William had no thought of representing Christians individually, as so many discrete units, or territorially, as the inhabitants of such and such districts." Rather, the demand of these writers was for a more perfectly ordered social organism, in the sense that the church would approximate this ideal if all the members and groups of Christianity were represented in a more adequate way.

The *legislator humanus* in Marsilius's thought, for instance, differed from the traditional view only in that his legitimacy derived from popular consent rather than from divine inspiration. His "role," to use a modern term, was more that of a judge than that of a delegate as we understand it today. Nicholas of Cusa's complaint largely centered in the point that the Pope represents the Church only "in a very confused fashion," whereas the universal council is more representative because "it is alway better in judgment than the single pontiff who is a more uncertain representative" (quoted in Sigmund, 1963: 166). In fact, then, the conception of representation used here is still in part one of impersonation. As one recent interpreter of Nicholas put it, "the council is not superior to the pope because it is made up of representatives chosen by others to take their places, but because a larger number are present who 'figure' or 'personify' the lesser hierarchical groupings in the church" (in Sigmund, 1963: 166-167). If anything, then, this conception is closer to the Burkean notion of "virtual representation" than to the view of representation as delegation. On the other hand, Nicholas also entertained ideas of delegation. His *legati*, members of Church councils, including the college of cardinals, do not simply personify the Christian community, but are presumably answerable to electors, or in the case of the cardinals, responsible to the *praesides*— the heads of the various hierarchical ranks in the provinces whose places they were taking in Rome.

The intellectual turmoil apparent in Nicholas of Cusa's treatment of representation suggests that the conciliar theorists did not completely surmount the traditional holistic paradigm of the political order. Though the authority of representatives was increasingly constructed as deriving from a mandate, taking for granted the sovereignty of the people and the contractual basis of rulership, both representative institutions and the collectivities represented were still seen as wholes. The council or assembly of representatives was treated as an analog of the *ecclesia universalis* or of the *universitas populi.* The method of theory construction was one of extrapolation from the macrocosm of a universal, hierarchical order to the microcosm of the particular assembly of representatives. In other words, the council or assembly was also a *universitas,* for it was only a substitute for the larger unit of which it was a part.[9] But this construction hardly disguises the changes in political relationships that were at the base of the theoretical efforts to free theory from the holistic paradigm. Nevertheless, as Gierke (1939: 244) has pointed out, referring to the difficulties involved in these constructions, "the persistent cult of the antique was a hindrance to the progress of the representative idea, while the absolutist doctrine of Bodin was positively hostile."

The medieval case is instructive because it suggests that a theory of the relationship between representative and represented cannot be fruitfully pursued independent of the prevailing status relations in a society. I am reluctant to link representation with considerations of status in this connection. But a theory of representation clearly cannot ignore what both representative and represented, be they superiors or subordinates, can in effect do to reach other as a result of occupying different status positions. For instance, reverting to the medieval case, representation as delegation is bound to fail if the represented occupy status positions that in effect prevent them from issuing instructions. Yet, as status relationships were in fact changing, medieval representational theory confronted the dilemma of taking account of these changes without, however, disturbing the social order as such. It was therefore supremely unconcerned with the problem of how the relationship between representative and represented could be instrumented. The solution, as I suggested, was found in isomorphic construction: smaller organisms were seen as replicas of the larger organism. But the question of effective linkage between representative and represented remained unanswered.

The isomorphic view of the representative assembly became a theoretical straitjacket that, later on, plagued representational theory. For once church, or sovereign people, or estates gave way to area as the unit of representation, and even after representatives were seen as delegates from geographic constituencies, the latter were assumed to be represented as wholes. But this conception, in turn, could only yield a paradox: if that which is represented constitutes a whole, particularistic interests within the whole cannot be articulated, and as Professor MacIver (1947: 210) has rightly observed, "the only policy he [i.e., the representative] can logically stand for is the presumptive interest of the whole he represents."

What becomes of interest, then, is how later theorists coped with this paradox. Clearly, no representative can speak for the whole except in a formalistic sense. As I shall point out, Edmund Burke tried to solve it by asserting that, in order to represent the whole, the representative must speak and act according to his own judgment. From this perspective, then, Burke's formulation was truly "progressive." Virtual representation, as he understood it, was the only alternative to a holistic view of representation, on the one hand, and to an individualistic view, on the other hand.

EDMUND BURKE ON REPRESENTATION

Before discussing Edmund Burke's theory of representation, we must once more take a leap through the centuries in order to appreciate the change in paradigms from the holistic conception of representation in the Middle Ages to the individualistic conception that took root in the seventeenth century. Yet, I shall not dwell on Hobbes' logical perversion of the individualistic paradigm or on Rousseau's sentimental radicalism that led him to reject the technique of representation as a violation of the individualistic principle.[10] I shall almost immediately turn to Burke, for a number of reasons. That our contemporary thinking about representation derives from Burke's suggesive polemic rather than from Hobbes or Rousseau is perhaps most relevant. But almost equally interesting is the location of Burke's statement in the development of representational theory. What Burke told the electors of Bristol in his famous speech of 1774 could not have been said without the profound change in paradigms that had taken place in the centuries between the conciliar movement and his own time. In other words, behind Burke's view of representation lay an altogether new view of social relationships. The individual, either as representative or as represented, had become the primary unit of theoretical analysis.

But Burke, unlike Hobbes and Rousseau, and perhaps also unlike Montesquieu, had to come to practical grips with the consequences of individualism for the representational process. If the individual is the unit of any representational relationship, the problem clearly is how it comes about that the community, also, is represented. Hobbes had solved the problem by liquidating the individual through contracting him out of the political process. Rousseau had simply denied that any problem existed, very much as the Greeks had done, though he knew better. Montesquieu (1962: 154-155) was perhaps the first theorist who presented a pragmatic conception of representation by geographic districts, on the ground that a locally elected representative is better acquainted with the needs of his own locality and with his own neighbors than any other would-be representative. But even though Montesquieu recognized the individual as the unit of the representational relationship, he viewed representation as resting on a collective mandate, in the sense that representatives act on behalf of the community which is itself vested with legislative power. Representation, then, is simply a convenience. The problem—just how individual representation gives rise to collective representation—is treated by absorption: the people as individuals may be capable of choosing representatives, but they are not themselves capable of taking an active part in government, despite their being vested with legislative power. In arguing against a delegate view of representation, Montesquieu simply postulated that representation somehow takes place, without paying attention to the question of how representative and represented are linked (see Gierke, 1939: 247).

All of these "solutions" were not solutions, though they gave the impression of being so. If we turn to Burke, I think the reason his formulation, in contrast to those of Hobbes, Rousseau, or Montesquieu, is still so suggestive today is the fact that he did *not* present a pseudosolution to the puzzle of how individual representation can become collective representation. Burke's failure is our legacy. To appreciate it, we must place Burke into the English historical context.

After emerging from the holistic preoccupations of the medieval period, representational theory was above all a theory of legal relationships, a theory of authority. Whether the legal accent was put, as by Hobbes, on the sovereignty of the ruler, or as by the Levellers on the sovereignty of the people, with parliament having only purely delegated authority, there was little theoretical concern with the instrumentation of the actual relationships between representative and represented.[11] The change in paradigm was evident enough. The Levellers, as Sabine (1937: 487) has stated, "conceived parliament as standing for the actual human beings that composed the nation, and not as representing corporations, vested interests, and rights of property or status." True, as Gierke (1939: 246) mentioned, certain "weighty maxims" gradually came to prevail in England, "to the effect that every member of parliament should represent the whole nation and not merely his district, that he is not bound to obey instructions or to render account to his constituents." But these weighty maxims did not cut much ice. Down to Burke's day, it seems, parliamentary representation was conceived as delegation—a type of relationship between representative and represented and not different from the ordinary legal relation of agency.

What, we wonder, touched off Burke's polemic and his attack on the mandate theory? One might argue, as Burke himself argued in his speech, that it was his fellow M.P. from Bristol who, Burke tells us, "expresses himself (if I understand him rightly) in favor of the coercive authority of such instructions." But why should this occasion Burke's outspoken attack on the notion of mandate—an attack which, as a clever politician, he might surely have expected to backfire? Why did he dwell on the problem of his relationship with the voters of Bristol at all? He could have remained silent.

Burke's attack was not a simple reply to a familiar and common doctrine reiterated by a colleague. He was not so naive politically as it might seem if we were to take his argument at face value. On the contrary, as I shall suggest, his argument was designed to conceal rather than reveal his true intentions as one of Bristol's representatives. Some years ago, employing the technique of textual exegesis, I thought that (Eulau et al., 1959: 744)

> Burke postulated two possible foci of representation: local, necessarily hostile interests, on the one hand; and a national interest, on the other hand. He rejected the former as an improper and advocated the latter as the proper focus of the representative's role. But in doing so, he also linked these foci of representation with partic-

ular representational styles. If the legislature is concerned with only one interest, that of the whole, and not with compromise among diverse interests, it follows that the representative cannot and must not be bound by instructions, from whatever source, but must be guided by what Burke called "his unbiased opinions, his mature judgment, his enlightened conscience." Moreover, Burke buttressed his argument by emphasizing the deliberative function of the legislature—presumably in contrast to its representational function.

I can no longer leave it at that. For if we leave the argument at this point, Burke's view of virtual representation could hardly be challenged, or to put it differently, his hypothesis could hardly be falsified. We must ask, therefore, just what Burke had in mind when he confronted the diverse interests of different constituencies with the one interest of the nation as a whole. His claim that this national interest would somehow emerge out of the deliberations of an assembly of men endowed with reason and judgment, provided they are unencumbered by instructions, does not sound true. For Burke's whole orientation to politics was a kind of pragmatic aristocratism. This aristocratism, by the third quarter of the eighteenth century, had found institutional expression in an incipient party system. Yet, nowhere in his speech to the voters of Bristol is there any acknowledgment of his commitment to a particular party.

Burke's speech oozes an air of political innocence. But how innocent was Burke? We are indebted to a delightful essay by Ernest Barker on "Burke and His Bristol Constituency" to disabuse us of any illusions we might cherish about Burke's political innocence. Who was the politician who, in 1774, stood for election in Bristol? After having been private secretary to the member for Petersfield, known as "single-speech Hamilton," Burke had entered similar confidential employment in 1765 with the Marquis of Rockingham, a week after this leader of one of the Whig factions had become Prime Minister. And soon, Barker (1945: 170) narrates,

> his nature working powerfully on Rockingham's affection, he became his right hand, his goad to action, his trumpeter, his manager, his plague, his inspiration. A seat in Parliament was immediately found for him, by the influence of Lord Verney, at the foot of the Chilterns, in the borough of Wendover.

Through his connection with Rockingham, Burke became a party man. The party leaders included Rockingham, the Duke of Portland, the Duke of Richmond, and when he was not engaged in fox hunting, Lord John Cavendish. These men were cajoled by Burke, Barker (pp. 172-173) tells us,

> that they would not stay immured in their castles, on the plea of health or foxes or private affairs; that they would come to London before the session began in order to concert a policy; that they would brave the Court and the crowd for the sake of their policy; in a word, that they would work for their party, live for their party, and, if necessary, die for their party, in the grand old manner of the seventeenth century. A passion of activity is natural to a zealous party organizer, and Burke, if we may use a modern name, was the Rockingham party organizer. He suggested policies, drafted

petitions, arranged for meetings, looked after elections, arranged everything and goaded everybody.

The man who was put up for election in Bristol was a party man. In fact, he was put up *because* he was a party man. In putting him up, his supporters broke a "polite arrangement" made toward the end of the reign of George II, "under which Whigs and Tories were to share its [i.e., Bristol's] two seats for the next three Parliaments." But the local Whigs had become ever more restless as the sitting Tory member had voted consistently for an anti-American policy that annoyed the merchants and traders of Bristol. In settling on Buurke as a second Whig candidate, his Bristol friends thought they knew what they were getting. As the virtual leader of the Rockingham faction, he was eminently sound on the American question; he "was the man with whom North corresponded on the business of the House, as a Prime Minister corresponds today with the Leader of the Opposition." Burke, in turn, was aware of the advantages that would accrue to his parliamentary position if "he could sit for one of the great popular constituencies, which would lend authority to his protests and weight to his policies" (p. 179).

But the alliance between Burke and Bristol was an uneasy one from the start. Even during the election an anonymous writer had urged, "it is plain that ye have greatly mistaken one another, and the best thing that can now be done is to make explanations and apologies on all sides and part" (pp. 183-184). Another pamphleteer had asked (pp. 184-185):

> Do you know that he is the agent and instrument of the Rockingham party? Do you know he has written a book recommending the principles of that party? That they amount to this . . . that they will invest themselves with the people's rights, who shall be free in their power but not otherwise, for that *they* shall have virtue and ability enough for you all?

But what does Burke's being a party man and being known as a party man tell us about his theory of representation? It tells us, I think, that taking words out of historical context, as we have done for so long, can be highly misleading. In coming down on the side of independent judgment as the proper style and in preaching the supremacy of the whole over the parts as the proper focus of representation, Burke in fact translated the interests of his party into a universal principle of politics. And in doing so, Burke would become the victim of his own dissemblances. Burke could say what he did say in his Bristol speech only because in 1774 he and his constituents happened to be of similar mind on economic questions. On the Irish issue and American matters, Burke's policies and the interests of the Bristol merchants chanced to coincide. But their agreement was only apparent. Burke was a free trader by conviction; his demand that parliament legislate for the whole nation in the national interest meant for him, in this context, a demand for free trade. But the merchants of Bristol favored free trade only as long as it served their particular interests; if they thought restricted trade served their interests better, they would favor rigid protection. Similarly, Burke's advocacy of toleration on the Catholic issue could only succeed if parliament would identify toleration with the national interest. Bristol's Protestants saw it otherwise. Burke was never defeated in Bristol, as is commonly believed. On Saturday, September 9, 1780, Barker (p. 204) recounts, "he appeared at the Guildhall, on the opening of the second day of the poll, and declined the election." He withdrew from the polls and retired from a contest which, he knew, could only end in defeat.

Burke's difficulties were not limited to the discrepancy between his policy views and those of his constituents. In the decade prior to the Bristol speech of 1774, the view that representatives should be instructed delegates had found wide acceptance. Burke's own view was that the representative is a free and responsible agent, to be left free in his decisions but accountable for them after they were made. No doubt, this conception had grown deep roots in his political thought. For eight years prior to 1774, he had been free, in the sense in which he thought the representative should be free, because the rotten borough of Wendover had hardly made demands on him. And he had associated himself with aristocrats who, by virtue of their status, considered themselves as free in the same sense. But, above all, freedom from local connections and instructions was for Burke a necessary and very practical condition to work for a parliamentary party, be its leader, and accept the commitments of a party man. Burke never envisaged the possibility that his own judgment and his party's policies could ever come into conflict.

Professor Barker, in his essay, on which I am drawing so much in this chapter, admires Burke's candor, for he might have circumvented the issue by avoidance. But he did not. He did not, and could not avoid it, it seems to me, because he knew that he would be challenged as a party man in any case, as indeed he was. Granted that he believed what he said, we cannot ignore what he did not say but might have said. And what he did not say was that he was bound to the principles of his party as strongly as he did not want to be bound to instructions from his constituents. True, as Barker (p. 197) points out, "the question raised between Burke and his constituents was more than personal and psychological; it was, in its essence, as we have seen, a grave constitutional question, which went to the impersonal roots of politics." But, as Barker (p. 199) had also to admit, "to espouse without reserve the cause of Burke against Bristol would be, in effect, to deny the casue of democracy." The real issue was the political question of who should rule England—and on this issue Burke (1803-1827, III: 335) had committed himself as much as any man of his time. At issue, too, was the future of his party—"a body of men united, for promoting by their joint endeavours the national interest, upon some particular principle in which they are all agreed"—and the role of his party in the future of England.

Needless to say, perhaps, Burke's notion of political party is far removed from our own notion of the party as an agent of interest aggregation in a pluralistic or polyarchic society. Yet it is an astounding fact, now confirmed by many empirical studies of representational roles, at least in the American context, that Burke's conception of the representative as a trustee is widely held. But, as in the case of Burke himself, what we must look for is not what the trustee orientation tells us about the representative who holds it, but what it does not tell us. What it does not tell us is anything significant about the exchanges that occur between the representative and those—party leaders, colleagues, lobbyists, even some constituents—from whom he receives his cues, and about the processes of politics that, in the end, lead to the self-serving assertion of independent judgment. The dichotomy in terms of which Burke has made us think—and this includes radical democratic thought as well—does not correspond to the political realities of our time. Burke's trustee was, in the end, a party man—in the sense of party as he understood it. But what is today's trustee? I do not think we can say. And so, Burke too, has failed in solving the problem of representation—how individual relationships are transformed into representation of the whole.

CONCLUSION

With Edmund Burke, theoretical thinking about representation reached an impasse. The pendulum of preference swung heavily in the direction of the mandate or delegate interpretation of the representational relationship. The theories of proportional and functional representation that became prominent in the later nineteenth and early twentieth centuries were either party-centered or interest-centered interpretations of the basic relationship between representative and represented. Their immediate purpose was to maximize meaningful popular participation in the governing process and to maximize governmental responsiveness. As normative doctrines they were largely obiter dicta, and no efforts were made to answer the question of whether schemes of representation based on these theories actually attained the promised objectives. On the other hand, a small but influential group of writers continued to advocate notions of virtual representation and actually succeeded in writing these notions into some modern constitutions.

My purpose in reviewing the failure of the ancients to develop a theory of representation, the struggle of the medieval writers to formulate a theory, and Burke's attempt to diagnose the basic issue, has not been to describe, but to point up the problematic situations involved in these theoretical postures and to suggest how theoretical formulations are anchored in problematic situations. My purpose has been to see just what it is that we, as empirical political scientists, can learn from the theoretical failures, struggles, or dilemmas of the past. It is my point of view that we can learn something from the history of political theories if we ask of it what we ask of empirical science. The first demand which we must make on ourselves as empirical researchers is that we have as accurate, as unembellished, a picture of the problematic conditions that give rise to our theorizing in the first place. This, it seems to me, is all too often forgotten as we practice "normal science." Normal science necessarily sees the world in terms of its own conventional, agreed-on ways. But we can be sensitive to the presuppositions that determine what we see in the real world. In part, the difficulties of the past were the result of the fact that presuppositions of an epistemological kind—essentialism in the Greek case, holism in the medieval case, and rationalism in Burke's case—powerfully circumscribed the diagnoses that were made of the problematic situations that were at the base of theorizing about representation.

We have witnessed, in the last ten years or so, an outpouring of empirical studies which, in one way or another, concerned themselves with a great variety of political relationships connected with problems of representation. Most of this research has been conducted in the American context, but some of it has also been undertaken abroad, especially in Western Europe. Most of this research has been conceived, wittingly or not, within the broad theoretical framework that Edmund Burke bequeathed to us. We have been practicing normal science. In doing so, we have largely taken for granted just what the problems are that interest us when studying representation, and we have largely overlooked the possibility that a change in basic paradigms may have taken place in the intervening years. And we have failed to make this change as explicit as might be desirable.

As a result, it seems to me, we are in a curiously ambiguous research situation. On the one hand, we have subjected to empirical testing a broad range or propositions translated from normative formulations, and we have found that these formulations do not square with our findings. This, you will recall, is what I had in mind in the opening of this chapter when I said that we know what representation is not. On the other hand, because we have not really addressed ourselves to problematic situations in our current reality, we have been unable to come up with relevant knowledge as to what representation means in our own time. In this respect, I believe, we are closer to the Greeks, for whom knowledge had become an idle pastime, than to the medievalists or to Burke, who were deeply involved in a search for solutions to troubling situations. In the medieval case, this was the quest for political integration and legitimization; in the case of Burke, it was the quest for solving the problems of party, responsiveness, responsibility, and the national interest.

Burke—I once more turn to him, because he defined our scientific problems for us in regard to representation—really formulated a dilemma, and this dilemma is still with us. If the critical real-life problem of representation—even under the very much changed conditions of our time—is the responsibility of the governors to the governed, then indeed virtual representation, as Burke understood it, is probably the appropriate style in an era when "mandate uncertainty"[12] and the complexity of governmental policy making create a deep and wide gap between representative and represented. In this situation, the representative can act responsibly only if he has sufficient freedom and discretion to act as he sees fit in the face of the intricate, rapidly changing issues which he must decide on. Prior consultation of the represented is out of the question.

But if we see as the critical problem the responsiveness of the representative to the represented, than a mandate or delegate conception would seem to be appropriate. Responsiveness implies that the representative be at least alert and sensitive to the preferences and wishes of the represented. Burke was eminently conscious of the conflict that necessarily arises out of these alternative formulations of the problem of representation.

In general, we have continued to formulate the problem in Burkean terms, in spite of all the evidence to the contrary. The circumstances of modern government are such that neither responsibility nor responsiveness can be assured through the technique of representation. Despite all the oratory of the politicians, they cannot possibly be responsive, in the traditional sense, to individual constituents whose numbers are in the hundreds of thousands or millions, whose interests are enormously diverse, and whose understanding of the complexities of public policy is minimal. At the same time, and for very much the same reasons, it is increasingly impossible to hold the representative responsible for his decisions. As we observe the electoral process, still considered the main technique to enforce responsibility, it is evident that the electorate is chiefly guided by rather vague and often confused moods about the drift of public policy in general rather than by a clear perception as to whether the individual representative has acted responsibly or not within his discretionary capabilities.

It seems to me, therefore, that much of our research on representation, geared as it is to the problem as formulated by Burke, does not really come close to the problematic situation of modern government. And although responsiveness and responsibility remain the norms in terms of which we would like to see government conducted, the difficulties involved in practicing these norms challenge us to discover just what it is that makes representative government tick. I cannot possibly present here a modern theory of representation, and doing so was not my assignment. However, I would at least like to suggest, in conclusion, the threshold for such a theory.

Whatever the scheme of representation, the core problem involved in representation is the relationship that exists between representative and represented. Burke and the research based on the Burkean formulation dealt primarily with the role of the representative. But the relationship between representative and represented is problematic because not only the roles but also the statuses of the counterplayers are likely to be ambiguous, so that the exchanges occurring between them are likely to be misperceived, creating all kinds of difficulties for the polity's other functional problems. Where there is little or no ambiguity in the relationship, it is not really very interesting from a theoretical point of view. For instance, if the representative is a dictator and the represented are subjects, and if this model really corresponded to an actual situation, our theoretical curiosity would hardly be mobilized. Similarly, if the "imperative mandate" guided the relationship between representative and represented, our research interest would not be aroused. The fact is, of course, that in reality—even in dictatorships or radical democracies—the representational relationship rarely corresponds to such models. On the contrary, it is likely to be ambiguous and, therefore, becomes theoretically interesting because of the tensions for the political system that arise out of the ambiguity. Dictators, for instance, are invariably concerned with their legitimacy; or assemblies based on mandate are concerned with their authority.

A viable theory of representation cannot ignore, therefore, the status of each party to the representational relationship. Status refers to the position of superordination, subordination, or equality of the actors; role refers to the expectations of how the incumbent of each status should behave in the relationship. Contemporary research is primarily concerned with representation as a system of role relationships and avoids the admittedly ticklish problem of representation as a status system. This, perhaps, is one of the reasons why the research literature on the new nations, where status is even more problematic than in the West, avoids dealing with representation. I mention this matter here only because we tend to take the status relationship between representative and represented in the modern democratic polity for granted, and because we take it for granted we fail to see it as a critical problem of representation. It seems to me that a future empirical theory of democratic representation should not foreclose the problematics of status in the representational relationship by simply identifying, *ex definitione,* the representative with governor, ruler or elite, and the represented with governed, ruled, or mass. Who governs whom in the representational relationship is an empirical question that cannot and should not be answered by definition.

At the bottom of all theories of democratic representation is the behavioral assumption that responsibility and responsiveness are best assured by some similarity, achieved mechanically through appropriate governmental structures or empathically through relevant psychological processes, between the characteristics, attributes, attitudes, or goals of the representative and the represented. I think that this behavioral assumption is totally false. On the contrary, I believe we must proceed from the behavioral assumption of a built-in difference between representative and represented—built-in in the sense that representation always involves a difference in status between representative and represented. And if this is so, a viable theory of democratic representation must be based on this assumption of an inevitable status difference rather than on the democratically pleasing, but false assumption of some basic similarity between representative and represented.

Let me put this a bit more concretely. It is an error, I think, to assume that the "chosen"—whether elected or selected—are or can ever be "like" their choosers. The very fact of their having been elected or selected—having been "elevated" through some mechanism of choice from one position into another—makes the "chosen" fundamentally different from their choosers. Having been chosen, the representative has at least one attribute that differentiates him from the represented, no matter how similar, socially, or psychologically, he may be in all other respects. Status differentiation, then, is a crucial property of any representational relationship. Whether he was born in the proverbial log cabin or in the mansion of the high and mighty, the fact of having been "chosen" sets the representative off as someone "special."

It is on the basis of this status relationship, then, that a viable empirical theory of democratic representation must build its axioms, theorems, and research hypotheses. These axioms, theorems, and hypotheses will have to deal with the tensions arising out of the status differentiation between representative and represented that representation entails and the role expectations that a democratic polity entertains with respect to its representative's conduct. I shall leave it at that. But one thing seems clear to me: Whatever solutions are found concerning the proper modes of conduct in the representational relationship, they are unlikely to be as simple as our conventional conceptions of the representative as either a delegate, bound by mandate to follow his constituency's instructions, or a trustee, committed to pursue the interests of his constituency, however he defines it, according to his own conscience or best judgment. Once status is introduced as a variable into the representational equation, the formula is bound to be more complex than we hitherto suspected.

We have come a long way in the last fifteen years since Oliver Garceau (1951: 78-79), in his seminal recommendations for research on the political process, enjoined us

> to observe the flow of communication from constituency to legislator and the pattern of response to these multiple pressures, together with a broad gauge field study of the constituency itself, its economy, social stratification, group organization, media of communication and party organization, in order to record simultaneously the circumstances originating this flow of information. In this way the multiple roles of the representative may be illuminated and judgments made in regard to our contradictory and normatively colored hypotheses of representation.

We have done all and more than what Garceau asked us to do. We have come to know what representation is not. This is the challenge to theory of these years of travail. Our conceptions of representation are obsolete. We have representative institutions, but like the Greeks we do not know what they are about. Continuing with normal science will not get us out of our theoretical quandary. I am not suggesting a moratorium on empirical research. But I do feel that we must break the spell of Burke, just as Aristotle's spell had to be broken by late medieval theory. This, I believe, is the lesson to be learned from the history of representational theory.

NOTES

1. I am gratified to note that the problem of representation is dealt with in its own terms by Pye, 1966: 21, 24-26. I also note that "representation" does not appear as an entry in the book's index, just as it does not appear in the indexes of any number of books on the new nations that I have perused. What I find fascinating is that the problems which Pye identifies resemble the problems with which medieval theorists had to cope.

2. Merz, 1896, I:7, quotes Goethe: "History must from time to time be rewritten, not because many new facts have been discovered, but because new aspects come into view, because the participant in the progress of an age is led to standpoints from which the past can be regarded and judged in a novel manner."

3. How often it is said that the social sciences do not "deserve" the kind and amount of research support which the physical and biological sciences receive because they are less "useful"! To just what useful applications can the social sciences point by comparison with the natural sciences? Even if their usefulness is not altogether denied, they cannot claim to have had the same revolutionary consequences for the shape of human affairs that can be attributed to the natural sciences.

4. In other words, I reject the argument that, because it is perhaps possible to reduce social to biological phenomena, the materials of the social sciences are not unlike those of the natural sciences.

5. Representation, wrote James Mill in 1820 (Mill, 1937: vi), is "the grand discovery of modern times" and "the solution of all the difficulties, both speculative and practical. . . ." Loewenstein, 1957: 40, states: "In retrospect it appears that the invention or discovery of the representative technique was as decisive for the political evolution of the West and, through it, of the world as the mechanical inventions—steam, electricity, the combustion engine, atomic power—have been for man's technological evolution."

6. Note the rather hopeless enterprise by Fairlie, 1940.

7. Voegelin, 1952: 54, refers, evidently for demonstration, to the early Asiatic empires which "understood themselves as representatives of a transcendent order, of the cosmos. . . ." In this conception, "the ruler himself represents the society, because on earth he represents the transcendent power which maintains the cosmic order."

8. For an opposite view, denigrating the role of ideas in institutional survival, see Sait, 1938: 475. However, Sait's chapter on representation is still one of the best succinct historical accounts I have seen.

9. For similar doctrinal difficulties with federalistic theories, see Eulau, 1941.

10. For an excellent discussion of Rousseau, see Bloom, 1963.

11. For a detailed treatment of their thought on representation, see Brailsford, 1961: 10-11, 275-287, 354-357.

12. I am indebted for this term to Janda, 1961: 169-179.

Chapter 3

THE PUZZLE OF REPRESENTATION:
Specifying Components of Responsiveness

HEINZ EULAU
PAUL D. KARPS

The puzzle: "We have representative institutions, but like the Greeks we do not know what they are about" (Eulau, 1967).

With the publication in 1963 of "Constituency Influence in Congress" by Miller and Stokes, the direction was set for a novel approach to the study of political representation.[1] The virtue of this original study notwithstanding, the approach had some quite unexpected consequences for subsequent theoretical development and empirical research. Much of this development and research was due less to the impact of Miller and Stokes' innovative approach as such than to its vulgarization. The questions addressed in this paper are two: first, we propose to unravel the continuing puzzle of representation which was probably made even more puzzling by the thoughtless use of the concept of "congruence" which Miller and Stokes had introduced into discourse about representation; and second, we propose to explicate the concept of "responsiveness" by decomposing it into four components which seem to correspond to four targets of representation.

THE MILLER-STOKES MODEL

Miller and Stokes (1963) themselves were well aware of the broader context of theory and research on representation,[2] but the focus of their particular analysis was a more limited one than "representation." They were interested in the degree to which "constituency control," rather than "party voting," determined congressional roll call behavior: "The fact that our House of Representatives . . . has irregular party voting does not of itself indicate that Congressmen deviate from party in response to local pressures" (p. 45). The analysis addressed an old question: which factor, party or constituency, contributes more to variance in roll-call voting (all other things being equal)? The question had been previously asked in numerous studies relying, of necessity, on aggregate surrogate indicators of presumed district predispositions, most of them demographic or ecological.[3]

Miller and Stokes' research was a giant stride in the study of representation because it freed analysis from dependence on surrogate variables as indicators of constituency attitudes or predispositions. Miller and Stokes interviewed a sample of congressional constituents (voters and non-voters) and their respective congressmen (as well as non-incumbent candidates) whose attitudes in three broad issue domains they compared with each other, with congressmen's perceptions of constituency attitudes, and with corresponding roll call votes. Their tool of analysis was the product moment correlation coefficient and their mode of treatment was "causal analysis," which was then being introduced into political science. Miller and Stokes found the relationships among the variables of their model to vary a good deal from issue area to issue area, being strongest in the case of civil rights, weaker in the case of social welfare, and weakest in the case of foreign involvement. They concluded:

> The findings of this analysis heavily underscore the fact that no single tradition of representation fully accords with the realities of American legislative politics. The American system *is* a mixture, to which the Burkean, instructed-delegate, and responsible-party models all can be said to have contributed elements. Moreover, variations in the representative relation are most likely to occur as we move from one policy domain to another (p. 56).

We have no quarrel with this general conclusion concerning the American system. We are bothered by the definition of what Miller and Stokes call "the representative relation" and its operational expression. This "relation" is the similarity or, as it is also called, the "congruence" between the four variables of the causal model that serves the purposes of analysis.[4] This specification of congruence as the expression of the representative relation has had great influence on later researchers, both those working in the tradition of, or with the data made available by, the Michigan group and those working independently with fresh data of their own.[5] The concern here is not this influence as such but rather the gradual erosion of alternative theoretical assumptions about representation of which Miller and Stokes themselves are fully cognizant. As a result of this erosion, what for Miller and Stokes (1963: 49) was only "a starting point for a wide range of analyses" became an exclusive definition of representation: high congruence was interpreted as evidence of the presence of representation, and low congruence was taken as proof of its absence.

Whatever congruence may be symbolizing, it is not a self-evident measure of representation. Later researchers, poorly tutored in theories and practices of representation, tended to ignore this. Miller and Stokes, in order to use congruence as a measure, had stipulated three conditions for constituency influence or control. First, control in the representational relationship can be exercised through recruitment—constituents choose that representative who shares their views so that, by following his "own convictions," the representative "does his constituents' will." Second, control can be obtained through depriving the representative of his office—the representative follows "his (at least tolerably accurate) perceptions of district attitude in order to win re-election." And third, "the constituency must in some measure take the policy views of candidates into account in choosing a Representative" (pp. 50-51).

The electoral connection is of course only one of the links between representative and represented. And it should by no means be taken for granted that it is the most critical, the most important, or the most effective means to insure constituency influence on or control over public policies and the conduct of representatives. It is so only if one or all of the conditions for constituency control specified by Miller and Stokes are satisfied. This is also precisely the reason why attitudinal or perceptual congruence is not an exclusive measure of representation; it is simply the "starting point," as Miller and Stokes knew, in the puzzle of representation. Anyone who has the least sensitivity to the representative process recognizes that representatives are influenced in their conduct by many forces or pressures or linkages other than those arising out of the electoral connection and should realize that restricting the study of representation to the electoral connection produces a very limited vision of the representational process. Miller and Stokes themselves were eminently aware of this, as their "Conclusion" indicated. Yet, only three years after publication of their analysis, when two other analysts (Cnudde and McCrone, 1966), subjecting the Miller-Stokes data to an alternative causal analysis, found no support for recruitment as a condition of representation, constituency control was reduced to a purely psychological function in the representative's mind, and the danger of limiting the "representative relation" to attitudinal and perceptual congruence was demonstrated. Moreover, these analysts altogether ignored Miller and Stokes' important third condition for constituency influence through the electoral connection: constituents' taking account of the candidate's policy views in choosing the representative.

Indeed, Miller and Stokes themselves had the most trouble with this last condition. The overwhelming evidence of their research and that of others denies the condition: most citizens are not competent to perform the function which the model assumes—that elections are in fact effective sanctioning mechanisms in the representational relationship. Miller and Stokes gave a number of "reasons" for why representatives seem to be so sensitive about their voting records—for if voters do not know the record, this sensitivity is surely puzzling. They suggested that the voting record may be known to the few voters who, in close contests, make the difference between victory or defeat, and that the Congressman is a "dealer in increments and margins." They also speculated that the voting record may be known to opinion leaders in the district who serve as gatekeepers and conveyors of evaluation in a two-step flow of communication. But there is no evidence for this in their own research.[6]

THE CRISIS IN REPRESENTATIONAL THEORY

It would not yield further theoretical dividends to review in any detail the empirical studies of representation that, in one way or another, are predicated on the attitudinal-perceptual formulation of congruence that had served Miller and Stokes as a starting point but that, for most of their successors, became a terminal point. Most of these studies are distinguished by lack of historical-theoretical knowledge of representation and of independent theoretical creativity. In particular, they are cavalier in regard to a number of dilemmas that, by the middle sixties, had forced themselves on the attention of scholars interested in theoretical understanding of the problem of representation. That these dilemmas were articulated by different scholars at about the same time was probably coincidental, but the coincidence is important because it emphasized the possibility of alternative research directions.

First, representational theory made assumptions about citizen behavior that were negated by the empirical evidence. Wahlke, examining the role of the represented in the representational relationship, concluded that the evidence did not justify treating citizens as significant sources of policy demands, positions or even broad orientations that could be somehow "represented" in the policy-making process. Citizens simply lack the necessary information for effective policy choices to be communicated to their representatives, even if they were to make the effort to communicate. This being the case, Wahlke concluded that the "simple demand-input model" of representation was deficient. This is of course precisely the model that Miller-Stokes had in fact constructed in order to organize and explain their data. Wahlke suggested that a "support-input model" might be more appropriate.[7]

Second, given the limited capacity of the represented to formulate policy, a viable theory could no longer ignore the asymmetry of the representational relationship. Eulau suggested, therefore, that research should proceed from the structural assumption of a built-in status difference between representative and represented in which the former rather than the latter give direction to the relationship. Representational theory would have to deal with the tensions arising out of status differentiation rather than deny their existence (Eulau, 1967). Once status is introduced as a variable into the representational equation, the model of the representational relationship can be recursive, and the causal ordering of the relevant variables is likely to be reversed.

Finally, in a linguistic study of the concept of representation, Pitkin (1967) found the traditional theories of representation flawed. She advanced the proposition that representation, referring to a social relationship rather than to an attribute of the individual person, could be meaningfully conceptualized only as a systemic property. Representation might or might not emerge at the level of the collectivity, the criterion of emergence being the collectivity's potential for "responsiveness." Political representation "is primarily a public, institutionalized arrangement involving many people and groups, and operating in the complex ways of large-scale social arrangements. What makes it representation is not any single action by any one participant, but the over-all structure and functioning of the system, the patterns emerging from the multiple activities of many people" (pp. 221-222). Moreover, after considering every conceivable definition, Pitkin concluded that political representation means "acting in the interest of the represented, in a manner responsive to them" (p. 209). However, there is also the stipulation that the representative "must not be found persistently at odds with the wishes of the represented without good reason in terms of their interest, without a good explanation of why their views are not in accord with their interests" (pp. 209-210).

Pitkin's formulation creates many measurement problems for empirical research. Concepts like "wishes," "good reason," "interest," or "views," are difficult to operationalize. She provides no clues as to how "responsiveness" as a systemic property of the political collectivity can be ascertained and how, indeed, it can be measured in ways enabling the scientific observer to conclude that representation has in fact emerged at the level of the political system. Pitkin's treatment seems to stress the condition in which the representative stands ready to be responsive when the constituents do have something to say. A legislature may, therefore, be responsive whether or not there are specific instances of response. In other words, Pitkin emphasized a potential for response rather than an act of response. There are considerable difficulties in empirically working with a concept stressing the possibility of an act rather than the act itself. Moremover, the formulation ignores Wahlke's injunction to jettison the demand-input model. Nevertheless, Pitkin's **work had an almost immediate and profound effect on subsequent empirical** research. (See Prewitt and Eulau, 1969; Muller, 1970; Peterson, 1970.)

Research on representation following the watershed year of 1967 has taken two major innovative routes. First, taking their cue from Wahlke's critique of the demand-input model, Patterson, Hedlund, and Boynton (1975) have used a support-input model that makes fewer requirements on the capacity of the represented to play a role in the representational process. However, their model continues to be based on congruence assumptions. Their analysis, conducted at the level of the individual, largely consists of comparison of the represented and representational elites in terms of relevant attitudes, perceptions and behavior patterns.

Second, taking a cue from Pitkin, Eulau and Prewitt (1973) transformed data collected at the level of individuals into grouped data, and conducted their analysis of representation at the macro level of small decision-making groups (city councils). In contrast to Patterson and his associates, Eulau and Prewitt stressed actual rather than potential response to constituent inputs, whether of the demand or support variety. In retrospect, it appears, they were harnessing "reactive" behavior rather than responsive behavior in Pitkin's sense, for they ignored the direction of the response—whether it was in fact "in the interest of" the constituents at the focus of representation. But these retrospective musings only suggest that the problem of conceptualizing representation in term of responsiveness remains on the agenda of theory and research. As Loewenberg (1972: 12) has summed up the situation more recently:

> Representation . . . is an ill-defined concept that has acquired conflicting meanings
> through long use. It may be employed to denote any relationship between rulers and
> ruled or it may connote responsiveness, authorization, legitimation, or accountability.

It may be used so broadly that any political institution performs representative functions or so narrowly that only an elected legislature can do so. To a surprising extent, the Burkean conceptualization of the representative function is still in use, and Eulau's call for a concept adequate to modern concerns about the relationship between legislators and their constituencies has not been answered.

RESPONSIVENESS AS CONGRUENCE

Although the expectations or behavioral patterns to which the term "responsiveness" refers were implicit in the concept of "representative government,"[8] the term as such had not been used by Miller and Stokes or others as the defining characteristics of representation. By 1967, when Pitkin's work was published, the term struck an attractive chord as the ideals of "participatory democracy" were once more being revived in neopopulist movements that had intellectual spokesmen in the social sciences. Even though one should not expect a close affinity between the vocabulary of participation and the vocabulary of representation on logical-theoretical grounds, a term like responsiveness stemming from considerations of representative democracy could easily blend in with considerations of participatory democracy. When analysts of political participation like Verba and Nie (1972) came to pay attention to empirical work on representation, they had little trouble in linking, by way of an adaptation of the assumption of congruence, the concept of responsiveness to their work on participation. Interestingly, although they did not cite or refer to Pitkin's linguistic analysis, Verba and Nie found, on the one hand, that "responsiveness, as far as we can tell, rarely has been defined precisely, almost never has been measured, and never has been related to participation" (p. 300). On the other hand, they acknowledged Miller and Stokes, who had not used the term: "Miller and Stokes in their analysis of the relationship between constituency attitudes and Congressmen, do deal with responsiveness in ways similar to ours" (p. 300, ft. 3).

Indeed, in examining and seeking to explain the effects of different degrees of citizen participation on the responsiveness of community leaders, Verba and Nie present a rechristened version of the congruence assumption of representation which they call "concurrence":

> Our measure of concurrence depends on how well the priorities of the citizens and the leaders match. Several types of concurrence are possible . . . our measure of the concurrence between citizens and community leaders measures the extent to which citizens and leaders in the community choose the same "agenda" of community priorities (p. 302).

But they immediately raise the critical problem of causality: "whether we have the warrant to consider our measure of *concurrence* to be a measure of responsiveness. Just because leaders agree with citizens and that agreement increases as citizens become more active, can we be sure that it is citizen activity that is causing leaders to *respond* by adopting the priorities of the citizen?" (p. 304).

In order to test for the causal relationship, Verba and Nie compared the correlation coefficients obtained for the relationship between "citizen activeness" and concurrence, on the one hand, and between "leader activeness" and concurrence, on the other hand. Finding that the correlations for citizens are "much stronger" than those for leaders, Verba and Nie concluded that their measure of concurrence "seems to be a valid measure of responsiveness to leaders" (pp. 331-332). But this mechanical comparison is not a test of causality at all in regard to the direction of responsiveness. In fact, it amounts to a false interpretation of the data. The correlations for citizens simply mean that more active citizens see things (priorities to be done in the community) more like leaders do than is the case with less active citizens; the correlations for leaders simply mean that the more active leaders see things more like citizens do than is the case with less active leaders. The strength of the coefficients, all of which are positive for both citizens and leaders, does not prove anything about the direction of causality—whether citizens influence leaders or leaders influence citizens, or whether citizens are responsive to leaders or leaders to citizens. It cannot be otherwise because Verba and Nie's measure of concurrence, like Miller and Stokes' measure of congruence, is neutral as to direction and requires that the direction of the relationships involved in the model be theoretically stipulated. There is no such stipulation in the Verba-Nie application of the concurrence measure to the question of linkage between leaders and led.

Causal analysis, then, does not free the analyst from defining his terms—be they power and influence, or be they responsiveness—in advance and stipulating the direction of expected relationships in advance.[9] The mechanical application of statistical tests of a possible causal structure does not necessarily model real-world relationships if the operational definitions of the model's components make no theoretical sense. Verba and Nie's two-edged use of responsiveness, operationalized in terms of the directionless concept of concurrence, is intrinsically characterized by ambiguity. If concurrence is a measure of responsiveness of leaders to citizens, it cannot be a measure of responsiveness of citizens to leaders. If one were to take their comparison of the correlations between participation and concurrence for citizens and leaders as an indication of anything, it would have to be that leaders are responsive to citizens and citizens are responsive to leaders, varying in degree with degree of participation.

Pitkin, it was noted, had raised the importance of responsiveness as the critical characteristic of representation, but she had left the term undefined. Representatives, in order to represent, were to be responsive to their constituents, but Pitkin did not specify the content or target of responsiveness. Verba and Nie had taken a step forward by specifying public policy issues as the target of responsiveness. In focusing exclusively on congruence or concurrence in regard to policy attitudes or preferences, they ignored other possible targets in the relationship between representatives and represented which may also give content to the notion of responsiveness. By emphasizing only one component of responsiveness as a substantive concept, they reduced a complex phenomenon like representation to one of its components and substituted the component for the whole. But if responsiveness is limited to one component, it cannot capture the complexities of the real world of politics. It is necessary, therefore, to view responsiveness as a complex, compositional phenomenon that entails a variety of possible targets in the relationship between representatives and represented. How else could one explain that representatives manage to stay in office in spite of the fact that they are *not* necessarily or always responsive to the represented as the conception of representation as congruence or concurrence of policy preferences requires?

It deserves mention that Miller and Stokes (1963) had themselves realized that there are possible targets of responsiveness other than policy issues. They emphasized the "necessity of specifying the acts *with respect to which* one actor has power or influence or control over another." Their target, they conceded, was only the set of issues lying within the three policy areas of civil rights, social welfare and foreign involvement. But significantly they added. "We are not able to say how much control the local constituency may or may not have over *all* actions of its Representative, and there may well be pork-barrel issues or other public matters of peculiar relevance to the district on which the relation of Congressman to constituency is quite distinctive" (p. 48). Miller and Stokes did not specify what they referred to as "other public matters." It is the task of the rest of this paper to suggest what some of these other targets of responsiveness might be.

COMPONENTS OF RESPONSIVENESS

There are four possible components of responsiveness which, as a whole, constitute representation. While each component can be treated as an independent target of responsiveness, all four must be considered together in the configurative type of analysis which, it seems to us, the complexity of the representational nexus requires. The first component is, or course, *policy responsiveness* where the target is the great public issues that agitate the political process. Second, there is *service responsiveness* which involves the efforts of the representative to secure particularized benefits for individuals or groups in his constituency. Third, there is *allocation responsiveness* which refers to the representative's effort to obtain benefits for his constituency through pork-barrel exchanges in the appropriations process or through administrative interventions. Finally, there is what we shall call *symbolic responsiveness* which involves public gestures of a sort that create a sense of trust and support in the relationship between representative and represented. It is possible that there are other targets of responsive conduct which, in composition with the four here tapped, constitute the matrix of representational relationships. But the main point we are trying to make is this: responsiveness refers not just to "this" or "that" target of political activity on the part of the representative but to a number of targets. Only when responsiveness is viewed as a compositional phenomenon can the approach to representation-as-responsiveness recommended by Pitkin be useful. It is the configuration of the component aspects of responsiveness that might yield a viable theory of representative government under modern conditions of societal complexity.

Policy Responsiveness

How the representative and the represented interact with respect to the making of public policy lies at the heart of most discussions of responsiveness. Responsiveness in this sense refers to the structure in which district positions on policy issues, specified as some measure of central tendency or dispersion, are related to the policy orientation of the representative—attitudinal or perceptual—and to his subsequent decision-making conduct in a given field of policy.

The premise underlying the specification of policy responsiveness is the presence of a meaningful connection between constituent policy preferences or demands and the representative's official behavior. This is what Miller and Stokes called "congruence" and what Verba and Nie called "concurrence." Whatever the term, the operational definition is the same: if the representative and his constituency agree on a particular policy, no matter how the agreement has come about, then the representative is responsive. There are, as has been noted, several problems with the model of representation built on the operationalization of responsiveness as congruence, notably the problem that congruence is neither a necessary nor a sufficient condition for responsiveness. The representative may react to constituency opinion, and hence evince congruent attitudes or behavior, yet not act in what is in the best interest of the constituency as he might wish to define that interest, thereby being in fact unresponsive. Further, the representative may make policy in response to groups and interests other than his constituents, including executive and bureaucratic agencies. Whether such conduct is also in the interest of his district as he sees it is an empirical question. But whatever the formulation and findings, it cannot be denied that policy responsiveness is an important component of representation.

The notion of policy responsiveness is implicit in some of the classic theories of representation. First of all, the controversy over mandate versus independence, whether the representative is a delegate or a trustee, though considered obsolete by Eulau (1967: 78-79) and in many respects resolved by Pitkin (1967: 144-167), is still intriguing and relevant to the present discussion. For the debate is over whether the representative should act according to what *he* thinks is in the "best interest" of the constituency, regardless of constituency "wants," or whether he should follow the "expressed wishes" of the district, regardless of how he personally feels. The debate really turns on the competence of the citizenry in matters of public policy. For while the citizenry may know what it wants, it may not know what it needs. Secondly, therefore, an appropriate definition of policy responsiveness will be related to the classic issue of "district interest" as against "district will." There is no denying that the notion of policy responsiveness pervades empirical research on legislative decision-making, even when the issue of representation as a theoretical one is not raised. (For recent research, see Turner and Schneier, 1970; Kingdon, 1973; Clausen, 1973; Jackson, 1974; Matthews and Stimson, 1975.) However, precisely because this is the case, it is important not to ignore other components of responsiveness in the representational relationship. Exclusive emphasis on the policy aspects of responsiveness may give a one-sided view and may not help in solving the puzzle of representation.

Service Responsiveness

A second target for responsiveness to define the representational relationship concerns the non-legislative services that a representative actually performs for individuals or groups in his district. Service responsiveness, then, refers to the advantages and benefits which the representative is able to obtain for particular constituents. There are a number of services that constituents may expect and that the representative considers an intrinsic part of his role. Some of them involve only modest, if time consuming, requests, such as responding to written inquiries involving constituents' personal concerns, or facilitating meetings and tours for visitors from the home district. Newsletters or columns in local newspapers may be used to inform constituents of legislation that may be of interest and use to them. Much of this work is routine and carried out in regular fashion.

Another link in the chain of service responsiveness is often referred to as case work. (See Clapp, 1963.) Given his official position and presumed influence, the representative is in a position to solve particular problems for members of his constituency. The representative intervenes between constituents and bureaucrats in such matters as difficulties with a tax agency, delays in welfare payments, securing a job in government, and so on. Providing constituent services and doing case work constitute for many representatives more significant aspects of their representational role than does legislative work like bill-drafting or attending committee hearings. These "errand boy" functions deserve more theoretical attention than they have been given in contemporary research. In some important situations the representative may actually serve as an advocate and even lobbyist for special interests in his district vis-à-vis the legislature, departmental bureaucracies or regulatory agencies. This type of responsiveness is indeed crucial in trying to understand modern representative government.

This notion of service responsiveness seemed to underlie Eulau and Prewitt's (1973: 424-427, 649-650) operational definition of responsiveness. In their study of San Francisco Bay Area city councils, they initially divided these small representative bodies into those which seemed to be somehow responsive to constituent needs or wants and those which did not seem to be responsive. They then distinguished among the former councils those which were responsive to important standing interests in the community or attentive publics, and those which more often were responsive only to temporary alliances having a particular grievance or request. This conception of responsiveness, then, is based on the kind of group or individuals whom the representative perceives as being primarily served by his activities. Zeigler and Jennings (1974: 77-94), in a study of school boards, present a similar conception of responsiveness, conceptually distinguishing more sharply between "group responsiveness" and "individualized responsiveness." Both of these research teams, then, defined responsiveness in terms of the significant recipients of representational services.

That service responsiveness is an important element in representation should be apparent. Moreover, there is every reason to believe that it is increasing rather than declining. Until the middle sixties, it was generally assumed that case work and the advocacy of special interests bring advantages and benefits only to those who take the initiative in soliciting the representative's help. But as Fiorina (1967: 180) has recently pointed out, at least with reference to the federal level, increased bureaucratic activity in the wake of increased federal largesse to all kinds of population groups has also motivated congressmen to "undoubtedly stimulate the demand for their bureaucratic fixit services." The representative does not just respond to demands for his good offices and services; he has become a kind of hustler who advertises and offers them on his own initiative.[10]

This explication of service responsiveness has been entirely focused on the relationship between the representative and particular constituents. The representative can also be responsive in his unique role as middleman in the allocation of more generalized benefits. We refer here to what has been traditionally called "pork-barrel politics" and to what we shall refer, for lack of a better term, as "allocation responsiveness." Both service responsiveness, whether initiated by the representative or not, and allocation responsiveness, which is always initiated by him, are important elements of representational behavior and important pillars in the representational relationship.

Allocation Responsiveness

It has long been recognized that pork-barrel politics in legislative allocations of public projects involves advantages and benefits presumably accruing to a representative's district as a whole. Although traditionally these allocations were seen as "public goods," with the expansion of the government's role in all sectors of society—industry, agriculture, commerce, health, education, welfare, internal security, and so on—the distinction between public and private benefits is difficult to maintain. Again, as Fiorina (1977: 180) has felicitously put it in connection with federal politics, "The pork-barreler need not limit himself to dams and post offices. There is LEEA money for the local police; urban renewal and housing money for local officials; and educational program grants for the local education bureaucracy. The congressman can stimulate applications for federal assistance, put in a good word during consideration, and announce favorable decisions amid great fanfare." Such allocations may benefit the district as a whole, or they may benefit some constituents more than others because they make more use of the benefits. The critical point to be made is that in being responsive as an "allocator," whether in the legislature or bureaucratic processes, the representative seeks to anticipate the needs of his clients and, in fact, can stimulate their wants.

Legislators' committee memberships sometimes serve as indicators of allocation responsiveness, as revealed in Fenno's (1973) studies of legislative conduct in committees of the U.S. House of Representatives. A representative from a district that has a particular stake in a committee's jurisdiction will often seek a post on a parent committee but also on a particularly suitable sub-committee; such membership presumably enables him to act in a manner responsive to the best interests of his district and some or all of his constituents.

However, one cannot automatically assume that a legislator serving on a committee "not relevant" to his district is necessarily unresponsive and not interested in securing allocations. Legislators often seek preferment on important committees like Rules, Appropriations, or Ways and Means not because these committees are directly "relevant" to the interests of their constituents, but because they place members in positions of power and influence vis-à-vis administrative agencies which distribute benefits, such as the Army Corps of Engineers, the Park Service, or the Veterans Administration. These secondary bonds are probably as critical in securing benefits for the district as are the primary bonds resulting from "relevant" committee assignments. However, the secondary bonds have less symbolic value than do the primary bonds. And symbolic pay-offs, we shall see, are an important fourth component of representational responsiveness.

Symbolic Responsiveness

The fourth component of responsiveness is more psychologically based than the others. The first three components all somehow tap a behavioral aspect of representation: policy responsiveness is oriented toward the decison-making behavior of the representative in matters of public controversy; while service and allocation responsiveness are oriented toward particularized or collective benefits obtained through the acts of the representative. The representational relationship is not, however, just one of such concrete transactions, but also one that is built on trust and confidence expressed in the support that the represented give to the representative and to which he responds by symbolic, significant gestures, in order to, in turn, generate and maintain continuing support.

The notion of symbolic responsiveness has been alluded to by Wahlke (1971) in examining the role of the constituency in the representational relationship. He found little evidence for presuming that a district makes specific policy demands on its representative. Rather, he suggested the relevance of Easton's concept of diffuse support (1965: 247-340) as a key component in the relationship between the represented and their representative. He states that the "symbolic satisfaction with the process of government is probably more important than specific instrumental satisfaction with the policy output of the process" (Wahlke, 1971: 288). The important question then becomes, ". . . how do representative bodies contribute to the generation and maintenance of support?" (p. 290).

In an era of cynicism about the functioning of representative institutions, the ways in which representatives manipulate political symbols in order to generate and maintain trust or support become critical aspects of responsiveness. Edelman (1964, 1971), following the earlier work of Merriam, Lasswell, and Smith (1950), has emphasized the importance of symbolic action in politics. The need for giving symbolic reassurance is being demonstrated by the "reach out" efforts of the new President of the United States—walking down Pennsylvania Avenue after his inauguration, fire-side chats, telephonic call-a-thons, visits to economically stricken areas, being "Jimmy" Carter, and so on. The purpose of all of these symbolic acts is to project an image that the President is truly the people's representative and ready to be responsive to them. By mobilizing trust and confidence it is presumably easier to go about the job of representation than would otherwise be the case.

Fenno, in a study of congressmen's "home style" (1977), emphasizes the importance of political support in the representational relationship. The representative's "home style"—how he behaves *in* his constituency—is designed not just to secure constituent support and re-election but also to give the representative more freedom in his legislative activities when he is away from home. Symbolic politics has the purpose of building up credit to be drawn on in future contingencies. Fenno's comments are all the more germane to the argument of this paper because it is interesting to note that this most eminent of legislative scholars deflates the prevailing obsession with policy responsiveness as the *sine qua non* of representation. In fact, such of what may appear to be policy responsiveness is largely symbolic responsiveness. From session to session, legislators on all levels of government—federal, state, and local—introduce thousands of bills which have not the slightest chance of ever being passed and, more often than not, are not intended to be passed. Yet representatives introduce these bills to please some constituents and to demonstrate their own responsiveness.[11]

RESPONSIVENESS AND FOCUS OF REPRESENTATION

Once the concept of representation-as-responsiveness is decomposed, policy responsiveness appears as only one component of representation and, perhaps, as by no means the dominant link between representative and represented. There is no intrinsic reason why responsiveness in one component of representation cannot go together with unresponsiveness in another. An individual or group may disagree with the representative's position and behavior on an issue of public policy and, as a result, may be unrepresented in this sense; yet, the same individual or group may be well represented by a person who is responsive by attending to their particular requests for some type of service. Similarly, it is possible for a representative to be responsive with regard to securing public goods for his constituency, while simultaneously being quite unresponsive with respect to issues of public policy. Finally, what matters in symbolic responsiveness is that the constituents feel represented, quite regardless of whether the representative is responsive in his policy stands or the services or public goods he provides for his constituency.

Moreover, even if attention is given only to policy responsiveness, research cannot simply neglect some of the classical questions of representational theory, such as the issue of representing the district's will as against its interest, or the issue of the focus of representation. It is easily conceivable that being responsive to a district's will—the wants of its people—may involve being unresponsive to a district's interest—the needs of its people. With regard to the focus of representation, being responsive to the electoral district may produce unresponsive behavior in the larger unit of which the district is a part and, of course, vice versa.[12]

In fact, a closer look at the question of representational focus will reveal further the potentially multidimensional character of the phenomenon of responsiveness. The representative can perceive his "constituency" in a multitude of ways,[13] thereby making the number of foci quite large. One might organize the possible foci into three categories. The first category entails a geographic focus; the representative may perceive his constituency in terms of nation, region, state, district, or any other territorial level of society. The second category would include particular solidary or functional groupings like ethnic, religious, economic, and ideological groups, whether organized or not. Finally, the representational relationship may have as foci individual persons ranging from distinguished notables to unknown clients in need of help and to personal friends.

Representational focus, then, can differ a great deal in each of these three ways. The crucial point, however, is that the focus of representation might vary with each of the four components of responsiveness. While one might find particular foci, according to the three categories, for policy responsiveness, one might find altogether different foci in regard to any of the other components of responsiveness. Any empirical combination is possible within relevant logical constraints. Empirical research has yet to address the relationship between modes of responsiveness and foci of representation, and untangle the web of complexity created by the relationship.

RESPONSIVENESS VERSUS RESPONSE

The generally confused and confusing use of "responsiveness," especially when linked to notions of "concurrence," is only symptomatic of a malaise that has come to characterize the "scientific" study of politics. The malaise is to substitute "theory construction" as a technique for substantive theory or theorizing. A younger scholar in the field, Fiorina (1974: 24), after reviewing the empirical research on representation of recent vintage, has come to a similar conclusion. We quote him precisely because he is not ignorant of or inimical to the new technological dispensations of our time:

> Too often it seems that the increasing availability of electronic computing facilities, data banks, and canned statistical packages has encouraged a concomitant decline in the use of our own capabilities. Rather than hypothesize we factor analyze, regress, or causal model. We speak of empirical theory as if it miraculously grows out of a cumulation of empirical findings, rather than as a logical structure one must carefully construct to explain those findings.

When Fiorina identifies "data banks" as one of the villains, he presumably implies that the user of these facilities has grown increasingly remote from his subjects of observation and lost touch with the humanity he is supposed to understand. Indeed, there are today users of survey research who have never interviewed a single person in their lives. Not surprisingly, therefore, causal models are being reified as if they described reality rather than being abstractions from reality. In the case of representational responsiveness, for instance, the causal direction has been assumed to point from the represented to the representative; the latter has been assumed to be the object of stimuli to which he responds (or does not respond) in the fashion of Pavlov's famous dog. But such a model, even if one provides for intervening attitudinal or perceptual processes, does not approximate representational relationships which are, above all, transactions not necessarily structured in the ways of the S-O-R paradigm.

To appreciate the complexity of representational relationships as transactions, it is simply erroneous to assume that responsivenes—whatever component may be involved—is somehow the dependent variable in a causal structure. "Responsiveness" and "response" are not the same thing. On the contrary, a representative whose behavior is purely *reactive*—a condition that is hard to conceive on reflection but one that the "concurrence model" postulates—is the very opposite of a politically responsive person in Pitkin's sense. As that person has been chosen, elected, or selected from the multitude or mass to be a representative, that is, as he occupies a superior position in the relationship by virtue of his "elevation," one should expect him not merely to be reactive but to take the initiative. Whether he does or not is, of course, an empirical question; but the question cannot be answered by simply substituting an inappropriate model of causation for empirical observation and a viable theory of representation that would guide both observation and analysis.

As already suggested, the attractiveness of the notion of responsiveness in the most recent period has been due in part to the fusion of participatory and representational ideas about democracy. But in the participatory theory of democracy the leader—insofar as the model admits of leadership at all—is largely a reactive agent guided by the collective wisdom of the group. He is at best the executor of the group's will, indeed a human facsimile of Pavlov's dog. He reacts, presumably, but he is not responsive. One is in fact back to the "instructed-delegate" model in which there is no room for discretion in the conduct of the representative. A causal model of representation that draws its arrows only in recursive fashion from the represented to the representative cannot capture, therefore, the meaning of responsiveness in Pitkin's sense. It excludes *ab initio* what is yet to be concluded.

It is a grievous error, against which Fiorina warned, to assume and to act as if the assumption were valid, that "causal analysis" will automatically yield "theory," or that by simple inversion of causal assumptions something meaningful will come out of a causal analysis. Theorizing involves something more than arbitrarily inverting the causal directions on the assumption that the resultant statistical structure will somehow reflect reality. It involves *giving reasons* and *justifying* the assumptions one brings into the causal analysis. It involves "going out on a limb," as it were, and saying something substantive about the phenomena being investigated, rather than hiding behind the artifactual "findings" of a causal analysis that may be inappropriate in the first place.

A next step in the study of representation as responsiveness must take off from the compositional nature of the phenomenon. This step cannot be limited to simplistic measures like congruence or concurrence in connection with one component of a complex set of transactional relationships. Any inferences one may make about the functions of any one component of responsiveness in "representative government" must be related to inferences one may make about the functions of other components. Otherwise the puzzle of representation—having representative government but not knowing what it is about—will continue to bewilder the political imagination.

NOTES

1. Miller and Stokes (1963). A revised version is included in Campbell, Converse, Miller, and Stokes (1966: 351-372). We shall be citing the original article because we are only interested here in the theoretical aspects of the analysis which remained unaffected by the revision. The particular analysis was part of a much larger study of representation conducted in connection with the 1958 congressional elections.

2. In footnote 2 of their original article Miller and Stokes refer to Eulau, Wahlke, Buchanan, and Ferguson (1959); Hanna F. Pitkin's then unpublished Ph.D. dissertation (1961), which presumably led to her later *The Concept of Representation* (1967); de Grazia (1951); and Fairlie (1940).

3. The two most significant studies of the fifties in this genre were: Turner (1951) and MacRae (1958).

4. The operational definition was expressed as follows: "in each policy domain, crossing the rankings of Congressmen and their constituencies gives an empirical measure of the extent of policy agreement between legislator and district." The measure itself was expressed as follows: "To summarize the degree of congruence between legislators and voters, a measure of correlation is introduced" (Miller and Stokes, 1963: 49 and ft. 10).

5. See, e.g., Stone (1976: 8), where one finds the bland statement: "Representation is conceived as congruence or agreement between the behavior of the legislator and the opinion of the constituency on comparable policy dimensions." Compare this also with Clausen (1973: 128): "Given the principal orientation of this book, the policy orientation, representation is further defined as the congruence of the policy requirements of the constituency with the policy decisions of the representative."

6. Instead, to illustrate the constituency's sanctioning power through elections, Miller and Stokes relied on data for a single Congressional district in a case which is both inappropriate and deviant, involving the defeat of Congressman Brook Hays in the Fifth Arkansas District where all *voters* in the sample (N=13) had read or heard "something" about Hays and his write-in opponent. But, as Miller and Stokes admit, the case was inappropriate: the voters probably knew little about Hays' legislative record in the previous Congress but punished him for his non-legislative role in the Little Rock school crisis. The Hays case indicated the power of an aroused electorate in an unusual situation; but even if they knew the legislative records of their representatives, electorates are rarely so aroused over any one of the many legislative issues with which representatives deal.

7. Wahlke (1971). The core ideas of this article were first presented by Wahlke in a 1967 paper before the Seventh World Congress of the International Political Science Association in Brussels, Belgium.

8. We could cite here, of course, an extensive "institutional" literature which has come to be neglected by "behavioral" students of representation. For a particularly useful recent introduction that paints a broad canvas, see Birch (1971).

9. The problem with causal analyses of phenomena like influence or responsiveness is that the direction of the relationships to which they presumably refer cannot be inferred from the causal structure of the statistical model that may be applied. The statistical model assumes the existence of a conceptual isomorphism between its ordering of the variables and their real-world ordering. The existence of a *possible* isomorphism between the direction of a political relationship and a causal relation between two variables in a statistical model was brought to the attention of political scientists in a series of papers by Herbert A. Simon. Attempting to define political power, Simon found that "the difficulty appeared to reside in a very specific technical point; influence, power, and authority are all intended as asymmetrical relations." It seemed to him that "the mathematical counterpart of this asymmetrical relation appeared to be the distinction between independent and dependent variables—the independent variable determines the dependent, and not the converse." But he pointed out in a significant passage that causal analysts seem at times to overlook, "in algebra, the distinction between independent and dependent variable is purely conventional—we can always rewrite our equations without altering their content in such a way as to reverse their roles." The problem, then, is one of giving operational meaning to the asymmetry that is implied in the definition of influence or power: "That is to say, for the assertion, 'A has power over B,' we can substitute the assertion, 'A's behavior causes B' behavior.' If we can define the causal relation, we can define influence, power, or authority, and *vice versa*." See Simon (1957: 5). The most significant term in Simon's explication of the causal relation is "vice versa." It suggests that the definition of the "causal relation" and the definition of the phenomenon to be causally treated (here influence) are interdependent events. In other words: "If we can define influence, we can define the causal relation."

10. Unfortunately Fiorina then characterizes the new-style Congressman as an "ombudsman." This attribution is inappropriate because an ombudsman, though presumably available for the settlement of grievances, is not the kind of "hustler" whom Fiorina sees as coming on the stage of representation. Of course, both roles seem to be involved—that of ombudsman and that of hustler.

11. For example, Froman (1967: 36) found that in the 88th Congress (1963-1964) 15,299 bills and resolutions were introduced in the House of Representatives, whereas only 1,742, or a little over 11 percent, were reported by committee.

12. For the distinction between "style" and "focus" of representation, see Eulau, Wahlke, Buchanan, and Ferguson (1959).

13. Fenno (1978) has also seen the need to decompose the concept of constituency. He suggests that congressmen perceive several distinct types of constituencies to which they respond in different ways.

Chapter 4

POLICY DEMANDS AND SYSTEM SUPPORT:

The Role of the Represented

JOHN C. WAHLKE

Discontent with the functioning of representative bodies is hardly new. Most of them were born and developed in the face of opposition denying their legitimacy and their feasibility.[1] Most have lived amid persistent unfriendly attitudes, ranging from the total hostility of anti-democrats to the pessimistic assessments of such diverse commentators as Lord Bryce, Walter Lippmann, and Charles de Gaulle.[2] Of particular interest today is the discontent with representative bodies expressed by the friends of democracy, the supporters of representative government, many of whom see in recent history a secular "decline of parliament" and in prospect the imminent demise of representative bodies.

Much of the pessimism among the friends of representative government appears, however, to be very poorly grounded. The notion that we are witnessing "the decline of parliament," it has been observed, "has never been based on careful inquiry into the function of parliaments in their presumed golden age, nor into their subsequent performance" (Loewenberg, 1967: 1). Neither has it rested on careful inquiry into the functions and roles of citizens, individually and collectively, in a representative democracy. Indeed, it is both possible and likely that, "If there is a crisis, . . . it is a crisis in the theory of representation and not in the institution of representation" (Eulau, 1967: 55). This paper suggests how (and why) we might begin to reformulate representation theory and to identify the critical questions which research must answer.

MODELS OF REPRESENTATION

Much of the disillusionment and dissatisfaction with modern representative government grows out of a fascination with the policy decisions of representative bodies which, in turn, reflects what may be called a "policy-demand-input" conception of government in general and the representative processes in particular. Theorists and researchers alike have long taken it for granted that the problem of representative government centers on the linkage between citizens' policy preferences and the public-policy decisions of representative bodies. Almost without exception they have conceived of the public side of this relationship in terms of "demands" and the assembly side in terms of "responses." Julius Turner (1951), for instance, has said that, "the representative process in twentieth-century America involves ... the attempt of the representative to mirror the political desires of those groups which can bring about his election or defeat." Almond and Verba (1963: 214), in the course of explicating new dimensions of civic behavior (to which we shall return) take the making of demands to be the characteristic act of citizens in democratic systems: "The competent citizen has a role in the formation of general policy. Furthermore, he plays an *influential* role in this decision-making process: he participates through the use of explicit or implicit threats of some form of deprivation if the official does not comply with his demands."[3]

The Simple Demand-Input Model

The basic elements in the general policy-demand-input conception can be described, in necessarily oversimplified form, as follows. The principal force in a representative system is (as it ought to be) the conscious desires and wishes of citizens, frequently examined in modern research on representation under the heading of "interest." Interests are thought of as constituting "policy demands" or "policy expectations," and the governmental process seems to "begin" with citizens exerting them on government. Government, in this view, is essentially a process for discovering policies which will maximally meet the policy expectations of citizens. There are several points at which emphases or interpretations may vary in important respects, but the critical assumptions of this view and the points at which such variations may occur can readily be outlined.

In the first place, the interests which constitute the fundamental stuff of democratic, representative politics, are most often thought of in terms of specific policy opinions or attitudes, i.e., preference or dislike for particular courses of government action. But it is also common to envision citizens holding less specific policy preferences, in the form of ideological orientations or belief systems.

Although "interests" are taken to be rooted in individual desires, they may be expressed in the form of either individual policy opinions (often aggregated by opinion analysts as "public opinion" or the opinion of some segment of the public), or organized group or association opinion, usually thought to be expressed on behalf of the individuals by group agents or spokesmen, or, of course, in both forms simultaneously.

Analytically, the core of the representative process is the communication of these various forms of interest to governmental actors, which is thought to occur in either or both of two principal ways. It may take place through constituency influence, i.e., the communication of aggregated individual views by constituents to their "representatives." (The latter term theoretically includes administrative agency personnel, police officials, judges, and countless other governmental actors, but we shall deal here only with members of representative bodies.) Communication may also occur through pressure or lobbying activities, conceived of as communication by group agents who are intermediaries between representatives and the aggregates of citizens for whom they (the group agents) speak.

The critical process for making representative government democratically responsible is, of course, election of the representatives. Elections are the indispensable mechanism for ensuring a continuing linkage between citizens' public-policy views (interests) and the public policy formulated by representatives (in cooperation, needless to say, with executives and administrators). The mechanism works in one or both of two ways. It may provide representatives with a mandate to enact into public policy at an early date the policy views expressed in the elections. It may also serve to legitimize, by stamping the *imprimatur* of citizen acceptance on, the policies must recently enacted by the representatives.

However logical and obvious such a conception of democratic representative governmental processes may seem, the observed behavior of citizens is in almost all critical respects inconsistent with it. Some of the more important established propositions about observed behavior which conflict with assumptions about the role of policy-demand inputs in politics may be listed here, even though there is no room to list in detail the evidence supporting them. They are, in most instances, propositions which are well known, although not normally brought to bear in discussions of representation:[4]

1. *Few citizens entertain interests that clearly represent "policy demands" or "policy expectations," or wishes and desires that are readily convertible into them.*
2. *Few people even have thought-out, consistent, and firmly held positions on most matters of public policy.*
3. *It is highly doubtful that policy demands are entertained even in the form of broad orientations, outlooks, or belief systems.*
4. *Large proportions of citizens lack the instrumental knowledge about political structures, processes, and actors that they would need to communicate policy demands or expectations if they had any.*
5. *Relatively few citizens communicate with their representatives.*
6. *Citizens are not especially interested or informed about the policy-making activities of their representatives as such.*
7. *Nor are citizens much interested in other day-to-day aspects of parliamentary functioning.*
8. *Relatively few citizens have any clear notion that they are making policy demands or policy choices when they vote.*

None of this, of course, is new or surprising information. But it is sometimes forgotten when working from slightly less naive models of the representational system than the one sketched out above. Each of the alternative models familiar to students of representative bodies, however, must sooner or later reckon with these facts.

A Responsible-Party Model

Whatever else they are doing in the electoral process, voters in most political systems are certainly choosing between candidates advanced by political parties. It is therefore easy to assume that electoral choice between party-candidates is the vehicle for making policy-choices and to derive logically plausible mechanisms by which that choice might be made. For such mechanisms of demand-input to operate, several requirements would have to be met. In the first place, there must be a party program formulated and it must be known to the voters. Second, representatives' policy-making behavior must reflect that program. Third, voters must identify candidates with programs and legislative records, and base their choices on reaction to them (Stokes and Miller, 1962). The arguments against the American party system and in favor of the British on grounds of systemic capacity for meeting these requirements are well known (Committee, 1950).

In most American contexts, the failure of party and legislative personnel to provide appropriate policy cues makes the applicability of the responsible-party model dubious to begin with, no matter what voters might be doing. But there are also signs of voter failure to respond appropriately to whatever such cues might be available. In one American state (Washington), for example, far less than half the public knew which party controlled either house of the state legislature at its most recent session (41 per cent in the case of the lower, 27 per cent for the upper house) (Showell, 1953). Shortly after the 1966 election in the United States, 31 per cent of the electorate did not know (or was wrong about) which party had a majority in Congress just before the election; more striking still, 34 per cent did not know which party had won most seats in that election and another 45 per cent misinterpreted Republican gains to believe the Republican Party had won a majority! With respect to public reaction to party at the national level, Miller and Stokes (1962: 209) have demonstrated that party symbols are almost devoid of policy content, which is not surprising in view of what they call the legislative party "cacophony." And Converse (1964), in one of the few relevant studies using panel data, found that party identification was far more stable among American voters sampled in 1958 and 1960 than their opinions on any "issues." We can only conclude, at least for the American case, that, with or without policy content, party symbols do not serve the American voter as the responsible party model would wish.

Of somewhat greater interest, however, is the situation in those countries where it seems more likely that party and legislative leaders provide voters the conditions under which they could, if they chose, behave as the responsible-party model would have them. The British political system is usually cited as the classic example. What, then, are the facts about the connection between voting and policy preferences of British voters? Perhaps because it has been so commonly taken for granted that every General Election in Britain constitutes an electoral mandate or at least an unfavorable judgement on past policy performance, surprisingly little evidence is available. The most direct testimony, from a nationwide survey of 1960, is that, given a question asking them to differentiate between the two major parties with respect to sixteen political ends or party traits, on only four of the statements did as many as two-thirds of the sample attribute a clear-cut goal to either party, and these were not stated in policy but in group (e.g., "middle class") or personal terms; on four, some one-half or more were unaware of any difference between the parties, and on the remaining eight, between 33 per cent and 45 per cent detected no differences (Abrams, 1962). There is strong reason, then, to doubt the applicability of the responsible-party model even in Great Britain.

But the most persuasive reason for questioning that model is what we know about the phenomenon of party identification itself. For the mere fact that one political party (or coalition) is replaced in government by another as a result of changing electoral fortunes, together with the fact that voters are making electoral choices between parties, does not in itself demonstrate anything at all about the relationship between election results and the public's view about party programs or policy stands. There is abundant evidence, on the contrary, that in many political systems voters identify with a political party much as they identify with a baseball or soccer team. Many voters in many lands are better described as "rooters," team supporters, than as policy advocates or program evaluators. The authors of *The American Voter* have acquainted us with the importance of that phenomenon in the United States. Of special interest here is their finding that, far from serving as a vehicle for the voter to express prior formed policy views, it is more likely that "party loyalty plays no small role in the formation of attitudes on specific policy matters" (Campbell et al., 1960: 169). More recent studies seem to show that party identification of German voters is in some respects similar (Zölnhofer, 1965). The very great stability of party loyalties in Great Britain suggests strongly the operation of similar mechanisms there (Milne and Mackenzie, 1955: 145):

> Not many people switch their votes in the course of their whole lives; therefore, the number changing in the short period between two successive elections is necessarily small. On this definition, only 4 per cent of the electors in the Bristol sample [Bristol Northeast, 1951] were floaters.

It can hardly be said, then, that the responsible-party model solves any of the theoretical problems encountered in the elementary atomistic model of representative democracy. If anything, it raises further and more serious ones.

Polyarchal and Elitist Models

Historically, the awareness that few human beings are politically involved or active was at the core of many anti-democratic theories. More recently it has been the starting assumption for various elitist conceptions of power structure, particularly at the level of local communities.[5] Still more recently the empirical accuracy of the assumption as well as the justifiability of "elitist" conclusions drawn from it has been questioned and subjected to empirical research (Dahl, 1956, 1961).

Our concern here is not with the general theoretical problems raised by such approaches, however.[6] It is rather with their implications for the demand-input conception of representative processes. The chief implication, of course, is that policy demands and policy expectations are manifested by a relative few and not by citizens in general. This implication is hardly to be questioned. Summarizing relevant knowledge on the point, one article (Verba et al., 1967: 318) noted that "Most recent academic studies of public attitudes . . . indicate differences between the political attitudes of elite groups and attitudes reflected in mass samples." And Converse and Dupeux (1962: 291) have said that "It appears likely that the more notable [Franco-American] differences stem from the actions of elites and require study and explanation primarily at this level, rather than at the level of the mass electorate."

The crucial question, then, concerns the extent to which and the mechanisms by which elites' policy-demanding activities are connected to the representational activities of the mass public. One possibility is that there is competition for different policy satisfactions among different elites, that this competition is settled initially in the governmental process, much as Latham (1952: 35) has described the group process:

> The principal function of official groups is to provide various levels of compromise in the writing of the rules, within the body of agreed principles that forms the consensus upon which the political community rests. In so performing this function, each of the three principal branches of government has a special role.

> The legislature referees the group struggle, ratifies the victories of the successful coalitions, and records the terms of the surrenders, compromises, and conquests in the form of statutes.

What Latham leaves unsaid is how members of the voting public enter into this process "within the body of agreed principles that forms the consensus upon which the political community rests." Does it, by electoral decision, provide the ultimate ratification of policies formulated in the process of compromise among elites (groups)? At the very most, one might look for some "potential" power in the hands of the general public which it could use, if it wished, to ratify or reject policies and programs thus put before it. But all the considerations which made the simple atomistic and responsible-party conceptions implausible apply with equal force and in identical fashion against such an interpretation.

Thus, when we look for public participation through electoral choice among competing elites, we encounter the same difficulties we have encountered before. So-called polyarchal or elite-democracy models are no more helpful in connecting policy-making to policy demands from the public than were the atomistic and party models.

PUBLIC VIEWS AND LEGISLATIVE POLICY

Demand-input emphases have tended also to color our views of what constitutes responsible behavior by elected representatives. Since the kind of findings just surveyed are well known, few modern studies consider Edmund Burke's "instructed delegate model" appropriate for modern legislators (Wahlke et al., 1962; Miller and Stokes, 1963). Most report without surprise the lack of connection between any sort of policy-demand input from the citizenry and the policy-making behavior of representatives.

Nevertheless, most empirical studies of representative behavior accept the premise that conformity between legislators' actions and the public's policy views is the central problem of representative government, usually envisioning some kind of role-conception or normative mechanism through which the agreement comes about. Thus Jewell and Patterson (1966: 351-352) argue that high concern of representatives for their constituency is plausible in spite of the fact that legislators have low saliency in constituents' eyes. And Miller and Stokes (1963: 368) suggest still more specifically that, in spite of these facts, "the idea of reward or punishment at the polls for legislative stands is familiar to members of Congress, who feel that they and their records are quite visible to their constituents." A study by John Kingdon (1967: 144) suggests one interesting mechanism through which the moral obligation to represent the constituency views might work: what he terms the "congratulation-rationalization effect" leads winners of Congressional elections to have higher estimates of voters' interest and information than do losers, and to attribute less importance to party label and more importance to policy issues in voters' actions at their election than do losers. Therefore,

> The incumbent is more likely than if he lost to believe that voters are watching him, that they are better informed, and that they make their own choices according to his own characteristics and even according to the issues of the election. Because of the congratulation-rationalization effect . . . [he] may pay greater attention to the constituency than otherwise, because he believes that his constituents are paying greater attention to him than he might think if he had lost.

Perhaps the most persuasive explanation of the mechanism linking public views to legislative policy is that offered by Miller and Stokes (1963). They compared representatives' votes in several policy domains to constituency opinion, representatives' personal opinion, and representatives' perceptions of their constituency's opinion, in order to determine the proportionate contribution of each to his voting. In brief, they found that constituency policy views play a large role for Congressmen in civil rights issues, but a negligible role in domestic welfare issues and no role in foreign policy issues. Cnudde and McCrone (1966), extending this line of research, demonstrated the primary importance of the Congressman's perceptions of his constituents' opinion in establishing whatever link there is from constituency through to legislative voting. That is, in civil rights issues, Congressmen appear to shape their attitude to fit the opinions they think their constituency holds.

These findings, while in some respects striking, are nonetheless ambiguous. From the standpoint of our understanding of representative government, the results of studies of the behavior of representatives are as unsatisfactory as the studies of citizen behavior seem disquieting. Many important questions are left unanswered, theoretically or empirically. Often the differences on which theoretically important distinctions are based are found to be small. Above all, in spite of the fact that legislative policy decisions are universally taken to be the most important type of legislative output, we know almost nothing about the character, let alone the conditions and causes, of how they vary in content. We now turn briefly to this problem.

THE CHARACTER OF
LEGISLATIVE POLICY DECISIONS

"Policies" have been described as the most important variety of political output and legislative policy decisions are commonly understood to be the most important type of legislative output (Easton, 1965: 125; 1966: 353 ff.). It has been argued, therefore, that a major problem for legislative research is "to achieve adequate conceptualization of legislative output, i.e., to specify the dimensions or variables of legislative output which are related to different consequences of that output" (Wahlke et al., 1962: 25). So it is rather startling to discover that the term "policy" remains almost totally unconceptualized, i.e., that the literature provides "no theoretically meaningful categories which distinguish between types of policies" (Froman, 1967).

There is, however, a recent series of methodologically sophisticated but theoretically unstructured inquiries into possible variations in public policy which tends still further to challenge the relevance of demand-input conceptions to understanding the representative process. Most of these studies utilize the readily available masses of quantitative data about American states to analyze relationships among policy outputs and many possible correlates. Variations in policy output have usually been measured by the amount of money spent by a system on different categories of substantive policy or program, such as public highways, health programs, welfare, etc. Political variables investigated have usually been "structural" in nature—for example, degree of two-party competition, degree of voter participation, extent of legislative malapportionment, and so on. Socioeconomic environmental (or "background") variables have included such things as degree of urbanization and industrialization, or education level.

It is the general import of these studies that, with only rare and minor exceptions, variations in public policy are *not* related to variations in political-structure variables, except insofar as socio-economic or environmental variables affect them and public policy variations together. Variations in policy output can be almost entirely "explained" (in the statistical sense) by environmental variables, without reference to the variables supposedly reflecting different systems and practices of representation. Most far-reaching of such studies is Dye's examination of the effects of economic development (industrialization, urbanization, income, education) and political-system (party division, party competition, political participation, and malapportionment) on ninety policy variables in four different policy fields. His conclusion (Dye, 1966: 293):

> [S]ystem characteristics have relatively little *independent* effect on policy outcomes in the states. Economic development shapes both political systems and policy outcomes, and most of the association that occurs between system characteristics and policy outcomes can be attributed to the influence of economic development.

It is possible, of course, that these remarkable findings are unique to the American political system. That such is not the case, however, is strongly suggested by Cutright's (1965) discovery that variations in the national security programs of seventy-six nations appear to be explainable directly in terms of economic-development level and to be unrelated to differences in ideology or type of political system (including differences between communist and capitalist systems). There is a curious hint of similar findings in a study suggesting that changes in foreign policy do not seem to be associated with instances of "leadership succession" so far as voting in the U.N. General Assembly is concerned; that is, there is apparently substantial continuity of foreign policy in any given system despite changes in political regime (see Blake, 1967).

In sum, then, the policy-environment correlation studies imply that stimuli which have been thought to be policy demands are really just automatically determined links in a chain of reactions from environment to policy output, a chain in which neither policy demands, policy expectations, or any other kind of policy orientation plays any significant role. There is no room, in other words, for any of the policy-related behaviors and attitudes of citizens which we examined in the preceding section of this paper to enter into the policy process.

THE ROLE OF SUPPORT

The foregoing arguments are not especially "anti-democratic" or "anti-representative." They are just as damaging to much antidemocratic theory and to elitist criticisms of representative democracy. It is not only policy-opinions of citizens in the mass public which are demoted in the rank order of policy determinants but policy opinions of elites and group leaderships as well. The principal implication is that "policy-process" studies whose aim is primarily to discover the political bases of policy decisions conceived of as choices between policy alternatives contended for by divergent political forces, or to explain why a particular decision went one way instead of another, comprehend too little of the political life of man, and that the part they do comprehend is probably not its most vital. The appropriate conclusion is not the grandiose notion that representative democracy is chimerical but the limited recognition that our conceptions of government, politics, and representation are somewhat deficient, that "policy making" plays a different and evidently smaller role in the governance of society than we thought.

Precisely what role we cannot yet say, for neglect to study the political consequences of policy making is "a practice very much in line with the tradition of
political science" (Meehan, 1967: 180). Research on representation has tended toward preoccupation with the results of legislative roll calls and other decisions, or
the results of elections and series of them. It has concentrated on the antecedents
of legislative "output" and left unexamined the political "outcomes" which above
all make output an appropriate object of political study.[7] It has explored the possible sources of variations as small as a few percentage points in the influence of
"factors" influencing legislative and electoral decision, but ignored the relationship, if any, between legislative output and the incidence of discontent, riots, wars,
civil wars, *coups d'etat,* revolutions, and decay or integration of human groups. Its
focus has been determined by "political theories of allocation," in almost total
disregard of the perspectives opened up by "theories of sytems persistence." This is
an essential part of de Jouvenel's (1961: 777) charge that political science has not so
far had the "dangerous" impact it might because it has so far been content to investigate only "weak political behavior."

A plausible working hypothesis which directs the study of representation
toward "strong political behavior" is provided by Easton's discussion of "support." Viewed from this perspective, previous studies are seen to presume that
political systems stand, fall, or change according to the "specific support" accorded
them, the "consent" granted "as a consequence from some specific satisfaction
obtained from the system with respect to a demand that the members make"
(Easton, 1966: 268). But the arguments above show that specific support, the
support attaching directly to citizens' reactions to policy decisions, does not adequately describe the relationship between citizen and government. We must also
recognize and take into account what Easton calls "diffuse support," the support
constituted by "generalized attachment to political objects, . . . not conditioned
upon specific returns at any moment."[9]

There is good warrant for the working hypothesis that (Easton, 1966: 273):

> Except in the long run, diffuse support is independent of the effects of daily outputs. It
> consists of a reserve of support that enables a system to weather the many storms when
> outputs cannot be balanced off against inputs of demands. It is a kind of support that a
> system does not have to buy with more or less direct benefits for the obligations and
> responsibilities the member incurs. If we wish, the outputs here may be considered
> psychic or symbolic, and in this sense, they may offer the individual immediate benefits
> strong enough to stimulate a supportive response.

The plausibility of such a starting point has been intimated by other observers.
Edelman's (1964) instructive discussion of the importance of "symbolic" as compared with "instrumental" satisfactions deriving from the administration of public
policies clearly argues for it. More directly concerning representative functions,
Thomas Anton (1967: 39) has shown, with respect to the roles of agency spokesmen, budget officers, legislators, and citizens in budgetary process of American
states that "what is at stake . . . is not so much the distribution of resources, about

which state actors have little to say, but the distribution of symbolic satisfaction among the involved actors and the audiences which observe their stylized behavior." And Alfred de Grazia (1951: 170) has discussed the ways in which "the election process is symbolic and psychological in meaning, rathe than a device for the purpose of instructing delegates."

That the problem of support is a proper springboard for representation research is suggested also by some commentators on the functions of representative bodies. Almost thirty years ago, T. V. Smith (1938: 187) spoke of the "cathartic function of legislators, which by themselves appearing as scapegoats, harmlessly conduct away disaffections that otherwise "might well totalize into attacks upon public order." More recently, Eulau and Hinckley (1966: 85-86) have pointed out that representative bodies perform "such latent functions . . . as consensus-building, interest aggregation, catharsis for anxieties and resentment, the crystallization and resolution of conflicts, and the legitimization of decisions made elsewhere in the political system." With respect to Great Britain, Beer (1966: 31) has described the main parliamentary task as that of "mobilizing consent," "certainly not the representative function by which in greater or lesser degree the legislature brings the grievances and wishes of the people to bear upon policy-making." And Patterson (1967: 126) has asserted that,

> A legislature is much more than a law-making factory. It is a symbol of representative, democratic government. Its symbolic 'output' may be related to the kinds of policies it makes, but it is related also to the representative adequacy of the legislature, to the respect citizens can have for individual legislators, and to the pride citizens can take in their legislatures.

David Truman (1966: 90) has drawn important implications from such a view for the behavior of representatives, arguing that the primary skill lying at the heart of representative government is not substantive, technical skill, but in combination with that,

> a special skill. This is skill in assaying what is asked or done in the name of substantive expertise and in reconciling or combining such claims or acts with the feasibilities that exist or can be created in the electorate, in the extra-governmental world in all its configurations.

The shift of attention from "demands" to "support" which all these insights suggest calls for a corresponding shift of research emphasis from the behavior of representatives which has hitherto preoccupied most of us, to the perceptions, attitudes, and behaviors of the people whom representatives collectively represent, about which as yet we really know very little. The most immediate task is a primarily conceptual one—to identify the dimensions of support behavior, to map the incidence and variations of support in specific systems, and through comparative analysis of support mechanisms in different systems, to formulate hypotheses about its conditions and correlates.

DIMENSIONS OF SUPPORT

David Easton's definition of support as affective orientation toward political objects, and his analytical distinction of political community, political regime, and political authorities as the three principal categories of such political objects is a useful starting point.[10] We can probably assume, to begin with, that support for the political community is the most pervasive, general (diffuse), and stable element in the overall support mechanism of any political system. Basic group-identification, the sort of "pre-political" sentiment giving all segments of the community "a we-feeling . . . , not that they are just a group but that they are a political entity that works together and will likely share a common political fate and destiny" (1966: 332) is surely a major dimension of this level of support. Everything we know about the historical evolution of nation-states, tribal societies, and all other political forms, as well as everything modern research tells us about the processes of political socialization indicates that the loyalties, identifications, and cognitive-affective structures which make up this communal-loyalty dimension are acquired and shaped in early childhood and are affected little, if at all, by any political events, let alone such little salient events as the functioning of representative bodies. The indispensability of this kind of support for any political system was noted by V. O. Key (1961: 549): "A basic prerequisite is that the population be pervaded by a national loyalty. Or perhaps, more accurately, that the population not consist of segments each with its own sense of separateness." Almond and Verba (1963: 101-105), whose concept of "systems affect" approximates the concept of support for political community, likewise appear to take for granted (at least in the five countries they studied) the existence of a nationality sentiment or similar community sense defining a political community toward which members respond with varying effect.

But what if no sentiment of political community binds together a group of people who are, in fact, being governed (as is the case in many new African nations, to give an obvious example)? Or if segments seem increasingly to develop "each with its own sense of separateness" (as may well be the case in Canada or Belgium)? Can we be sure that "the sense of community must also be in part a product of public policy?" (Almond and Verba, 1963: 551). If not "policy," what aspect then of governmental activity, and especially of representative bodies' activity, affects it? At this stage we can only wonder—and begin to design research to find out.

A second major dimension of political community support is suggested by Almond and Verba's typology of political cultures, comprising what we may interpret as the political roles of "parochial," "subject," and "participant." The authors' original formulation differentiates these three types primarily in terms of their relative participation in demand-input activities.[11] There is justification even in the original formulation, however, for viewing these roles as differentiated also by the extent of conscious support for the political community, or "the gradation from 'public' to 'private' ": "The overwhelming majority of the members of all political systems live out their lives, discover, develop, and express their feelings and aspirations in the intimate groups of the community. It is the rare individual who is fully recruited into the political system and becomes a political man" (1963: 143). Viewed this way, the second component of community support, which might be labelled "political commitment," appears as an autonomously defined political variable, a kind of participation through sensitivity and alertness to political events and objects as well as participation in civic and political roles—participation in politics per se, not necessarily in the sense of power seeking, however, and not participation in primarily instrumental activities. It is a kind of "political interest," but, "it is interest not in the form of gains in material well-being, power, or status, but it is rather in personal satisfaction and growth attained from active engagement in the political process" (Bachrach, 1967: 38).

A number of familiar concepts bear on this second dimension of political-community support. Most of the phenomena usually treated under the heading of "political alienation," for example, represent an extreme negative value, ranking above only such anti-supportive positions as rebellion itself. "Political apathy," in a sense related to Almond and Verba's "parochialism," is more supportive than alienation but less so than "compliance." More supportive still is active "interest and involvement," although one must be careful to remember that support for the political community here is perfectly compatible (perhaps often associated?) with failure of support for regime or authorities. Beyond active spectator interest there is participation of varying degrees—ranging from nothing more than sporadic voting to regular and intensive political communication, to participation in authority or other "trans-civic" roles.

Such a conception of supportive political commitment seems perfectly consistent with what we do know about the relevant behavior of citizens. For example, once-depressing statistics about "low levels" of citizen interest take on quite different meaning in this light. The finding that "only" 27 per cent of the American public could be considered politically active (Woodward and Roper, 1950), that during 1945 and 1946 sometimes "as few as" 19 per cent and "never more than" 36 per cent of the American Zone population in West Germany claimed to be personally interested in politics (Cantril and Strunk, 1951: 582), that in 1958 35 per cent of the West Germans had no interest at all in attending Bundestag sessions even if it cost them nothing (Noelle and Neuman, 1958: 265), or the countless similar readings of political interest and involvement in the other political systems, must now, if there is no other different evidence on the point, be read not as sure signs of "apathy" or "negativism" but as probable indications of moderate support for the political community.

Still, on balance, we know much less than we should about the dynamics of support for the political community. Though we can recognize that communal loyalty and political commitment constitute important dimensions of it, we do not know how one dimension relates to the other, or how the day-to-day functioning of government, including the input-output functioning of representative institutions, relates to either.

The situation is not much different when we consider the problem of support for the "political regime." One major dimension here appears to be the level of conscious support for broad norms and values which apply to the political world generally, i.e., to "rules-of-the-game," or standards by which regimes are judged. But the meaning of what information we have here is ambiguous. How much consensus, in the sense of "agreement on fundamentals," may vary, and what is the effect of such variation, are questions which do not yet have clear answers.[12]

The level of support for the institutional apparatus of government seems to be another major dimension of regime support, empirically distinguishable from generalized "agreement on fundamentals." Citizens are apparently able to dislike something or other about the actions of government and at the same time support its continuation institutionally unchanged, and their levels of support in this respect apparently fluctuate over time. An instructive example is the differences in French responses to identical questions put at different times concerning which political regimes seemed to be functioning better or worse than the French regime. From January 1958, to January 1965, the percentage saying each country named worked better than the French dropped in every case and the percentage saying the French regime worked better increased in every case.[13] Again, although 41 per cent of a sample in a small midwestern American city said, in 1966, that there were things Congress had done which they did not like (about some of which they claimed to feel strongly), only 20 per cent of them thought any proposals for changing Congress should be given serious attention; although 44 per cent said the city council had done something they particularly disliked, and only 20 per cent thought the council was doing a good or excellent job, less than a third thought the form of government should be changed.[14] This perspective also leads us to view not as deviant, undemocratic views, but as probably indicators of probably normal regime support, the fact that more Americans think the majority of people usually *in*correct in their ideas on important questions (42 per cent) than think the majority correct (38 per cent), or that Congress is thought more correct than "the people" in its "views on broad national issues" (42 per cent as against 38 per cent).[15] Similarly, it becomes understandable why, when only half the American public thinks it makes much difference at all which party wins the election, some two-thirds to three-fourths of them make a point of voting at all elections, whether or not they have any specific interest in them,[16] and almost nine-tenths of them (87 per cent) think having elections makes government pay some or a good deal of attention to what the people think.[17] Although Almond and Verba (1963: 101) consider such indicators as these under the heading of "input affect," meaning essentially demand-input ("the feelings people have both about those agencies and processes that are involved in the election of public officials, and about the enactment of public policies"), they seem much more intelligible viewed under the heading of regime support, i.e., support for the apparatus of government in general.

Our information about regime support phenomena, then, is no more adequate or satisfactory than our information about support for the political community. What there is of it, however, does seem to indicate that symbolic satisfaction with the process of government is probably more important than specific, instrumental satisfaction with the policy output of the process. Thus Thomas Anton (1967: 39-40) has noticed, concerning the budget process, that "it is not the document which creates satisfaction, but the process of putting it together . . . [The] budget, as document and process, creates symbolic satisfaction built upon the idea that affairs of state are being dealt with, that responsibility is being exercised, and that rationality prevails." Dye's (1966: 30) conclusion after studying a voluminous array of the content of policy outputs, was that "The *way* in which a society authoritatively allocates values may be an even more important question than the outcomes of these value allocations. Our commitments to democratic processes are essentially commitments to a mode of decision-making. The legitimacy of the democratic form of government has never really depended upon the policy outcomes which it is expected to produce." And deGrazia (1951: 170) has said, more poetically, "the whole *process* of representation becomes an acting out of a play in which the actors are independent within the limits of the state, the setting, and the changing tastes of the audience. Their role is meaningful but it has no direct connection with the ticket the audience files for admission."

Whereas political research has by and large neglected to study support for the political community and the political regime, it has paid considerable attention to support for "political authorities." Elections, of course, are considered an indispensable feature of representtaive government by anybody's definition, and election results in representative systems are almost universally interpreted as indices of support for incumbent authorities. The innumerable public opinion polls between elections which ask the level of voters' satisfaction or dissatisfaction with the ruling Government's performance in general, with the performance of various individual office holders or agencies, or with the handling of particular problems, are likewise taken as indicators of the rising and falling level of support for authorities.

No doubt such data are properly interpreted as measures of such support. But the question is, what should be read into them beyond that simple indication? "Democracy," says Schumpeter (1947: 285), "means only that the people have the opportunity of accepting or refusing the men who are to rule them." Our earlier discussion of the role of issues and policies in elections cautions us not to hastily assume voters are voting up one set of policies and voting down another when they go to the polls. A unique series of data about British opinion in 1966 strongly intimates we ought not even assume that they are voting up one set of officeholders and voting down another in quite the simple, straightforward, preferential fashion we have always taken for granted. The data shown in Figure 4.1 clearly demonstrate that, at least in Britain in 1966, many voters seem to be giving up or withdrawing support from the whole apparatus of government officialdom and not, as one might at first think, transferring support from one set of authorities to another. To a remarkable degree, support for Government goes up as support for Opposition goes up, and support for Opposition goes down as support for Government goes down. One is strongly tempted to conclude, though it may be premature, that the support for authorities is much more closely related to regime support and much less related to individual voter preferences for individual authority figures than anyone has hitherto suspected.

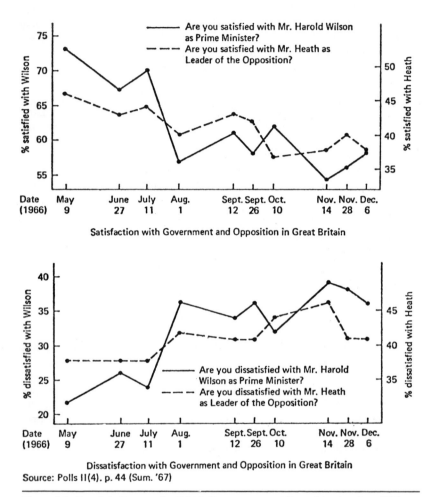

Satisfaction with Government and Opposition in Great Britain

Dissatisfaction with Government and Opposition in Great Britain
Source: Polls II(4). p. 44 (Sum. '67)

Figure 4.1: Trends in Support for British Government and Opposition Leaders, 1966

CONCLUSION

The conceptualization of support sketched out here is only that. It is not a theory, nor even a few hypotheses. Indeed, it is not even a very complete conceptualization, since many important questions are left open—how do we visualize support in a complex, multi-level, pluralistic government? What is the connection between support for local as against national (and, in federal systems, intermediate) authorities, regime, and political community? Between support for different segments of the regime at different levels? What is the relevance of the notion to supranational and intergovernmental politics?

What bearing has all this on representative government? Surely it does not suggest that to maintain representative democracy is more difficult, or that representative democracy is less desirable, just because it might seem to depend less on support deriving from mechanically satisfying demand-inputs than it does on the generation of support through quite different mechanisms. The question still is, how do representative bodies contribute to the generation and maintenance of support? In what respects and for what particular aspects of the task are they superior to non-representative institutions? These are questions to be answered by empirical research.

NOTES

1. The best analytical surveys of representation are those of Birch, 1964; and de Grazia, 1951.

2. See Bryce, 1921, II: 335-357; Lippmann, 1946: 216-220. While General de Gaulle has, of course, not contributed formally to literature of this kind, Gaullist views are well known from various speeches, debates, and publication preceding the creation of the Fifth Republic. They are conveniently discussed in Macridis and Brown, 1960: 124-131.

3. More recently Almond has specifically identified this kind of model as a sort of paradigm for developed representative political systems. See Almond, 1965: 197.

4. See, for example, the familiar discussion in Berelson, Lazarsfeld and McPhee, 1954: 305-323. The particular propositions listed here are supported, in every instance, by survey data from various political systems collected at different times. Although systematically analyzed in the original research for this paper, the data are not reported here because of limitations of space. The more relevant compilations and commentaries include the following: Cantril, 1965: 167-171; Cantril and Strunk, 1951; Campbell, Converse, Miller and Stokes, 1960; Converse and Dupeux, 1962; Converse, 1964; Bauer, Pool and Dexter, 1963; Stokes, 1963; Axelrod, 1967; Noelle and Neumann, 1965; McPhee and Glaser, 1962; Epstein, 1964; Buchanan, 1965.

5. See Hunter, 1953. For a general commentary on this line of studies, see Polsby, 1963.

6. Such problems are discussed in Plamenatz, 1958; Sartori, 1958; Walker, 1966; Dahl, 1966; Bachrach, 1967.

7. Easton (1966: 349, 351) describes this distinction as that between "a stream of activities flowing from the authorities in a system" (outputs) and "the infinite chain of effects that might flow from an authoritative allocation" (outcomes).

8. See Lindberg, 1966: 108. The same point has been made in Wahlke, 1962, and is indirectly made by Jewell and Patterson, 1966: 528-531.

9. Easton, 1966: 272, 273. Easton himself later (1966: 434n.) makes the much stronger assertion still that, "Under some circumstances the need for outputs to bolster support may be reduced to the vanishing point."

10. "Political community" refers to "some minimal readiness or ability (of a group of people) to continue working together to solve their political problems" (Easton, 1966: 172). "Political regime" refers to the values and principles, norms ("operating rules and rules of the game") and structures of authority (authority-*roles*) by which, over a period of time authori-

tative decisions are made in the political community (Easton, 1966: 190-211). Political authorities are the persons who occupy the authoritative roles at any given point in time (Easton, 1966: 212-19).

11. The "participant" is "an active participant in the political input process," the "subject" hardly at all oriented toward input objects but positively (if passively) oriented affectively "toward the output, administrative, or "downward flow" side of the political system," and the "parochial" detached from political roles of every sort, on both input and output sides. See Almond and Verba, 1963: 161, 19, 17 respectively.

12. Key's (1961: 30ff.) discussion of "supportive," "permissive," "negative" and "decisional" consensus is most instructive here. See also McClosky, 1964; and Prothro and Grigg, 1960.

13. Drop in proportion saying other regime better than France, 25 per cent for G.B.; 28 per cent for U.S.A.; 7 per cent for Italy; 31 per cent for West Germany; 16 per cent for USSR. Increase in proportion saying French worked better; 15 per cent for G.B.; 13 per cent for U.S.A.; 1 per cent for Italy; 14 per cent for West Germany; 9 per cent for USSR. *Sondages*, XXVI (1), 1966.

14. Iowa City Form of Government Study, 1966, Code Book. University of Iowa Laboratory for Political Research.

15. A.I.P.O. 17 July 1939, and 8 August 1939, reported in "The Quarter's Polls," *Public Opinion Quarterly*, X (4): 632. The remainder of responses in each instance were DK and NA.

16. 49 per cent and 51 per cent in two separate polls in September 1946, for example. A.I.P.O. reported in "The Quarter's Polls," *Public Opinion Quarterly,* III (4): 580.

17. Survey Research Center, 1966, SRC Study 0504, ICPR Preliminary Code Book.

Chapter 5

POLARITY IN REPRESEN-
TATIONAL FEDERALISM:
A Neglected Theme of Political Theory

HEINZ EULAU

After almost 200 years of experimentation, America's "experiment in federalism" remains experimental. This is surely the conclusion one must reach on viewing the great variety of patterns in federal-state-local relations that in the past decade accompanied the expansion of governmental activity into new fields of public policy. American federalism has involved an ever-changing series of innovations in governmental structures and functions, some successful and some unsuccessful. Success and failure alike have brought forth, from the beginning of the republic, a great many hypotheses to explain the American experiment in federalism. Indeed, because American federalism has been and continues to be multifaceted, it can accommodate many alternative propositions and interpretations.

Whatever the truth or falsity of the hypotheses about the historically specific case of American federalism, it was and still is *the solution of a fundamentally theoretical problem* that distinguishes the American experiment from earlier and later attempts in federalistic organization elsewhere. To what extent the Founding Fathers were aware of having solved, in the Constitution of 1787, not only a practical problem but also a theoretical problem, is difficult to say. But had they not solved the theoretical problem as they were solving the practical problem, the American experiment in federalism might not have proceeded as it did.

The great innovation in political theory implicit in the American Constitution consisted in the theoretical fusion of two basic principles of governmental engineering—the principle of federation and the principle of representation. The two principles were known, though only crudely articulated, as separate principles before being joined in the Constitution. It had been the previous failure of political theory to weld the two principles into a single model of governance that had proved to be of disastrous consequence in earlier federalistic experiments. Any federal arrangement likely to have long-term survival prospects is predicated on representation as a necessary condition. A federated order unable to accommodate in its structure the representation of its constituent parts, whether collectivities or individuals, is *ab origine* doomed to fall apart. This is not to say that representation is the only condition of federal engineering. It is to say that federation without representation is theoretically unthinkable. At issue is, of course, what should be represented and how it should be represented.

My inclination is to believe, by inference from *The Federalist*, that at least its authors were well aware of the theoretical solution of the relationship between federalism and representation implicit in the Constitution of 1787. Not that all of what its authors asserted in this connection was historically correct and theoretically sound. But it is curious that so learned a commentator as Max Beloff altogether missed the theoretical significance of just those papers in *The Federalist* which explicated the great breakthrough in political theory made in this respect in the Constitution. I am referring to papers No. 52 to 67, and especially those concerning the House of Representatives. These papers, Beloff wrote in his introduction, "are of interest to the student of the American constitution as revealing the original prognostications of its likely development, *rather than to the student of polical theory*."[1] Rarely, I think, has a commentator so missed the theoretical boat.

A common flaw of most political theory is its *post-facto* nature and low predictive capability. Both representation and federalism as theories only emerged *after* the political phenomena to which they refer had already been institutionalized and, in some cases, declined. What usually stands in the way of recognition, if not prediction, of new political structures is some powerful paradigm, like the Aristotelian conception of the *polis*, or at least a fashionable theoretical perspective. But occasionally constitution-builders can draw on novel ideas that, whatever their existential roots, prove serviceable beyond the moment of their use, especially if they are adaptable to prevailing conditions and practical necessities. The makers of the American federal constitution drew on the contractual and mechanistic metaphors of Hobbes, Locke, Harrington and Montesquieu, but in their hands— or better, in the bargaining situation in which they worked—these metaphors were translated into viable formulae of governmental engineering. They were, indeed, self-fulfilling prophecies that give *The Federalist*, for instance, an aura of some predictive power. Not that all of its predictions were fulfilled; but enough were to make it, in retrospect, more than a tract for the times. The passage of almost 200 years and altogether unanticipated developments notwithstanding, *The Federalist* as a treatise of political theory remains an amazingly suggestive work.

This is particularly true of its deft and subtle meshing of the principles of federation and representation. While other aspects of theory found in *The Federalist* have been justly celebrated, it is sometimes overlooked that it was the linkage of federalism and representation that in Madison's view constitutes "a republican remedy for the diseases most incident to republican government" (No. 10: 48). Much has been made, and probably rightly so, of the great compromise by which the small states were given equal representation in the Senate in exchange for the power of the House to initiate money bills. The compromise avoided what otherwise might have become an insurmountable deadlock in the Philadelphia convention. But, in retrospect, the role of the Senate in the federal-representational scheme of things is less significant than the role of the House of Representatives. Despite the guaranteed equality of the states in the Senate, the "upper house" became a much more nationalized and nationalizing institution than the House. It is in the House where federalism and representation meet.

The vice of sacred documents like the Constitution or commentaries like *The Federalist* is their ambiguity which so readily permits revisionist interpretations. But if one assumes that history as an approach to human affairs is inherently revisionist because history as a subject of study is always liable to be reinterpreted, the vice of ambiguity becomes a virtue. It forces the revisionist to clarify assumptions, even though such clarification runs the double risk either of being historically false or of not even being an accurate reflection of current reality. It is idle to speculate, therefore, whether *The Federalist* articulated the doctrine of "dual federalism" read into the Constitution for 150 years or so after its adoption. As Daniel J. Elazar (1962) has shown, that doctrine was not an accurate description of the working of American federalism even in the middle of the nineteenth century because the federal and state governments were already working jointly in fields like banking, railroad construction, internal improvements, and others.

Any reading of *The Federalist* today is, therefore, necessarily influenced by current conceptions of the evolving structure of national-state-local arrangements. The late Morton Grodzins and Elazar have made a persuasive case for viewing the emergent structures of American federalism in terms of such theoretical concepts as partnership, sharing and cooperation. If their diagnoses and prognoses have not as yet yielded a full-fledged contemporary theory of federalism, by which is meants an internally consistent theory that joins the representational and federational principles, it is probably all to the good. For even as they were writing, American federal arrangements were undergoing fast and vast changes in the name of a "creative federalism" whose implications and consequences for the American commonwealth are yet to be theoretically understood.

If anything, the "little chaos" that Grodzins (1966) and Elazar (1966) found to make for the responsiveness of American federalism had become even more chaotic in the late sixties, raising the question whether the multiplicity of arrangements among federal departments, state agencies, local authorities and even non-governmental organizations did not require drastic steps in coordination in order to overcome administrative confusion, bureaucratic jealousies and jurisdictional conflicts. It is interesting that the emphasis of those seeking an answer is almost exclusively on the administrative aspects of the problem and seems to neglect the issue of representation which is so intrinsically tied up with the problems of federalism.

James L. Sundquist (1969), for instance, enjoins us to view American federal arrangements as a "single system." What recommends the system notion is that it would alert policy-makers or administrators to otherwise unanticipated and presumably dysfunctional consequences for some parts of the system as a result of changes in other parts. The system of American federalism, Sundquist admits, "is so complex that it can be altered only piecemeal. Yet the piecemeal changes should be guided by some model. . . . The federal system is an intricate web of institutional relationships among levels of government, jurisdictions, agencies, and programs—relationships that comprise a single system, whether or not it is designed as one," (1969: 31). It is not useful to dwell on the appropriateness or inappropriateness of the system metaphor, even if the administrative reforms recommended by Sundquist were to make for a system rather than for what he calls a "jumble." For, one suspects, even if the American federal system were guided "according to a consistent set of principles and governing doctrine" (1969: 278), it would probably remain multicentered, loose, fluid or porous—in other words, a system that is not very systemic.

However, this is not the critical point. The point is that the administrative view of federalism ignores the multiple legislative-representational components of American federalism from the houses of Congress down through the state houses to city councils, school boards and other legislative bodies. Sundquist (1969: 278) gives the federal game away, so to speak, when he concludes that the guidance of the federal system "can come from but a single source of authority—the President. It is he who must apply the principles and the doctrine in proposing legislation to the Congress and in directing the execution of the laws." This is clearly a counsel for the demise of federalism in the name of federalism; and perhaps it would be more candid to argue, as Harold J. Laski (1939) did some decades ago, that federalism in America is obsolete.

Before reaching this dismal conclusion, however, it may be desirable to take another theoretical look at federalism as a *political* process. One cannot ignore the politican parties that serve as decentralizing institutions, or the universe of pluralistic interests that seek access to government, or the hose of constituencies represented in the House of Representatives. I shall not deal here with the roles of the parties, so well treated by Grodzins, and the role of cultural and social interests whose importance in the federal scheme of things Elazar has emphasized. Rather, I want to return to *The Federalist's* treatment of the House of Representatives and the role assigned to it in the federal system.

THE FEDERALIST REVISITED

The purpose of the exercise is neither conceptual exegesis for its own sake nor some kind of patriotic semanticism. While exegesis is a necessary prerequisite of theory *development*, it all too often degenerates into exegetical competition among commentators as to what some text "really means." This is not the purpose here. And while semantic clarity is important, to call what one likes in politics "federal" or, for that matter, "democratic," serves no good purpose. What makes it difficult to construct the drift of the theoretical argument concerning the relationship between federalism and representation in *The Federalist*, however, is the fact that these papers were written in response to objections to the Constitution. Yet, it would be too tedious to review all of the objections and answers because they are not germane to the objective. One must therefore be selective.

Four themes concerning the relationship between federation and representation can be derived from *The Federalist* in connection with its discussion of the House of Representatives. I shall briefly and separately outline these themes and then comment on the model that seems to be implicit in them. This procedure omits discussions in *The Federalist* that deal with representation or federation as separate topics.

First, it is unmistakably clear that the House of Representatives is in no way to be dependent on the state governments, but rather on the people in the states, though the states can maximize the representation of their interests in the House by making full use of the number of representatives in the House. The definition of the right of suffrage was written into the Constitution and not left to state discretion because "it would have rendered too dependent on the state governments that branch of the federal government, which ought to be dependent on the people alone" (No. 52: 269). Subsequently referring to the constitutional article which provides that "the Congress may at any time by law make or alter such regulations" for elections, a task generally assigned to the state legislatures, *The Federalist* defends the propriety of the provision on the ground that "every government ought to contain in itself the means of its own preservation" (No. 59: 302). If the state legislatures had exclusive power of regulating elections, "every period of making them would be a delicate crisis in the national situation" (No. 59: 305).

Dependence on the people is, of course, the corollary of the independence of the House from the state legislatures. The House, it is pointed out in connection with a defense of biennial elections, "should have an immediate dependence on, and an intimate sympathy with the people. Frequent elections are unquestionably the only policy by which this dependence and sympathy can be effectually secured," (No. 52: 269-270). Moreover, the people not only elect but also evict their representatives. The House is so constituted "as to support in the members an habitual recollection of their dependence on the people."[2]

But this apparently sharp distinction between the House's dependence on the state legislatures and the people is qualified. Elsewhere *The Federalist* suggests that despite the constitutional division, the state will (should?) have an interest in what goes on in the House. Pointing to a "peculiarity in the federal constitution" that in the House "larger states will have most weight," while in the Senate "the advantage will be in favor of the smaller states," *The Federalist* continues: "From this circumstance it may *with certainty* be *inferred* that the larger states will be strenuous advocates for increasing the number and weight of that part of the legislature, in which their influence predominates" (No. 58: 298). It is inferred further that, formal equality of authority between the two houses notwithstanding (except for originating money bills in the House), "it cannot be doubted that the house composed of the greater number, when supported by the more powerful states, and speaking the known and determined sense of a majority of people, will have no small advantage in a question depending on the comparative firmness of the two houses" (No. 58: 298-299).

What is of interest in these passages is not only the manifest inferences made, but also the unspoken premise that, through their popularly elected delegations, the states have a presence in the House as they do in the Senate—in other words, that legislative representation at the national level cuts across the formal division of powers. The House, being rooted in the people, serves as a kind of hyphen between the federal and representational principles of the Constitution. *The Federalist* did evidently not fully accept the notion of "dual federalism" that the general government and the states are "separate and distinct sovereignties, acting separately and independently of each other, within their respective spheres."[3] Rather, especially the larger states are expected to have a very real interest in and influence on the conduct of the House of Representatives, and through the House on national affairs.

A second theme deals with the social composition of the electorate and the consequences of this composition on the federal quality of representation in the House. To refute the objection that the House may consist of representatives "taken from that class of citizens which will have the least sympathy with the mass of the people," *The Federalist* rejects the anticipated evil as ill-conceived because "the elective mode of obtaining rulers in the characteristic policy of republican government." The inference evidently to be made is that the House will be a true mirror of the electorate. Who, it is asked, "are to be the electors of the federal representatives?" The answer is one of the classical passages in *The Federalist* (No. 57: 292):

> Not the rich, more than the poor; not the learned, more than the ignorant; not the haughty heirs of distinguished names, more than the humble sons of obscure and unpropitious fortune. The electors are to be the great body of the people of the United States. They are to be the same, who exercise the right in every state of electing the correspondent branch of the legislature of the state.

Because the same people vote for "correspondent" branches, another paper continues, "no rational calculation of probabilities would lead us to imagine" that the union would use its power to regulate elections "to promote the election of some favorite class of men in exclusion of others." That it would happen "is altogether inconceivable and incredible." But were it to happen, "it could never be made without causing an immediate revolt of the great body of the people, headed and directed by the state governments." And there is another reason why it will not happen—the pluralistic nature of the union (No. 60: 307):

> There is sufficient diversity in the state of property, in the genius, manners, and habits of the people of the different parts of the union, to occasion a material diversity of disposition in their representatives towards the different ranks and conditions in society.

In other words, federalism is promoted by the representational mix that stems from the diversity of the people who elect the members of the House. There is the expectation that "an intimate intercourse under the same government will promote a gradual assimilation of temper and sentiment," but this tendency of federation will not destroy the pattern of diversity in representation. *The Federalist* envisages the interpenetration of polar tendencies—the federal tendency toward assimilation of temper and sentiment," and the representational tendency toward "material diversity of disposition."

The third theme centers in the consequences for representation of the size of the House, notably that a small number of representatives "will be an unsafe depository of the public interests," and that "they will not possess a proper knowledge of the local circumstances of their numerous constituents," (No. 55: 283). The first objection is set aside on the ground that "nothing can be more fallacious than to found our political calculations on arithmetical principles" (a somewhat hypocritical argument given all the other arithmetic in many of the papers). But *The Federalist* is more candid; the familiar fear of "the confusion and intemperance of a multitude" is enough reason to keep the House relatively small: "Had every Athenian citizen been a Socrates; every Athenian assembly would still have been a mob" (No. 55: 284).

The second objection to a small House is dealt with more seriously. *The Federalist* admits that "it is a sound and important principle that the representative ought to be acquainted with the interests and circumstances of his constituents." But it is emphasized that "this principle can extend no farther than to those circumstances and interests to which the authority and care of the representative relate," (No. 56: 288). This restriction seems to involve the definition of "dual federalism" as a limit on the role of the federal representative. But weaving into consideration that in a *federal* legislature the representatives come from several states, *The Federalist* recognizes the severity of the knowledge problem in a compound polity. The federal representative, precisely because he is a *federal* official, cannot avoid being cognizant of what goes on in the states (and presumably the different constituencies) other than his own (No. 56: 290):

> This information, so far as it may relate to local objects is rendered necessary and difficult, not by a difference of laws and local circumstances within a single state, but of those among different states. . . . Whilst a few representatives, therefore, from each state, may bring with them a due knowledge of their own state, *every* representative will have much information to acquire concerning *all* the *other* states.

The passage is prescriptive and recommends that the federal representative should have two foci of attention, not only his own state but also all other states in the aggregate. His role is multilateral. Again one notes the effort to combine federational and representational criteria in appraising the place of the House of Representatives in the Constitution.

The fourth and final theme occurs in a passage addressed to the problem of the potential abuse of power by the House. Some of the reasons given for why this should not occur are the familiar ones—the House's limited legislative authority, its dependence on the people, and the separation of powers within the national government. But to these is added another that is less known. The House is unlikely to abuse its power because it " will be moreover watched and controlled by the several collateral legislatures, which other legislative bodies are not," (No. 52: 272). The sentence is ambiguous and difficult to interpret, for an interpretation must turn on (a) the meaning of "control," (b) the meaning of "collateral," and (c) some implicit premise as to what "collateral legislatures" can do to each other.

One can rule out the conception of collateral as meaning "secondary" or "subordinate," for the House and the State assemblies are generally treated in *The Federalist* as parallel legislative bodies, each with its own sphere of competence. More suggestive is the notion that collateral means "belonging to the same ancestral stock but not in a direct line of descent." If, in this connection, this be the meaning of *The Federalist*'s use of collateral, both the federal House and state assemblies were thought to be of the same genus though of different species, and one may infer that what makes them belong to the same genus is their representational base in a *shared* electorate. The "control" of the federal House exercised by the "several collateral legislatures" is presumably not direct, for this would violate the federal principle; it is presumably indirect and made possible by the representational principle of collateral legislatures having a common electorate that controls the abuse of power by the representative bodies. It is the interpenetration of federal and representational structures envisaged by *The Federalist* that makes for a particular kind of control that "collateral legislatures" exercise less *over* each other than *on* each other. And this interpretation would be consonant with the general notion of balance and equilibrium that pervades *The Federalist*.

THE CONTRIBUTION OF THE FEDERALIST

If one reads the relevant papers of *The Federalist* with care, what is impressive is their effort to integrate both federal and representational principles into a single model of republican governance. It is not that first the federal aspects of representation and then the representational aspects of federation are treated. Although the emphasis necessarily shifts from one to the other and back again, for it is impossible to speak about everything at once, the argument is clearly predicated on the meshing of the federal and representational principles in a polar rather than dualistic model of government. I shall come back to this in the last section, but here I wish to assess more generally *The Federalist*'s contribution to political theory.

What is throughout impressive is *The Federalist*'s high level of theoretical self-consciousness in pursuing a variety of themes. Evidence of this self-consciousness is not just the persistent references to actual historical experiences with federation and representation from the ancients down to the American colonists, but the effort to exploit these experiences from a theoretical standpoint. If some of the inferences seem false or labored, it is less the logic of the argument than the fragility of the empirical base from which the inferences are drawn that must be faulted. But given the state of historical scholarship in the eighteenth century, *The Federalist* can hardly be censured on that account. What is of importance is that *The Federalist* was a theoretical treatise that, in suggesting and analyzing the interdependence of the federal and representational principles in the new Constitution, has remained a force of its own in shaping the course of the American experiment in federalism.

Without theoretical explication, political experience must be an unassimilated, almost random experience that cannot serve as a guide to the future. By being devoted to political theorizing, *The Federalist* made possible the transmission of the Founders' political experience and its serviceability in subsequent governmental engineering. It is the merit of theory that, by abstracting from practical experience, it distills what is significant and abandons what is not significant. It therefore makes for comprehension long after the particular and concrete conditions involved in an experience can no longer be readily apprehended, no matter how much insight or emphathy may be brought to bear.

Although theory cannot altogether neglect the context of its emergence, the logic of a theory need not be dependent on the context. For instance, if one reads what No. 62 of *The Federalist* has to say about the make-up of the Senate as against what is said about the make-up of the House in the preceding papers, one is impressed by the practical arguments for the composition of the Senate, things in the real world of the American states at the time being what they were. By way of contrast, the arguments concerning the House of Representatives are eminently theoretical—more a matter of logic than, as in the case of the Senate, a matter of prudence. When, in due time, the Senate came to be elected by the vote of the people, it was possible to abandon the prudential stance, so necessary in 1787, and argue the case for the popular election of senators on the logical grounds advanced about the election of the House of Representatives. Without theory, the experience in constructing the House and its application to the Senate may have been lost.

To appreciate the importance of theory in political engineering, one may well compare the American experience with that of the Greeks on whome *The Federalist* drew so much of its own formulation of a "compound republic," as the creation of 1787 is occasionally called. It is pointed out that "the scheme of representation, as a substitute for a meeting of the citizens in person, [was] but imperfectly known to ancient polity," and there is an immediate turn to "more modern times" for instructive examples" (No. 52: 270). *The Federalist* was essentially correct. Although recent scholarship has shown that the Greeks, and later the Romans, did in fact have representative institutions in the modern sense, their theoretical meaning was never understood. If anything, representation seems to have been designed to limit rather than extend citizen participation in government (see Eulau, 1967). This theoretical failure was one reason, though probably not the only one, why the various late Hellenic confederacies could not surmount the structural handicaps inherent in their large size that exceeded the size of the familiar polis. These confederacies did provide for representative assemblies based on population, but in the absence of a theory of representation they were unable to cope with the problem of making collective decisions (Larsen, 1955). As Carl J. Friedrich (1946: 267) has pointed out, "the attempts at solving this problem [i.e., of governing a large unit] through a federal organization foundered upon the inability of the ancients to work out a representative scheme."

Representation again emerged in the Middle Ages for reasons that need not be spelled out here, except to say that it gave rise to a variety of theories that were known to the framers of the Constitution. Yet, though much of the discussion centered on the problem of the relationship between representative and represented, medieval political theory could not conceive of governance in other than hierarchical terms, with the result that it failed to observe and elaborate the emerging federational character of the Holy Roman Empire. Just as the Greeks had been unable to construct a viable theory of representation that might have undergirded their experiments in federation, so the medieval writers were unable to construct a theory of federalism that might have served in solving the Empire's structural problems. What stood in the way was, once more, the Aristotelian conception of the unitary state that, medieval feudalism and corporatism notwithstanding, provided the pervasive paradigm of medieval theory. Ironically, federalism as a working concept for understanding the structure of the Empire did not emerge until the second half of the seventeenth century when disintegration had gone so far as to make the Empire little more than a mere shadow of its medieval organization (Eulau, 1941).

Both the Greek failure to conceive a theory of representation and the medieval failure to conceive a theory of federation had not only practical consequences for contemporary and subsequent governmental engineering, but they pinpoint the achievement of the Founding Fathers in creating a constitutional framework that was built on a federational-representational symbiosis. The symbiosis that was achieved gives added significance to its theoretical statement in *The Federalist*. This does not mean that *The Federalist* fully understood the creation which it justified and defended, or that it accurately anticipated the course of the American experiment in popular self-government through representational federalism. But it suggests that *The Federalist* deserves our close attention as a masterpiece not only of constitutional wisdom but also of empirical theory construction.

THE POLARITY PRINCIPLE IN AMERICAN FEDERALISM

The image of the federal order that emerges from *The Federalist*'s four themes focused on representation in the House of Representatives is not one of a dual structure but of a polar structure. Nation and states are opposites that, like the poles of the magnetic field, are yet linked. What links the poles of the federal system is representation of the people—what *The Federalist* refers to as "proportional" representation (as against the "equal" representation of the states in the Senate) (No. 62: 316). This formulation was, of course, simplistic and did not anticipate the plural system of representation that has developed in the United States over the last 180 years, notably the emergence of political parties and interest groups as mediating agencies in addition to direct constituency linkages between representatives and represented. But the underlying model is not a structural dualism that presumes the existence of two *kinds* of entities whose interaction is made difficult by some immanent qualitative difference. Rather, the underlying model is one of structural continuity which presumes that poles of the federal structure are yet linked by the workings of a plural system of representation.

The polarity principle is a heuristic tool which assumes that in all determination of empirical reality there are opposing elements or categories. It differs therefore from a conception like "system" which also assumes that in the real world different things are more or less connected, but which cannot explain any particular thing. The notion of system can give direction to the scientific effort; it is not helpful in the search for adequate explanation. By way of contrast, by assuming that all determinate effects are necessarily opposed yet mutually entailed, the polarity principle is implicit in the testing of relevant hypotheses. In a bivariate relationship, for instance, one value or "force" is assumed to pull the association in the direction of the hypothesis, while the second value is assumed to pull it in the opposite direction.[4] For this reason, the principle of polarity is a supplement to the principle of causality rather than an alternative mode of explanation (Cohen, 1949: 12): "Not only must every natural event have a cause which determines that it should happen, but the cause must be opposed by some factor which prevents it from producing any greater effect than it actually does."

By calling attention to the basic interdependence of opposites and their mutual entailment, the polarity principle sensitizes the observer to the complexity of seemingly paradoxical facts as well as to the possibility of alternative hypotheses. In contrast to dualistic thinking, the polarity principle aids the analyst in avoiding one-sided and easily false formulations.[5] The notion that the poles of a phenomenon (like magnetism or federalism) are distinct and opposed, yet mutually entailed and inseparable, denies false dichotomies like individual vs. society, fact vs. value, means vs. ends, constancy vs. change, form vs. content, growth vs. decay, unity vs. plurality, homogeneity vs. heterogeneity, activity vs. passivity, simplicity vs. complexity, cause vs. purpose, organism vs. environment, and so on and so forth. If conceived as polar opposites, each category involves the other when applied to a significant phenomenon; each is impossible without the other; there is no action without reaction, no force without resistance, no identity without difference, no individuality without universality, no centralization without decentralization, no division without combination of powers and so on.

The workings of the polarity principle also differ from the workings of the dialectic in its Hegelian-Marxian version. The dialectic is uncomfortable with the contradictions immanent in a phenomenon and seeks to absorb or transcend them in their unity.[6] The polarity principle accepts as given the coexistence of opposites. In contrast to the dialectic, it stresses the interdependence of the poles in what is a continuous phenomenon; and it does not deny the existence of the poles but calls for their measurement.[7]

Application of the polarity principle to social phenomena has two further advantages over dialectic thinking. First, as Morris Cohen (1933: 263) pointed out, polarity thinking implies "wise scepticism about sharp antitheses. Certainty and flexibility may be difficult qualities to bring together, but they are not really logical contradictions." Rather than being real contradictions, many traditional dilemmas involving opposites may only be difficulties and, therefore, soluble. But unless the effort is made to solve them, they remain seeming contradictions (Cohen, 1933: 145; 1949: 16): "For a man to cross the water and not get wet was a patent contradiction before the invention of boats."

Moreover, difficulties must be distinguished from *impossibilities* if facile reconciliation of incompatible alternatives is to be avoided. "How to live long without getting old," or "how to eat the cake and have it too," are real impossibilities. Apart from such impossibilities, however, the polar mode of thought is helpful in that it avoids both exaggerating and underestimating difficulties in human affairs. On the one hand, it is a mistake to treat real difficulties as absolute impossibilities; on the other hand, it is a mistake to minimize difficulties by calling them false alternatives. For instance, it is not sufficient to say that unity and diversity are false alternatives and that both are needed. Although unity and diversity are mutually entailed, it may be frequently difficult to have both, at least at the same time. "Social problems are generally difficulties which arise because we do not know how to attain what we want without also having something which we do not want" (Cohen, 1931: 399).

American federalism is predicated on the coexistence of localities, states and nation (and, more recently, also many other jurisdictional units) as mutually entailed entities. The political order envisaged by *The Federalist* is one of polar federalism rather than dual federalism. Polar federalism is predicated on the complementarity of institutions and especially of representational institutions. The model of representational federalism induced from a few passages in *The Federalist* is admittedly amorphous and truncated. *The Federalist*'s concern was only with the relationship between two levels, and what it said directly about the implicit model was cryptic. What is obviously needed is an elaboration of polar federalism in the perspective of representation as the process by which government can be made responsive to the people,[8] its extension to the multi-level structure of present-day American federalism[9] and, above all, empirical demonstration of its theoretical viability.

There is every reason to believe that the polarity principle can go a long way in explaining the paradoxical fact that as the federal center is strengthened there is yet also a noticeable strengthening of the federal periphery. However, belief is not enough. Research should address itself to the mutual entailment of centralization and decentralization in the federal system. Insofar as the glue that holds the system together is the representation of multiple constituencies—geographic, demographic, social and associational interests and so on—the linkages involved in representation are of paramount research concern. Yet, perhaps due to the long-prevailing dualistic conception of the federal structure, there has never been commensurate research. Representation has been studied in isolation at each level of the federal system—national, state, and local—but it has not been studied as a network of linkages among the three levels of American government.

An appropriate research design would select a policy area in which federal, state and local representatives are significant decision-makers. For instance, if the policy area were primary and secondary education, one would want to interview the members of the Education Committee in the U.S. House of Representatives, and, perhaps, a random sample of Congressmen who are not members of the committee. These respondents would be queried along two main lines: first, about their actual and symbolic relationships with state legislators and school board members in their districts; and second, about their actual and symbolic relationship with educational constituencies and clienteles. As a second step, a sample of state legislators *in* the Congressmen's district would be interviewed and asked essentially the same questions. Finally, a sample of school board members *in* the state legislative districts would be selected for parallel interviewing. This procedure would not only yield information about the linkages among representatives at the three levels (which may or may not exist—no one presently knows), but it would also indicate whether the representatives on the three levels share or do not share the same constituents and clienteles (again, no one presently knows).

In addition, the persons or groups named by representatives at each level would in turn provide the anchor points for snowball-sample interviewing of the cross-level constituents and clients, thereby making possible, first, a check on the reciprocity of relations between representatives and represented, and second, the construction of the total sociometric network of representational relationships. Figure 5.1 is a rough approximation of the research design.

The data generated by this investigation would permit an appraisal of the federal representational system in its entirety in a given policy arena. It would presumably show the simultaneous ebb and flow of centralizing and decentralizing tendencies in the federal system as these are mediated by the working of representation. It would show both the equilibrating and disequilibrating forces in the division of authority and functions among the three levels of the federal representational system. If the polarity principle can serve not only as a heuristic but also as an explanatory tool of political analysis, it should be possible both to describe the state of the federal system in a given policy arena and to explain this state of the system in terms of the particular set of relationships among the representatives and represented who are the significant actors in this policy arena. A more ambitious effort would, of course, want to replicate the analysis in other policy fields. And, again, the polarity principle would not rule out—indeed, it might lead one to discover—the possibility that centralizing trends in one policy arena are contemporary with decentralizing trends in another. Comparative analysis of centralizing and decentralizing tendencies, in different policy fields themselves joined in polar opposition, would maximize our understanding of the enormously complex federal representational system and possibly contribute to an explanation of why centralizing and decentralizing forces serve as change mechanisms in national-state-local relationships.

It is only if the complexity of the federal system is harnessed in a research design commensurate with this complexity that the theoretical insights of *The Federalist* into the interface between federalism and representation can be extended in line with modern developments in the real world of public affairs and in line with modern developments in political theory and methodology.

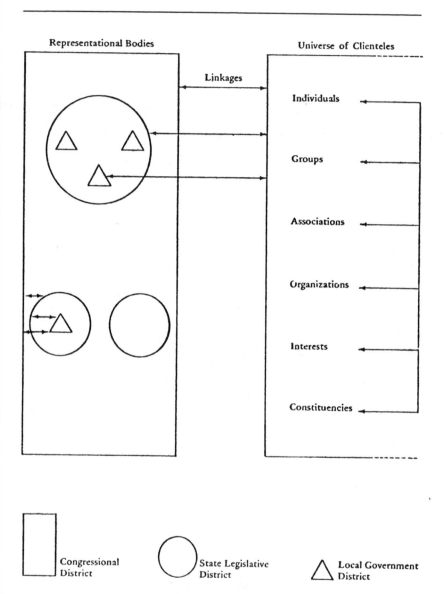

Figure 5.1: Graphic View of the Federal Representational System with Network of Governmental and Clientele Linkages

NOTES

1. Beloff, ed., 1948: xliii, "Introduction." Italics added. All references in the text are to this edition.

2. No. 57: 293. The passage continues: "Before the sentiments impressed on their minds by the mode of their evaluation, can be effaced by the exercise of power, they will be compelled to anticipate the moment when their power is to cease, when their exercise of it is to be reviewed, and when they must descend to the level from which they were raised; there for ever to remain unless a faithful discharge of their trust shall have established their title to a renewal of it."

3. See Ableman v. Booth, 21 How. 506 (1859). Chief Justice Taney speaking.

4. In the gamma statistic, for instance, the measure of association is simply the cross-product of these pulls. The bivariate case can be generalized to more complex multivariate situations. See Galtung, 1969: 195-196.

5. I have stressed this elsewhere; see Eulau, 1969: 123-124.

6. See Cohen, 1949: 14: "The opposition between contrary categories is neither absorbed nor in any way transcended by their unity, any more than abstract unity can be generated by abstract difference."

7. See Cohen, 1931: 166: "Thus physical science employs this principle when it eliminates the vagueness and indetermination of popular categories like *high* and *low*, *hot* and *cold*, *large* and *small*, *far* and *near*, etc. It does so by substituting a definite determination such as a determinate number of yards or degrees of temperature. The indetermination and consequent inconclusiveness of metaphysical and of a good deal of sociological discussion results from uncritically adhering to simple alternatives instead of resorting to the laborious process of integrating opposite assertions by finding the proper distinctions and qualifications."

8. For an empirical test of representation as systemic responsiveness, see Prewitt and Eulau, 1969; this volume Chapter 7.

9. Sundquist, 1969: 242, points out that today "added to the traditional federal-state-local or federal-state-county-town structure of federalism are new bodies with jurisdiction over new areas—multicounty bodies interposed between the states and their local governments, and neighborhood bodies acting as a link between the people and their local governments within the larger cities."

PART II.
Research

INTRODUCTORY NOTE

The separation of theory and research is largely one of convenience and not of principle. "Pure theory" is possible only in the most abstract fields like logic or mathematics. In the social sciences the distinction between theory and research simply refers to whether one is satisfied with theorizing that relates itself to the world of experience in an intuitive, speculative or illustrative manner, or whether theorizing relates itself to empirical observations in a probative, demonstrative or evidential mode. In either case there is an interchange between concept and object of conceptualization which may be more or less casual or rigorous. Not at issue is whether the procedure used in this interchange is inductive or deductive.

Behavioral research in political science, whether grounding theory in research or testing theory through research, seeks to overcome the dualism between theory and research. In retaining it here for the purpose of organizing the chapters, we merely follow a rule of thumb. The chapters in this second part seem to stress empirical research findings more than the chapters in the first part in which theorizing seems to predominate. The separation does not mean, therefore, that the "theoretical chapters" are not grounded in empirical research or oriented toward such research; and it does not mean, as will be apparent, that the "empirical chapters" are not enlightened by theory or not designed to test hypotheses derived from theory.

"The Role of Representative: Some Empirical Observations on the Theory of Edmund Burke" (Chapter 6) by Eulau, Wahlke, Buchanan and Ferguson, exemplifies the interchange between theory and research as well as the integration of behavioral theorizing with classical political theory that Wahlke (Chapter 1) calls for. The study adapts some of Burke's formulations of representation to contemporary conditions and, in turn, reconceptualizes these formulations. Best known is the tripartite typology of representational roles and the important distinction between style and focus of representation. The study has become something of a classic in its own right and the point of departure for a great many replications, extensions and innovations but also, as pointed out in the Introduction, the source of misconceptions and misconstructions in research on representation.

One of the studies following up on the Burke study is Prewitt and Eulau's "Political Matrix and Political Representation: Prolegomenon to a New Departure from an Old Problem (Chapter 7). A preliminary report from the City Council Research Project, Prewitt and Eulau address some of the problematics in theorizing about representation that had come to be recognized in the middle sixties, and that have already been mentioned earlier. But they also face the challenge of Pitkin's (1967) definition of representation as responsiveness at the macrolevel of the polity. Although their measure of systemic responsiveness is crude, being a barely ordinal scale built from informant data collected at the level of individual legislators, they find "representational response style" to vary systematically with such independent variables as city size, electoral competition, community support and recruitment practices. Prewitt and Eulau use the findings to speculate about conditions of democratic governance, but they also imply that Pitkin's notion of representation as an emergent property of the political system is an operationally variable hypothesis. However, from the research point of view, responsiveness should not be treated simply as an absolute property that may or may not emerge but as a property whose emergence is a matter of varying form and degree.

Most research findings on legislatures and representation are usually partial, tentative, heuristic or merely suggestive because available data bases are incomplete and limited. No single study of a single legislative system, the characteristic mode of inquiry, and not even a relatively comprehensive comparative or statistical study is ever "final" in any meaningful sense. More often than not, even if many variables can be introduced and controlled, conditions and contexts from one study to another are sufficiently different to caution against exaggerated conclusions or inferences. Wahlke's study of the Iowa General Assembly, "Policy Determinants and Legislative Decisions" (Chapter 8), is a model of inferential modesty. It would be an exaggeration to claim that the study constitutes proof of Wahlke's proposition that legislative behavior can be better explained by the representative's efforts to mobilize continuing support among constitutents and interest groups than by his or her attempts to discover the policy demands presumably made by citizens. For his strategy of inquiry is one of explicit indirection rather than direct proof or disproof. He simply does not find enough evidence to warrant the conventional proposition that legislatures convert demand-inputs into policy outputs.

Much of legislative responsiveness is symbolic and allocative (see Chapter 3), oriented toward assuring diffuse support by indulging democratic aspirations or providing concrete benefits to particular clienteles rather than reactive to policy demands. The meanings of policy contents also appear to be much more variable, from time to time and place to place, than has been assumed in studies that seek to link structural features of the polity or economic and ecological variables to policy outputs. Conflicts over policy issues along party, urban-rural or interest-group lines are only minimally related to legislative decision-making, much of which is unanimous. Combined with the low information level of the great majority of citizens, all of these and other considerations stemming from relevant research combine to cast doubt on the theoretical viability of the familiar demand-input model. Of course, all of this does not mean that the modern legislature is an anachronism or an institutional misfit. Rather, it means that its decisions can be responsive without being reactive, anticipative of support that will be forthcoming if citizen needs and interests are reasonbly satisfied. Iowa, as Wahlke makes clear, is a highly homogeneous state and constitutes a special case; but a special case is not necessarily a deviant case. The Iowa findings therefore probably constitute one end of a continuum whose middle and other end are yet to be explored.

With a research design altogether different from Wahlke's but with similar theoretical suspicions about the validity of causal-modelling the public policy process in a demand input-output frame of reference, Eulau examines the interaction of ecological conditions and policy development of eighty-two San Francisco Bay area cities and their joint interaction with the policy maps (perceptions, images and positions) of city councils in "Policy-making in American Cities: Comparisons in a Quasi-longitudinal, Quasi-experimental Design" (Chapter 9). The study, part of a much larger research report (Eulau and Prewitt, 1973), is of interest because it is probably the only research of its kind that treats the confluence of environmental challenges and constraints, legislative policy outputs, and legislative groups' policy maps at the macrolevel of analysis. The resultant perspective of the legislative policy process is considerably more complex than that of simplistic input-output models. The variables entering the legislative policy configuration constitute a manifold of events within which policy is not "made" but emerges as a product of both causal and purposive forces which are themselves interactive with ongoing policies—the policy environment.

The possibilities of configurative analysis at the macro level with a built-in temporal dimension are explored in Karps and Eulau's "Policy Representation as an Emergent: Toward a Situational Analysis" (Chapter 10). This is a reanalysis of some variables in the important data set assembled in a 1956-1958-1960 panel study of policy representation by Miller and Stokes (1963). Whereas Miller and Stokes used the data in developing a causal model of the relationships assumed to exist between constituents' issue attitudes, representatives' perceptions of these attitudes, representatives' own policy attitudes and their policy positions on relevant roll calls, Karps and Eulau attempt to examine the emergence of representation in the relationship between representatives and represented. They therefore use the data to construct "representational situations" which are assumed to constitute dynamic contexts for other aspects of representation. Much of their chapter is devoted to the theoretical exposition, operationalization and empirical validation of the typology of representational situations, identified as pervasive, conflictual, dissonant and blocked. When applied to the relationship between the familiar role style of Trustee and several indicators of policy responsiveness and one indicator of service responsiveness, situational analysis clearly aids in discovering both regularities in legislative behavior and deviant outcomes as well as in exploring "pockets of interest" rooted in situational conditions which are not easily discoverable by itemistic procedures.

The kind of analysis undertaken by Karps and Eulau presents many problems of construction and interpretation because it is based on data never envisaged to serve the uses to which they are being put. Two things are to be said in this connection. First, it is preferable to explore theoretical and methodological matters with the help of data, even if the data are marginal to the task at hand, than without them. And second, the very limitations in the data base of the study underline the need for massive data collections geared to research at the macrolevel of legislative processes and representation. There is no substitute for continuing, theory-guided fieldwork. Secondary analysis can only do so much and not more. Political analysis needs theory and method, but it is never better than the data that are made available by research.

Chapter 6

THE ROLE OF THE REPRESENTATIVE:
Some Empirical Observations on the Theory of Edmund Burke

HEINZ EULAU, JOHN C. WAHLKE, WILLIAM BUCHANAN, and LeROY C. FERGUSON

The problem of representation is central to all discussions of the functions of legislatures or the behavior of legislators. For it is commonly taken for granted that, in democratic political systems, legislatures are both legitimate and authoritative decision-making institutions, and that it is their representative character which makes them authoritative and legitimate. Through the process of representation, presumably, legislatures are empowered to act for the whole body politic and are legitimized. And because, by virtue of representation, they participate in legislation, the represented accept legislative decisions as authoritative. But agreement about the meaning of the term "representation" hardly goes beyond a general consensus regarding the context within which it is appropriately used. The history of political theory is studded with definitions of representation (Fairlie, 1940), usually embedded in ideological assumptions and postulates which cannot serve the uses of empirical research without conceptual clarifications (see DeGrazia, 1951).

REPRESENTATIVE AND NON-REPRESENTATIVE BODIES

Many familiar formulations treat representation in a non-functional fashion, viewing it as something valuable in itself, as an ultimate end, and seek to discover or specify its "nature" or "essence." Functional theory, on the other hand, deals with representation from the point of view of the political system as a whole or its component units. Herman Finer (1949) for instance, has suggested that "responsibility is the chief and wider aim, and representativeness merely a convenient means to attain this. . . . The desire for responsible government is paramount; people not merely wish to represent their views, but actually to make and unmake governments." But while functional formulations treat representation as a means for the

111

attainment of some other political objective, failure to test functional propositions by way of empirical research leaves the problems raised by theory in the realm of hypothesis rather than reliable knowledge. In connection with Finer's proposition, for example, there has been little, if any, empirical analysis of the extent to which the represented do, in fact, want to enforce political responsibility, and how capable they are, under modern conditions, of exercising the necessary control. Nevertheless, once relevant concepts are clarified, a functional formulation of representation can open up areas of research which, in turn, may contribute to theoretical cumulation.

The relationship between the representative and the represented is at the core of representational theory. The term "representation" directs attention, first of all, to the attitudes, expectations and behaviors of the represented—to their acceptance of representatives' decisions as legitimate and authoritative for themselves. More particularly, representation concerns not the mere fact that they do accept such decisions, but rather the reasons they have for doing so, their rationalizations of the legitimacy and authority of the decisions made by their representatives.

Sometimes the adjective "representative" denotes nothing more than the publicly approved process by which representatives are to be chosen—as when a distinction is made between a "representative body" (meaning a group of men elected by specific modes of popular election) and a "non-representative body" (meaning a group of men selected by royal or executive appointment, entailed inheritance, or some other non-electoral process). Such usage implies that citizens' attitudes and expectations include, and may extend no farther than, the belief that representatives' decisions must be accepted as legitimate and authoritative if the representatives have been selected in the approved manner. In other words, elected officials are called "representatives" primarily because of the way they have been chosen. Even in a looser usage an appointed commission may be approvingly called a body of "representative" citizens, or may be attacked as "unrepresentative," depending on whether its members might conceivably have been chosen and they been subject to election rather than appointment; and their views will correspondingly be accorded or denied a measure of authority and legitimacy.

But the appropriate process of selecting public decision-makers has never been the really fundamental question for theories of representation. Behind every proposal for altering the method of selecting officials is some assumption, at least, about the effect of such changes on what decision-makers or decision-making institutions do, and how they do it. Proposals for reform must assume,or show that the proposed change will bring it about,that *what* representatives decide and *the way* they reach decisions is more nearly in accord with expectations and demands of the represented than has been the case under the system to be reformed. The various defenses of existing systems of selection which postulate "virtual representation" have in common some shading of the belief that the process of selection is not of major significance in determining what representatives do or how they do it, or that decisions made by representatives can be brought in harmony with public expectations, without altering whatever process of selection is being defended by the advocacy of virtual representation.

The relationship between the process of selection of legislators and the modes and consequences of legislative behavior, or the relationship between public expectations and legislative decisions, offer wide and fertile fields for empirical research. Our purpose here, however, is less ambitious than a full-scale investigation of such relationships. It is to eliminate those particular ambiguities in the concept of representation which concern the actions or behavior of representatives, by use of the concept of "role," and to demonstrate the utility of this approach for further research relevant to the theory of representation.

BURKE'S FORMULATION

A convenient and useful starting point in theoretical clarification is Edmund Burke's theory of representation. For, in following his classic argument, later theorists have literally accepted Burke's formulation and ignored its contextual basis and polemical bias. Burke ingeniously combined two notions which, for analytical purposes, should be kept distinct. In effect, he combined a conception of the *focus* of representation with a conception of the *style* of representation. Parliament, Burke (1774) said in a famous passage,

> is not a *congress* of ambassadors from different and hostile interests; which interests each must maintain, as an agent and advocate, against other agents and advocates; but parliament is *deliberative* assembly of *one* nation, with *one* interest, that of the whole; where, not local purposes, not local prejudices ought to guide but the general good, resulting from the general reason of the whole.

The sentence indicates that Burke postulated two possible foci of representation: local, necessarily hostile interests, on the one hand; and a national interest, on the other hand. He rejected the former as an improper and advocated the latter as the proper focus of the representative's role. But in doing so, he also linked these foci of representation with particular representational styles. If the legislature is concerned with only one interest, that of the whole, and not with compromise among diverse interests, it follows that the representative cannot and must not be guided by what Burke called "his unbiased opinion, his mature judgment, his enlightened conscience." Moreover, Burke buttressed his argument by emphasizing the deliberative function of the legislature—presumably in contrast to its representational function. Yet if one rejects his notion of the legislature as only a deliberative body whose representational focus is the whole rather than its constituent parts, the logic of Burke's formulation is no longer necessary or relevant.

Today, many "publics" constitute significant foci of orientation for the representative as he approaches his legislative task. Under the conditions of a plural political and social order, these foci of representation may be other than geographical interests, be they electoral districts or the larger commonwealth. The modern representative faces similar choices concerning the style of his representational role not only *vis-à-vis* his constituency or state and nation, but *vis-à-vis* other clienteles, notably political parties, pressure groups and administrative agencies. From an analytical point of view—though not, of course, from an empirical standpoint—the style of the representative's role is neutral as far as these different foci of representation are concerned. Regardless of his focus of representation—a geographical unit, a party, a pressure group, or an administrative organization—he is not committed to take either the role of free agent, following his own convictions, or the role of delegate, bound by instructions. In other words, Burke's linkage of a particular areal focus of representation with a particular representational style constitutes only a special case in a generic series of empirically viable relationships between possible and different foci of representation and appropriate styles of representation.

Of course, different foci of representation need not be mutually exclusive. They may occur simultaneously, and appropriate role orientations may be held simultaneously. For instance, a party may be so strong in a district that, in the representative's mind, the interests of district and party are identical. Or a pressure group may have such pervasive influence—as, for example, the Farm Bureau in a predominantly agricultural constituency, or the AFL-CIO in a predominantly working class district—that, again the interests of district and pressure group become identified. Moreover, it is possible that different focal role orientations are activated *seriatim* as circumstances require. In particular, one may assume that on matters of no relevance to the representative's district, roles oriented towards party or lobby as foci of representation may serve as major premises of choice.

The generic extension of Burke's special case, broken down into analytic components, suggests that the focal and stylistic dimensions of representation must be kept separate in empirical research. Burke combined them for polemical reasons: he was writing in opposition to the idea of mandatory representation which had much popular support in the middle of the eighteenth century (see Beer, 1957). The result of this polemical commitment was that the problem of *how* the representative should behave *vis-à-vis* his clienteles became a substantive problem—*what* he should do for the clienteles. But the fact that a representative sees himself as reaching a decision by following his own convictions or judgment does not mean that the content of his decisions is necessarily oriented towards a general rather than a particular interest, just as his acceptance of instructions from a clientele group does not necessarily mean that he is oriented towards a special rather than the public interest. A representative may base his decisions on his own conscience or judgment, but the cause he promotes may be parochial. Or he may follow instructions, but the mandate may be directed towards the realization of the general welfare.

The distinction between the focal and stylistic dimensions of the representative's role allows us to suggest that representation is not concerned with what decisions should be made, but with how decisions are to be made. Now, it is axiomatic that decisions made in institutional contexts, such as legislatures provide, are made in terms of a set of premises which guide the behavior of decision-makers. The notion —explicit in Burke and other traditional formulations—that legislative decisions can be purely rational is not tenable in view of the fact that rationality, while not altogether absent, is invariably bounded by the legislature's institutional environment.[1] One of these boundaries is the representational fabric of the legislature. The representative system provides the representative with some of the assumptions in terms of which he defines his role. The roles he takes, in turn, whether in the focal or stylistic dimensions of representation, provide the premises for decision.

Premises underlying decisions made by legislatures, then, may be of two kinds: (1) they may be premises relevant to the focus of representation; and (2) they may be relevant to the style of representation. With regard to the first kind, for instance, a representative may be guided by premises such as that legislation should benefit either his district or the state, that it should be "liberal" or "conservative," that it should or should not favor special interests, that it should or should not be in performance of his party's campaign pledges, and so on. With regard to the second kind of premises, the representative's choices may be circumscribed by his stylistic role orientation, whether he sees himself following his own conscience or instructions. In this dimension the premises involved in his decisional behavior refer not to the focus but to the style of his role as representative.

REPRESENTATION AND GEOGRAPHICAL DISTRICTS

The issue of styles of representation—free agency versus mandate—has been confounded by the fact that the enabling source of a representative's power is the electorate of a geographical district. Representation of geographical areas introduces a certain amount of ambiguity into the relationship between representative and represented which is likley to be absent under schemes of proportional or vocational representation (see Gosnell, 1948: 124-142). Part of this ambiguity is the widely held expectation, contested by Burke but shared by many citizens and politicians alike, that the representative is a spokesman of the presumed "interests" of the area from which he has been elected. Of course, implicit in this expectation is the assumption that a geographical unit has interests which are distinct and different from those of other units, and which should be represented in public decision-making. This assumption has been challenged on a variety of grounds: that the geographical area as such, as an electoral unit, is artificial; that it cannot and does not generate interests shared by its residents; that it has no unique interests; and so on. Schemes of proportional or vocational representation have been advanced to make possible the representation of allegedly more "natural" interest groupings, such as minority groups, skill groups or economic groups.[2]

The assumption that geographical districts have particular characteristics— such as population attributes and industrial, agricultural or commercial properties —and, hence, unique interests which are, or ought to be, factors influencing the direction of public decisions continues to be shared not only by voters, politicians and others involved in policy-making, but also by scientific students of the political process. It underlies many studies which seek to relate legislative roll-call votes to the socio-economic characteristics of electoral districts (see Turner, 1951; MacRae, 1958), as well as those studies which analyze the socio-economic composition of legislatures (see Matthews, 1954; Hyneman, 1940).

It is a further assumption of these studies that legislators, having lived in their districts for all or substantial parts of their lives, share the values, beliefs, habits and concerns of the people who elected them and whom they presumably represent. Indeed, a literal interpretation of "represent" is to make something present that is not actually present. But this interpretation is most tenuous under modern conditions. Electoral districts tend to be so heterogeneous in population attributes, so pluralistic in the character of their group life, so diverse in the kinds of values and beliefs held, that whatever measures of central tendency are used to classify a district are more likely to conceal than to reveal its real character. The notion that elections are held as a method to discover persons whose attributes and attitudes mirror those most widely shared by people in their district appears to be of dubious validity.

This does not mean, of course, that the geographical district is dysfunctional from the point of view of maintaining the political system. The very circumstance of heterogeneity in the district tends to free the representative from being readily bound by a mandate, to make for discretion and political responsibility, and to enable him to integrate conflicting demands. The function of representation in modern political systems is not to make the legislature a mathematically exact copy of the electorate.

But the difficulty of finding an identity between representative and represented does not also mean that a representative's point of reference in making decisions cannot be his district. It may or may not be, and whether it is or not is a matter of empirical inquiry. We merely doubt that what orients a representative towards his district rather than some other focus of attention is the similarity between his district's characteristics and his own. We cannot assume, therefore, that even if a representative incorporates in himself the characteristics of his district—which, for argument's sake, may be admitted when he comes from a relatively homogeneous area—he will be more oriented towards the district than a representative who, from the point of view of district characteristics, is a deviant. In fact, the latter may be more concerned with his district and seek to discover its "interests," if they are discoverable, than the former. And if a district interest, so-called, can be specifically singled out, it is more likley to be the interest of a politically salient group in the district than of the district as an undifferentiated entity.

In so far as the district rather than some other unit, such as the entire commonwealth, is at the representative's focus of attention, it is more likely to be a function of political than of demographic or socio-economic variables. The problem is one of discovering under what conditions the representative can afford to disregard the district and still hope to maintain the confidence of his constituents. We might speculate, for instance, that in so far as he cherishes the position of power he holds, he is unlikely to ignore his district. We should expect, therefore, that representatives from districts where competition between the parties is keen are more district-oriented than representatives from one-party districts. Yet, we also know that competitive districts are more likely to be found in the heterogeneous metropolitan areas where district "interests" are difficult to ascertain (Eulau, 1957). In other words, what tends to orient the representative towards his district is likely to be the mechanism of political responsibility effectuated by political competition. District-oriented representatives from metropolitan areas where party competition is strong are, therefore, likely to rely on their own judgment, for a mandate must yield here to discretion to satisfy the demands of political responsibility. Discretion, of course, does not mean that the representative is wholly free to act as he pleases. On the contrary, it means that he will have due regard for all the considerations relevant in the making of legislative decisions. And among these considerations, certainly, the "interests" of his electorate or segments of the electorate, as well as his own estimate of the limits which these interests set to his actions, are important. As Burke admitted,

> it ought to be the happiness and glory of a representative to live in the strictest union, the closest correspondence, and the most unreserved communication with his constituents. Their wishes ought to have great weight with him; their opinion high respect, their business unremitted attention.

Though analytically the foci and the style of the representative's role are distinct, they can be expected to be related empirically in a system of mutually interpenetrating orientations. In other words, just as we need not assume that a commitment to district invariably involves the representative's following instructions from his district (the role orientation of Delegate), or that a commonweal-oriented representative is invariably a free agent (the role orientation of Trustee), so also we need not assume that the foci of a representative's role are invariably unrelated to his representational style. In fact, it is the functionally related network of roles which makes for a representational *system*. We can assume, for instance, that a representative who is highly sensitive to the conflict of pressure groups, but not committed to any one, is more likely to be a Trustee in his representational role than the representative who feels close to a particular group and, consequently, is more likely to be a Delegate. Similarly, we might expect that a representative not strongly attached to a party, but not independent of it, is likely to shift between his own judgment and instructions (the role orientation of Politico).

TRUSTEE, DELEGATE, AND POLITICO

An opportunity to test the validity of the theoretical distinction here made, between the focus and style of representation, as well as of the representative's role, was afforded in connection with a comparative research project undertaken by the authors during the 1957 sessions of the state legislatures in California, New Jersey, Ohio and Tennessee.[3] State legislators in these four states were asked the following question, among others: "How would you describe the job of being a legislator—what are the most important things you should do here?" Of the 474 respondents, 295 gave answers relevant to the stylistic dimension of the representative's role, and 197 of these gave additional answers referring to the areal focus of their role.[4]

Responses concerning the stylistic dimension yielded three major representational role types: Trustee, Delegate, and Politico.[5] These types may be described as follows:

(1) *Trustee:* This role finds expression in two major conceptions which may occur separately or jointly. First, a moralistic interpretation: the representative is a free agent, he follows what he considers right or just—his convictions or principles, the dictates of his conscience. Second, a rational conception: he follows his own judgments based on an assessment of the facts in each case, his understanding of the problems involved, his thoughtful appraisal of the sides at issue.

The orientation of Trustee derives not only from a purely normative definition, but is often grounded in conditions which make it functionally necessary. The represented may not have the information to give intelligent instructions; the representative is unable to discover what his clienteles want; preferences remain unexpressed; there is no need for instructions because of a presumed harmony of interests between representative and represented—all of these circumstances may be cited as sources of the role orientation of Trustee.

(2) *Delegate:* Just as the Trustee is by no means an empirically pure type, the orientation of Delegate allows for a number of conceptions. All Delegates are, of course, agreed that they should *not* use their independent judgment or convictions as criteria of decision-making. But this does not mean that they feel equally committed to follow instructions, from whatever clientele. Some merely speak of consulting their constituents, though implying that such consultation will have a mandatory effect on their behavior. Others frankly acknowledge their direct dependence on instructions and accept them as a necessary or desirable premise for their decisions. Some may even follow instructions counter to their own judgment or principles. In other words, the

possibility of conflict in role orientations is clearly envisaged and resolved in favor of subordinating one's independence to what is considered a superior authority.

(3) *Politico:* The classical dichotomization of the concept of representation in terms of free agency and mandate was unlikely to exhaust the possibilities of representational styles. Depending on circumstances, a representative may hold the Trustee orientation at one time, and the Delegate orientation at another time. Or he might seek to reconcile both in terms of a third. One can think of representation as a continuum, with the Trustee and Delegate orientations as poles, and a midpoint where the orientations tend to overlap and, within a range, give rise to a third role. Within this middle range the roles may be taken simultaneously, possibly making for conflict, or they may be taken serially, one after another as conditions call for.

Because the data do not permit sharp discrimination between the two possibilities, we shall speak of representatives who express both orientations, either simultaneously or serially, as Politicos. In general, then, the Politico as a representational role type differs from both the Trustee and the Delegate in that he is more sensitive to conflicting alternatives in role assumption, more flexible in the way he resolves the conflict of alternatives, and less dogmatic in his representational style as it is relevant to his decision-making behavior.

The spell of the Burkean formulation on the interpretation of representation tended to create reactions which, it seems, are almost as arbitrary as Burke's formula itself. In particular, the functional notion, itself quite realistic under modern conditions, that the legislature is an agency for the coordination and integration of diverse social, economic and political interests makes apparent the simple-mindedness of Burke's theory, now as then. Carl J. Friedrich (1950: 297), for instance, has pointed out that "the pious formula that representatives are not bound by mandate, that they are subject only to their conscience and are supposed to serve the common weal, which is repeated in so many European constitutions, while significant as a norm, may lead to differentiating as well as to integrating results." Yet, in concentrating on the multiplicity of potential representational foci, Friedrich went too far in his rejection of Burke. For, once the distinction is made between the style of the representative's role and its focus, Burke's "pious formula" is still relevant. Both the focus and the style are likely to be influenced by the character of politics at a given time and by the demands of contemporary political circumstances on the representative as a decision-maker. Functional analysis cannot limit itself to the foci of representation alone, but must also pay attention to those political requirements which may be relevant to the representative's style.

Our hypothesis may be stated as follows: the exigencies of modern government, even on the relatively low level of state government, are exceedingly complex. Taxation and finance, education and public welfare, legal reform, licensing and regulatory problems, transportation, and so on, are topics more often than not, beyond the comprehension of the average citizen. Unable to understand their problems and helpless to cope with them, people are likely to entrust the affairs of government to the elected representatives who, presumably, are better informed than their constituents. People may pay lip service to the notion that a representative should *not* use his independent judgment,[6] but in fact they are unable, or do not care, to give him instructions as may once have been possible when the tasks of government were comparatively simpler. It is likely, therefore, that the representative has become less and less a Delegate and more and more a Trustee as the business of government has become more and more intricate and technical. Rather than being a "pious formula," the role orientation of Trustee may be a functional necessity, and one should expect it to be held by state legislators more frequently than that of Politico, and latter more frequently than that of Delegate.

A test of this general proposition is possible by way of comparative analysis of the distribution of representational role styles in the four states. As Table 6.1 indicates the role orientation of Trustee is held by a greater number of legislators than that of either Politico or Delegate. In all four states it appears more frequently, and significantly more frequently, than the other two. Moreover, the Politico appears somewhat more frequently in all states than the Delegate.

The Trustee orientation appears significantly more frequently in Tennessee than in the other three states, a fact that seems to contradict the proposition that the orientation of Trustee varies with the complexity of governmental affairs. As Tennessee is less urbanized and industrialized than the other states, one should expect Tennessee legislators to be less often Trustees and more often Delegates than legislators in California, New Jersey or Ohio. But it may also be that "complexity" is a function of perceptions, regardless of the real situation. If so, then to Tennesseans the relatively less complex character of socio-economic life may appear more complex than it actually is, compared with the other states. The more frequent appearance of the Trustee orientation there may only be symptomatic of an even greater feeling of helplessness and inefficacy on the part of people *vis-à-vis* governmental problems, as it is perceived by state representatives. Such perceptions may be a reflection of the lower educational level in Tennessee; but to demonstrate this is beyond the limits of the analysis.[7]

Table 6.1: Distribution of Representational Role Orientations in Four States

Representational Role Orientation	Calif. (N=49)	N.J. (N=54)	Ohio (N=114)	Tenn. (N=78)	Total (N=295)
Trustee	55%	61%	56%	81%	63%
Politico	25	22	29	13	23
Delegate	20	17	15	6	14
Total	100%	100%	100%	100%	100%

AREAL-FOCAL ORIENTATIONS

If, as suggested earlier, a representative's areal-focal orientation does not automatically derive from ascertainable district interests or from personal characteristics he may share with his constituents, the question arises where such orientations do come from, and how they intrude on the representative's conception of his role. For the purpose of this study, it was possible to delineate three areal-focal orientations which may be described as follows:

(1) *District-orientation:* District-oriented representatives had essentially two alternatives: either they could simply mention their districts or counties as being relevant in their conception of their jobs, or they could explicitly place their districts as being above the state as an important factor in their legislative behavior. Among the former, the most frequent responses suggested that it is the representative's job to take care of his district's needs and pass legislation which will benefit his district or county. Others emphasized the policy problems involved in legislation and the necessity to protect what they considered district interests from the policy point of view. Or the emphasis was on the services which these representatives think they are expected to render for their district. Another group of district-oriented representatives specifically pointed to the importance of placing the interests of their district above those of the state, though they usually admitted that state concerns should also be given consideration.

(2) *State-orientation:* As in the case of the district-oriented respondents, state-oriented representatives may either mention the state alone as the salient focus, or they may also mention the district, but clearly tend to place state above district. Some emphasized the need of state policy or state programs as an overriding consideration. A second group pointed to both state and district as relevant foci, but tended to give the benefit of doubt to the state. Finally, some state-oriented representatives explicitly emphasized the desirability of overcoming parochial considerations in favor of the state.

(3) *District-and-state-orientation:* A third major group of respondents who spontaneously concerned themselves with the areal focus of their role mentioned both district and state, but, apparently, did not envisage a possibility of conflict and thought that they could attent to both foci without undue difficulty. Yet, the generality of the responses given in this connection may be deceptive, and coding them under this rubric may have been somewhat arbitrary in a number of cases. Though the actual language used tended in the direction of the state as the focus of role orientation, the tone often appeared to be more indicative of a latent district orientation. One should expect these hyphenated representatives to resemble district- more than state-oriented representatives.

Areal role orientations may be assumed to be a function of the dynamics of the democratic political system with its emphasis on the responsibility of the representatives to the represented. Political responsibility—a set of relationships in which the elected are aware of the sanctions which make responsibility a reality—is predicated on the existence of a competitive political system where constituents have a genuine choice, *i.e.,* where the representatives are periodically confronted with the real possibility of removal from office. The sanction of removal inherent in a competitive party system serves to focus representative's attention on their district rather than the state as the crucial point of reference. Representatives from competitive areas are more likely to be district-oriented than representatives from one-party areas, while representatives from one-party areas are more likely to be state-oriented than those from competitive areas.

An initial, though crude, test of this hypothesis is possible by examining the distribution of areal role orientations in the four states. Tennessee representatives might be expected to be less district-oriented than representatives in the other states, in view of the predominant one-party character of Tennessee politics. As Table 6.2 indicates, the data support this hypothesis. Though the percentage differences are small and statistically not significant, except in the California-Tennessee contrast, only 21 per cent of the Tennessee representatives are district-oriented as against 35 per cent in California, 27 per cent in New Jersey, and 28 per cent in Ohio. But the most noticeable aspect of Table 6.2 is the fact that Tennessee representatives in significantly greater proportion failed to express themselves spontaneously in this connection. Why this is so can, at this point, be only a matter of speculation. Tennessee representatives may take whatever areal foci they have so much for granted that they feel no need to mention them, or they may simply be less articulate than representatives elsewhere. Finally, while there is a somewhat sharper differentiation between district and state role orientations in California than in New Jersey and Ohio (where the combined category figures more prominently), relatively few representatives in all states mentioned the state alone as the focus of their areal orientation.

A more severe test of the hypothesis is possible by relating areal role orientations to the political character of representatives' home districts. Because party competition as an independent variable has no room for operation in predominantly one-party Tennessee,[8] Table 6.3 presents the combined data for California, New Jersey and Ohio alone.[9] As Table 6.3 shows, 53 per cent of the representatives from competitive districts were district-oriented, while only 33 per cent of those from one-

Table 6.2: Distribution of Areal Role Orientations in Four States

Areal Role Orientation	Calif. (N=113)	N.J. (N=79)	Ohio (N=162)	Tenn. (N=120)	Total (N=474)
District	35%	27%	28%	21%	27%
District-and-State	14	28	25	8	19
State	20	14	16	9	15
No mention	31	31	31	62	39
Total	100%	100%	100%	100%	100%

Table 6.3: Political Character of Electoral Districts and Areal Role
Orientations in Three States*

Areal Role Orientation	Political Character of District		
	Competitive (N=72)	Semi-competitive (N=77)	One-party (N=96)
District	53%	48%	33%
District-and-State	28	34	33
State	19	18	34
Total	100%	100%	100%

*California, New Jersey and Ohio. "Non-respondents" on the areal dimension have been omitted.

party districts were so classified. On the other hand, one-party district representatives held in significantly greater proportion a state orientation than those from competitive districts.[10] The data support the hypothesis that areal orientation varies with the political character of the district in which representatives are elected.[11]

THE ROLE SYSTEM

The analytical distinction between the foci and the style of representation is helpful in dissecting the representative's role. Actual behavior is not a function of discrete role orientations, however, but of a system of such orientations. It is the network of interpenetrating roles which gives patterns and coherence to the representational process. It is essential, therefore, to relate areal and stylistic role orientations to each other in terms of significant hypotheses about conditions of their covariation in the representational system.

It has been suggested earlier that, analytically, stylistic role orientations are neutral. What correlation may be found empirically, therefore, should depend on some crucial attribute in the independent variable—in this connection the areal role orientation. It may be suggested that this crucial attribute is the condition of effective political responsibility. In so far as they differ, district-oriented representatives are ultimately responsible to their constituents, while state-oriented representatives are not responsible to an equivalent state-wide constituency. The state-oriented representative cannot point to a state-wide clientele from which he could possible receive a mandate.[12] Hence the hypothesis may be advanced that state-oriented representatives are more likely to be Trustees than district-oriented representatives, whereas the latter are more likely to be Delegates than the former. As Table 6.4 demonstrates this is in fact the case. While 84 per cent of the state-oriented representatives are Trustees, only 37 per cent of the district-oriented and 55 per cent of the district-and-state-oriented representatives are so. And while 36 per cent of the district-oriented representatives are Delegates, only 8 per cent of

Table 6.4: Areal-Focal and Representational Role Orientations
in Four States*

Representational Role Orientation	District-oriented (N=89)	State-District-oriented (N=64)	State oriented (N=44)
Trustee	37%	55%	84%
Delegate	36	8	——
Politico	27	37	16
Total	100%	100%	100%

*χ^2 for the entire array = 37.759; d.f. = 4; p < .001.

the district-and-state-oriented and none of the state-oriented hold a mandatory view of their representational role.

Moreover, Table 6.4 supports some corollary hypotheses. In the first place, because a representative is district-oriented, he need not be a Delegate any more frequently than a Trustee. This simply means that though a representative may clearly have his district at his focus of attention, he may nevertheless act on behalf of the district, in his own conception, as a free agent. Such a representative will say that he knows and understands what the district needs and wants, and he rejects the notion that anybody in the district can tell him what to do. As Table 6.4 shows, among the district-oriented representatives, almost equal proportions, 37 per cent and 36 per cent respectively, are Trustees and Delegates. On the other hand, state-oriented representatives are more likely to be Trustees than anything else. This hypothesis is based on the assumption that the state-oriented representatives do not and cannot recognize a state-wide areal clientele which could give them instructions. As Table 6.4 indicates, none of the state-oriented representatives is a Delegate, and only 16 per cent are Politicos.

Finally, if the representative's areal focus is both his district and the state, one should expect that he will take the role of Politico more frequently than either the district- or the state-oriented representative. For, because he stresses both foci, he is likley to be subject to cross-pressures: as a district-oriented representative he will take the role of Delegate at least as frequently as that of Trustee; as a state-oriented representative he will take the role of Trustee more frequently than any other. We should expect, therefore, that this representative will not only be a Politico more frequently than the other two areal-oriented types, but also that he will take the Trustee role more frequently than the Delegate role. Both hypotheses find support in the data reported in Table 6.4. While the differences are small, 37 per cent of the district-and-state-oriented representatives are Politicos, while only 16 per cent and 27 per cent of the other two groups admit to this representational style. Moreover, a majority are also Trustees, while only 8 per cent are Delegates—evidence of the differential effect of areal role orientations on the particular stylistic roles which seem most appropriate.

This analysis supports the notion that the areal-focal and stylistic dimensions of representation give rise to role orientations which, though analytically distinct, constitute a role system, and that this system gives the process of representation both its structure and its function.

NOTES

1. For the conception of "bounded rationality" as well as the notion that roles constitute some of the premises of decision-making behavior, we are indebted to Simon, 1957.

2. Most theories of functional or proportional representation are motivated or supported by tacit and untested assumptions about the relationship of legislators' behavior to the process by which they are selected. This is merely a special case of the general democratic assumption that political responsibility is the mechanism *par excellence* for bringing legislators' actions in line with the expectations of the represented.

3. The samples for the four legislators are 91 per cent in Tennessee, 94 per cent in California and Ohio, and 100 per cent in New Jersey. The four states composing the total sample represent different regions of the country, different ratios of metropolitan and non-metropolitan population, and different degrees of party competition. The interviews, using fixed schedules, uniform in all four states and including both open-ended, focussed-type questions as well as closed, or fixed-answer type questions, averaged about two hours.

4. The reduction in the number of respondents from the total samples is, of course, due to the open-endedness of the question. Hence not all respondents could be used in the construction of the role types as they emerged from representatives' own definitions, and in the analysis.

5. In constructing stylistic and areal-focal role orientation types, the responses to the question were coded in terms of (a) characterization of job; (b) objectives of job; and (c) critieria of decision. Each total answer was broken up into individual statements and coded in terms of manifest content rather than latent meanings, though meaning was taken into consideration in locating manifest statements. Role orientation types were constructed by combining relevant manifest statements which seemed to make for a major orientational dimension. In general, data concerning criteria of decision yielded the stylistic orientation, and data concerning the objectives of the job yielded the areal orientation.

6. In the years before the second World War, public opinion polls several times sampled expectations in this regard. Relevant poll questions were: (1) Do you believe that a Congressman should vote on any question as the majority of his constituents desire or vote according to his own judgment? (2) Should members of Congress vote according to their own best judgment or according to the way the people in the district feel? (3) In cases when a Congressman's opinion is different from that of the majority of the people in his district, do you think he should usually vote according to his own best judgment, or according to the way the majority of his district feels? In three of four polls, 61, 63 and 66 per cent, respectively, of the respondents said the Congressman should vote the way people feel. In the fourth poll, only 37 per cent gave this answer. See Cantril, 1951.

7. As the Trustee orientation includes reponses stressing traditional moral values, it might be assumed that these virtues—such as following one's conscience or what one feels to be "right"—are more valued in rural Tennessee than in the three more urbanized states. But inspection of the frequency with which this attitude appears in Tennessee as against the other states does not reveal significantly different distributions of relevant responses: California—18%; New Jersey—8%; Ohio—28%; and Tennessee—23%.

8. Of the 46 Tennessee respondents who mentioned an areal orientation, only four came from competitive and five from semi-competitive districts.

9. Competition in district was severally defined in the four states on the basis of past election returns. Space limitations prevent us from specifying the criteria here. They may be obtained from the authors.

10. $x^2 = 9.238$ for the entire array, where d.f. = 4, $p \geqslant .05$. If the middle categories are omitted and only competitive and one-party districts are compared with respect to state and district orientation alone, $x^2 = 7.12$; d.f. = 1; $p < .01$.

11. However, this finding may be spurious. It might be less a function of the political character of the district than of its ecological character. Competitive districts are, more often than not, located in metropolitan areas, while one-party districts are more frequent in non-metropolitan areas. It seemed advisable, therefore, to control the districts' political character by their ecological character. For this purpose, the districts were divided on the basis of the 1950 Census specifications. The hypothesis concerning the relationship between political character of district and areal orientation was clearly maintained in both metropolitan and non-metropolitan districts. However, while the pattern proved similar in both ecological categories, a greater proportion of district-and-state-oriented representatives appeared in the non-metropolitan than in the metropolitan areas, suggesting a pull towards greater dichotomization of areal orientations in the metropolitan environment. In view of the intimate connection in industrialized states between metropolitan and state-wide problems, this result is not surprising. It seems that the state is more salient as a focus of attention for representatives from metropolitan districts (no matter what their political character) than from non-metropolitan districts.

12. He might, of course, receive instructions from a state-wide clientele such as a pressure group or political party, but these constitute other dimensions of his attention foci.

Chapter 7

POLITICAL MATRIX AND POLITICAL REPRESENTATION:
Prolegomenon to a New Departure from an Old Problem

KENNETH PREWITT
HEINZ EULAU

Scholars interested in theorizing about political representation in terms relevant to democratic governance in mid-twentieth-century America find themselves in a quandary. We are surrounded by functioning representative institutions, or at least by institutions formally described as representative. Individuals who presumably "represent" other citizens govern some ninety thousand different political units—they sit on school and special district boards, on township and city councils, on county directorates, on state and national assemblies, and so forth. But the flourishing activity of representation has not yet been matched by a sustained effort to explain what makes the representational process tick.

Despite the proliferation of representative governments over the past century, *theory* about representation has not moved much beyond the eighteenth-century formulation of Edmund Burke. Certainly most empirical research has been cast in the Burkean vocabulary (see Eulau et al. 1959; Miller and Stokes, 1963). But in order to think in novel ways about representative government in the twentieth century, we may have to admit that present conceptions guiding empirical research may be obsolete. This in turn means that the spell of Burke's vocabulary over scientific work on representation must be broken (see Eulau, 1967).

To look afresh at representation, it is necessary to be sensitive to the unresolved tension between the two main currents of contemporary thinking about representational relationships. On the one hand, representation is treated as a relationship between any one individual, the represented, and another individual, the representative—an *interindividual* relationship. On the other hand, representatives are treated as a group, brought together in the assembly, to represent the interest of the community as a whole—an *intergroup* relationship. Most theoretical formulations since Burke are cast in one or the other of these terms.

Current empirical studies of representation by and large make individualistic assumptions. Partly these presuppositions are rooted in the individualistic culture of democratic politics; but they are also eminently congenial to the methodology of survey research that takes the individual as the empirical unit of analysis. In concentrating on the individual, be he representative or represented, contemporary research has gained much insight into the ideology of representation and possibly into representational behavior. We know, for instance, that the representative may see himself as a "trustee" or "delegate" (or some mixture) and that such self-images serve the public official in defining political situations, in guiding his actions, or in justifying his decisions.[1] But research into the rationalizations of the representatives has not led to an adequate theory that would explain the functioning of contemporary representative government. Other investigations are less "individualistic" in their presuppositions. In particular the theoretical discussions of "public interest" or "general will" suggest an understanding of representation as a relationship between collectivities. These investigations, however, have not provided the empirically grounded theory of representation we feel is needed.

A viable theory of representation, it seems to us, cannot be constructed from individualistic assumptions alone. It must be constructed out of an understanding of representation as a relationship between two collectives—the representative assembly and the represented citizenry. However, neither can a viable theory be advanced in the absence of empirical investigation into the thinking and the acting of the individuals in the collectives. What we grope toward, then, is a theoretically adequate treatment of representation as a property of the political system, but a treatment tutored by systematic data.

A FRESH LOOK AT REPRESENTATION

Our beginning point is a highly suggestive passage in Professor Pitkin's (1967: 224) recently published explication of the concept of representation. She elaborates on representation as something that "must be understood at the public level":

> The representative system must look after the public interest and be responsive to public opinion, except insofar as non-responsiveness can be justified in terms of the public interest. At both ends, the process is public and institutional. The individual legislator does not act alone, but as a member of a representative body.

By elevating representation from the level of individual relationships to the level of the political system, Pitkin (pp. 221-222) suggests that representation is, in her own words,

> primarily a public, institutional arrangement involving many people and groups, and operating in the complex ways of large-scale social arrangements. What makes it representation is not any single action by any one participant, but the overall structure and functioning of the system, the patterns emerging from the multiple activities of many people.

Having pointed out that representation is a systemic phenomenon, Pitkin (p. 224) goes on to note that representation *may or may not emerge* from whatever is the relationship between citizens and public officials. "I am not suggesting," she writes, that representation "must emerge from any particular system; there is no guarantee that it will. But it may emerge, and to the extent that it does we consider that system as being a representative government."

If, as Pitkin suggests, representation is a collective and public phenomenon that may or may not emerge in a political community, and if emergence of a representative relationship is conditioned by the "over-all structure and functioning of the system," our attention should be directed to properties of the political system that either facilitate or impede representation. This we propose to do.

Some Methodological Considerations

In describing representation as an emergent property of the political system, Pitkin anticipates a course of methodological inquiry that has engaged us for a number of years and that underlies the procedures adopted in present research on the governance of cities. First, our analysis assumes that representation as well as other variables we consider are group rather than individual properties; thus we make statements about governing bodies and not individual public officials. Second, although we study 82 governments formally defined as "representative," we see representation not as something existing by definition but as something which emerges in the relationship between governing assemblies and governed citizens. Third, whether the particular relationship we might call representation does emerge is affected by the political matrix within which representatives and represented act. Finally, the analysis is configurative, not causal; we want to determine how a particular configuration of system properties, including representation, are linked together.

Of course not all properties of the political community are likely to be equally relevant to the emergence of representation. Our reading of the theoretical literature about American politics directed us to four variables usually considered germane to representation: the degree of social pluralism, the effectiveness of elections as sanctioning mechanisms, the support available to the governing group, and the recruitment processes that select public officials. For present purposes, we consider these four variables—taken together—to constitute a political matrix. The configuration of the political matrix, then, should be critical to how the governing group responds to social pressures and political demands.

Two of these properties—degree of social pluralism and election effectiveness—are first-order system variables that can be directly measured with relevant indicators. The other two properties—recruitment and support—in addition to representation, are *constructed* into group properties from individual data. The data base for our measures of these three variables are interviews with 423 city councilmen in 82 cities of the San Francisco Bay metropolitan region. In order to make the relevant information appropriate for systemic analysis it was necessary to convert the responses of individuals into group properties. This we did in one of two ways. In the case of representation and support we treated the councilmen as informants. We read appropriate questions in the interview schedule for the council *as a whole* and assigned the council to a code category. Because in this analysis we use only one measure of representation, no further index construction was necessary. Our measure of support is constructed from five separate indicators that are sufficiently cumulative to permit a simple summation index. Recruitment as a systemic property, on the other hand, was measured by aggregating the codings of each individual councilman's recruitment pattern into a single council measure. We describe the procedures more fully as we introduce the measures in the analysis.

To employ these coding procedures, of course, is to take certain liberties. For example, although we sometimes speak of community support for the council, we actually are inferring level of support from responses of the councilmen themselves. This is not the place to engage in a complicated defense of whether "definitions of the situation" do indeed serve as the "reality" for those who see it as such. Our intent is to explore in a tentative fashion the relationship among several variables; level of community support being one of these variables, we sought the best measure possible within the confines of our data. A second methodological assumption made is that single group measures can be constructed from the individual responses of those who belong to the group without doing violence to the data. Again, this is not the time to present an extended discussion of "group properties" and how to construct them. Our general strategy is to pursue certain theoretical questions as vigorously as possible, but to report specific findings in a tentative way, paying full heed to the data difficulties.

REPRESENTATION AS RESPONSE

Whether the relationship between the governing few and the governed many can be said to be a representative one depends of course on how the term is defined. Representation has been subject to a variety of definitions. Some studies have described a legislative assembly as representative when the social and economic characteristics of the constituency were fairly well mirrored in the assembly. Other studies, pursuing the logic of "mirror representation", have been less concerned with demographic representation and instead have examined whether in ideology or general values the assembly reflected the constituents. Yet other studies, dropping the mirror analogy, have defined representation in terms of equal access to the assembly by all members of the constituency.

The definition of representation which guides the theoretical endeavors in this paper differs from these formulations. In coding the interviews we made what to us was a surprising discovery; of the 82 councils, as many as 36 did not in any discernible manner seem to act in response to any politically organized views in the public. These 36 councils seemed to rely on their own sense of what the community needs were. This finding alerted us to Pitkin's observation that representation is an emergent property whose appearance cannot be taken for granted. The finding further suggested the importance of looking at the representative relationship in terms of whether the elected assembly acts in response to public views, especially views as delivered in some identifiable manner.

Pitkin left no stone unturned in her effort to salvage the concept of representation as a viable tool for theorizing about problems of democratic governance. After reviewing and interpreting almost any conceivable formulation of the concept's meaning, she settles for this definition: "representing here means acting in the interest of the represented, in a manner responsive to them" (Pitkin, 1967:209). We find this definition useful because it seems to conceive of representation in two related ways: first, the representative assembly defines *what* it should do—"acting in the interest of the represented"; that is, it decides on the political agenda and, in so doing, formulates community goals. Second, the assembly does so in a manner *responsive* to the sentiments of the constituents.[2]

In studying the protocols from the councils, it became clear that, as they govern, councils can act in response to two types of politically organized and publicly voiced opinions. First, councils can consider the views and wishes of attentive publics, of fairly well-defined and permanent interest clusters in the community. These attentive publics may have differing views of how the community should be governed, in which case the council must compromise and adjust. Or the attentive publics may be more or less of the same view, in which case the council need only determine what this view is and act upon it. In either case, we say that the council, by acting in response to the viewpoints and thinking of attentive publics represents these publics. Second, the council may not concern itself with cohesive attentive publics but may, instead, act in response to *ad hoc* pressures and petitions. Neighborhood groups, for instance, may organize on a sporadic basis, make a claim on the council for some service or benefit, and expect to be listened to by "their representatives." Under these conditions, councils placate or respond to specialized and transitory citizen groups. If in the first case the council represents attentive publics, in this case it represents issue-specific groups of citizens.

There is a third type of representative relationship with the public. As previously noted, some councils appear to be altogether immune from external pressures; no identifiable groups of citizens, permanently or sporadically organized, appear to intrude on council deliberations about community affairs. In such cases, councils may or may not be acting *in the interest* of the represented (an issue we do not explore here); they are not, however, acting *in response to* the represented. Rather, these councils entertain a self-defined image of what community needs are. It is in terms of its own image that the council tackles the problems which come to its attention.

The 82 councils divided into the three categories as follows.[3]

Councils responsive to attentive publics	20	24%
Councils responsive to *ad hoc* issue groups	26	32%
Councils entertaining self-defined image	36	44%

The distribution of the councils into this three-category classification essentially sets the question. For the present analytic purposes, representation is taken to mean a relationship between governed and governors wherein the governing group responds to ("represents") politically organized viewpoints among citizens, that is, responds to something *other* than its own image of what the community needs. With representation so understood, we ask: under what political conditions is a representative relationship between governors and governed likely to emerge in a community? Our analysis examines the patterns among the four variables that we have singled out as relevant for representation and examines the connections between the political matrix, as constructed from these four indicators, and the emergence of representation.

REPRESENTATIONAL RESPONSE STYLE AND SOCIAL PLURALISM

An assumption which frequently appears in discussions of representation and modern society might be stated as follows: increasing complexity and differentiation in modern societies makes it more and more difficult for representative bodies to respond to the variety of interests which constitute the political community. Persons who make such observations usually assume representation to be a relationship between individuals. We were interested to see if representation, treated at the systemic level, was indeed less likely to emerge in larger and more complex communities. Table 7.1 presents relevant data.

Using population size as an indicator of a community's social pluralism,[4] it is clear that responding to interests voiced from the community is *facilitated* in the more pluralistic communities. How are we to reconcile this finding with the assumption that social complexity impedes the exercise of the representational function? It may be correct that the larger and more complex a social system, the more difficult it is for any *one* citizen to make his wishes known or for any *one* representative to respond to individual constituents. The data in Table 7.1 emphasize why an individualistic conception of representation is obsolete. Representation as a relationship between two collectivities—the represented and the representatives—appears to emerge more easily in the larger, more complex communities than in the smaller, more homogeneous communities. To understand representation as a systemic property we may have to rethink many of our conventional assumptions. Indeed, the responsiveness of the representative assembly is facilitated under just those conditions assumed to impede individual responsiveness.

Table 7.1: City Size as Indicator of Social Pluralism and
Council Response Style

Representational Response Style	City Size		
	< 10,000 N=32	10–50,000 N=33	> 50,000 N=17
Self-defined Image	56%	39%	29%
Ad hoc Issue Groups	31	36	24
Attentive Publics	13	25	47
Total	100%	100%	100%

$$\frac{\chi^2}{d.f.} = \frac{8.10}{4} = 2.03$$

Gamma = +.38

The pattern in Table 7.1 makes considerable sense. It may well be that in the smaller and more homogeneous communities, the social structure is such that there is simply little opportunity for the council to respond to stable, attentive publics or to *ad hoc*, spontaneous issue groups. Unlike in larger and heterogeneous cities, where various social groups are present and likely to make their demands known to the city council, in the smaller, more homogeneous settings, the group life is likely to be less developed and the public pressures brought on the council are probably less frequent or urgent. If this is so, councils in small cities are unable to identify groups to which they might *wish* to respond, if they only could, and will have to rely on their own images of what is in the best interest of the represented. As Table 7.1 shows, this is in fact the case: the smaller the city, the more councils act in their self-images; the larger the city, the more councils are responsive to groups that articulate interests.[5]

REPRESENTATIONAL RESPONSE STYLE AND ELECTORAL TOLERANCE

It is customary to entertain many assumptions, which often remain untested, about the consequences of elections for representation. Different nominating procedures (primaries vs. conventions), voting rules (list vs. transferable vote), electoral arrangements (at-large, multimember vs. single-member constituencies), counting procedures (majority vs. proportional), election types (partisan vs. nonpartisan), and so on, are said to produce very different types of elected representatives.

Even more to the point, assumptions about elections are very central in writings that consider such issues as "accountability" and "responsiveness." As Dahl (1956: 131) has written, elections "are crucial processes for insuring that political leaders will be somewhat *responsive to the preferences of some ordinary citizens.*"[6] The assumption made by Dahl and by many other writers on democratic politics is that public officials choose policies in anticipation of likely electorate response at the next election. Schlesinger (1966: 2) employs similar reasoning and states the point even more strongly: "The desire for election and, more important, for re-election becomes the electorate's restraint upon its public officials."[7] In democratic theory, then, elections are viewed as the sanction available to the public. In the absence of this sanction, office-holders would not be accountable. And, if the governors are not accountable, it is difficult to imagine them being responsive. "The point of holding [the elected official] to account after he acts is to make him act in a certain way—look after his constituents, or do what they want" (Pitkin, 1967: 57).

The difficulty with these assumptions about representative democracy is that they, in turn, make the assumption that elections do indeed remove or threaten to remove men from public office. We have serious doubts that this is the case. For one thing, and a fact too often overlooked by theorists who emphasize elections as a sanction, a very sizable group of office-holders retire from office voluntarily. As Charles Hyneman sharply pointed out three decades ago, turnover in legis- latures is due not to election defeats, or even to fear of same, but because men simply decide to leave public office. The real task, Hyneman (1938: 30) wrote in 1938, "is to find out why so many legislators, senators and representatives alike, choose not to run again."[8] In his analysis of eight states covering the period 1925- 1933 he found that *more than 60 per cent* of the retirements from both lower houses and Senates were due to failure to seek reelection.[9]

Alerted by Hyneman to the question of voluntary retirement, we checked to see how frequently city councilmen retired from office for reasons other than election defeat. In 82 cities over a ten-year period (approximately five elections per city), more than half of the councilmen retired voluntarily from office. Although a few leave the council to seek higher office, survey data indicate this number is not large. And though a few might retire out of threat of election defeat, survey data indicate that this occurs very infrequently.[10]

This high and persistent rate of voluntary retirement from elected office cer- tainly should caution us against the easy assumption that "elections make public officials responsive" and thus guarantee representative government. For if the representative body plans to depart from office in any case, why should it be concerned with voter approval of its policies? To explore the relationship between elections and representative response style, we need to determine whether the voting public does indeed ever remove incumbents from office.

We constructed an index of "forced turnover" based on the number of incumbents who won, divided by the number of incumbents who sought reelection over a ten- year period (five elections). (The index does not include incumbents who were appointed to office in the expired term)[11] In 21 cities no incumbent seeking reelection was defeated. On the other hand, in only four cities did as many as half of the incumbents suffer defeat. The distribution, therefore, is highly skewed toward success in being reelected. Nevertheless the spread of election defeats is sufficient to permit us to classify cities into three theoretically useful groups: those in which a bid for reelection never failed, those in which it sometimes failed but less often than twenty-five per cent of the time, and those in which it failed for at least one of every four incumbents.

We derive from general democratic theory a simple hypothesis. Cities with the highest rate of forced turnover, where electoral tolerance is relatively low, should have councils tending to act in response to public pressures and petitions. Conversely, councils which govern in a milieu where elections never force anyone from office will act in response only to their own image of what the community needs. This, as Table 7.2 shows, is the case.

Thus, on the one hand, conventional democratic theory appears to be confirmed. The presence of an electorate which removes men from office leads to more acts of reponse by the representative body. On the other hand, conventional theory also holds that councils not responding to political groups would be ousted from office. If we read Table 7.2 in reverse it is evident that this does not happen; elections do not necessarily remove councils which respond only to their own image of community needs. The inability of conventional theorizing about elections to help us explain Table 7.2 is due to an oversight in much of the contemporary literature about representative democracy. Nowhere that we could find have scholars systematically examined the implications for representation *if elections are not used to force turnover* on representative bodies. But the reluctance, or inability, of the electorate to remove public officials is something we must take into account if our theory of representation is not to make unfounded empirical assumptions. Just why nonresponsive councils are seldom removed from office is a question

Table 7.2: Forced Turnover and Representational Response Style

Representational Response Style	Per Centage of Forced Turnover		
	None N=21	1—24 N=39	25+ N=22
To self-defined image	71%	41%	23%
To *ad hoc* issue groups	19	31	45
To attentive publics	10	28	32
Total	100%	100%	100%

$$\frac{\chi^2}{d.f.} = \frac{10.96}{4} = 2.74$$

Gamma = +.44

to which we turn momentarily, but first we take a quick look at the relationship between social pluralism and electoral tolerance.

We expect that the electorate uses its voting powers to force turnover more often in larger cities, where pressures on the governing bodies are diverse and frequent, than in the more homogeneous and politically quiet environment of the smaller community. Table 7.3 shows this to be the case. The medium-sized and larger cities are characterized by higher rates of forced turnover than are the smaller cities, though even in the latter election defeats are not uncommon. Interpreting Tables 7.2 and 7.3 together, it seems that electoral tolerance is negatively related to the degree of representational response. Where councils need not fear the vote of the people, they are also less likely to act in response to the voice of the people.

REPRESENTATIONAL RESPONSE STYLE AND COMMUNITY SUPPORT

For purposes of our theoretical exploration, let us assume that the first three tables provide findings on which we can build. Governing bodies with self-defined images of the public interest are found in smaller communities and are less subject to electoral sanctions than councils which act in response to public pressures. This is a paradox for representational theory. In order to solve the paradox, it is necessary to consider another aspect of the political matrix that may be related to a council's representational response style—a system property we characterize as "community support." We expect, for instance, that where a council is generally supported in what it does by the citizenry, it is relatively free to define the community interest in its own image. And if this is so, it helps explain why a council, though nonresponsive, faces little risk in being ousted from office.

Table 7.3: City Size and Forced Turnover

	City Size		
Percentage of Forced Turnover	<10,000 N=32	10–50,000 N=33	>50,000 N=17
None of incumbents	37%	25%	7%
1–24	41	45	64
25 or more	22	30	29
Total	100%	100%	100%

$$\frac{\chi^2}{d.f.} = \frac{6.26}{4} = 1.57$$

Gamma = +.28

In order to characterize the citizenry of the 82 cities as more or less supportive of the council, we assumed that support was forthcoming if, according to council reports, any one or all of the following conditions were met: (1) that the public held a favorable and respectful image of the council; (2) that the public was generally agreed with the council on its duties; (3) that the public did not include disruptive elements; (4) that there were not many groups steadily critical of the council; and (5) that the public seemed appreciative of the council's policies. We combined these items into a single index of community support.[12]

The measure of community support allows us to investigate the paradox that councils acting on the basis of their own images are less exposed to electoral sanctioning than councils which placate *ad hoc* issue groups or are attentive to more stable interest groups. As Table 7.4 shows, communities in which the electorate does not force incumbents from office are seen as overwhelmingly supportive of their councils; in communities where some or relatively many incumbents are forced from office, the citizens are seen as almost evenly split in the support they are giving their councils.

In communities, then, in which the citizenry is on the whole satisfied with council operations and policies and is apparently giving the council its support we can assume that citizens do feel "represented" by the council even though the council follows its own definition of what is in the best interests of the governed. If this inference is sound, it helps explain why councils which do not act in response to community groups are yet free of threats of election defeats. It is precisely because it does not hear from the public that the council is able to rely on its own judgment. As Table 7.5 indicates, there is a very significant difference in council's representational response styles between the more and less supportive political milieux, and the relationship is exceptionally strong. The table and our analysis suggest that, in dealing with representation as a system property, we must at all times keep in mind that it is embedded, as Pitkin so well put it, "in the complex

Table 7.4: Forced Turnover and Community Support

Level of Community Support	Percentage of Forced Turnover		
	None N=21	1–24 N=39	25+ N=22
Relatively high	81%	49%	45%
Relatively low	19	51	55
Total	100%	100%	100%

$$\frac{\chi^2}{d.f.} = \frac{7.14}{2} = 3.57$$

Gamma = −.42

Table 7.5: Community Support and Representational Response Style

Representational Response Style	Community Support	
	Relatively High N=46	Relatively Low N=36
To self-defined image	63%	19%
To ad hoc issue groups	17	50
To attentive publics	20	31
Total	100%	100%

$$\frac{\chi^2}{d.f.} = \frac{16.52}{2} = 8.26$$

Gamma = .54

ways of large social arrangements." It remains, therefore, to ascertain in what type of community support is forthcoming. From all that we know about small, relatively homogeneous cities we expect that they are more likely to have a supportive citizenry than will larger, more heterogeneous cities. Table 7.6 shows that our expectations are met: the relationship between support and social pluralism is as strong as between support and response style. Small communities, it appears, generate relatively high levels of political support that, in turn, leave the governing body free to pursue community interests as it sees fit.

RECRUITMENT AND REPRESENTATION

The study of political representation must, at some time, confront the naked fact that in any political community a handful of men are chosen to govern over a very large number of citizens. As Lord Bryce (1924: 542) observed:

> In all assemblies and groups and organized bodies of men, from a nation down to a committee of a club, direction and decision rest in the hands of a small percentage, less and less in proportion to larger size of the body, till in a great population it becomes an infinitesimally small proportion of the whole number. This is and always has been true of all forms of government, though in different degrees.

The phenomenon that so impressed Bryce alerts us to the fascinating research problem of linking political recruitment and political representation. Since it is clear that a few men are chosen to govern the many and since, at least under democratic rules, the few are charged to "represent" the many, it is important for a theory of representation that we investigate how the few are chosen. This directs our attention to political recruitment—the process or set of processes by which in a city of, say, 30,000 inhabitants, the population is narrowed to only

Table 7.6: City Size and Community Support

Level of Community Support	City Size		
	$<$10,000 N=32	10–50,000 N=33	$>$50,000 N=17
Relatively high	72%	58%	23%
Relatively low	28	42	77
Total	100%	100%	100%

$$\frac{\chi^2}{d.f.} = \frac{10.59}{4} = 5.30$$

Gamma = −.53

5 men who, as councillors, assume formal authority to govern the remaining 29,995 citizens.

In spite of the obvious logical connection between how the governors are recruited from the people and how they represent the people, the linkage has received little attention in empirical political studies. Some years ago, one of us had occasion to point out that "the relationship between the process of selection of legislators and the modes and consequences of legislative behavior . . . offer wide and fertile fields for empirical research," but the relevant questions were not pursued in *The Legislative System* (Wahlke et al., 1962: 269) or, as far as we can tell, in any other subsequent work.

One of the main reasons for this inattention to the link between recruitment and representation is the tendency of scholars to treat recruitment as an individual characteristic. There are studies of the political career, of the selective effect of personality on political success, of nominations of candidates, of the ascent and descent of political leaders, and so on.[13] Although these studies are productive in their own right, the preoccupation with recruitment at the individual level blocks theorizing activity and empirical research which could connect recruitment and representation. If the position taken in this paper that representation is a systemic property be accepted, however, it is evident that recruitment must also be conceptualized at that level.

We should note that there are studies which treat recruitment and representation at least as aggregate variables. These are the studies which examine the socioeconomic attributes of elected officials and compare them with a demographic profile of their constituents.[14] The difficulty with this research design is that it locks the analyst into a very narrow definition of both recruitment and representation. As to recruitment, it means studying who is selected but not the processes by which this happens. For representation it means that the analysis is limited to a "mirror theory" wherein the very complex process of representation is reduced to a very simple formula of statistical "representativeness." This approach can yield only limited understanding.

Our own conception of recruitment centers in the problem of "sponsorship"— the degree to which the recruitment process is open or unsponsored and the degree to which it is closed or sponsored. Where sponsorship is highly developed, persons already in established political positions exercise considerable control over who will sit on the council. Sponsorship implies that there are fairly determined or even institutionalized pathways to office. The route to the council might be through an apprenticeship on the planning commission or by being an officer of the Chamber of Commerce or by being active in the local ethnic association. For a man to gain a council seat in a community where sponsorship dominates political recruitment, it is important and maybe even necessary for him to first join the inner circles. Sponsorship does not mean, however, that restrictive criteria are being applied, at least as we normally think of restriction in political recruitment. Our analysis is not concerned with whether persons with the "wrong" social traits are eliminated from consideration. In addition, sponsorship is not a notion which masks some conspiracy theory. A community can rely heavily on sponsorship as a means for recruiting political talent without there being manipulation by powerful persons behind the scene.

Sponsorship is an issue of considerable theoretical interest to students of political recruitment. A problem for most elected governing groups is how to maintain some policy continuity despite personnel turnover. This is an especially difficult problem for city councils where, as we have seen, the rate of voluntary retirement is high and where the average tenure is fairly low. (The average number of years of service is 6.5). Continuity of policy viewpoint can be maintained despite turnover if control can be exercised over successive recruits. A procession of like-minded men through office is equally as effective in stablizing city policies as is low turnover. If indeed sponsorship aids a governing group to maintain control over both its members and its policies, sponsorship should also relate to how the group defines its representational function. A reasonable hypothesis is that sponsored recruitment insulates the council from certain political experiences and that this insulation will in turn lead to a representational response style that minimizes the impact of organized demands from the public on the council thinking.

The measure of sponsorship used here was derived by aggregating individual recruitment patterns at the council level. Just as any one councilman could, on the one extreme, be an "outside challenger" who initiated his own career and attained a council seat with minimum prior contact between himself and those already in office, so the council group as a whole could have followed this career line. At the other extreme, just as an individual might have been asked to run for office by current incumbents or even appointed to office, so the council as a group could have had this experience. Between these extremes more or less prior involvement with city affairs could be characteristics of individual councilmen or the council as a whole. Sponsorship is admittedly a highly multidimensional measure as it pertains to the council, but it undoubtedly captures at the group level something of the rich variety of recruitment patterns that are possible.[15]

Recruitment patterns, of course, are part of the political matrix and are likely to be related to other system properties. In communities where elections are not a sanctioning mechanism and where there is, as a result, little or no forced turnover, the recruitment pattern is likely to be characterized by considerable sponsorship, while in politically volatile systems relatively little sponsorship is likely to be practiced. As Table 7.7 reveals, these expectations are reasonably well substantiated by the data.

Similarly, we expect that sponsorship is more likely to appear in a supportive political environment than in a critical one. In a community seen as supportive, where the council is relatively free to do as it pleases precisely because what the council does pleases the citizenry, incumbents are likely to bring into the council men who have already had experience in local community affairs and who can be counted on to continue the policies which seem so satisfactory. On the other hand, and the relatively weaker relationships shown in Table 7.8 underline the point, a council more exposed to criticism and social pressures may *also* seek to perpetuate its policy views by bringing like-minded and trusted members into the council fold. On balance, then, either alternative is possible. Support as a system property and recruitment through sponsorship are moderately related.

Recruitment practices might also be related to the degree of social heterogeneity or homogeneity of a community. In small communities where men are more likely to share each other's characteristics, know each other better and are more likely to be of similar mind, sponsorship should be practiced more frequently than in more pluralistic settings. Again the data suggest, as Table 7.9 shows, that

Table 7.7: Forced Turnover and Political Recruitment

	Percentage of Forced Turnover		
	None N=21	1—24 N=39	25+ N=22
Amount of Sponsorship			
Little	5%	36%	27%
Some	38	51	59
Much	57	13	14
Total	100%	100%	100%

$$\frac{\chi^2}{d.f.} = \frac{18.59}{4} = 4.65$$

Gamma = −.44

Table 7.8: Community Support and Political Recruitment

Amount of Sponsorship	Community Support	
	Relatively High N=46	Relatively Low N=36
Little	19%	33%
Some	48	53
Much	33	14
Total	100%	100%

$$\frac{\chi^2}{d.f.} = \frac{4.50}{2} = 2.25$$

Gamma = +.38

Table 7.9: City Size and Political Recruitment

Amount of Sponsorship	City Size		
	$<$10,000 N=32	10–50,000 N=33	$>$50,000 N=17
Little	19%	30%	29%
Some	37	61	53
Much	44	9	18
Total	100%	100%	100%

$$\frac{\chi^2}{d.f.} = \frac{11.14}{4} = 2.79$$

Gamma = −.34

this seems to be the case, though a good deal of sponsorship is evidently also practiced in the larger and medium-sized cities.

We noted in connection with Table 7.1 that the response style of a council depends in some important measure on the actual presence of groups or publics to which the representative group can respond. We assumed that the same reasoning would hold for recruitment practices; a socially diverse community would sustain a relatively open recruitment process. Although the reasoning is not incorrect, Table 7.9 indicates that recruitment practices may be less affected than response style by community charcteristics. This being the case, the relationship between recruitment and representation is perhaps more problematical than our initial theoretical reasoning might suggest.

Where a council is free to recruit its own successors, with a view toward maintaining continuity in policy leadership by like-minded and trusted men, it should

Table 7.10: Political Recruitment and Representational Response Style

Representational Response Style	Amount of Sponsorship		
	Little N=21	Some N=41	Much N=20
To self-defined image	38%	37%	65%
To *ad hoc* issue groups	33	36	20
To attentive publics	29	27	15
Total	100%	100%	100%

$$\frac{\chi^2}{d.f.} = \frac{4.85}{4} = 1.21$$

Gamma = −.25

also be free from those public pressures which would force it to consider views other than its own when selecting policies. But, it seems, sponsorship is practiced to some degree in the larger, more pluralistic cities where councils are exposed to a politically more active environment. It is not surprising, therefore, that, as Table 7.10 shows, the relationship between recruitment and representation is relatively weak. Although the data point in the theoretically expected direction— councils practicing "much" sponsorship seem more likely to follow their own image of the community interest, while councils characterized by "little" sponsor- ship are more likely to respond in one way or another—the relationship between the two variables is lower than that between any other unveiled in the total con- figuration of the analysis.

Because of the small number of cases, we are generally reluctant to subject the data to a multivariate analysis which would permit us to untangle the rela- tionship between recruitment and representation. However, since councils in the larger cities reported more sponsorship than expected, we decided to control the relationship between recruitment and representation by city size, collapsing however both the size and the representation variables. Table 7.11 reports the results.

It appears that where *much* sponsorship is practiced in a city's recruitment process, size does not have an independent effect on representational style. In large and small cities, councils practicing a great deal of sponsorship tend to follow their own image of community interests. But where sponsorship is less frequently practiced, councils in large cities are more responsive to issue groups or attentive publics than councils in the smaller cities. In the latter, one half of the ten councils with open recruitment practices yet are able to pursue their own conceptions of the community interest. This may be due, of course to the fact, suggested in regard to Table 7.1, that in smaller cities there may just not be any groups or publics sufficiently active to be paid attention to by the council. In general, we can

Table 7.11: Political Recruitment and Representational Response Style, Controlled by City Size

Sponsorship	City Size					
	<25,000			>25,000		
Representational Response Style	Little N=10	Some N=27	Much N=15	Little N=11	Some N=14	Much N=5
To self-defined image	50%	41%	67%	27%	29%	60%
To issue groups and publics	50	59	33	73	71	40
Total	100%	100%	100%	100%	100%	100%

Gamma = —.25   Gamma = —.32

conclude that the uncontrolled results of Table 7.10 do not give too distorted a picture of the relationship between recruitment and representation.

Because community support seems strongly related to the kind of representation that emerges, whereas recruitment seems less critical, we controlled the recruitment-representation relationship by our support variable. Table 7.12 shows some interesting outcomes. Where the community is supportive, sponsorship has no effect at all on representational style. Regardless of whether much or little sponsorship occurs, councils in supportive communities are pursuing their own notions of the public interest. There is, of course, one very plausible interpretation of why sponsorship is so unrelated to response style in such communities. In small cities, recruitment processes need not be controlled to insure a succession of like-minded men through office. In the socially homogeneous and politically satisfied community, anyone who presents himself for office is acceptable. Selection of public leadership by some random method is as likely to produce men with roughly the same views as does selection by sponsorship. Thus the high-support but low-sponsorship communities do not present an anomaly at all.

In communities where support from the citizenry is relatively low, however, sponsorship has the expected consequences for representational behavior. Councils with little sponsorship are almost always those which respond to public pressures, while those with more sponsorship apparently are those less likely to respond (but the small number of cases does not permit us to be confident that this result is sufficiently stable to allow a firm inference). While recruitment does seem to play a role in representation, the degree of support that a community is willing to give is clearly a more important factor in shaping representational style.

Support in turn is attenuated by the political system's electoral tolerance. As Table 7.13 indicates, in a relatively supportive environment where retirement is forced upon incumbents by electoral defeat, councils tend to be attentive rather than self-sufficient in their representational behavior. In less supportive com-

Table 7.12: Political Recruitment and Representational Response Style, Controlled by Community Support

| Sponsorship | Community Support | | | | | |
| | Relatively High | | | Relatively Low | | |
Representational Response Style	Little N=9	Some N=22	Much N=15	Little N=12	Some N=19	Much N=5
To self-defined image	78%	50%	73%	8%	21%	40%
To issue groups and publics	22	50	27	92	79	60
Total	100%	100%	100%	100%	100%	100%

Gamma = .00   Gamma = —.52

Table 7.13: Forced Turnover and Representational Response, Controlled by Community Support

| Percentage Forced Turnover | Community Support | | | | | |
| | Relatively High | | | Relatively Low | | |
Representational Response Style	None N=17	1—24 N=19	25+ N=10	None N=4	1—24 N+20	25+ N=12
To self-defined image	82%	58%	40%	25%	25%	8%
To issue groups and publics	18	42	60	75	75	92
Total	100%	100%	100%	100%	100%	100%

Gamma = +.55   Gamma = +.42

munities forced turnover accentuates the tendency for councils to act in response to community groups. Eleven of twelve councils with high forced turnover rates indicated responsiveness to issue groups or attentive publics, fifteen per cent more than reported in the original Table 7.2. The fact that our measure of forced turnover is truly independent of our representational style and support measures makes this result all the more significant.

SUMMARY AND CONCLUSIONS

The analysis suggests that the four components of the political matrix—the complexity of the social environment, the impact of elections in forcing incumbents from office, the degree of public support perceived by the council, and the amount of sponsorship in political recruitment—may explain a great deal about whether a responsive relationship between governors and governed will emerge. Since the analysis has been configurative, on the assumption that representational "responding to" emerges, if it does, in the context of the "overall structure and functioning of the system," we do not assess the relative impact of any given variable. Rather we stress two things: first, there seems to be a theoretically meaningful cluster of political phenomena that is strongly related to the response style adopted by the governing body; and second, under certain, very identifiable political conditions the governing body may remain indifferent to any views of the public good except its own and yet not suffer at the hands of an antagonistic electorate. What then do we make of these findings for a theory of representation?

In order to pursue a theory of representation we have chosen a particular concept of representation. The concept with which we work stresses that political representation is a relationship between two collectivities—i.e., representation occurs when the few who are chosen to govern respond to some organized demands or preferences of the many who permit themselves to be governed. The theory to which this concept directs us is one which emphasizes that a politically responsive relationship may or may not emerge, and that the type of community in which it does emerge is characterized by an identifiable matrix of properties.

The analysis led to some unexpected findings; we summarize them here, but remind the reader that they are tentative. What we have attempted is to break new ground in theorizing about representation in modern society; the specific findings to which our theorizing activity gives rise will undoubtedly be modified as additional empirical work along these lines takes place. The findings, then, are presented as suggestive of what we may expect from a rethinking of "representation" rather than as confirmed facts about the political world.

(1) By the definition we introduced, an elected assembly is representative when it acts in response to publicly expressed and more or less organized viewpoints from the citizenry. We found that the governing councils most often act in response to interest groups or attentive publics in the larger, more diverse communities. In the smaller, homogeneous cities, councils tend to rely on their own image of what the community requires. Thus, as an initial observation, we suggest that as a system property representation is more likely to emerge under just those conditions often presumed to impede responsiveness at the individual level.

(2) A theory of representation as an emergent property may have to be adjusted in the light of certain facts about elections too long ignored. We are not sure, as one author (Pennock, 1968: 8) has recently stated it, that "elections are thought of as providing the great sanction for assuring representative behavior." The patterns uncovered in our analysis suggest a considerably more complex relationship between elections and representative government. Where an aroused electorate does, from time to time, unseat incumbents, the governing groups do tend to be attentive. However, it does not follow that elected assemblies concerned only with their own definition of the political

situation will be turned out of office, for such self-images may indeed coincide with public preferences.

(3) A council tends not to be responsive, as we use the term, where the public is viewed as being most supportive. This finding suggests a major qualification to the assumption that "elections force representativeness." Representative government can function quite independently of elections, though only under certain conditions. A politically satisfied community is apparently unconcerned about whether the council acts in response. If the job is being done, the citizens would just as soon not be bothered. It appears then not to be the inattentive council which is thrown out of office but only the council whose performance is suspect.

(4) A fourth finding is one which validates the observations just made; communities in which the council sees itself as generally supported tend to leave to the council itself the selection of its successors. The pattern of sponsored recruitment, in which candidates are insulated from the competitive struggle for a council seat, tends to be associated with a representational style also suggesting a certain insulation from public pressures.

Students of democratic politics are deeply interested in the processes available to the public for controlling and holding accountable the political leadership. The analysis presented here is closely related to an understanding of these processes. It appears that members of the public dissatisfied with their representative assembly can intrude into its deliberations and force attentiveness in two ways at least, (1) by playing a role in determining who is selected to the representative body, and (2) by defeating incumbents when they stand for reelection. Put differently, when members of the public control the constituting of the representative assembly, they also influence how that assembly will define its representational role. When, however, citizens do not exercise that control, allowing the assembly more or less to determine its own members and seldom unseating an incumbent, they thereby permit the representative group the privilege of defining for itself the goals and programs of the community.

NOTES

1. We may note, in making this statement, that of 474 state legislators interviewed in the late fifties, 38 per cent *failed* to articulate any kind of representational role in response to an open question about how they would describe the job of being a legislator. See Wahlke et al., 1962: 281. Ten years later, of 435 city councilmen interviewed in connection with this study, as many as 59 per cent failed to make any spontaneous mention of their putative representational role in response to the same question. As far as we know, no student of representatioal behavior has as yet examined the implications of the evidently *low salience* of thinking about representation among political practitioners.

2. Pitkin's treatment of responsiveness appears to stress the condition in which the representative assembly stands ready to be responsive when the constituents do have something to say. An assembly may, threfore, be responsive whether or not there are specific

instances of response. Our analysis, as will be clearer shortly, stresses the actual act of response rather than simply the potential for it. The difficulties of empirically working with a concept stressing the possibility of an act rather than the act itself dictated our decision to modify Pitkin's theoretically suggestive definition.

3. The coding procedure used was as follows: Both investigators, reading jointly, read through all parts of the interview schedules pertinent to how councilmen defined their relations with the public for all members of any given council. If the councilmen seldom mentioned any groups or groupings in the public or if they failed to describe an actual case where they had been responsive to public pressures or if they simply asserted (a not unusual occurrence) that they knew what was best for the community and acted upon it, the council was placed in the "self-defined image" code. If the councilmen made references to neighborhood groups or to transitory groups wanting, say, a stoplight at a given corner, or to election groups and if the councilmen indicated that they responded to pressures from such groups and attempted to placate them, then the council was coded in the "responsive to issue-groups" category. If the councilmen defined for us a fairly well organized public, attentive to what the council was doing, and if the councilmen indicated (usually by citing an illustrative case) that they were responsive to these attentive publics, the council was placed in the "responsive to attentive publics" code. The procedure, then, used the councilmen as individual informants about the responsive style of the council. It is quite possible, though not a frequent occurrence, for a given individual councilman to not feel responsive to, say, attentive publics but to describe the council as acting in that way.

4. That size is an adequate indicator of "social pluralism" may not be self-evident. We refer the reader to Hadden and Borgatta, 1965, for evidence of the correlative power of size as an indicator of a city's demographic and ecological diversity and pluralism.

5. In Table 7.1 and all following tables our interpretation of the data is largely based on comparison of the distributions in "high" and "low" categories of the "independent" (column) variable. However, we are attaching to each table two statistics: the raw   score adjusted for degree of freedom which can tell us something about the relative order of the data; that is, by dividing chi square by the table's degree of freedom, it is possible to compare tables of different numbers of cells as long as the "N" remains the same or nearly so. Because we are not essentially dealing with a sample but with a universe (82 out of 90 cases in the defined universe), we are not concerned with the sampling problem of whether the distribution in any table is due to chance or not at some set level of confidence. Gamma is introduced as a measure of relationship because it seems especially suitable to data ordered by ordinal or weak ordinal scales.

6. At another point (p. 72) Dahl argues, "The effective political elites, then, operate within limits often vague and broad, although occasionally narrow and well defined, set by their expectations as to the reactions of the group of politically active citizens who go to the polls."

7. Schlesinger's study is a very careful and ingenious examination of how the political opportunity structure in the U.S. might facilitate or impede political ambitions and thus affect the workings of democracy. He does not, however, consider the consequences for democratic politics if men in public office are not ambitious.

8. Hyneman also remarks that his finding "completely knocks out the supposition that the transiency of legislative personnel is due to the fickleness of the voter at the polls . . . Only 16.1 per cent of the 1,965 House members and 14.7 per cent of the 511 senators

who quit service during this period were eliminated by defeat in the general election" (pp. 25-27).

9. Possibly one of the reasons Hyneman's findings have had such little impact on theories about elections is that he was concerned with the implications of turnover for questions of legislative experience. Students who followed Hyneman's lead also addressed themselves to this question. As far as we have discovered, no political scientist has yet considered how the high rates of voluntary retirement might affect the attention of law-makers to voter preferences.

10. The mean per cent of voluntary retirements is .53; the standard deviation is .18. The rate of voluntary retirement is not related to any major demographic characteristic of the city, not to size, population density, per cent of the working force in manufacturing occupations, nor to median income. The stability of this rate across all types of cities suggests that it is a very permanent, even institutionalized, feature of nonpartisan city politics in the Bay Area. By the way, only 3 of the 82 cities studied have limitations on tenure. The survey data which help us understand the reasons for the high rates of voluntary retirement are presented and analyzed in Prewitt (1970).

11. Appointed incumbents were excluded because of the high rate of appointment to the councils—24 per cent for all cities averaged over the ten year period. Appointment can be a strategy designed, in this context, to assure election. Omitting these appointed incumbents therefore strengthens the index of forced turnover. The aggregate election data which were used in constructing these analyses were initially collected by Gordon Black in collaboration with William Hawley, Institute of Governmental Studies, Berkeley. We are indebted to both Black and Hawley for their help.

12. Four of the five items used in the support index were coded by using the informant procedure described in footnote 3. Councils were classified according to whether they reported (1) the public to have a respectful view toward councilmen, (2) the public to be in agreement with the council's definition of its duties, (3) the public to include disruptive and unfriendly elements, and (4) the public to be generally supportive in its behavior toward the council. The fifth item, whether there are critical groups in the community, was initially an aggregate measure of individual responses to a question about the number of critical groups. Councils were ranked in terms of this aggregate measure and those above the median were said to have supportive publics, those below, to be operating in a nonsupportive environment. Each council was given a score of 1 for each plus on the five items. The support scores were then dichotomized to provide the "relatively high" and "relatively low" classifications used in the analysis.

13. The literature, of course, is quite large. Representative studies are reviewed in Prewitt, 1965.

14. See, for instance, Marvick, 1961; Matthews, 1954; and the chapter by Dye in Jacob and Vines, eds., 1965. This issue is explored with the city council data in chapter 2 of Prewitt, 1970.

15. The measure of sponsorship is particularly problematic since we are summing not just individual experiences to get a group score but individual experiences which took place over a considerable span of time in some cases. It may be that the aggregation of individual career experiences into a council recruitment measure disguises more variance in the original data than the index should be burdened with. Councilmen enter the council at very different points in time and recruitment, as a system property, may have undergone major changes since the

entry experiences of the older members. For the present, however, we are trapped by our own data; when we began the study we still were thinking of recruitment as an individual attribute and thus mainly collected data about individual careers. Despite the relatively weaker nature of our sponsorship measure, we are reluctant to give up our theoretical posture. We simply note, then, that the weaker relationships in tables using the sponsorship measure may be traced to these methodological difficulties. A council was given a sponsorship measure by computing the mean of six alternate paths to office. The "sponsorship continuum" ranged from the case in which an outside challenger initiates his own career and attains a council seat with minimum contact between himself and those already in established positions, to the case in which a councilman was deliberately selected—either asked to run or appointed to the council—by those already in office. The means were then ranked and, for present purposes, the lowest quartile in the rank constitutes the low sponsorship councils; the highest quartile constitutes the high sponsorship councils; the remainder we assigned to the middle group.

Chapter 8

POLICY DETERMINANTS AND LEGISLATIVE DECISIONS

JOHN C. WAHLKE

THE LEGISLATURE AND
THE POLITICAL SYSTEM

The prevailing conception of the modern representative body and its place in the governmental system envisions the legislature as essentially a "demand-input processor." Legislators are seen as so many targets (and receivers) of communications from constituents, lobbyists, governors, administrators, and many other demand-inputters or demand "within-putters." What these communications put into the legislative conversion mill, in this view, is, above all, indices of demanders' desire or aversion (demands for or against specific policy decisions). Thus, it must be assumed tacitly, the cardinal function of the legislature as a body is to "make policy decisions." Therefore, it seems to follow implicitly that legislative activity consists primarily of choice-making behavior by its members.

On such assumptions, the bulk of legislative research, particularly in America, has been concerned with discovering, for one or another specific time and place, how the specific legislature in view presumably made particular choices among the particular alternatives presumably confronting it. Generally, the key "dependent variable" of legislative research has been the particular legislative "policy decision" or class of decisions. A common form of research questions is which demand-input factor or agency (political party, gubernatorial influence, constituency pressure, etc.) seems most influential in producing the decision (or pattern of decisions reached in particular legislative bodies).

Viewed from a perspective wider than that of the legislative process itself, legislative policy decisions are generally thought of as "policy output." In this context, it is usually taken for granted that the "decision" as "output" relates simply and directly, through "feedback" mechanisms to "support" for government in general and incumbent officials in particular. The view seems to be that the citizenry, whose input of demands for the enactment of public policy generated the power to put (or keep) the legislative mill in operation to begin with, evaluates the policy output for the closeness of its fit with current policy demands.[1]

One reason for questioning the utility of such a "demand-input processor" model of the legislature, as has been suggested elsewhere, is that citizens nowhere seem to constitute the kind of demand-expressing, policy-choosing, decision-evaluating behavior which the model requires of them logically.[2] The average citizen, both as spectator and as voter, seems neither to know enough about issues or candidates in particular nor to care enough about political campaigning, elections, and governmental activity in general to mount the kind of policy demands which seem to be expected of him.

A series of recent studies, empirical rather than theoretical in orientation, calls into question the adequacy of demand-input processor conceptions from a different direction. These studies utilize readily available masses of quantitative data about American states to analyze relationships among policy outputs and many possible correlates. Variations in policy output usually have been measured by the amount of money spent by a system on different categories of substantive policy or program, such as public highways, health programs, welfare, etc. Political variables investigated as possible correlates of policy output usually have been "structural" in nature—for example, degree of two-party competition, degree of voter participation, extent of legislative malapportionment, and so on. Socio-economic environmental (or "background") variables have included such things as degree of urbanization and industrialization, or education level.

The general conclusion of these studies is that, with only rare and minor exceptions, variations in public policy are not related to variations in political-structure variables, except insofar as socio-economic or environmental variables affect them and public policy variations together. Variations in policy output can be "explained" (in the statistical sense) almost entirely by environmental variables, without reference to the variable supposedly reflecting different systems and practices of representation. (See Dawson and Robinson, 1963; Hofferbert, 1966; Dye, 1966; Cutright, 1965.) One major implication of these and similar studies would seem to be that "policy output" is not determined by "legislative decisions" at all. Whatever legislative bodies are doing when they debate and vote on proposals to spend more or less money on this or that program, it is no longer easy to think of them as "deciding" or "choosing" to do so. If their collective action is predictable ultimately from key features of the socio-economic environment within which the legislature operates—whether or not it is somewhat predictable proximately from elements of the political structure underlying the legislative and other institutions in its particular political system—their individual behavior hardly can be the product of free, voluntary choice among competing demands. Or, at the very least, the linkage between policy demands and policy output is much more complex and circuitous than we have taken it to be hitherto.

In point of fact, the import of such studies may be even more radical and far-reaching. What they really call into question is the adequacy of our basic theoretical conceptions—of demand-processing and conversion as the chief function of representative bodies and of "policy decisions" as the basic units of analysis of the legislative process.

This chapter, therefore, takes a different approach toward the activity of legislative bodies and the behavior of members composing them. It does not seek to explain why the body examined (the Iowa House of Representatives) reached the decisions it reached at a particular time (the 60th session of the Iowa General Assembly, 1963). Rather, it seeks clues about the place of policy-making in the overall legislative process and the place of the legislature in the political system. Its approach is perforce sketchy and tentative. Its data pertain to the proceedings of only one chamber in only one session. The choice of object and time were dictated almost entirely by the ready availability of copious data.[3] But since the purpose is above all exploratory and speculative, the limitations should do no serious harm.

In some respects, the Iowa legislature of 1963 is more suitable for our purposes than some other American state legislatures. It might be called "underdeveloped" or "unprofessionalized." It met then biennially, for a relatively short session (January 14 to May 18 of the year in question).[4] It provides minimal services or facilities for individual members. Its leadership structure and system for division of labor (committees, etc.) is relatively simple, a considerable amount of business actually being transacted on the floor in plenary sessions. Its procedures are simple, with relatively few and relatively formal requirements; rather than being complex, with informal and unwritten understandings whose intricacies might be known only to insider old hands. In short, its structure and processes are such that one reasonably can hope to get useful information from the formal record of floor proceedings.

Moreover, the political substructure to which the Iowa legislature presumably responds in some fashion is relatively simple and loosely structured. The state is more homogeneous economically and socially than most American states. The political organization and voting habits of Iowans seemed in 1963 to be largely Republican, with a party balance in the House of Representatives of 79 Republicans to only 29 Democrats, although the elections of 1964 produced startling alterations in this picture. In any case, no lines were drawn very clearly within the legislature, structuring the day-to-day business of the chambers in clearly discernible ways. Some issues might see Democrats pitted against Republicans, but on many others party allegiance was wholly irrelevant.

WHAT DOES THE LEGISLATURE DO?

We begin, then, by asking in very general terms, what a legislature like this in a political community like Iowa is doing when it assembles every two years for four or five months of business. How large does the function of "making policy decisions" bulk in the overall pattern of its activities? What else might it be doing besides settling policy questions? How important to the functioning of the legislature and of the government system are the different classes of legislative activities and in what ways?

We may assume safely that the indispensable grist for the legislative mill, if the legislature is to be accepted by other governmental institutions and officers and by the citizens as a legitimate enterprise, worthy of support, is that which is contained in the formal agenda of bills and resolutions. A random sample of 1,001 Iowans was asked in 1966, "How would you describe the job of the state legislature, that is, what are the things it should do when it meets in Des Moines?". Those who responded overwhelmingly mentioned legislative output resulting from that agenda—usually by reference to specific policy decisions thought to be called for, not merely by such general responses as "to make laws." Similarly, when asked, "Thinking of the state legislature in general—not any one session of it—what are the things about the Iowa legislature that you are most proud of?" and "What are some of the things you do not like about the state legislature . . . ?," those who responded overwhelmingly mentioned legislative output resulting from that agenda, rather than legislator's qualities and characteristics, practices and procedures for doing business, or other terms. (See Table 8.1.)

The raw material for legislative processing provided by the formal agenda of proposed legislation for the 1963 Iowa House is substantial, even though far less formidable than the comparable tally in, say California or New York. Table 8.2 gives a very rough picture of the size of that agenda, as well as of the actions of the House in very general terms. Before examining the legislative processing summarized there, however, let us note some important legislative activity which does not usually show up on such tallies.

As for any other institutionalized group, some level and form of interpersonal comity is prerequisite to the performance of the functions of a state legislature. Research on several American state legislatures has shown the existence and importance of various informal "rules of the game" for managing interpersonal relations and promoting group solidarity.[5] A considerable part of the activity

Table 8.1: The Importance of Legislative Output In Iowans' Conceptions of the Legislature

	Question Concerning		
	Job of Legislature	Things Liked About Legislature	Things Disliked About Legislature
Percentage of *respondents* giving some answer	69.2%	47.1%	56.9%
Percentage of *responses* citing legislative output in some form	58.2%	48.4%	59.3%

Table 8.2: Summary of Measures Introduced and Actions Taken, Iowa House of Representatives, 60th General Assembly, 1963

	House Bills	Senate Bills[1]	House Joint Reso-lutions	Senate Joint Reso-lutions	House Conc. Reso-lutions	Senate Conc. Reso-lutions	Total
Submitted	596	267	19	6	23	33	944
Acted upon on floor	276	210	3	5	23	33	550
Passed	163[2]	204[3]	2	5	18	33	425

1. Figures are for Senate Bills messaged to House.
2. Two measures (H.F. 48, H.F. 156) passed both houses, were vetoed by Governor.
3. One measure (S.F. 1) passed both houses, was vetoed. One (S.F. 434) was vetoed but passed over the Governor's veto.

occurring within the legislative halls likewise clearly constitutes not decision-making or policy debating but institutional-maintenance rituals. The ubiquitous daily prayer or invocation serves such functions among others. Resolutions in memory of relatives of the lawmakers (not just particularly close relatives) obviously tend to reassure the legislator with the thought that his fellow lawmakers feel sympathy for him. Presentations of birthday greetings and birthday cakes are more common, as well as more festive and jocular rituals but they serve the same function.

The importance of non-legislative or extra-legislative services to constituents and other citizens is another generally well recognized feature of legislative life. The "errand boy function" is not only familiar to legislators, but often lamented and resented by them, even though they recognize the value of such services in building diffuse support for their office and their own incumbency. But legislators collectively may serve citizens merely by being on the job, going about their business, even if constituents and citizens don't know (or care) what they are doing in any practical sense, let alone in terms of specific policy-making activities. Murray Edelman (1964) has pointed to the importance of symbolic as distinguished from instrumental output of governmental activities, and Thomas Anton (1967: 39) has said of legislative budgetary activies,

> it is not the document which creates satisfaction, but the process of putting it together. . . . [The] budget, as a document and process, creates symbolic satisfaction built upon the idea that affairs of state are being dealt with, that responsibility is being exercised, and that rationality prevails.

Dye (1966: 300) reached the same conclusion in more general form from his study of the voluminous array of policy-output contents previously mentioned:

The *way* in which a society authoritatively allocates values may be an even more important question than the outcomes of these value allocations. Our commitments to democratic processes are essentially commitments to a mode of decision-making. The legitimacy of the democractic form of government has never really depended upon the policy outcomes which it is expected to produce.

The same sample of the Iowa general public which responded to the question about its conception of the job of the legislature mainly in terms of legislative policy output at the same time couched 36.4 percent of its responses in the most vague and general terms of general representative posture or activity. The responses suggest that many citizens habitually lend diffuse support to the legislative institution so long as its activities satisfy expectations (however vaguely defined) which concern the form of legislative existence and activity, rather than the substance of decisions it produces.

A considerable amount of legislative energy appears to be spent in activities serving mainly to generate goodwill and diffuse support in largely symbolic fashion. Proposals granting or seeking symbolic recognition of community values, such as the resolution (not adopted!) memorializing Congress to designate the corn tassel the national floral emblem, are one variety. Spreading on the record and actual elocutionary readings on the floor of moralistic, hortatory, or other value-diffusing poetry and literature is another. But the most common activity serving to generate diffuse support among constituents and the wider state public is the public introduction of distinguished, and often not so distinguished, visitors in the gallery to the House.

Given the ubiquity of these forms of behavior and the proportion of precious legislative time devoted to them, legislative research might well pay more attention to them and to their net effects on public conceptions of the legislature. In at least some instances, behavior of the kinds described probably could be used as indices of the form and amount of legislative evaluation of the current state of diffuse support and of the current need for support-building activity, as well as of the relative importance in legislative eyes of symbolic and ritualistic mechanisms for building diffuse support compared with more pragmatic and instrumental means of generating specific support. Cross-national comparisons, particularly among representative bodies in widely divergent systems of government, might yield particularly fruitful information about fundamental political processes and functions. Here, however, we can do no more than suggest such possible avenues for future research. In the remainder of this paper we shall focus our attention on the activities in plenary session which seem, at least at first glance, to be neither ritualistic, institutional maintenance activities nor symbolic, generalized-support building activities, but decision-making activities relating directly to the policy-output from the legislative process.

POLICY OUTPUT

The following analysis utilizes all the roll calls taken in the 1963 session of the Iowa House of Representatives and the documentation pertaining to each as found in the *House Journal*. Omitted from consideration are the 394 measures submitted to the House but not finally disposed of on the floor (see Table 8.2), and a few voice-vote decisions on resolutions of various sorts. (Senate- and House-File measures are disposed of on the floor only by roll-call votes.) This omission leaves out, chiefly, an unknown amount of committee activity, lobby and smoking-room activity, as well as some (not much) largely desultory floor activity which led to no final action. No doubt, some measures this omits might be fully as "important" as the measures analyzed merely because they were disposed of by recorded vote in plenary session. Extensive perusal of the *Journal* (not systematically tabulated or content analyzed) suggests, however, that the measures left in limbo by this method of data selection were consigned there primarily by the accidents of legislative scheduling and the arbitrary pressures of time. Although the present analysis cannot demonstrate this, the picture formed from the data which have been used probably would not be changed substantially had the analysis been designed to include all measures submitted, whether or not they had left any legislative trace after introduction and referral.

In any event, the criterion used yielded 466 measures for analysis, on which a total of 641 roll calls were taken. The simplicity of the Iowa legislative process is further evidenced by the scarcity of procedural motions. Of the 641 roll-calls, 613 were substantive motions to pass or amend the measure before the house, and only 28 were procedural (table, rerefer to committee, reconsider, etc.).

When these actions are classified by subject matter, it becomes evident that a good deal of the legislature's decisional activity is not exactly related to "policy decision" in the usual sense of the term. For example, forty-eight of the measures (and forty-nine of the roll calls) constituted *pro forma* validation or legalization of actions already taken by other governmental bodies but requiring legitimizing approval from the legislature. Seven of these concerned actions of state government agencies (e.g. confirming real estate patents issued by various state agencies, transferring state hospital lands, etc.); eleven concerned claims to various persons; and the rest concerned actions by specific cities, towns, counties, or special districts. Legislative action in all these instances was unanimous, save on two measures.

The remaining 418 measures (and 592 roll calls) are, for the most part, more substantive in nature, more likely to reveal the pattern of legislative decision-making using the term "decision" in its more descriptive sense. Ideally, we should begin by mapping the distribution of legislative attention to different substantive areas, *i.e.*, the distribution of legislative attention over various policy issues, comparing the results of such an examination with similar mappings for other legislative bodies. Unfortunately, despite the longstanding concern of legislative researchers for questions about policy output, not only is there no reliable gauge of the degree of legislative concern for various problems; there is not even an accepted scheme for classifying legislative subject matter.

We can depict approximately the pattern of legislative concern for different classes of legislative subject matter by means of several simple measures for each class—the average number of roll calls per measure, the proportion of measures settled by only one roll call, the average number of absences per roll call, and the average percentage of voting representatives in the minority (hereafter called "percent dissenting"). The logic behind each of these measures requires very little explanation. The simpler a decision (other things, as usual, remaining equal), the fewer are the amendments calling for discussion and vote that are likely to be proposed. Similarly, the simpler and less controversial a given measure appears to members, the less the likelihood of delaying motions, procedural maneuvering, and other roll-call-eliciting tactics. Again, the more a measure appears important or interesting to members, the less they seem likely to absent themselves from discussion and voting on it. Finally, in politics as in business, sports, and many other human affairs, conflict seems to be inherently more interesting or attention getting than concord. Moreover, contests over legislative decisions are not uncommonly considered to be the very heart and soul of the legislature's business. So we have prima facie grounds for thinking that all three indices will tell us something about issue salience. That all three measures tend to measure the same dimensions is indicated clearly by their inter-correlation, shown in Table 8.3. Table 8.4 presents these measures, as well as some additional related information for all the roll calls, on all the categories and subcategories of policy issue in the 1963 session of the Iowa House. As one might surmise, the classification contains

Table 8.3: Inter-correlations of Four Measures of Salience of Legislative Issues*

	Percentage of Measures with Only One Roll Call	Mean No. of Roll Calls per Measure	Mean No. of Absences per Roll Call
Mean Percentage Dissenting	−0.780	0.907	−0.856
Percentage of Measures with Only one Roll Call	X	−0.669	0.436
Mean Number of Roll Calls per Measure		X	−0.747
Mean Number of Absences per Roll Call			X

*Pearson's "r"

Table 8.4: Amount of Legislative Activity and Degree of Salience for Different Classes of Legislative Issue in the 1963 session of the Iowa House of Representatives

	No. of Measures	No. of Roll Calls	% of Measures 1 Roll Call	Mean No. of Roll Calls/ Measures	Max. No. of Roll Calls/ Measures	Mean % Dissenting Roll Calls	Max. % Dissent-ing	Mean No. of Absences
Substantive Motions	445	613	--	--	--	11.2%	50%	12.0
Procedural Motions	21	28	--	--	--	33.6%	50%	9.4
Appropriation Measures	40	46	85.0%	1.15	2	4.8%	40%	16.6
All Other Measures	426	595	71.7%	1.39	31	12.8%	50%	11.6
GRAND TOTAL	466	641	81.8%	1.37	31	12.2%	50%	11.9
LEGALIZATION/VALIDATION								
State Gov. Agencies	7	7	100.0%	1.00	1	0	0	17.9
Local Govt./Special Dist:								
Counties	7	7	100.0%	1.00	1	0	0	14.3
Cities/towns	7	8	85.6%	1.14	2	3.0%	20%	14.3
Spec. Distrs.	16	16	100.0%	1.00	1	0	0	12.8
(Sub-total)	(30)	(31)	(96.7%)	(1.03)	(2)	(0.8%)	(20%)	(13.4)
Claims	11	11	100.0%	1.00	1	0	0	13.0
TOTAL	48	49	97.9%	1.02	2	0.5%	20%	13.9

Table 8.4 (Continued)

	No. of Measures	No. of Roll Calls	% of Measures 1 Roll Call	Mean No. of Roll Calls/ Measures	Max. No. Roll Calls/ Measures	Mean % Dissenting Roll Calls	Max. % Dissent-ing	Mean No. of Absences
AGRICULTURE AND LAND								
General Regulation/Prom.	12	32	50.0%	2.67	13	21.7%	50%	10.5
Conservation	8	9	87.5%	1.13	2	13.2%	45%	12.0
Recreation	9	13	66.7%	1.44	3	10.0%	37%	15.6
TOTAL	29	54	65.5%	1.86	13	17.4%	50%	12.0
LABOR	11	17	72.7%	1.55	3	18.4%	48%	10.8
TAXATION	40	83	75.0%	2.08	31	18.5%	50%	11.1
BUSINESS, INDUSTRY, PROFESSIONAL								
General Regulation/Prom.	6	7	83.3%	1.17	2	19.7%	36%	7.1
Public Util./National Resource	4	8	75.0%	2.00	5	19.3%	41%	8.9
Licensing Trades/Prof'ns.	38	51	78.9%	1.34	4	9.3%	48%	14.2
Highway Transportation	38	48	75.7%	1.26	3	5.6%	42%	10.8
Railroads, Air Transp.	3	3	100.0%	1.00	1	10.7%	28%	11.3
Business/Commercial Law	7	8	85.7%	1.14	2	10.0%	43%	10.1
Banking and Insurance	7	8	87.5%	1.14	2	0.1%	1%	8.8
TOTAL	103	133	81.6%	1.29	5	8.7%	48%	12.4

Table 8.4 (Continued)

	No. of Measures	No. of Roll Calls	% of Measures 1 Roll Call	Mean No. of Roll Calls/ Measures	Max. No. Roll Calls/ Measures	Mean % Dissenting Roll Calls	Max. % Dissent- ing	Mean No. of Absences
PUBLIC ORDER, WELFARE								
Crime, Crim. Law, Enforcement	9	13	66.7%	1.44	3	21.3%	47%	10.3
Education	15	15	100.0%	1.00	1	3.9%	48%	18.3
Health and Sanitation	1	1	100.0%	1.00	1	0	0	10.0
Housing	3	4	66.7%	1.33	2	2.0%	6%	10.8
Liquor	9	26	77.8%	2.89	11	27.3%	48%	4.2
Welfare (public assist.)	20	26	70.0%	1.30	2	5.5%	40%	11.9
Miscellaneous	8	10	75.0%	1.25	2	6.4%	33%	9.8
TOTAL	65	95	81.5%	1.46	11	13.8%	48%	10.7
GOVERNMENTAL STRUCTURES, PROCESS								
General Measures	10	11	90.0%	1.10	2	7.7%	28%	11.6
State Legislature	12	14	91.7%	1.17	3	15.2%	40%	9.6
State Judic./Legal System	16	21	87.5%	1.31	5	9.0%	48%	13.7
State Admin., Agencies	41	53	78.0%	1.29	3	9.2%	48%	12.6
State Institutions	18	20	88.9%	1.11	2	4.5%	29%	14.5
Local Governments:								
General	11	15	63.6%	1.36	2	7.6%	46%	12.6
County	8	11	77.8%	1.33	3	2.6%	14%	14.3
Cities/towns	28	33	85.7%	1.18	3	5.0%	41%	15.6
School Distrs./Boards	12	14	91.7%	1.17	3	15.5%	46%	14.6
Other Spec. Distrs.	9	13	55.6%	1.44	2	0.5%	3%	11.1
(Subtotal)	(68)	(86)	(78.3%)	(1.26)	(3)	(6.1%)	(46%)	(14.1)
TOTAL	170	210	82.5%	1.23	5	7.9%	48%	13.2

some ambiguities. But inspection of the detailed, measure-by-measure arrays of roll calls in each category supports strongly the "eyeball" conclusion that the ambiguities are so few that their possible influence on the overall picture is minor.

The table reveals that, in the course of a session, different legislative issues appear to receive different degrees of contention. It also suggests a few general features of legislative concern during this session. The areas of primary concern appear to be problems of liquor sale and control (mean dissent 27 percent) and crime (21.3 percent), regulation and promotion of agriculture (21.7 percent), regulation and promotion of business and industry (19.7 percent), public utilities and natural resources (19.3 percent), taxation (18.5 percent), and labor (18.4 percent). Attention and contention in some areas appears to be highly specific to the particular measure rather than general for a broad issue. Thus, although licensing of trades and professions averages only 9.3 percent dissent, the practice of barbering, architecture, and pharmacy each generated considerably more legislative activity than that average. Moralistic issues (liquor, crime, capital punishment) tend to receive legislators' concern more than any other types of issue. At any rate, such matters are the only class of issues which yield almost no unanimous or very low-dissent divisions, which are not settled on one roll call, and which lure more than usual numbers of members to the floor to vote (note that the average absence rate on liquor roll calls was only 4.21). But whether a given issue is "moralistic" or not depends on the prevailing cultural norms. The record shows that some legislators think of certain types of welfare programs in highly moralistic terms (*viz.* the frequent allusions to the low moral character of persons who habitually "feed at the public trough"). Considerably more information about public and legislative guiding conceptions in such matters is needed before even the simplest generalization along these lines can be formulated.

In truth, the most surprising features of the picture are the dispersion of legislative attention, the absence of concentration on measures grouped into broad policy classes, and the very great range of interest and contention within each policy domain. The latter feature can be shown better by regrouping the data in the summary fashion shown in Table 8.5. What such a table does not show, and what cannot be shown without impossibly cumbersome listing of many measures, is that in almost every policy domain, however contentious some measures may be, numerous noncontentious measures quietly receive unanimous and near-unanimous approval. The formal record alone does not show how, if at all, they differ in content from the more contentious measures on the same subject.

Table 8.4 contains one other bit of information which bears on the questions about legislative policy decisions raised by the studies of Dye and others described previously, namely, the surprisingly low level of salience and contest over the monetary aspects of legislative programs. Not only is the mean level of dissent on appropriation measures only 4.8 percent as against an average of 12.8 percent for all others, but on every measure shown appropriation measures rank strikingly lower than others. Nor does the contention that occurs center on the "major"

Table 8.5: Number of Roll Calls and Levels of Dissent in Different Classes of Policy Issues

	Level of Dissent						
	Unan.	1 Mbr.	2 Mbr.	3-10%	11-24%	25-50%	Mean %
Legalization/ Validation	46	0	2	0	1	0	0.5%
Agriculture and Land	15	4	2	8	4	21	17.4%
Business, Indus., Professional	71	8	2	18	11	23	8.7%
Labor	9	0	0	1	0	7	18.4%
Taxation	29	3	2	5	11	33	11.1%
Public Order, Welfare	35	—	4	14	12	24	13.8%
Govt. Struct./Proc.	114	11	12	26	12	35	7.9%
TOTAL	319	32	24	72	51	143	12.2%

bills. The measure ranking highest (40 percent) concerned an amendment to the bill funding various programs of the Department of Social Welfare (SF 453). The bill itself passed unanimously after the amendment failed. The next highest dissent figure was 35 percent on a proposed amendment to a bill (SF 476) appropriating money to the Superintendent of Buildings and Grounds for capital improvements. Dissent level on all other appropriations measures was less than 30 percent (and on only four does it exceed 6 percent).

Our data do not permit further exploration of this pattern. Conceivably legislative decision-making did, in fact, take place at stages in the legislative process preceding floor action, especially, in committee. But, in that event, why did many other measures produce active debate and controversy both in committee and on the floor, whereas similarly interesting and contentious decisions about appropriations for policy programs were "decided" finally before reaching the floor. More likely, very little legislative "deciding" occurs on these matters. Such an interpretation supports the description of legislative functioning in budgetary matters offered by Thomas Anton (1967) as well as the paradigm of legislative legitimization on budgetary levels implied by the concept of "incremental budgeting."[6] Also, it is consistent with the dependence, especially when measured in monetary terms (as is the case for most policy variables examined by Dye, Hofferbert, and others), of policy variations on factors outside the legislature, with internal legislative cleavages on policy decision able to play at best an intermediate role in the "decisional process" viewed in its largest sense. That is, *if* the content of public policy in many areas really is responsive to socio-economic and other environmental variables, its relation to activities occuring wholly within the legislative body should be unclear, to say the least. If we are to exploit and interpret politically the suggestive findings of the environmental-determinist studies, we need some notion about just how legislative behavior is affected by such factors, in more sophisticated and realistic terms than are provided by simple policy-demand input notions of legislative functioning. A tentative working hypothesis might well be that the environment enters the legislative world not so much through legislators' specific responses to constituency (or pressure group or other citizen) policy demands as through their general cultural orientations—their picture of the state as a political and economic community, their expectations and aspirations for it. Quite possibly, even while paying lip service to the familiar dogma that representatives should be delegates of their constituents, they adjust to the constituents' failure to give them cues by using the best guidelines available to them, a vague but pervasive conception that they are custodians of the interest of the public. Such an assumption is certainly consistent with the available information about how legislators actually see their jobs.[7]

In any case, one is drawn to the conclusion that the subject matter of legislative decisions probably is a very inadequate guide to the legislature's functioning. Our past assumptions that legislative activity comprises primarily decisions to have or not to have such and such a policy on such and such a subject seem highly dubious. Legislative attention and legislative energy seems much to sporadically and unpredictably associated with any given policy issue, if we accept the evidence of the single instance examined here, for us to take conscious "policy making" or specific "value allocation" as the obvious and directly-served principal legislative function.

Plainly major work must be done to conceptualize "policy output." The foregoing discussion points toward examining that output not in terms of its supposed intrinsic, objective "content" but in terms of how it is perceived by specific publics at specific times. A given policy proposal may well appear to be one thing to one set of circumstances, and something altogether different to other people in other times and places.

A number of suggestions have been made for classifying policy output, very few of them tested in exhaustive research application, which seem to lead in this direction. Lowi (1964), for example, has suggested the importance of distinguishing "distributive," "regulatory," and "redistributive" policies, suggesting that the arena of power (locus of decision-making) varies by type of policy. Froman (1968) has distinguished "area policies" (which affect the total population of the system simultaneously in a "single-shot" action) from "segmental policies." These classification schemes shift attention from the supposedly inherent "content" of policies to their impact, i.e., their effects on (including, by logical implication, their interpretation by) the general public. Other suggested distinctions shift attention in this direction even more radically. Edelman's (1964: 84) distinction between citizens' "material satisfaction" and "symbolic satisfaction" from policy, already noted, clearly requires any operational measurement or classification of policies to refer empirically to citizens' cognitive and evaluative perceptions of policy output. So, too, does the distinction between "style issues" and "position issues" drawn by the authors of *Voting* (Berelson et al., 1954).

At this point, however, we can do no more than suggest that future theoretical efforts might produce more useful conceptions of the links between "policy output," public perceptions of it, and legislators' behavior which produces it than those presently afforded by concepts formulated within the "demand-input processor" model of the representative body.

PARTY INFLUENCE

The chief question for studies pursued within the framework of the model usually has been, "Why has a certain decision (or group of them) come out the way it did, rather than the other way?" Somewhat tautologically, particular results of legislative decision-making have been "explained" by characterizing the makeup of the winning and losing sides. This approach tends to give a somewhat misleading picture of the activity of the legislature by excessive concentration on hotly contested (i.e., closely divided) issues, and by presuming that such events are confrontations between legislators who want different things, presumably because they are seeking to implement policy demands made by contesting groups of interests and persons outside the legislature. The meaning of the vast amount of business done unanimously or nearly so remains unexplored. (As Table 8.2 showed, of 641 roll calls in the 1963 Iowa House, 319 were decided unanimously, 32 with but a single member dissenting, 24 with but two members dissenting.) As Eulau (1964: 28n) has noted,

> In part, this lack of evidence is probably due to prevailing research strategies. Studies of legislative decision-making by way of roll call votes are usually limited to the relatively few situations in which legislatures are divided. The criteria used to determine whether a roll call is to be considered controversial vary, and different research methods employed by different students have led to divergent findings about the importance of one or another factor that is assumed to make for division.

Customarily, the influence of party differences on policy outcomes is examined on the assumption that party provides "the most common and durable source" of legislative conflict, to borrow James Madison's language about factions. In the Iowa House during the 1963 session, eighty-one of the 641 roll calls were "party roll calls," i.e., divisions in which a majority of one party voted on the opposite side from the majority of the other (only members voting were used in this calculation). That figure in itself, of course, tells us little. The relative influence of party as a basis for division in these roll calls (and the others, for that matter) can be shown conveniently and simply by means of Rice's index of likeness, which measures the extent to which any two groups (here the two party delegations) resemble each other in their voting on a given roll call.[8] These statistics reveal readily that party is a somewhat erratic producer of conflict and cleavage, at least in the particular case we are dealing with. The average Index of Party Likeness for the 81 "party roll calls" is only .586, and the 81 "party roll calls" include 15 with Index of Likeness values greater than .800 (the range is from .034 to .985). The mean of the Indices of Likeness for all roll calls is .767 and for the roll calls which were not party roll calls, .893 (for twenty-five of them, less than .800).

The Indices of Likeness data reveal quite a bit about the relationship between party contention and policy decision in the Iowa House in this particular session. Table 8.6 displays the I.P.L. scores for all the 37 roll calls on which I.P.L. was no greater than .600. In spite of the leniency of the criterion, on only twenty-one measures was party cleavage on any roll call sufficient to reduce the resemblance between parties to as low as .600 (hardly a very stringent criterion!). These tend to be measures relating not to the substance of public policy but to the contest between parties as organizations, *viz.*, Numbers 1, 2, 6, 8, 9, 11 in Table 8.6. Notably missing are the grander issues of public policy around which textbook and journalistic discussions of legislative party conflict often revolve. Measure Number 7 in Table 8.6, the proposal to increase taxes on cigarettes and numerous other commodities in replacement of the School Property Tax Fund, and Numbers 4, 5, 10, 14, 15, and 17, come as close as any on the list to being such matters. Most of the substantive matters, however, either are narrowly specific issues, whose connection to the lines of party contention must be almost wholly local and idiosyncratic (e.g., Numbers 12, 16, 19) or as much symbolic as practical in their relation to public policy issues (Numbers 3 and 21, proclaiming suspicion of federal programs), or basically substantive but minor by most ordinary standards of importance (e.g., Numbers 13, 14, 15, 20).

Thus the picture is one in which legislators appear to entertain party identifications but not often to be much influenced by them in their legislative decision making. Whatever structured the attention and activity of the Iowa House in 1963, political party played a very minor part, to say the least. But, if the legislative struggle almost never pitted Republicans against Democrats, who did win and lose on the various roll calls concerning public policy? A common assumption, never formulated carefully for research purposes, is that the economic interests of citizens, expressed through representatives of constituencies, underlie these contests. Where constituencies are large, socially heterogeneous, and economically complex, the precise way in which district socio-economic interests might be linked up to a representative's behavior cannot be visualized easily. But where, as in Iowa, most constituencies tend to be relatively homogeneous and not exceedingly complex, perhaps legislative battles are waged between socio-economic interests.

Table 8.6: Indices of Party Likeness for All Roll Calls of I.P.L. Less Than .600

		Measure	Index of Party Likeness		
1.	— —	Rerefer to Contest Committee a report on contested seat	.034		
2.	SF 434	Confirmation by Senate, eligibility for interim appointment	.059, .196		
3.	SCR 23	Oppose US laws infringing right of state to administer own Workmen's Compensation Laws	.230		
4.	SF 411	Amend appropriations to Dept. Soc. Welfare, medical assistance to aged	.243		
5.	HF 491	Change law re unemployment compensation benefits	.249, .265		
6.	SJR 1	Composition, apportionment, legis.	.258, .539, .566		
7.	HF 550	Increase tax on cigarettes, etc. to replace School Property Tax Fund	.258, .275, .275 .275, .285, .364 .399, .481, .504 .518, .533		
8.	— —	Amend a change to House Rules	.330		
9.	HF 374	Reject report of Judiciary Committee One	.355		
10.	SF 453	Appropriations, Dept. Social Welfare, various programs	.393		
11.	— —	Amend a change to House Rules	.400		
12.	SF 175	Salaries, utility plant boards of trustees in cities	.456		
13.	HF 48	Licensing, inspecting county homes	.491, .563		
14.	SF 461	Regulation, taxation of travel trailers	.503		
15.	HF 96	Exemption of educational institutions from property taxation	.544		
16.	HF 101	Appointment of night deputy sheriffs	.544, .592		
17.	HF 498	Establish Employment Safety Commission	.549		
18.	SF 466	Appropriations, Board of Control for	.553		
19.	HF 76	Hours of duty, fire dept. members	.577		
20.	HF 47	Authorize School Districts to buy annuities for employees	.580		
21.	HF 424	Authorize Conservation Commissioner cooperate with US government	.595		

Insofar, however, as this conception envisions specific social or economic groups based in a constituency pursuing narrowly and specifically defined interests, our data are not adquate to explore the hypothesis very far. Inspection of the measures acted upon reveals many measures which very well might be designed for such purposes, including not merely specific "local bills" but general provisions respecting taxation, local-government guidelines (contracts, etc.), welfare programs, and others. A major problem with this interpretation of the legislative process, however, is that it is silent about an apparently significant feature: even if social and economic "interests" initiate and promote measures designed for their own advantage, remarkably few interests appear on the scene to contest them. Is that because of a basic harmony of interests, after all, so that only rarely authoritative allocation of values results in conflict? The interest-group conception of government assumes just the opposite, that scarcity of resources breeds conflict necessarily and conflict necessitates that values be allocated authoritatively.

To the extent that socio-economic interests are defined in broad, class terms, Iowa offers a very crude indication of the extent that this kind of difference affects legislative decision-making. We can calculate median level of family income for all constituencies from census data readily. Then, we can divide constituencies into the rich and the poor (47 with median family income below $3,600 or more) and compute indices of lineness between these groups. This computation yields only 22 roll calls on which a majority of "rich-district" representation lined up against a majority of "poor-district" representatives ("SES Roll Calls" analogous to "Party Roll Calls"). The average score of these Indices of SES Likeness was .860, meaning that the two groups really differed very little even on these few roll calls. Furthermore, the average I-SES-L overall for 641 roll calls was .911 and an I-SES-L score of .704 represents the greatest difference found (on HF 498, concerning establishment of an Employment Safety Commission—IPL on this was .549). So, social-class interest expressed through constituency representation is totally inadequate to account for the decisions reached in this session of the Iowa House.

On the other hand, the relative urban or rural character of constituencies does play some role in dividing the legislature. Table 8.7 lists the 19 measures and 67 roll calls on which a majority of urban representatives opposed a majority of rural representatives (analogous to the criterion for Party Roll Calls) and the Index of Urban-Rural Likeness was less than .700. Altogether, 34 measures had at least one "Urban vs. Rural" roll call (a total of 72 Urban vs. Rural roll calls) and the average I-UR-L for these was .710. (The average I-UR-L for all roll calls was .803.)

In numbers of actions affected, urban-rural differences appear to be almost as influential as party differences (which influence, remember, was not especially great). But the level of urban-rural conflict is not notably high. Even on the most contentious issue I-UR-L is only .381. Note that the method of calculating the values of I-UR-L deliberately was chosen to exaggerate these values, by omitting from the computation five legislators from mixed urban-rural districts and 27 from rural non-farm districts so as to distinguish urban and rural constituencies as sharply as possible.[9] Even measures on which the I-UR-L scores suggest relatively great urban-rural conflict, often have generated other roll calls where urban-rural cleavage is practically non-existent. For example, on Number 7 in Table 8.7, SF 437 concerning home rule liquor control and licensing, in addition to the two

Table 8.7: Indices of Urban-Rural Likeness for all Roll Calls Where Majority of Urban Opposed Majority of Rural Members and I—UR—L is Less Than 70.0

		Measure	Indices of Likeness
1.	SJR 1	Composition, apportionment of legislature	.381, .481
2.	HF 550	Increase tax on cigarettes and other commodities to replace School Property Tax	.489, .586, .589 .623, .634, .656 .669, .737, .758
3.	HF 498	Establish Employment Safety Commission	.532, .552, .658
4.	SF 94	Bovine brucellosis control	.540
5.	— —	Amend a House Rule	.582
6.	HF 13	Increase limitation on school bond indebtedness to 10 mills	.606
7.	SF 437	Home rule liquor control licensing	.610, .676
8.	HF 47	Authorize school districts to buy annuity contracts for employees	.626
9.	SF 114	Retirement of judges	.642
10.	SF 18	Create an appointive State Board of Public Instruction	.643, .685
11.	SF 69	Publication of real property valuations	.648
12.	HF 76	Re hours of duty, fire dept. members	.651
13.	SF 1	Re controlled access highways	.652
14.	HF 491	Change law re unemployment compensation benefits	.660
15.	SF 466	Appropriations to Board of Control, capital improvements	.662
16.	SF 404	Marketing of dairy products	.664, .685, .685 .693, .697
17.	HF 48	Re licensing, inspecting county homes	.693
18.	SF 275	Re overall length, combination vehicles	.693
19.	HF 96	Exemption of educational institutions from property taxation	.697

roll calls shown in Table 8.7, a third roll call yielded an I-UR-L of .917 and 8 other roll calls did not divide along urban-rural lines.

Of still greater interest, however, is the subject matter of the measures contended over more or less in urban-rural terms. The most contentious concerns reapportionment, supposedly a perennial bone of urban-rural contention, although not directly "substantive" in policy terms. Very few other measures listed in Table 8.7 have any very obvious conflict of urban vs. rural economic interest. Indeed, in one case, Number 4 (brucellosis control), besides the one moderately contentious roll call shown, on five other roll calls urban members did not vote against rural members at all. Several measures appear to involve not so much clashing economic interests as differential effects of measures which intrinsically are neither particularly urban nor rural, such as Numbers 2, 6, and 8. Others appear to be related to urban-rural differences in life style and mores, as much as anything (particularly Number 7).

In general, however one is drawn again to the general conclusion that conflicting urban and rural demands cannot account for very much legislative decision-making. Table 8.8, comparing some summary statistics based on the indices of likeness, shows just how slight, on balance, is the influence of party, urban-rural influences, and socio-economic class factors, in legislative divisions in the session under view. That these factors are by no means unrelated to one another is indicated by the number of measures that appear in all three categories of roll call division. The data show plainly that, in general, party more than urban-rural differences tend to divide the legislators most. Among the relatively highly divisive roll calls, the Index of Urban-Rural Likeness approaches the Index of Party Likeness only on reapportionment (SJR1). But, again, the relatively low

Table 8.8: Comparisons of Indices of Likeness for Three Variables in the 1963 Session of the Iowa House

	IPL Legislator's Party	I—UR—L Constituency Urban-Rural Status	I—SES—L Constituency Socioeconomic Status
Mean Index of Likeness, all roll calls	.767	.710	.911
Number of measures split (majority v. majority)	41	34	17
Number of roll calls split	81	72	22
Mean Index of Likeness, split roll calls	.586	.803	.860
Range of Index of Likeness Split roll calls	.034—.985	.381—.917	.704—.813
All other roll calls	.582—.100	.547—.999	.743—.100

Table 8.9: Urban-Rural Characteristics of Districts Represented by Democrats and Republicans

	Democrats N=29	Republicans N=79
Urban (% Urban greater than % Rural by at least 10%)	34.5%	21.5%
Mixed (% Urban and % Rural within 10% of one another)	3.4%	5.1%
Rural Farm (% Rural at least 10% greater than % urban and number of rural farm greater than rural nonfarm)	41.8%	46.8%
Rural Nonfarm ("Rural," but rural non-farm outnumber rural farm population)	20.7%	26.6%
TOTAL	100.0%	100.0%

degree to which all these factors really account for the roll call divisions undoubtedly is more important.

The muddiness of the associations in constituency and legislator terms is indicated by the average of constituency family-income means which differs between Republicans and Democrats by only approximately $89 ($3,760 for the Democrats, $3,849 for the Republicans). While Republican constituencies are more rural than Democratic constituencies, neither party is predominantly urban or rural in terms of the character of legislative districts it represents, as Table 8.9 shows. But exploration of the precise character and extent of inter-relationships among these constituency characteristics must await more sophisticated analysis than can be attempted here. At this point, as justification for such work later, we point out the divergence of the picture obtained by the methods used above from that suggested by Wayne Francis's study of "important issues," which relied on questionnaires to legislators who were members of the very session we have been examining. His study does not report the number of Iowans who actually responded to the questionnaire, but does report that Iowa ranks exceptionally high among the fifty states in conflict on important issues (sixth), and fairly low on his "Index of Agreement." The legislators who responded did think, however, that conflict was based more on factions and pressure groups than on regions or parties (Francis, 1967: 44-45).

REDUCTION OF CONFLICT

The diffuseness of contention in the legislative situation just described, when added to the well known but little considered phenomenon of unanimous "decision-making" reinforces the conclusion that research aimed at identifying winners and losers in the legislative game must be overlooking something. If things are unclear generally, as they seem to be, why should legislators go on playing the game? Why should citizens watch it at all? The phenomenon of persistently high levels of popular support for legislative institutions and legislative actions about which people know practically nothing is further reason to believe that legislative output is reaching them as something other than "policy decisions" which they approve or disapprove in the light of their previous demands.[10]

A clue as to what is going on is suggested by the ease with which samples of mass publics answer questions about "important issues" or "matters requiring government action" not in terms of personal interests convertible into private demands on government but in terms of general "problems" confronting "the country" or "the state."[11] They seem to evaluate government clearly and lend it their support in terms of generalized feelings about whether it is dealing adequately with the most pressing problems. Also, it is quite plausible, as well as consistent with what little information we have, that many legislators view the legislative task as one of identifying and dealing with problems.[12] Conflicts can arise from different technical estimates about the adequacy of means to reach agreed ends, from different estimates of what problems are most pressing, and from other differences of opinion among legislators not at all related to representatives' association with this or that "interest" or "demand" as well as from outright confrontations of irreconcilable interests.

Moreover, even if the task of the legislature is defined as dealing with clashing interests, the primary goal almost inexorably becomes reconciliation, reduction of conflict, not mere registry of preponderant demands. All to easily we forget, in the search for winners and losers of legislative decision, that, to participant legislators, the group goal is not the imposition of interest-directed, demand-sensitive wills but the resolution of differences, the search for the most widely acceptable ultimate settlements of opinion differences, the reconciliation and ultimate reduction of conflict. Legislative research has not studied this process of conflict crystallization and resolution and the ways in which it is related through the processes of representation to public support for government, to legitimacy.

Such study clearly is not within the province of this paper. but the data used above do contain some suggestive hints about the shape of the legislative process. The crystallization and subsequent resolution of tension shows clearly with some issues, whereas with others conflicts, once focused, remain essentially unresolved, producing ultimately only a final registering of the disagreements. Bearing in mind that we are really dealing with a *process*, and not a static condition of disagreement, we can look at the legislative record of the 1963 Iowa House from a different perspective than that used in the preceding sections of this paper.

In terms of the process by which the legislature disposed of them, the various measures dealt with in the 1963 session fall into several different patterns. In the most common, the matter is disposed of unanimously in a single floor action. The session we are examining handled 293 such measures. Closely akin are those settled in one roll call, but with a handful of dissenters, let us say anything under 10 percent; there were 39 such measures. Of the measures requiring two roll calls, twenty-five were contested by no more than two members on either ballot; they therefore properly belong with the unanimous or near unanimour measures. In addition, one measure received 3 roll calls, of which none were contested. At least from the record alone, none of these can tell us much about the *process* of conflict resolution in the legislature.[13] Neither can the forty measures characterized by some degree of dissent (more than 10 percent), but nonetheless settled in the one roll call which both registered the dissent and disposed of the matter. The remaining 60 measures might be illuminating, however.

These measures received at least two roll calls, at least one of which was contested. They permit us to compare levels of contention on each of them at different points in the legislative process. On this basis, they fall into three groups. The largest, thirty-one measures, consists of those in which dissent on the final vote was lower than the mean level of dissent for all other roll calls on that measure. The level of contention on these was reduced in every case to no more than 5 percent on the final vote, although dissent may have been quite high on one or more earlier roll calls. On another five measures, dissent on the final action was considerably lower in each case than the average dissent of all other roll calls in that measure, but nevertheless remained as high as 10 percent or more. The third and fourth groups include measures on which dissent remained high through final floor action. In the case of 11 measures the level of dissent decreased slightly by the final roll call, but on 13 measures dissent was actually higher on the final action than the average of preceding roll calls on that measure.

A policy-subject pattern in the data is difficult to detect. Agricultural bills are as likely to appear in the list of unresolved conflicts as in the list of those fully resolved (or the unlisted set of those settled unanimously and expeditiously). The same is true for other subject matters. Equally interesting, the extent of conflict resolution on any set of measures does not appear to relate to the supposed bases for contest—party and urban-rural differences, in particular. What, then, does determine the development and resolution of legislative contention over time? Are different patterns of conflict management, in this sense, perceived differently by the general public? How may we account for the tendency of legislators to register in procedural terms those conflicts which seem least soluble, rather than totting up directly the "ayes" and "nays" on the substantive measure itself? How is the function of registering and resolving conflict performed in legislatures which, unlike Iowa, conduct their business by repetitious divisions into sides which remain the same regardless of the issue (e.g., tight bipartisan bodies)? Indeed, how does a party revolution, such as Iowa experienced in 1964, affect this picture?

To answer such questions will require more intensive investigation than the tentative beginning attempted here. More and diffferent data are needed. Comparative analysis of different kinds of legislative bodies under different kinds of circumstances is required. For the moment, our main conclusion is relatively simple, however: the questions asked by legislative research should change from those preoccupied with explaining why a representative body may have decided as it did to questions about what happens to it and to its public when it decides things as it does. It may be more difficult to attack such questions through political research. But, also we are more likely to learn something important about the political system from doing so.

NOTES

1. Although the terminology in these paragraphs closely follows David Easton's, the conception in question is much more general than Easton's "political system." The description applies equally well, for example, to "group approach" studies, empirical roll call studies, and most others.

2. See Wahlke, 1971; reproduced in this volume as Chapter 4.

3. I am indebted to my Iowa colleagues, Professors Samuel C. Patterson and G.R. Boynton, for their making available the Iowa State Legislative Research Project data on which this chapter is based.

4. The 60th General Session did meet in extraordinary session February 24 through April 8, 1964, however, following the U.S. Supreme Court's decision concerning Iowa's malapportionment.

5. See especially Wahlke et al., 1962: 155-165.

6. For discussions of incrementalism as a method of decision-making, see Dahl and Lindblom, 1953: 82ff; Lindblom and Braybrooke, 1963; Lindblom, 1965; and Wildavsky, 1964.

7. Wahlke et al., 1962: 267-310. The strength of this myth among the Iowa public is attested by the responses to several questions in the 1966 study mentioned earlier. Asked how important they thought it that a legislator "know the will of the people in his district," 73 percent said "very important" and 23 percent "pretty important," while a mere 1.6 percent said "not too important" (the rest didn't know). On the other hand, 78 percent of them disagreed in some degree with the proposition that, "If the Iowa Legislature continually passed laws that the people disagreed with, it might be better to do away with the legislature altogether." See Boynton et al., 1968.

8. See Rice, 1925. Its value can range from 0 (100 percent of one party versus 100 percent of the other, i.e., maximum intergroup difference) to 1.0 (50 percent of one versus 50 percent of the other, indicating the groups's behaving identically). It has been calculated here as the complement (from 100 percent) of the difference between the percentage of one party voting "Aye" and the percentage of the other party voting "Aye," ignoring non-voting members of both parties. The values obtained by percentaging the winning vote instead of always the "Aye" votes are essentially the same as those obtained here. Omission of non-voters apparently tends, where it has any effect, to exaggerate the inter-party difference.

9. Districts classified as "urban" are those in which, by 1960 census figures, percent-population-urban was greater than percentage-population-rural by at least 10 percent; "rural" were those where the reverse was true. Districts where neither urban nor rural propor-

tions exceed the other by more than 10 percent were classified as "mixed," and those rural districts in which the nonfarm population was larger than the farm population were classified as "rural nonfarm."

10. See Boynton et al., 1968, for discussion of support in Iowa, and Wahlke, 1971 (Chapter 4), for general discussion of the theoretical utility of studying support.

11. In addition to the questions regularly reported in Harris and Gallup polls, see Cantril, 1965.

12. See the discussion of representational role conceptions and of legislators' recognition of technical expertise as a basis for legislative judgment in Wahlke et al., 1962: 193-215, 267-285.

13. But they might well be analyzed in the light of Eulau's taxonomy of unanimous decisions. See Eulau, 1964.

Chapter 9

POLICY-MAKING IN AMERICAN CITIES:
Comparisons in a Quasi-Longitudinal, Quasi-Experimental Design

HEINZ EULAU

In recent years several efforts have been made to explain public policies by the use of a study design which treats the outputs of policy as dependent variables, usually by relating them to such independent variables as a polity's socio-economic or political-structural characteristics. One of the weaknesses of this research has been that it does not include data on the political attitudes and orientations of policy-makers themselves, for one might expect that their positions on public issues make a difference in policy outputs. Hence conclusions reached about the importance of 'politics' in the formation of policies are incomplete at best.

But this weakness, partly remedied in the research reported here, is not my major concern. Rather, what interests me is the attempt to explain public policy by way of causal models, for this strikes me as something of an anomaly. At issue, therefore, is the question of whether the design of research involved in causal modelling of public policy is sufficiently isomorphic with policy as a behavioural process in the real world to warrant confidence in the inferences that are made about the emergence of policy.

The plausibility of causal modelling being an appropriate technique for explaining public policy is largely predicated on acceptance of the familiar conception of the political system that deals in inputs and outputs. This conception is congenial to causal modelling because it permits a quick and easy step from treating inputs as 'causes' to treating outputs as 'effects.' In other words, policy outcomes are assumed to be the ultimate dependent variable to be accounted for,[1] and the research question is whether exogenous variables (environmental, economic, social, etc.) or endogenous variables (political structures and processes) account for variance in policy. The prior question—whether the input-output system model corresponds to what goes on in the real world of policy—is largely ignored. Also ignored is Easton's (1965: 89) caveat that this "approach to the analysis of political systems will not help us to understand why any specific policies are adopted by the politically relevant members in a system."

The problem of whether causal modelling is the proper technique for explaining public policy is exacerbated by the perplexing and discomforting findings that political variables seem to account for little or none of the variance in policy outputs.[2] "This, I submit," comments Salisbury (1968: 164) after reviewing the relevant research, "is a devastating set of findings and cannot be dismissed as not meaning what it plainly says—that analysis of political systems will not explain policy decisions made by those systems."

In spite of Easton's own caveat and Salisbury's blunt conclusion, policy research continues causal modelling. Instead of raising questions about the conception of policy implicit in causal modelling, the failure to find relationships between political variables and policy outputs is attributed to the inadequacy of input or output indicators or to error in measurement. Much effort, perhaps misspent, is devoted to the search for more valid indicators of both independent political and dependent policy variables, and to the correction of measurement errors.

If modelling is to be used in the analysis of public policy, it should follow rather than precede an empirically viable conception of policy. Such a conception is not likely to emerge, in *deus ex machine* fashion, from causal modelling all kinds of indicators of presumed inputs and outputs that may or may not be germane. Of critical importance are not the indicators but the designs for their analysis. An analytical design is a way to produce the readings of the empirical indicators. Like a definition, it may be wilful, but it must not be arbitrary. Thoughtlessly imposing a causal model on the policy process is not likely to yield valid knowledge.

This paper describes alternate ways of exploring, if not explaining, public policy. Following Stouffer's (1962: 297) injunction that "exploratory research is of necessity fumbling, but . . . the waste motion can be reduced by the self-denying ordinance of deliberately limiting ourselves to a few variables at a time," it initially presents a rather simplistic causal model of policy that employs only five variables. It also presents a rather intricate post facto quasi-longitudinal design for observing variations in components of the causal model. This design seeks to make the best of empirical data which are basically static, but it is inspired by another Stouffer (1962: 297) comment that we need "many more descriptive studies involving random ratlike movements on the part of the researcher before we can even begin to state our problems so that they are in decent shape for fitting into an ideal design." Before proceeding, it is necessary to explain the conception of policy that is employed and introduce the variables that are being manipulated in the analyses.

A CONCEPTION OF POLICY

Policy is a strictly theoretical construct that is inferred from the patterns of choice behaviour by political actors and the consequences of choice behaviour. Choice behaviour is manifest in actual decisions such as the vote counts in legislative bodies, budgetary allocations, or the assignment of personnel to specified tasks. The consequences of choice behaviour are manifest in the behaviour that follows upon choice, especially compliance or non-compliance. If the behavioural patterns are consistent and regular, the existence of policy is inferred and identified. But behavioural patterns themselves, whether intended or not, are not policy but manifestations from which the nature or direction of policy is inferred.

So defined, policy is distinguished from the intentions, goals, or preferences that political actors may entertain in making choices. Although intentions, goals, or preferences may influence choice, policy cannot be inferred from them. Policy may be consonant with intentions, goals, or preferences, but this can only mean that they have been realized in practice. This conception of policy differs from the conventional usage, when we say, for instance, that it is the policy of government to end discrimination in housing. It may be the intention of the government to end discrimination, but behaviour in pursuit of this intention may or may not occur. Because something is intended, it does not follow that it is in fact the policy.

As a process, policy is the collectivity's response to conditions of the physical and social environment. A policy is operative as long as it is successful, that is, as long as the response that it represents proves rewarding. In fact, it is the rewarding of the response that makes policy what it is—a set of consistent and regular behavioural patterns through which governing units cope with environmental conditions. Changes in policy, that is, changes in response, presumably occur when there are changes in environmental conditions. If there is no appropriate response, and if the old response pattern or policy continues, no reward is likely to be forthcoming. As the policy no longer proffers rewards, it may actually become dysfunctional, if insisted upon, or it may simply be obsolete. In responding to environmental conditions, the characteristics of the governing unit may affect the form of response—its political structure, its human and physical resources, the degree of mass or elite involvement in governance, the vitality of private interests making public demands, and, last but not least, the perceptions, orientations, and preferences of policy-makers themselves.

The problems of policy-making arise out of the relationship between changes in the environment that call for some response, the ways in which these changes are experienced as problems requiring solutions, and the values that policy-makers may seek in responding to changes. Policy, then, functions as a response to environmental conditions, both physical and social, that has built into it an anticipation of a future state of affairs. If this is the case, a change in policy is both causal and purposive: it is "caused" by environmental stimuli, but it is also directed towards a goal and shaped by a purpose. The tension arising out of the simultaneity of causal and purposive "forcings" is a basic property of policy.

The problem of causal modelling policy is congruent with the nature of policy in the real world. Policy as a response to environmental challenges inferred from behavioural patterns manifest in outputs or outcomes of choice processes is truly "caused." However, as the response is also in pursuit of a goal, value, or end-in-view, it is purposive. But behaviour in pursuit of a goal, or purposive behaviour, is "caused" in a sense quite different from that we have in mind when we say that a change in environmental conditions brings about or causes policy as a response. When we say, therefore, that a purpose "informs" or "orients" a response, we do not mean that the response is "caused" by a purpose in the same sense that it is caused by an environmental stimulus. If this is so, grave doubts may be raised about the applicability of causal assumptions to policy analysis. For causal modelling does not and probably cannot discriminate between genuinely causal and what are, in effect teleological assumptions about policy.

The problem is confounded by the fact that the relationship between environment and policy is probably symmetrical. In the sense that policy is a response, it is caused by environmental conditions; but as policy is itself a sequence of behavioural patterns through time, it has a reactive effect on the environment. Put differently, it is best to assume that policy and environment are interdetermined. As policies cumulate through time they come to constitute an environment of their own that persists because, insofar as policy proves rewarding, the behavioural patterns involved in responding to environmental challenges have proved rewarding and therefore are continued. But it is just for this reason that the values or goals that policy-makers pursue in responding to the environment are not independent of the interdetermined relationship between environment and policy. If this is so, it goes a long way in explaining what has been called "incremental decision-making," though this formulation places the explanatory accent elsewhere (Lindblom, 1965; Wildavsky, 1964). Empirically, it means that current policies do not deviate widely from the goals implicit in policy as a response to the environment. Hence the finding that past expenditure patterns are the best predictors of future expenditures, apparently leaving little room for other variables to affect policy (Sharkansky, 1969: 113-125). Psychologically, it means that policy is inert, unless environmental challeges are so overwhelming that innovative behavioural responses are called out. Given the fact that goals are implied in ongoing policy, it is simply "easier" or "cheaper" to behave incrementally than to act otherwise.

The model of the policy process that emerges from these considerations consist of three major variables—the physical-natural environment, the policy environment (i.e., the configuration of relevant policies that emerges through time), and what may be called the "policy map" of policy-makers. The policy map, in turn, consists of three components: first, policy-makers' perceptions of the environmental challenges or problems which they are called to act upon; second, the goals or images of the future which they have in mind as they respond or fail to respond to the environment; and third, the positions they take in making choices in regard to the problems confronting them. The operational definitions of these variables and the measures used will be introduced in the next section.

The propositions that can be derived from our conception of policy and that constitute a theoretical model of the policy process are as follows:

(1) The physical-social environment and the policy environment are interdetermined. For instance, there is a reciprocal relationship between urbanization as an environmental stimulus and policy as a response. But policy can also influence the course of urbanization as when land is set aside for industrial or commercial growth or when taxing policies favour urbanization. As an interdeterminate relationship, it is subject to the conditions of a moving equilibrium: a change in environmental stimuli engenders a change in policy, and a change in policy alters the environment.

(2) An environmental challenge calling for a policy response has the expected effect only if it is perceived by policy-makers as constituting a problem situation. Unless environmental challenges are experienced as problems, policy responses are not likely to be forthcoming.

(3) Environmental challenges may be, but need not be, directly related to policy-makers' images of the future. They need not be related because goals or images refer to the future and can be independent of past or present conditions. But images may be related indirectly to environmental conditions if the latter are perceived as problems and suggest a reformulation of images.

(4) Environmental challenges are not directly related to policy positions, for positions need only be taken if the challenges are seen as problems and become issues to be settled.

(5) The policy environment, i.e., the set of ongoing policies that has emerged through time, may be, but need not be, related to the perception of challenges from the environment as problems. Policy environment will not be related to problem perceptions if the relationship between it and the environmental challenge is in equilibrium; it will be related if the latter relationship is disturbed. Put differently, if ongoing polices successfully cope with environmental challenges, the latter are unlikely to be perceived as problems.

(6) The policy environment is related to policy-makers' images of or goals for the future. The policy environment is, by definition, rewarding. And if the policy environment is rewarding, images and goals are not likely to deviate widely from the goals or images that are implicit in ongoing policies and, in fact, are likely to be congruent with them.

(7) The policy environment is not directly related to policy positions. For positions are at best intentions that may or may not be consonant with ongoing policies.

(8) The relationship between the perception of problems and policy images is highly problematic. On the one hand, one can assume that images as views of the future are totally independent of perceptions of current problems. On the other hand, one can also assume that the perception of strong challenges from the environment lead to a reformulation of images or that the perception of problems, even if rooted in the reality of environmental challenges, is "coloured" by preferances or expectations inherent in images. Put differently, what policy-makers perceive as problems and what they envisage for the future may be at loggerheads; but perceptions of problems may reshape images, or images may shape the perception of problems. As a result, the relationship between problem perceptions and policy images as such is indeterminate and depends largely on antecedent conditions.

(9) Policy images are directly related to policy positions. Because positions are policy-makers' declarations of how they intend to cope with environmental challenges, they are likely to be tutored by their images or ends-in-view.

(10) Perceptions of problems, stimulated by environmental challenges, are directly related to policy positions. For if no problems stemming from environmental conditions are perceived, there is no need to adopt policy positions.

DATA AND MEASURES

The data for the two analyses that follow were collected by the City Council Research Project in 1966-1967. Interviews were conducted with 435 city councilmen in 87 cities of the San Francisco Bay region. The interviews covered a wide range of questions of political interest (for a full report of the Project, see Eulau and Prewitt, 1973). For the purposes of this chapter, individual responses were aggregated at the council level so that the council rather than the councilman serves as the empirical unit of analysis. The method of coding and aggregation will be described in connection with the measures used. In addition to the interview data, ecological, demographic, and budget data were collected.

In the following analyses, not all of the 87 city councils in which interviews were conducted could be used. The reduction in numbers is due to a variety of reasons, as follows:

Number of councils in which not enough individual councilmen were interviewed to warrant aggregation at council level   5
Number of councils for which census or budget data are missing (recently incorporated cities)   3
Number of councils with code categories on one or another of the three policy map components too small to permit meaningful analysis   16
Number of councils with environmental characteristics of no interest in the quasi-longitudinal analysis   6

As a result the number of councils available for analysis was reduced to 65 in the first analysis and further reduced to 59 in the second analysis.

Variable 1: City Size as an Indicator of Urbanization

We assume that city size is an appropriate indicator of the level of urbanization that represents the intensity of environmental challenges. There is overwhelming evidence that city size correlates highly not only with other indicators of urbanization such as population density, industrialization, and commercialization but also with the community's "social pluralism."[3] The larger the city, the more demanding and more complex is not only its physical environment but also its social environment. City size data come from the 1965 Census of Population. The set of 82 cities included in the main study was dichotomized at the median. As a result

41 cities with a population of over 17,000 were characterized as "more urbanized," and 41 cities below the median with a poplulation of under 17,000 were characterized as "less urbanized."

Variable 2: State of Policy Development as Indicator of Policy Environment

This variable derives from a complex analysis of city expenditure ratios for development planning and amenities over a period of eight years, 1958-1965. Space limitations here do not permit a full explanation of the measures.[4] In general, cities with limited expenditures in planning and amenities, judged by the grand median for all cities, which remained in the same expenditure category over the period of eight years were categorized as "retarded." At the opposite end, cities above the grand median in planning and amenities expenditures for the whole period were categorized as "advanced." Cities moving across the grand medians on either planning or amenities expenditures were variously categorized as "emergent," "progressed," or "maturing." For the purpose of analysis here the five categories were collapsed into two: cities whose policy environment, defined by the cumulative effect of planning and amenities expenditures, is "more developed" (maturing and advanced), and those whose policy environment is "less developed" (retarded, emergent, and progressed).

Variable 3: Perception of Policy Problems

The data stem from an interview question that reads: "Mr. Councilman, before talking about your work as a councilman and the work of the Council itself, we would like to ask you about some of the problems facing this community. In your opinion, what are the two most pressing problems here in [city]?" Once individual responses had been coded, they were categorized into four major types: problems relating to services and utilities, urban growth, social and remedial matters, and governmental or intergovernmental affairs. For the purpose of aggregation, the type receiving most individual responses was recorded, provided it received at least 30 per cent of all responses. As a result of this aggregation, only problems related to services and utilities, on the one hand, and growth, on the other hand, appeared frequently enough to warrant analysis. A council was characterized, then, as stressing either one or the other type of these two problem perceptions in its policy map. 49 councils saw growth as problematic, 23 councils perceived services or utilities as problems, and 10 councils fell into the other two categories which were omitted. For convenience of expression, we shall speak only of growth problems and service problems.

Variable 4: Policy Images

The data come from an interview question which reads: "Now, taking the broadest view possible, how do you see [city] in the future? I mean, what kind of a city would you personally like [city] to be in the next twenty-five years or so?" Once individual responses had been coded, it appeared that there were, for all practical purposes, only three types of response into which the individual responses could be aggregated: councils with a residential image or goal for the future, councils with a balanced residential-industrial image, and councils which were split. A council was categorized as having a residential image if 51 per cent or more of the individual councilmen favoured this image and as having a balanced image if 51 per cent or more favoured it. Of the councils, 32 held a residential image and 37 a balanced image. Thirteen of the councils could not be so categorized and were omitted from the analysis.

Variable 5: Policy Positions

The data come from an interview question which reads: "Now, looking toward the future, what one community-wide improvement, in your opinion, does the city 'need most' to be attractive to its citizens?" Once individual responses had been coded, they were categorized into five major types: positions relating to services and utilities, amenities, promotion and development, social and remedial matters, and governmental or intergovernmental affairs. A council was characterized as stressing one or another position on the basis of the highest proportion of responses in one or another of the five categories. As a result of this aggregation, only positions relating to amenities and development appeared often enough to be included in the anlaysis; 43 of the councils favoured amenities as position, 30 favoured development, and 9 fell into other categories omitted from the analysis.

ALTERNATE DESIGNS FOR POLICY RESEARCH

The task at hand is to ascertain just what kind of analytic design represents the "best fit" with the theoretical model of the policy process. Moreover, the design should be appropriate for the data that are available. The causal designs implicit in most policy research have in fact been dictated by available data, and to admit this is the better part of wisdom (but a wisdom rarely articulated in policy studies). However, even if data collection precedes rather than follows the formulation of the design, it should specify its criteria of proof in advance.

Causal modelling recommends itself as an analytic design in manipulating non-experimental data, and the more explicit the assumptions associated with diferent causal models, the more trustworthy are the inferences that can be drawn. On the other hand, this should not lead to a situation where alternate designs making use of the same data are ruled out. There has been a strong tendency to do this, largely because of failure to recognize that the design implicit in causal modelling is, at best, just one truncated design derivative of the classical experimental design. In fact, causal models are only one alternative in adaptations of the classical experimental design to real-world policy analysis. A few examples can demonstrate this.

Research on public policy is severely hampered by obstacles to genuine experimentation that inhere in real-world conditions. If public policy is a political unit's response to challenges from the environment, and if it is to be proved that policy is due to the intervention of policymakers, research in terms of the classical design would have to deal with at least two political units whose behaviour is to be compared—an experimental unit in which policy-makers intervene much like an experimental stimulus is introduced in the laboratory experiment, and a control unit in which the stimulus is absent. The design would look as shown in Figure 9.1. If, on measurement, $A_{0+1} - A_0$ is significantly different from $B_{0+1} - B_0$, the result may be taken as proof that the difference in outcomes is due to the intervention of policy-makers.

An experimental design of this kind is extraordinarily difficult to execute in the real world of politics. There is no need to dwell at length on the many obstacles involved in meeting the requirements of this design, such as the random assignment of the experimental stimulus so that any change in the experimental unit's condition at $time_{0+1}$ can be attributed with confidence to the intervention of policy-makers (see Fisher, 1937: 20-24), or the problem of obtaining a sufficient number of units through time so that the intervention of policy-makers in the experimental units can be observed and measured.

The purpose of reviewing the classical experimental design is not to set up an unduly perfectionist criterion of proof. Rather, it is to show that any research design, no matter how simple, is a derivative of the classical design. This is true even of the design which, in practice, is no design at all and which has only minimal truth value. For instance, the proposition is advanced that there is today a "generation gap" that is greater than it was yesterday, and an attempt is made to explain the gap

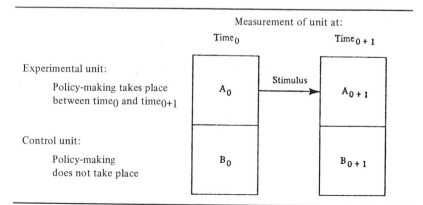

Figure 9.1: The Classical Experimental Design

in terms of some cause. The design implicit in this proposition is represented in Figure 9.2 In stating the proposition, the observer "fills in" the "before situation" with imagined data (represented by the cell with the broken lines). The design is highly truncated, for there is no control group to make sure that the hypothesized cause is in fact operative and the presumed difference between yesterday and today is not due to extraneous factors.

Suspicious as we rightly are of the highly truncated case study design, it may come as a shock to learn that the design most commonly used in contemporary policy research, though considerably more sophisticated and creditable, is also truncated in that it lacks a "before situation." In this design, let us call it the after-correlational design, two units or sets of unit are compared by way of cross-tabulation or correlation, and statistical controls are used in order to hold any number of variables constant so that the effect of a test variable can be identified and measured. As Figure 9.3 shows, the two units are compared in terms of a test variable at $time_{0+1}$, but nothing is known about the state of the units at $time_0$. Causal modelling is only a special case of the after-correlational design.

There are several other truncated designs, but only one other will be reviewed here because it is relevant to the design to be employed later in this paper. In this design, let us call it the random-panel design (as distinct from the longitudinal-panel design in which the same unit is observed at two points in time),[5] two different units or sets of unit are compared at different times. As shown in Figure 9.4, the assumption is made that if the unit observed at $time_0$ has also been observed at $time_{0+1}$, it would have the characteristics of the second unit actually observed at that time. Vice versa, the assumption is made, of course, that if the unit actually observed at $time_{0+1}$ had been observed "before" at $time_0$, it would have been identical in properties with the unit actually observed at that time.

The juxtaposition of a number of truncated or quasi-experimental designs and the classical experimental design serves to sensitize the analyst to the truth value of the proof involved in his design. None of the quasi-experimental designs satisfy the theoretical assumptions and technical requirements of the classical design.

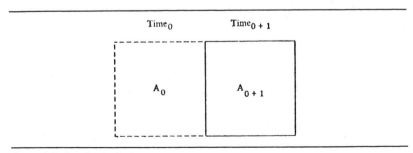

Figure 9.2: Case Study Design

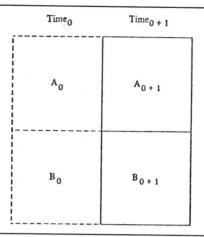

Figure 9.3: After-Correlational Design

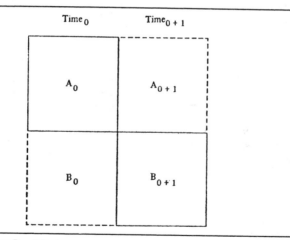

Figure 9.4: Random Panel Design

However, because they are not satisfactory from the perfectionist's perspective, it does not follow that they are not creditable; it only follows that the proof of any hypothesis tested by the design is at best partial.

The validity of the propositions advanced earlier cannot, therefore, be proved in any strict sense. The best proof can be harnessed by subjecting the propositions to alternate designs in order to determine whether they predict observations. There are two designs possible with the kind of data that are available. Both designs are predicated on the initial empirical observation of a close and strong relationship between urbanization as the environmental challenge and policy development as the response. Table 9.1 presents the data. The strength of the relationship alerts us to two observations. First, it is important to keep in mind that the data used to measure level of urbanization and degree of policy development refer to a time period clearly prior to the time period in which the data for the policy map components were collected. In other words, the possibility that any one of the policy components has an antecedent effect on either urbanization or policy development, or both, can be ruled out, and the relationship between urbanization and policy development need not be subjected to "control" in order to determine whether it is spurious. And second, the strength of the relationship suggests that there may be a strong "interaction effect" on observed relationships between each of the two variables and the components of the policy map and among the latter themselves.

Because so much current policy research is cast in the after-correlational design, we shall first examine the fit between the theoretical model derived from our conception of policy and the empirical causal model that can be constructed from the data. We shall then present an alternate design which, by introducing further assumptions about the nature of quasi-experimental designs, may represent a stronger test for the propositions of the theoretical model.

THE CAUSAL MODEL

For the purpose of modelling the relationships among the variables of the theoretical model, we shall treat level of urbanization and state of policy environment as independent variables, problem perceptions and policy images as intervening variables, and policy positions as the dependent variable.

Our first task is to determine the independence of the relationships between the two independent variables and the dependent variable (propositions 4 and 7), for only if these relationships are zero, as hypothesized, can it be assumed that problem perceptions and policy images are truly intervening variables. To test

Table 9.1: Policy Development and Urbanization (size) in Percentages

City Size	Retarded N=10	Emergent N=15	Progressed N=27	Mature N=15	Advanced N=15
<10,000	90	80	37	7	0
10-50,000	10	20	52	53	47
>50,000	0	0	11	40	53
g = 0.82	100	100	100	100	100

the null hypothesis, we control the relationships by both problem perceptions and policy images. The resulting second-order partial correlation coefficients are 0.07 for the urbanization-position relationship, and –0.03 for the policy environment-position relationship. Clearly, we cannot reject the null hypothesis of no direct relationship between the two independent variables and the dependent variable. Problem perceptions and policy images can be assumed to function as intervening variables.

We shall deal next with the bothersome question of the relationship between the two intervening variables (proposition 8). It will be recalled that the relationship was characterized as indeterminate. Because this relationship has important implications for all the model's linkages, we shall present it as a zero-order relationship, and as a partial relationship controlling successively for the other three variables individually and jointly.

It appears from Table 9.2 that, if uncontrolled, the relationship between problem perception and policy image is quite weak. In other words, there is only a very slight tendency for policy-makers with a balanced (rather than residential) image to perceive growth problems (rather than service-related matters). When the possible reactive effect of policy position on the relationship is partialled out, the relationship becomes somewhat stronger. However, it declines when controlled for the possible effect of policy environment, and it altogether vanishes when controlled for level of urbanization. To explore the relationship further, it was controlled for the possible simultaneous effect of urbanization and policy environment. The result, as Table 9.2 shows, is highly instructive. The relationship continues to remain weak, but significantly changes in direction. It now appears that it is policy-makers with a residential (rather than balanced) image who perceive problems of growth confronting them, while those with a balanced image now perceived service-connected matters as problems. However, the weakness of the relationship confirms our initial proposition that the direction of the relationship is quite indeterminate.

The implications of this indeterminacy require elaboration. One way of doing this is to examine the relationship between problem perception and policy position. If this relationship is controlled for the possible effect of policy image, it appears to be quite strong ($g = -0.61$) as expected (proposition 10). But its direction is confounding. One might have expected that policy-makers perceiving growth problems would advocate further development. This is clearly not the case. Instead, those perceiving growth as a problem take an amenities position, and those perceiving service problems favour further development (hence the negative sign of the coefficient).

We can also shed at least some light on the indeterminate relationship between problem perception and policy image by examining the relationship between policy image and policy position. The relationship is moderately strong ($g = 0.54$) and reveals that those with a residential image take a position favouring amenities, while those with a balanced image favour further development.

Table 9.2: Zero-Order and Partial Relationships Among Components of Policy Map

$g_{PI,PP} = 0.24$	$g_{PP,PoP} = -0.43$	$g_{PI,PoP} = 0.54$
$g_{PI,PP}/PoP = 0.50$	$g_{PP,PoP}/PI = -0.61$	$g_{PI,PoP}/PP = 0.54$
$g_{PI,PP}/PoEn = 0.32$	$g_{PP,PoP}/PoEn = -0.35$	$g_{PI,PoP}/PoEn = 0.54$
$g_{PI,PP}/Urb = 0.04$	$g_{PP,PoP}/Urb = -0.51$	$g_{PI,PoP}/Urb = 0.52$
$g_{PI,PP}/PoEn, Urb = -0.32$	$g_{PP,PoP}/PoEn, Urb = -0.62$	$g_{PI,PoP}/PoEn, Urb = 0.57$
$g_{PI,PP}/PoP, PoEn, Urb = -0.26$	$g_{PP,PoP}/PI, PoEn, Urb = -0.90$	$g_{PI,PoP}/PP, PoEn, Urb = 0.66$

NOTE: PI = Policy image; PP = Problem perception; PoP = Policy position; PoEn = Policy environment; Urb = Urbanization.

If we juxtapose the findings concerning the relationship between problem perception and policy position, on the one hand, and between policy image and policy position, on the other hand, the indeterminacy of the problem perception-image relationship becomes explicable. It appears that policy-makers with a residential image perceive problems of growth because these problems probably jeopardize the residential image of the future that they prefer. They therefore take an amenities position that is congenial to their image of the future. Vice versa, those seeing or preferring a balanced city do not perceive problems of growth as threatening and, seeing service problems, favour further development as their position, presumably because further development will maximize the city's resources needed for the effective provision of services. It would seem, therefore, that policy positions are "doubled-caused" by problem perceptions and policy images. This seems to be a true double-causation relationship and explains, therefore, the weak relationship between problem perceptions and policy images, for this relationship does not need to exist in a model of this kind at all.

However, it would be unduly hasty to accept this interpretation. As both policy images and problem perceptions were assumed to be related to policy environment (propositions 5 and 6), a third-order partial test controlling for policy environment, level of urbanization, and successively for each component of the policy map seemed indicated. Table 9.2 shows the outcome. Not only is the relationship between policy image and problem perceptions further weakened ($g = -0.26$), but the relationships among the policy map's other components are strengthened ($g = -0.90$ and 0.66 respectively). We infer that the major pathway of environmental conditions and ongoing policies move, in fact, through the cognitive screen of problem perceptions, although the effect of policy images on policy positions is also strong. The relationship between policy image and problem perceptions is not a crucial link in the chain of causation.

We shall turn now to the independent variables of the model. We have noted already that levels of urbanization and policy environment are not directly related to policy positions. However, both independent variables, being highly related to each other and interdeterminate (proposition 1), are likely to be stimuli for problem perceptions (propositions 3 and 6). The question of causal ordering the effect of the independent on the intervening variables is hardly at issue because the time order of the variables is unambiguous.

Of interest, therefore, is largely the question of which of the two independent variables contributes more to the variance in problem perceptions and policy images. Table 9.3 presents the zero-order correlation coefficients, the first-order partials (controlling for one of the independent and one of the intervening variables). Some of the consequences of the sequentially introduced controls are noteworthy. In the first place (see Table 9.3A) a fairly strong positive relationship links level of urbanization and problem perceptions and withstands all controls (in support of proposition 2). The more urbanized the environment, i.e., the more

Table 9.3: Zero-Order and Partial Relationships Between Urbanization, Policy Environment, and Components of Policy Map

A	$g_{Urb,PP} = 0.57$	C	$g_{PoEn,PP} = 0.08$
	$g_{Urb,PP}/PoEn = 0.73$		$g_{PoEn,PP}/Urb = -0.32$
	$g_{Urb,PP}/PoEn, PI = 0.64$		$g_{PoEn,PP}/Urb, PI = -0.53$
B	$g_{Urb,PI} = 0.58$	D	$g_{PoEn,PI} = 0.81$
	$g_{Urb,PI}/PoEn = 0.30$		$g_{PoEn,PI}/Urb = 0.75$
	$g_{Urb,PI}/PoEn, PP = 0.10$		$g_{PoEn,PI}/Urb, PP = 0.80$

intense environmental challenges, the more likely will policy-makers perceive problems connected with growth. Second, (see Table 9.3, B), the relationship between urbanization and policy image, weak in the first place, almost vanishes when it is controlled (in support of part of proposition 3). Third, (see Table 9.3, D) the state of the policy environment has a strong effect on the formulation of policy images and withstands successive controls (in support of proposition 6). In other words, the more mature or advanced the policy environment, the more do policy-makers hold a balanced image of the city's future. In entertaining policy goals, it seems, policy-makers do not entertain "far-out" views. Finally (see Table 9.3, C), and this is perhaps the most interesting finding, the relationship between policy environment and problem perceptions, evidently non-existent when uncontrolled, grows increasingly stronger as it is controlled by urbanization and policy image. As suggested in proposition 7, this relationship is likely to vary with the degree of equilibrium in the relationship between environmental challenges and policy environment. The negative coefficients show that the less mature or the less advanced the policy environment, the more are policy-makers likely to perceive problems related to growth.

This result, however, pinpoints a problem that the causal model cannot successfully tackle. We can best state the problem in the form of a syllogism that reflects the data, as follows:

The more urbanized the environment, the more developed is the policy environment ($g = 0.80$).
The more urbanized the environment, the more are problems related to growth perceived ($g = 0.64$).
The more developed the policy environment, the more are problems related to growth perceived.

The data, however, show that the logical conclusion derived from the premises is not empirically viable. In fact, the opposite is true: the less developed the policy environment, the more are problems of growth at policy-makers' focus of attention ($g = -0.53$). It would seem, therefore, that there is a condition present in the relationship between urbanization and policy environment that eludes the causal model. Proposition 7 suggested that this condition may be the degree of equilibrium in the relationship. The equilibrium condition is concealed in the causal model and can only be ascertained by a design that manipulates the data in a different way. As we shall see in the next section, there are a number of cities which are, in fact, in disequilibrium—those that are highly urbanized but whose policy environment is less developed than one should expect from an equilibrium point of view.

Figure 9.5 summarizes all the relationships obtained by partial correlation analysis. It is of the utmost importance to emphasize the tentative nature of the results because "all other things" are probably not equal, and relevant error terms are probably not uncorrelated. Determining causal directions under these conditions is likely to be controversial. While in the present model there is no doubt as to the true independence and priority of the urbanization and policy environment variables, and while direct relationships between them and the dependent variable—policy position—probably would not exist even if additional variables were introduced, the flow of causation through the two intervening variables is not self-evident. For instance, are the effects of urbanization or policy environment on the taking of policy positions mediated more through policy images or problem perceptions? To answer this question, we can compare the predictions that are possible with the actual results that were obtained for the intermediate links of the causal sequence.

If problem perceptions or policy images are truly intervening between the independent and the dependent variables, we should predict that the relationship between the independent variable x and the dependent variable y equals the product of the correlations between each and the intervening variable z. In other words, we predict that $r_{xy} = (r_{xz}) . (r_{zy})$. Table 9.4 presents the calculations.

Comparison of the predicted and actual outcomes shows that, while far from perfect, the fit is excellent for the chain in which urbanization and policy positions are linked by problem perceptions and good for the chain that runs through policy images. The fit is fair for the chain that links policy environment to policy positions through policy images so that we need not reject it. But it is poor for the chain from policy environment to policy positions through problem perceptions. We conclude, therefore, that policy positions are primarily taken in response to the perceptions of problems that stem from environmental challenges, and are secondarily influenced by policy images weakly related to the nature of environmental challenges (urbanization), but strongly to ongoing policies (policy environment). We can reject the assumption that ongoing policies have an effect on policy position through the intervention of problem perceptions.

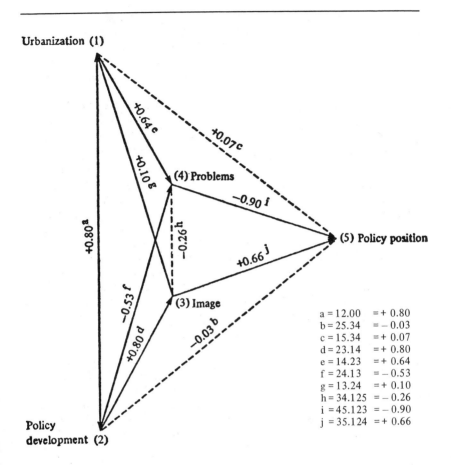

Urbanization (1)

+0.64 e

+0.07 c

+0.10 g

(4) Problems

−0.90 i

+0.80 a

−0.26 h

(5) Policy position

−0.53 f

+0.66 j

(3) Image

+0.80 d

−0.03 b

Policy
development (2)

a = 12.00   = + 0.80
b = 25.34   = − 0.03
c = 15.34   = + 0.07
d = 23.14   = + 0.80
e = 14.23   = + 0.64
f = 24.13   = − 0.53
g = 13.24   = + 0.10
h = 34.125   = − 0.26
i = 45.123   = − 0.90
j = 35.124   = + 0.66

Code for interpreting direction of coefficients:

Image–problem perception:
(+) = Balance-trowth or residential-service
(−) = Balance-service or residential-growth

Image–policy position:
(+) = Balance-development or residential-amenities
(−) = Balance-amenities or residential-development

Problem perception–policy position:
(+) = Growth-development or service-amenities
(−) = Growth-amenities or service-development

Figure 9.5: Causal Model of Policy Process

Table 9.4: Test of Models of Policy Process

	Predicted	Actual	Fit

1   Urbanization x
    ↓0.57
Problem perception z
    ↓0.42
Policy position y
	$r_{xy} = 0.24$	$=0.25$	Excellent

2   Urbanization x
    ↓0.58
Policy image z
    ↓0.54
Policy position y
	$r_{xy} = 0.31$	$=0.25$	Good

3   Policy environment x
    ↓0.08
Problem perception z
    ↓0.42
Policy position y
	$r_{xy} = 0.03$	$=0.29$	Poor

4   Policy environment x
    ↓0.81
Policy image z
    ↓0.54
Policy position y
	$r_{xy} = 0.44$	$=0.29$	Fair

NOTE: Predictions are based on uncontrolled correlations between variables.

A HYPOTHETICAL-LONGITUDINAL DESIGN

Although the causal model, if cautiously interpreted, fits the theoretical model of the policy process quite well and may be accepted as constituting some explanation, it lacks longitudinal depth. Assumptions were made about the time ordering of the relationships between each of the two independent variables and the two intervening variables, but not about any time ordering between the two independent variables alone. They were treated as synchronic, although it was suggested that the reciprocal relationship between them could alternately be one of equilibrium and disequilibrium. But if this assumption is made, it follows that the relationship at any one point in time is only a special case of "alternating asymmetries" at different points in time (see Rosenberg, 1968: 8-9). Is there a design, then, appropriate to treating the data in such a way that inferences can be made from the observed relationship between the independent variables that is synchronic to hypothetical relationships that are diachronic?

One of the drawbacks of the causal model cast in the after-correlational design is that it disguises original relationships in the data among the variables of the model. For instance, as shown in Table 9.1, the relationship between level of urbanization (measured by city size) and the state of the policy environment is so strong from the correlational perspective that we are prone to ignore the cases that deviate from the regression line. In order to pinpoint these deviant cases more sharply, Figure 9.6 presents the cross-tabulation of the data in bivariate form. It shows that we are dealing with two kinds of deviant situations. First, in cell C we note six cases of cities which are "more developed" in spite of limited environmental challenges. These cases are "truly deviant." They cannot be accounted for by the contingent relationship between urbanization and policy environment. In other words, the observed outcome can be attributed simply to policymakers' purposes, preferences, and efforts.

But this is not possible with the seventeen cases in cell B. Although they are statistically deviant, they could be considered truly deviant only if one were to assume that the relationship between urbanization and policy environment is invariably in equilibrium. But this is a quite unrealistic assumption. If we conceive of a reciprocal relationship as a succession of "alternating asymmetries," it is much more realistic to assume that there is likely to be a lag between stimulus and response, that as urbanization proceeds and challenges the policy-maker, an appropriate response is not immediately forthcoming. This reasonable assumption allows us to construct a dynamic model of the policy process. (1) As long as environmental challenges are weak (the city is small; less urbanized), the policy

		Size Dichotomized:	
		Less Urban $<$17,000 N=41	More Urban $>$17,000 N=41
Development dichotomized:			
Retarded, emergent, progressed	Less (N=52)	A 35	B 17
Mature, advanced	More (N=30)	C 6	D 24

Figure 9.6: Policy Environment and Urbanization (size), Variables Dichotomized

environment is "less developed"—challenge and response are, indeed, in equilibrium. (2) As the city grows and environmental challenges become urgent (the city is now large, more urbanized), there is an initial lag in policy response—the policy environment remains "less developed" so that challenge and response are in disequilibrium. (3) As the challenges from the environment are not likely to abate, and as ongoing policies are not appropriate, policy-makers as purposive actors will, sooner or later, adopt positions that re-establish the equilibrium between urbanization and policy environment.

This transformation of the static into a dynamic model of the relationship between environmental conditions and the policy environment suggests that the seventeen cases in cell B cannot be considered truly deviant. They represent situations that can be expected to occur "normally" in the sequence of events that link past and future. In searching for a design appropriate to the analysis of data that are synchronic but which, nonetheless, should be interpreted diachronically, it is clearly advantageous to make a number of assumptions that combine familiar assumptions made for the after-correlational design with assumptions made for the random-panel design, as follows:

(1) As in the panel design, the less urbanized, less developed cities are assumed to be "control groups." Having not been exposed to the stimulus of urbanization, they have no opportunity to respond. The two sets of cities that are more urbanized (whether less or more developed) are assumed to be experimental groups. Both have been exposed to the stimulus of urbanization.

(2) As in the panel design, it is assumed that if both experimental group cities have been observed at an earlier time, they would have looked like the control group cities; or the second experimental group of cities (more urbanized, more developed) would have looked like the first experimental group (more urbanized, less developed) at an earlier time. A corollary assumption is that if it were possible to observe the control group cities at a later time, after more urbanization has taken place, they would in sequence look like the two experimental group cities.

(3) As in the after-correlational design, it is assumed that the two experimental group cities are similar in all respects except for the differences in policy environment; the control group and the first experimental group cities are assumed to be similar in all respects except for the difference in level of urbanization.

(4) As in the after-correlational design, the difference in outcome (policy environment) between the two experimental group cities is assumed to be due to a third factor (or several other factors) which is the test variable—in our case the components of the policy map, and especially the relationships among these components themselves.

Although the set of assumptions made in constructing the design is complex, it merely combines a number of assumptions now routinely made in quasi-experimental designs for the analysis of real-world data. What the design shows is that once latent assumptions are made explicit, comparison of evidently static situations can be used to test hypotheses about change in the real world for which direct data are not available. Although the three sets of cities being compared are actually observed at the same point in historical time, longitudinal assumptions derived from adaptations of the classical experimental design serve to infuse an element of dynamic interpretation into comparative analysis—a recognition of the fact that comparative statics is, indeed, a special case of dynamics.

As Figure 9.7 shows, the design permits three kinds of comparison by way of test variables: (1) Comparison of A_0 and B_{0+1}; (2) comparison of A_0 and C_{0+2}; and (3) comparison of B_{0+1} and C_{0+2}. As we postulate that urbanization is a necessary but not sufficient condition for policy change, the comparison between A_0 and C_{0+2} is not enlightening for, while the two situations can be expected to differ significantly on test variables, we cannot say whether the difference in the policy environment is due to the test factors or change in urbanization. Moreover, both situations are in equilibrium. Of the other two comparisons that are possible, that between A_0 and B_{0+1} serves as a control test. As no change in policy environment is observed, yet there is a change in urbanization, it follows that increased urbanization is not sufficient to bring about a change in policies. The comparison between B_{0+1} and C_{0+2} is the most relevant because it is the appropriate test for rejecting the null hypothesis that a change in the policy environment is not due to purposive action.

The research question asked is why it is that in situation B_{0+1} the policy environment has not changed in spite of a change in the necessary condition for such change, i.e., increased urbanization. Our hypothesis is, of course, that policy change has not taken place because of policy positions taken by policy-makers that impede it.

	$Time_0$	$Time_{0+1}$	$Time_{0+2}$
Control group: Less urban, less developed	A_0	A_{0+1}	A_{0+2}
Experimental group I: More urban, less developed	B_0	B_{0+1}	B_{0+2}
Experimental group II: More urban, more developed	C_0	C_{0+1}	C_{0+2}

Figure 9.7: Quasi-Longitudinal Design of Policy Process

QUASI-LONGITUDINAL ANALYSIS

The data will be analysed within the constraints of the quasi-longitudinal design in three ways: first, as marginal distributions; second, as conjunctive patterns; and third, as correlations.

Marginal Analysis

Table 9.5 shows the marginal distributions of the councils on the three components of the policy map. They will be treated as if the data were genuinely longitudinal. From this perspective, Table 9.5 is highly informative.

First, growth is experienced as a problem by majorities of the councils in all three periods, but it is most felt in $time_{0+1}$ when the "eco-policy system" (as we shall call the relationship between urbanization and policy environment) is in disequilibrium. In the third period, when there has been an appropriate policy response to restore the equilibrium, the urgency of problems connected with growth is somewhat reduced, but these problems continue to concern policy-makers.

Second, in view of the prominence of growth problems at $time_{0+1}$, it is revealing that so few councils (36 per cent) at that time take policy positions in favour of development. In fact, they do not differ at all from $time_0$. Only in the third period, when the eco-policy system is again in equilibrium, do a majority of councils take positions that are presumably capable of coping with the problems of growth. It may be noted that a discrepancy between perceiving growth as a problem and taking prodevelopment positions also occurs in the equilibrium situations at $time_0$ and $time_{0+2}$, but it is considerably less than in the disequilibrium state at $time_{0+1}$ (19 and 22 per cent, respectively, versus 57 per cent). The need for services and not growth-related problems, the earlier causal analysis has shown, makes for policy positions favouring development. But as service problems are not seen as critial at $time_{0+1}$, it becomes understandably why positions preferring amenities are more widely held in this period by comparison with the third period.

Table 9.5: Distribution of Councils on Policy Map Components by States of Eco-Policy System (in percentages)

Components of Policy Map	$Time_0$ Less Urban, Less Developed N=27	$Time_{0+1}$ More Urban, Less Developed N=14	$Time_{0+2}$ More Urban, More Developed N=18
Growth is problem	56	93	78
Development is position	37	36	56
Balance is image	33	50	89
Problem-position differential	19	57	22

Third, as Table 9.5 shows, policy images change dramatically and systematically through time. While at $time_0$, only 33 per cent of the councils envisage a balanced future for their cities, 89 per cent do so at $time_{0+2}$. Of particular interest, however, is the fact that at $time_{0+1}$, when the eco-policy system is in disequilibrium, the councils are exactly split, with half holding an image of a balanced, and another half holding an image of a residential, future. In the disequilibrium situation, councils tend to behave quite randomly. For instance, councils do not unequivocally adopt policy positions in favour of development, in spite of the fact that they are keenly aware of problems connected with growth. These problems, it would seem, are looked upon as nuisances that can be wished away by pursuing amenities policies, and if problems connected with service are not perceived, further development is an option that does not enter the policy map.

Although we cannot prove, with the data at hand, that the policy environment as a response to the challenge of urbanization is facilitated or impeded by the policy map, we can look at the data as if they could be used as tests, provided we read them cautiously. In treating the same data in this hypothetical manner (as if the policy map components were the independent variables and the eco-policy system the dependent variable), we should read Table 9.6 as follows. For instance, while of the councils with a residential image 67 per cent are "found" at $time_0$ (in the less urbanized, less developed state of the eco-policy system), of those holding a balanced image 50 per cent are "found" at $time_{0+2}$ (when the system is more urban, more developed); and so on. If we read the data in this way, it is evident that the image component of the policy map discriminates most strongly among the three states or periods of the eco-policy system ($g = -0.69$), that problem perceptions discriminate moderately ($g = -0.45$), and that policy positions discriminate very little ($g = -0.24$)This is not surprising; as we noted in the causal model (Figure 9.5),

Table 9.6: Distribution of Councils on States of Eco-Policy System by Policy Map Components (in percentages)

| Eco-Policy System | Policy Map Components | | | | | |
| | Image | | Problem | | Position | |
	Balanced N=32	Residential N=27	Growth N=42	Services N=17	Developed N=25	Amenities N=34
$Time_0$	28	67	36	71	40	50
$Time_{0+1}$	22	26	31	5	20	26
$Time_{0+2}$	50	7	33	24	40	24
Total	100	100	100	100	100	100
	$g = -0.69$		$g = -0.45$		$g = -0.24$	

neither urbanization nor policy environment as separate variables have a direct effect on policy positions. As the causal model demonstrated, the perception of problems and policy images are critical intervening variables that link reality to policy positions. But the marginal distributions also suggest that the topography of the policy map may be quite different at different periods or in different states of the eco-policy system. We shall pursue this theme further by looking next at the conjunctive patterns in the policy map that can be observed at different time periods.

Conjunctive Patterns

The data can be looked at in terms of the particular combinations found by the components of the policy map. These conjunctive patterns probably constitute the most "realistic" representations of the policy maps as "wholes." Eight such patterns are possible, and our interest is in the frequency of particular patterns at different points in time or in different states of the eco-policy system. Table 9.7 presents the data.

It appears from Table 9.7, that some conjunctive patterns occur only at $time_0$, that some occur mainly at $time_0$ and $time_{0+1}$, and that some occur in all three periods, although dominantly at $time_{0+2}$. One pattern (BSA) does not occur at all. Councils with a residential image which perceive service problems are exclusively found at $time_0$, regardless of their positions on policy. However, when councils with a residential image experience growth problems, they are not only found at $time_0$ but also at $time_{0+1}$ when the eco-policy system is in disequilibrium. Again, policy positions seem to make little difference. As a balanced image is adopted but problems of growth continue to be experienced, councils are now more often found at $time_{0+1}$ and $time_{0+2}$, but especially in the later period. When a balanced

Table 9.7: Distribution of Councils by Conjunctive Patterns of Policy Map Components in Three States of Eco-Policy System (in percentages)

Conjunctive Patterns		$Time_0$	$Time_{0+1}$	$Time_{0+2}$	Total
RSD	(N=3)	100	0	0	100
RSA	(N=7)	100	0	0	100
RGD	(N=4)	50	25	25	100
RGA	(N=13)	46	46	8	100
BGD	(N=11)	27	27	46	100
BGA	(N=14)	29	21	50	100
BSD	(N=7)	14	29	57	100
BSA	(N=0)	0	0	0	100

NOTE: R = Residential image; S = Service problems; A = Amenities position; B = Balanced image; G = Growth problems; D = Development position.

image is combined with a recognition of service as a problem and a pro-development position is taken, the majority of councils has reached the state of the eco-policy system that is characteristic of the last time period, although some remain in the earlier states as well. While the configuration of patterns is by no means monotonic, it is far from random (yielding a gamma coefficient of 0.56). Above all it gives more detailed insight than do the marginal distributions into why it is that some councils experience disequilibrium in their eco-policy system, i.e., why it is that the policy environment is not in step with the challenges of the urbanizing environment and all that urbanization implies. These are evidently councils in which, because residential images prevail, growth is experienced not as a problem to be handled by appropriate policies, but as a problem that is unwelcome. However, when a balanced image comes to be accepted, policies to cope with growth problems are adopted and, in due time, the eco-policy system regains equilibrium.

Correlation Analysis

It remains to look at the transformation through time of the relationships among the components of the policy map. It is likely that at different times one or the other component is more relevant to the adoption of a particular policy position. Moreover, as the relationships among policy map components are more or less interdependent, it is desirable to observe the flow of the effects of one component on the other. Figure 9.8 presents the models using the phi coefficient.[6]

The diagrams suggest that the relationships among map components not only assume different values at different times, but that the map itself seems to undergo structural change. At time$_0$, when the challenges of urbanization are weak and the policy environment is relatively little developed, councils perceiving growth as a problem tend to entertain a balanced image of their city's future and favour devel-

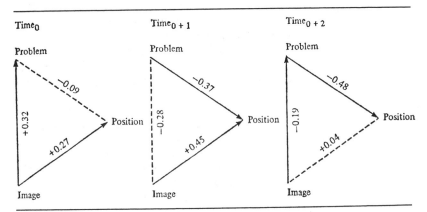

Figure 9.8: Structure of Policy Map in Three States of Eco-Policy System

opment, while councils perceiving service-connected problems tend to hold a residential image and favour amenities as their policy positions (phi = 0.32). The perception of problems is unrelated to policy positions (phi = -0.09). In fact, of course, and whatever the internal structure of the policy map, we know that the policy environment is little developed—ongoing policies, compared with those at later periods, do not particularly stress either development or amenities. Available resources are invested in meeting the minimal service needs of these communities. The policy environment is static and in equilibrium with the urban condition.

At time $_{0+1}$, the challenges of urbanization come to be felt, the structure of the map changes drastically. Councils perceiving problems of growth now tend to hold a residential image (phi = -0.28), a rather anomalous behaviour, and they tend to favour amenities policies. This is, of course, the RGA pattern observed in Table 9.8 that seems to be so characteristic of this period. The anomaly may be due to the effect that policy images seem to have in time $_{0+1}$. Although problems are seen quite realistically, policy images tend to have a fairly strong effect on the policy positions that are taken (phi = 0.45). On the other hand, councils perceiving service problems now have a balanced image. But, more significantly, there is now a linkage between problem perceptions and policy positions. Councils seeing growth problems still favour amenities positions, while councils perceiving service problems advocate further development (phi = -0.37).

An anomalous situation is unlikely to persist. Sooner or later the policy map will be restructured to fit the exigencies of urbanization. Our quasi-longitudinal design permits us to observe how the policy map is restructured. Most notable at time $_{0+2}$ is the fact that the relationship between policy images and policy positions vanishes (phi = 0.04), while the relationship between problem perceptions and policy positions becomes stronger (phi = -0.48). Moreover, the relationship between problem perceptions and images is also almost vanishing (phi = -0.19). The fact that two of the relationships among map components more or less disappear is due, of course, to the emergence of balanced images in council policy maps in this state of the eco-policy system. As we saw in Table 9.5, sixteen of the eighteen councils (89 per cent) entertain an image of balance at time $_{0+2}$. As a result, there is little room for images to discriminate among policy positions or problem perceptions. And, as a further result, it is the perception of problems that now almost alone influences the policy positions that are taken. Councils seeing service-connected problems favour development policies, presumably to mobilize the resources needed to pay for swelling demands for such services in the wake of increased urbanization; while councils experiencing the pangs of growth tend to favour amenities, presumably to offset the unpleasantness of growing urbanization. The policy environment at this time is, not unexpectedly, in congruence with the policy map. By operational definition, it is in an environment in which ongoing policies are geared to both development and amenities policies. In any case, the policy map no longer blocks, as it did at time $_{0+1}$, the taking of positions congenial to the emergence of a policy environment that is in equilibrium with the challenges stemming from heightened urbanization.

If we say that not only the values in the relationships among policy map components change but that the structure of the map itself changes, we mean, of course, that different models define the linkages between the map's points. To determine the adequacy of alternate models, Table 9.8 presents predicted and actual results for the following three models of three-variable relationships (Figure 9.9).

Table 9.8 shows that the dual effect model best characterizes the policy-map structure at time $_0$. Policy images, it seems, have a pervasive effect on the structure of the map, influencing both the perception of problems and the positions that are taken. The fit of prediction and result is only fair, but it is adequate enough to retain the model. A time $_{0+1}$, the effect of the policy image on policy positions is complemented by a relatively independent effect of problem perceptions, as predicted in the dual cause model. In the last period, insofar as policy images are still relevant, their effect is totally mediated through the intervention of problem perceptions. They have no independent effect on policy positions which are strongly determined by problem perceptions. The fit of the intervention model at time $_{0+2}$ is very good.

Although it has been repeatedly pointed out that the data cannot be used to test the validity of the inferences made about the course of policy through historical time, it appears that comparative cross-sectional data can be analysed by way of a post-facto, quasi-longitudinal design, and that this analysis yields a model of policy which is not only plausible, but which is in principle testable in a genuine natural-state experiment if appropriate data are collected at the proper time. We can summarize the model as in Table 9.9.

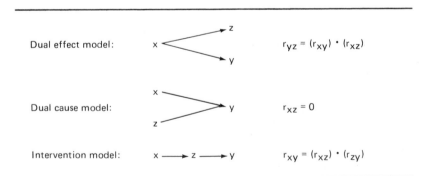

Figure 9.9: Three Models of Three Variable Relationships

Table 9.8: Predicted and Actual Relationships Between Policy Map Components in Alternate Models During Three States of Eco-Policy System

	Predicted	Actual	Fit
Dual Effect Model at Time			
0	0.08	−0.09	Fair
0 + 1	−0.13	−0.37	Poor
0 + 2	−0.00	−0.48	Poor
Dual Cause Model at Time			
0	−0.02	0.32	Poor
0 + 1	−0.17	−0.28	Good
0 + 2	−0.02	−0.19	Fair
Intervention Model at Time			
0	−0.03	0.27	Poor
0 + 1	−0.10	0.45	Poor
0 + 2	0.09	0.04	Very good

Table 9.9: Predictive Model of Policy Development

	Observations on Policy Map at		
	$Time_0$	$Time_{0+1}$	$Time_{0+2}$
Policy image	Residential	Ambivalent	Balanced
Problem perception	Services	Growth	Services and growth
Policy position	Amenities	Amenities	Development and amenities
Predicted eco-policy state	Less urban, less developed	More urban, less developed	More urban, more developed

CONCLUSION

Policy as a response to challenges from the physical and social environment is an emergent property of politics contingent on political behaviour that is, in part, purposive but that, in part, is not unrelated to changing environmental conditions. Because political behaviour is imbued with purposes that are its goals or ends-in-view, policy inferred from behavioural patterns may, at times, be at odds with environmental requirements for appropriate responses. The resultant disequilibrium in the relationship between environment and policy is resolved as the configuration of relevant orientations—what we have termed the policy map—undergoes structural change. This change, it appears, is largely due to cognitive adjustments to environmental pressures. It serves to ease behavioural rigidities in the relationship between policy and environment so that a satisfactory equilibrium can be re-established. Put differently, "what is" and "what ought to be" are dimensions of political behaviour which constitute an interlocking series of events through time. In this moving manifold of events, policy emerges as a resultant of causal and purposive forcings which are themselves interrelated in ways that seem commensurate with ongoing policies—what we have termed the policy environment.

NOTES

1. See, for instance, Dye, 1966: 3-4. The nomenclature of policy research is ambiguous. Output and outcome are sometimes treated as synonyms, sometimes as antonyms, as when outcome is conceived of as a consequence of output. Our own use of policy-related concepts will be explained below.

2. The output of relevant studies is considerable. See especially the work of Thomas R. Dye, Richard I. Hofferbert, Ira Sharkansky, Richard E. Dawson and James A. Robinson, and others. For a critical evaluation, see Jacob and Lipsky, 1968.

3. See, for instance, Hadden and Borgatta, 1965, for evidence of the correlative power of size as an indicator of a city's demographic and ecological diversity and pluralism.

4. For a detailed discussion of how the policy development typology was constructed and cities assigned to a stage or phase of policy development, see Eyestone and Eulau, 1968.

5. This is the design usually employed by the University of Michigan's Center for Political Studies in its famous election studies. A national random sample of respondents is interviewed prior to the election, and the same sample is interviewed after the election. Changes in response to the same question are assumed to be due to events, including the election itself. See Campbell et al., 1960: 16-17.

6. We opt here for the phi measure because it is not subject to a difficulty arising in gamma for a 2-by-2 table, also known as Yule's Q. For, in the case of the latter, if one of the cells vanishes, the measure appears as unity (+1 or −1) in spite of an imperfect relationship between the variables. Phi, like Q, is a symmetric measure and may be interpreted as the Pearson r. Its values are likely to be less than those of Q. Hence the phi and gamma values are not directly comparable.

Chapter 10

POLICY REPRESENTATION
AS AN EMERGENT:
Toward a Situational Analysis

PAUL D. KARPS
HEINZ EULAU

Contemporary research on political representation follows essentially itemistic procedures. Individual actors—representatives and/or represented—serve as the units of analysis, and their attributes or conduct are subjected to modes of treatment establishing relationships that range from being simple bivariate to complex multivariate. With very few exceptions, research has not heeded Pitkin's conception of representation as a property of the political system that may or may not emerge out of the individual-level relationships between legislators and voters (Pitkin, 1967: 224).[1]

Although theorizing about representation involves assertions about the relations that exist, under specified conditions, between the represented and their representatives, empirical research that would treat these linkages in emergent and systemic terms has been elusive because the data needed for this purpose have not been available; or, if available, as in the Miller-Stokes American Representation Study of some twenty years ago, have been treated by the itemistic procedures of correlational analysis.[2]

This chapter explores the feasibility of using the extraordinarily complex data sets of the 1956-1958-1960 Miller-Stokes study for the purpose of validating a dynamic model of representation as an emergent system of policy responsiveness.[3]

Most remarkable about the unusual data sets assembled by Miller and Stokes, used only very partially in their influential article (1963), is that they have never been widely exploited. As Miller (1977) has informed us, "given the fact that the data have been in the public domain as long as they have, I am at a loss to explain why others didn't stumble upon at least some of the nuggets that seem to be so accessible." Yet, it seems to us, there is an explanation. Miller and Stokes had presented their model in terms of behavioral patterns at the individual level of analysis—the representative's conduct on roll calls being the behavior of an object unit (the unit whose behavior is to be explained), while the subject unit (the unit whose behavior is used to explain the conduct of the object unit) was a transformed property of a macrounit—the district or constituency.[4] What Miller and Stokes did was something largely unfamiliar at the time to political scientists mostly schooled to deal *either* with individual-level survey data *or* with aggregate, census-type data. The congressional district as a macrounit was difficult to conceive as a unit useful to explain individual behavior in a multilevel analysis because of prevailing methodological preconceptions stemming from individualistic behavioralism. Moreover, Miller and Stokes themselves as well as those following them and adopting the policy congruence model of representation interpreted it in individualistic terms. There is nothing "wrong" with this usage of the data except that it obscures the multilevel character of the model. Actually, by aggregating citizen preferences at the district level and using the district as a unit of analysis, Miller and Stokes (unwittingly) anticipated in part the procedures that would be required to operationalize Pitkin's systemic conception of representation.

It is impossible to compare or correlate the properties of units whose behavior is observed and measured on different levels of analysis. Because of this constraint, Miller and Stokes had to treat *both* the properties of the subject units (aggregated district preferences) and the properties of the object units (representatives' preferences and roll calls) at the same level. In choosing the microlevel, they had to think of "Congressman with a constituency whose preference is favorable to civil rights," or of "Congressman with a constituency that is opposed to social welfare." These are, for theoretical purposes, cumbersome expressions, but they spell out precisely just what was done to make individual attitudes aggregated at the level of the geographical constituency amenable to correlational treatment: having been transformed from the micro- to the macrolevel as properties of the district, the properties so created were then *assigned* as contextual variables to a microunit—in this case the individual Congressman.

There is, however, an alternative mode of dealing with the same data—at the level of the macrounit, the congressional district. For this purpose, it is again necessary to use cumbersome but theoretically viable expressions such as "District with representative who is favorable to civil rights," or "District with representative who votes against social welfare." Here the procedure involves the assignment of micro- or subunit properties, the attitudes and votes of individual representatives, to the macrounit, and the analysis is conducted at the level of the macrounit. This is the procedure adopted in constructing the representational situations to be examined and validated here, for the objective is to create emergent and systemic contexts within which the behavior of individual representatives can then be observed and explained.

Let us state somewhat differently and more explicitly how our use of the Miller-Stokes data sets differs from the itemistic procedure of correlational analysis. In correlational or path-analytic models, *each item,* such as constituency preference, representative's attitude, or representative's roll call score, is separately linked to every other item, either directly or indirectly by treating some variables as intervening. Each pair of items is expressed in terms of a correlation coefficient or a regression coefficient, and the product of all relationships is expressed by some summary statistic like Multiple R, compound path coefficient or a simultaneous equation. Because in the Miller-Stokes model representation is defined as "congruence" or "agreement" between the individual components of the model or as the "sum" of congruences expressed in a summary statistic, a high coefficient is interpreted as evidence of representation being present and a vanishing coefficient as evidence of representation being absent. As a result, and because the temporal priority of the model components in "real time" is not captured by the summary statistic even if the variables were introduced into a regression in temporal order (rather than in terms of computer estimates of the original correlation coefficients), the itemistic approach cannot construct representational situations as emergent systems in different stages of development.

THE CONCEPT OF
REPRESENTATIONAL SITUATION

That it is feasible and, in fact, necessary to think of representation in terms of "situations" really follows from Pitkin's postulate of representation being an emergent property of the political system. Emergence is a process in time.[5] A process in time is constituted by a series of events that are sequential and may be "objective" (as legislative roll calls are) or "subjective" (as policy preferences are). Our intention here is to deal with representation as a process in time, even if, like a snapshot, it has to be treated as a "moment,"[6] rather than as a timeless institution or political pattern. If the events are differentially linked, they produce different situations. A situation may thus be described in terms of the structural relationships existing between "event-variables" observed at different points in time. A situation, then, is a temporally bounded set of event-variables, with a beginning and an ending to the sequence of events being observed. The duration of a situation may be relatively long or short, depending on the "life expectancy" of the event-variables. Life expectancy of the event-variables, in turn, is largely determined by the periodicity of situations as wholes. In the case of the representational situations to be constructed out of relevant event-variables, the situations are of about two years duration as a function of the biennial periodicity of Congressional elections and congressional terms.[7]

Another way to conceive of a situation, especially in regard to representational situations, is as a "context in transition." It is not fortuitous that, etymologically, situation derives from the Latin noun *situs*, which can be variously translated as "position" or "station," that is, in spatial terms; or as "situation" or "condition," that is, in temporal terms. A situation is thus both a configuration and a sequence of event-variables that constitute a context within which other events occur and

	Event Variables		
Representational Period	Constituency Preferences	Roll Call Votes	Congressman's Preferences
1956-1958 (85th Congress)	1956 ⟶	1957-1958 ⟶	1958
1958-1960 (86th Congress)	1960 ⟵	1959-1960 ⟵	1958

Figure 10.1: Component Event-Variables of Representational Situations

that presumably has an impact on the shape of these events. A "situation politics" is a model of politics in which political acts or events are treated within structurally defined and temporally bounded contexts.

To make this abstract explication of the concept of situation concrete, let us draw on the variables available from the Miller-Stokes American Representation Study. (For description of the measures, see Appendix.) These variables are "events" because they were collected at different points in time—constituency preferences in connection with the 1956, 1958 and 1960 elections; congressional roll call votes for the 85th (1957-1958) and the 86th (1959-1960) terms; and Congressmen's preferences about the time of the 1958 elections. Now, what is significant for the construction of representational situations is the fact that the variables can be temporally ordered and that they are periodicitous in being bounded by the length of the two Congressional terms at the focus of research attention. Figure 10.1 describes the flow of events observed for the two periods under consideration.

The three event-variables to be linked for the purpose of constructing representational situations do not follow each other in the same sequence in the two periods. This is due to the fact that there is only one measurement of Congressmen's preferences.[8] While the situations to be constructed will be composed of generically identical event-variables and will constitute the same configuration, the different, in fact symmetrically reversed, sequencing of the events probably has theoretically significant implications for the interpretation of the representational situations in the two time periods. However, as a situation is conceived as a "moment," as a single configuration of events, the representational situations are directly comparable across the two time periods and not affected in this regard by the temporal order of the variables.

Nevertheless, situations are dynamic properties of the political system in the sense of being contexts in transition. Just as contexts are stable states that impinge on actors and their actions, so situations are creations of actors and the resultants of their actions. Situations, then, are brought about by the interactions and relationships among actors over time. Just what situations "look like" and how they come about depends on the nature of the relationships that occur among the "enacted" events that constitute situations. In the case of the representational situations, the events have certain valences; roll calls, constituents' preferences and representatives' preferences are either in favor of or opposed to given objects of contention (here civil rights, social welfare, foreign involvement) that are given different valuations.

As all three event-variables are positively or negatively valenced, it follows that when brought into structural relationships with each other, the linkages themselves will be positively or negatively valenced. For example, if a constituency favors civil rights and has a representative who also favors it as well as acts on his own and his district's preferences, the emerging representational situation is itself fully valenced in favor of civil rights, or there may be disharmonies in the representational situation as when, for instance, the constituency is opposed to civil rights, yet the representative is favorable. When he then votes with his constituents, the emerging situation will be different from when he votes against them in accord with his own preferences.

Our concern is not with the positively or negatively valenced policy direction of an emergent representational situation but with congruence regardless of valences. In other words, a situation in which all or some of the component event-variables are negatively valenced is treated in the same manner as when all or some of them are positively valenced. This will become more clear as we proceed with the actual construction of the four representational situations. Suffice it to say here that by constructing representational situations in terms of congruence and incongruence among the variables regardless of policy valence, pro or con, we are seeking to establish continuity with Miller and Stokes' causal model of representation rather than celebrate discontinuity. However, while the procedure used by Miller and Stokes was itemistic and analytic in relying on correlational analysis, our procedure is configurational and synthetic.

Finally, something must be said about the "perception of constituency attitudes" variable that served Miller and Stokes as an important intervening component of their model. Miller and Stokes certainly demonstrated the significance of representatives' perceptions of constituencies' policy preferences as an important facet of representation. Our definition of representational situation as a configuration and sequence of valenced policy positions, behavioral or attitudinal, does not require the use of the cognitive component. In fact, rather than treating perceptions of constituency preferences as intervening variables, we are interested in the contextual effect of different representational situations on the accuracy of the perceptions and the relationship between perceptions and other aspects of representation within representational situations.

CONSTRUCTION AND EXPLICATION
OF REPRESENTATIONAL SITUATIONS

Dualistic theories of representation provide for two alternatives in the conduct of the representative: either he can, should or will act in such a way that his legislative conduct reflects the preferences of his constituents; or he can, should or will act in such a way that his legislative behavior corresponds to his own preferences. We can diagram these alternatives as in Figure 10.2, where CP = constituency preference, RP = representative's preference, and RC = roll call votes. The diagrams show that these alternatives constrain the relationship between the constituency's and the representative's own preferences: it has to be negative. But there is nothing in the real world that limits representation at the individual level to these alternatives. First, the representative may act in such a way that his conduct satisfies both his own preferences and those of his constituency. In this case, of course, the representative's preferences and those of his constituency will also be congruent. But, second, there is the possibility of the representative's legislative conduct not being in agreement with either his own or his constituency's preferences; rather, it is in agreement with the preferences of political actors not directly involved in the relationship between himself and his constituency, such as executive or administrative officials, special interest group spokesmen, national (nonlegislative or legislative) party leaders, and so on. In this case, the representative's and the constituency's preferences are also congruent, but so strong is the "external" pressure that neither can prevail in his roll call behavior. These two possibilities can be diagrammed as in Figure 10.3.

Each of the four possibilities presented in Diagrams 1 to 4 (Figures 10.2 and 10.3) constitutes a type of representational situation. By stipulating that the relationship between the representative's and the constituency's preferences is necessarily and invariably constrained by the other two relationships in any given situation, it is also possible to stipulate that each of the four types of situation is dominated by the other two linkages—between the constituency's preference and the representative's roll call conduct, on the one hand, and between the representative's own preferences and his roll call behavior, on the other hand. Emerging from these stipulations is a typology of representational situations, as follows:

(1) Both CP↔RC and RP↔RC are positive (in which case CP↔RP also will be positive): a situation called *pervasive* because it is permeated by congruent relationships throughout (Diagram 3).

(2) Both CP↔RC and RP↔RC are negative (in which case CP↔RP will be positive): a situation called *blocked* because the effect of both constituency and representative's preferences on legislative conduct are obstructed (Diagram 4).

(3) The CP↔RC relationship is positive, but the RP↔RC linkage is negative (in which case the CP↔RP connection is also negative): a situation which is called *dissonant*

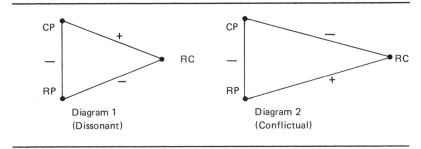

Figure 10.2.

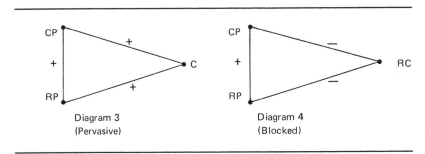

Figure 10.3.

because the representative may feel uncomfortable in having to act counter to his own preferences (Diagram 1).

(4) The CP↔RC relationship is negative, but the RP↔RC bonding is positive (in which case the CP↔RP linkage is negative): a situation called *conflictual* because the representative is in disagreement with his constituency (Diagram 2).

Given the two-dimensionality of the relationships out of which the representational situations emerge, we can chart the typology of representational situations, as in Figure 10.4.

To construct the situations empirically, crude classificatory combinations of the originally scaled variables were thought to yield more robust syntheses than would more refined techniques.[9] For this purpose, the three original scale or index scores were dichotomized at the median of the range, and all cases were placed in an eight-cell crosstabulation matrix made possible by the dichotomization (Figure 10.5). Because our concern is in the congruence of preferences and roll calls regardless of their valences, the eight individual cells of Figure 10.5 can be collapsed into the four paired cells conceptualized in connection with Figure 10.4.

Relationship Between Representative's Preferences and Representative's Legislative Conduct	Relationship Between Constituency Preferences and Representative's Legislative Conduct	
	Congruent	Incongruent
Congruent	Pervasive (Diagram 3)	Conflictual (Diagram 2)
Incongruent	Dissonant (Diagram 1)	Blocked (Diagram 4)

Figure 10.4: Theoretical Construction of Representational Typology

Congressman's Preferences	Constituency Preferences			
	Pro		Con	
Congressman's Roll Calls	Pro	Con	Pro	Con
Pro	Pervasive	Dissonant	Conflictual	Blocked
Con	Blocked	Conflictual	Dissonant	Pervasive

Figure 10.5: Empirical Construction of Representational Typology

This construction of representational situations is not unrelated to the tradition in theorizing about representation that centers in the presumed antinomy of mandate and trusteeship as basic principles of representation. Although the typology developed here rejects the classical antinomy as false and obsolete, it incorporates some potentially valid aspects of each of the opposed principles. On one side of the antinomy is the assumption that the represented alone can know what is in their best interest, that they can state this interest in the form of preferences, and that they can, will and perhaps should express these preferences by way of instructions to their representatives. By implication, only the representative following instructions is responsive to the interests of the represented, and the representative refusing to accept instructions cannot possibly be responsive in this sense. It is the validity of this implication of the mandate theory that is denied by the conception of representation as trusteeship. In this conception, the representative, following his own judgment, decides by himself alone whether the wishes of his constituents are in fact in their best interest. As Burke told his constituents in Bristol, the representative's unbiased opinion, his mature judgment, his enlightened conscience, he ought not to sacrifice to you, to any man, or to any set of men living. These he does not derive from your pleasure; no, nor from the law and the constitution. They are a trust from Providence, for the abuse of which he is deeply answerable.

Two things are to be said briefly about Burke's injunction. First, it does not preclude the representative, even if receiving his trust from Providence, from substituting other preferences—his own, or his party's, or the King's—for the preferences of his constituents in the making of decisions. (Burke was, after all, a very clever fellow; see Eulau, 1967.) And second, the Burkean prescription does not specify to whom, other than Providence, the representative is in fact answerable. The proposition that by following his unbiased opinion and mature judgment the representative acts in the best interest of the represented is no more tenable than the proposition that the represented are alone competent to know their best interest. Logical as the derivations of the mandate and trusteeship theories may be in their own theoretical contexts, they defy the logic of political experience.

In the logic of experience, no representative will ever concede that his or her views, preferences or positions would or could be counter to the "best interest" of the represented. This is the reason why Pitkin's (1967: 209) definition of political representation as "acting in the interest of the represented, in a manner responsive to them," creates many operational problems and produces propositions that are not empirically falsifiable; that is, they are tautological. It may also explain why "policy congruence" between representative and represented has been so attractive as a definition of representation, as if no other considerations need be applied in formulating what representation is about. For is not policy congruence presumptive evidence of responsiveness *regardless* of whether the representative has followed instructions or his own judgment in taking positions on public issues in legislative roll calls? And is this presumptive evidence not all the more persuasive when policy agreement exists not only between the preferences of constituents and the representative's roll call positions but also between both of these and the representative's own declared preferences?

The answer to these questions has to be positive, but it requires the most emphatic proviso that *under no condition must policy congruence of any kind be taken as a direct or even surrogate indicator of responsiveness in the interest of the represented.* All that congruence permits one to assume (and this is a great deal) is that when it occurs, in one or another of the four situational modes of representation developed here (see Figure 10.4), it may affect other behavior that is perhaps "responsive" in one way or another, or that it is indirectly conducive to responsiveness in Pitkin's sense of "acting in the interest of the represented, in a manner responsive to them." Policy congruence, then, as Miller and Stokes (1963: 49) recognized but as their descendants have failed to do, is only "a starting point for a wide range of analyses" and not an end point.

ORDERING THE TYPOLOGY
BY FREQUENCY DISTRIBUTIONS

If expectations are to be entertained about the influence that any one type of representational situation will have on the behavior of representatives as they go about the business of representation other than making legislative decisions, a first step is to specify the ordering potential of the typology. It is not unreasonable to deduce from the construction of the four types in terms of the two critical relationships ($CP \leftrightarrow RC$ and $RP \leftrightarrow RC$) that the pervasive situation is the least stressful in both a sociological and a psychological sense because it is permeated by positive relationships among the three event-variables; and that the blocked situation is the most stressful because it is dominated by negative relationships. There is no difficulty, then, in locating these two situations at opposite ends of the typology.

The other two types emerging from the confluence of the component event-variables are fungible. They cannot be ordered intrinsically because their stress potential, though probably more than that of the pervasive and less than that of the blocked situations, is likely to vary with the salience of the positive and negative relationships for the political actors in one or the other situation. In one situation, the fact that the representative votes against district preferences, while acting on his own, may be the affectively or cognitively most salient aspect; in the other situation, the fact that the representative disregards his own preferences in deference to his constituency's wishes may be most salient.

Ordering the typology is of course also complicated because any pair of situations shares some but not other congruent or incongruent linkages, as follows:

(1) Pervasive and blocked situations share $CP \overset{+}{\leftrightarrow} RP$.

(2) Pervasive and dissonant situations share $CP \overset{+}{\leftrightarrow} RC$.

(3) Pervasive and conflictual situations share $RP \overset{+}{\leftrightarrow} RC$.

(4) Conflictual and blocked situations share $CP \leftrightarrow RC$.

(5) Conflictual and dissonant situations share $CP \leftrightarrow RP$.

(6) Dissonant and blocked situations share $RP \leftrightarrow RC$.

These conditions in the typology prevent it from being fully ordinal.

What our interpretation of the representational situations points to is making the frequency distributions of the cases in each situation the ordering criterion. If the situations are characterized by more or less stress in a social-psychological sense, and if one assumes that there is a tendency for less stressful situations to prevail over more stressful ones, ordering the typology by the frequency distributions of the cases in the four types over the three issue areas in the two time periods is not an unreasonable procedure. Using the criterion of descending proportionality, we order the typology as reported in Table 10.1. Because we assume

Table 10.1: Distributions of Cases in Representational Situations, by Region, Period, Issue Area

	Pervasive	Conflictual	Dissonant	Blocked	Total	N =	No. Errors
North, 1956-1958							
Civil rights	49%	26	17	8	100%	1,470	0
Social welfare	48%	36	10	6	100%	1,591	0
Foreign involvement	27%	41	24	8	100%	1,182	1
North, 1958-1960							
Civil rights	54%	24	22	0	100%	1,657	0
Social welfare	50%	39	9	2	100%	1,700	0
Foreign involvement	40%	34	19	7	100%	1,273	0
South, 1956-1958							
Civil rights	80%	17	3	0	100%	688	0
Social welfare	15%	51	10	24	100%	723	3
Foreign involvement	31%	42	0	27	100%	723	3
South, 1958-1960							
Civil rights	48%	48%	4	0	100%	655	0
Social welfare	64%	20	0	16	100%	612	1
Foreign involvement	39%	39	1	21	100%	655	1
Times ranking first	9 (2 ties)	5 (2 ties)	0	0			
Times ranking second	2	7	0	1			
Times ranking third	1	0	8	3			
Times ranking fourth	0	0	4	8			

that civil rights but also the social welfare issue would be differently experienced and interpreted in North and South, the data are presented by region as well. Table 10.1 reveals:

(1) With some notable exceptions, pervasive situations include pluralities of cases in nine out of twelve opportunities (including two ties); in two opportunities the pervasive situation ranks second. Overall, the pervasive situation stands first in the typology on the basis of the frequency criterion.

(2) By way of contrast, blocked situations include the smallest proportions of cases in eight out of the twelve opportunities, and they are in third place three times. By the frequency criterion, the blocked situation is located at the end of the typology opposite the pervasive situation.

(3) Conflictual situations are in first place (including two ties) in five of the twelve opportunities, and in second place seven times. All conflictual situations include larger proportions of cases than the dissonant and blocked ones. The conflictual situation clearly ranks second in the typology by the frequency criterion.

(4) Dissonant situations are in third place in eight out of the twelve opportunities and in fourth place four times. The dissonant situation is located in the third position of the typology.

By the frequency criterion, then, it is fairly easy to order the representational situations in the typology. As Table 10.1 shows, there are nine "errors" in the 72 pairwise comparisons involving the order of frequencies in the distributions of the cases, or an error ratio of 12 percent. The order of the typology so established by the frequency criterion is informative in regard to the assumption made about the stress potential of each representational situation. If stress avoidance is to be considered evidence of situational rationality, one should indeed expect more cases to fall in the pervasive than in the other situations and the fewest in the blocked situations. By the frequency criterion, then, the conflictual situation would seem to be less stressful than the dissonant. It should be recalled that in the conflictual situation the representative votes against the preferences of his constituents and in line with his own preferences. It appears that the conflictual is more tolerable than the dissonant situation where the representative pleases his constituents but displeases himself.

Nevertheless, one must ask why so many cases do fall into the conflictual type of representational situation. We offer two, more or less speculative, hypotheses. First, a great deal of research has shown that, except on issues of great salience to their districts, legislative representatives are not particularly inclined to take cues from their constituents (see Wahlke, 1971). Moreover, as constituents are generally ill-informed about the particulars of their representatives' legislative conduct, the situation here called conflictual seems to be "easier to live with" social-psychologically than the dissonant and blocked situations.

Second, no assumptions are made about the degree of responsiveness to be found in the different representational situations; though the representative does not appear to be responsive to the policy preferences of his constituency in conflictual situations, he or she may well be responsive in other aspects, such as being the provider of services, obtaining budget allocations for his district, or being his constituency's symbolic agent (see Eulau and Karps, 1977). Because the representative may serve these other needs of his constituency, a conflictual representational situation is not necessarily a politically, and especially electorally, precarious one.

There are some other observations to be made about the order of the representational typology created by the application of the frequency criterion. First, the order is maintained in all four civil rights possibilities, regardless of period and region. Civil rights was, in the middle and late fifties, an issue domain in which the avoidance of stress, or at least its reduction, was crucial for political survival, especially in the South. As Table 10.1 shows, four-fifths of the Southern cases in the first period are in the pervasive situation in which the representative votes both his own and the constituency's preferences. There are other aspects in connection with the civil rights issue which will be dealt with later.

Second, as Table 10.1 also shows, eight out of the nine errors in the frequency distributions occur in the South in connection with the social welfare and foreign involvement issues. What is there in Southern situations, assuming that the data are reliable,[10] that makes for these results, especially if compared with the results in the North? The clue comes from the fact that so comparatively many of the Southern cases are found in the blocked situation where the representative, though sharing his constituents' preferences, votes against both his own and his constituents' predilections (and, presumably, in favor of the preferences of "third" parties). Having paid their dues to the constituency and having followed their own preferences on civil rights,[11] Southern Congressmen in the fifties had considerably more freedom than their Northern colleagues on other issues of relatively less interest to their constituents. This made Southern representatives eminently "available" for the kind of bargaining and compromising that is the spice of legislative politics. Being in harmony with their constituents on the central issue that mattered, having come through the crucible of primary elections, being unopposed or weakly opposed in general elections, and having accumulated seniority in the Congress, some Southern Congressmen were evidently free to vote in ways independent of constituency preferences and counter even to their own predilections. Although the data in Table 10.1 are merely suggestive, one may assume that the cases in blocked situations involved Southern Congressmen who, being Democrats, voted along with their Republican colleagues as part of the conservative coalition in the social welfare area; or who, in the foreign involvement domain, supported other interests. The potential flexibility of Southern Congressmen and their independence from their constituencies in the social welfare and foreign involvement areas are also evident in the high proportion of cases falling into conflictual situations.

VALIDATION THROUGH
TURNOVER ANALYSIS

The ways in which the component event-variables of representational situations are put together may be arbitrary; but the results must not be whimsical. That is, as the typology is intended to be serviceable as a research instrument beyond the time- and place-specific circumstances that yielded the data from which the representational situations are constructed, it must have some universal properties to be valid as a theoretical structure in its own right. As representational situations are configurations that involve sequences of events, stability and change are properties that transcend time and place, and that can serve as explanatory concepts to validate the typology apart from immediately observable data. One may then ask two questions: first, are the representational situations as conceptualized sufficiently stable from one period to another to warrant being considered theoretical and not merely empirical constructs? And second, if there is situational change, is the direction, if not determined by laws of change, at least theoretically plausible? To answer these questions, we proceed in two ways: first, by inspecting the *patterns* and *distributions* that appear in the turnover matrices (Tables 10.2 and

Table 10.2: Stability and Change in Representational Situations, 1956-1958 to 1958-1960, in North, by Issue Area

	Situation 1958-1960					
	Pervasive	Conflictual	Dissonant	Blocked	Total	N=
Civil Rights, 1956-1958						
Pervasive	83%	13	(4)	0	100%	714
Conflictual	40%	60	0	0	100%	380
Dissonant	2%	11	87[a]	0	100%	255
Blocked	11%	36	47	6	100%	121
Social Welfare, 1956-1958						
Pervasive	68%	32	0	0	100%	778
Conflictual	44	41	(15)	0	100%	566
Dissonant	0	64	36	0	100%	156
Blocked	28	(42)	4	26	100%	91
Foreign Involvement, 1956-1958						
Pervasive	55%	45	0	0	100%	319
Conflictual	41%	51	0	(8)	100%	471
Dissonant	(28%)	5	52	(15)	100%	289
Blocked	0%	33	55	12	100%	90

a = exception from hypothesized diagonal pattern.
( ) = turnover errors.

10.3); and second, by pinpointing particular circumstances where the patterns seem to be broken and a "deviant" condition seems to confirm the overall pattern.

The Stability-Change Criterion

All things being equal (issue area, region and unknown externalities), one might expect the pervasive situation to be the most stable and the blocked situation to be the least stable, with degree of stability or change in the conflictual and disso- nant situations difficult to anticipate. As situational transformations are due to changes at the level of the individual person, stressful situations are more likely to turn over than situations of low stress. Therefore, and as our measure of stability or change is the proportion of cases that remain in the same situational category from one period to another or the proportion that move, we would expect least turnover in the pervasive and most in the blocked situations of the first period.

The proportions reported in the main diagonal of Table 10.2 reporting the turnovers in the North, indicate that, with one exception (marked "a"), there is most stability in the pervasive-pervasive and least stability in the blocked-blocked

Table 10.3: Stability and Change in Representational Situations, 1956-1958 to 1958-1960, in South, by Issue Area

| | Situation 1958-1960 | | | | | |
	Pervasive	Conflictual	Dissonant	Blocked	Total	N=
Civil Rights, 1956-1958						
Pervasive	40%	60	0	0	100%	479
Conflictual	75%	25	0	0	100%	118
Dissonant	0%	0	100	0	100%	23
Blocked	0%	0	0	0	0%	0
Social Welfare, 1956-1958						
Pervasive	82%	18	0	0	100%	110
Conflictual	80%	20	0	0	100%	260
Dissonant	33%	67	0	0	100%	70
Blocked	(42%)	0	0	58[b]	100%	172
Foreign Involvement, 1956-1958						
Pervasive	51%	49	0	0	100%	155
Conflictual	41%	59	0	0	100%	304
Dissonant	0%	0	0	0	0%	0
Blocked	(26%)	0	5	69[b]	100%	196

b = calls attention to unusually high %; see text.
( ) = turnover errors.

circumstances, with varying results in the conflictual-conflictual and dissonant-dissonant conditions—the variations being a function of the issue domains. The patterns are somewhat less pronounced in the South (Table 10.3), but vanishing numbers of cases, especially in the dissonant cells, reduce confidence in the reliability of the results. The expected difference between pervasive-pervasive and blocked-blocked circumstances only occurs in two of the turnover tables for the South (in the civil rights and social welfare domains), but there are surprisingly high percentages of cases in the blocked-blocked cells for social welfare and foreign involvement (marked "b"). One is being informed here about an evidently "deviant" condition in the South already foreshadowed by the unusually large proportion of cases in the blocked situations for both periods noted in Table 10.1. The suggestion was made that this was due to the availability of Southern politicians in the game of legislative exchange in the social welfare and foreign involvement domains. The relatively high proportions of cases in the blocked-blocked cells of the turnover matrix of Table 10.3 suggests that, in this respect at least, there was little change; or, to put it differently in the perspective of validation, the blocked situation remained blocked in many cases where one should expect it to remain blocked. Politically speaking, there was simply no incentive in the South for situational change under conditions at the micro level which, in the North, would have been found "impossible," and which, as Table 10.2 shows, were in fact highly unstable. The deviant situation in the South would seem to confirm rather than falsify the proposition that blocked situations are the least stable in the typology.

Just why, in the North, so relatively many dissonant situations remained stable is more of a puzzle, especially in connection with civil rights. The commonsensical interpretation would be this: inasmuch as the representative in a first-period dissonant situation deferred, on the strongly constituency-salient issue of civil rights, to his district, presumably in a pro direction in the North and a con direction in the South, he would have no reason to change his conduct on civil rights roll calls if his constituency did not change. But as other components of the situation can also change, the matter requires more detailed examination at the microlevel of analysis.

In general, to judge by the stability-change criterion, the different situations are quite sensitive to pressures for stability or change in expected ways. Even deviant results would seem to confirm rather than negate the theoretically expected patterns.

The Direction-of-Change Criterion

Turnover analysis to validate the representational typology can be guided by a second criterion which postulates two requirements: first, changes will be away from the more stressful toward the less stressful situations among the available alternatives, or, if in the "false" direction, will be toward the least stressful among the available alternatives; and second, changes will be "one step at a time" or only between adjoining cells in the turnover matrix. If these requirements were met, the following changes would be observed in the movement of cases from one situation in the earlier period to another situation in the later period:

(1) *Blocked* situations will change primarily into dissonant situations and secondarily into conflictual and pervasive, in that order.

(2) *Dissonant* situations will change primarily into conflictual and secondarily into pervasive situations, in that order; if the change is false, it can only be to the blocked situation.

(3) *Conflictual* situations will change into pervasive ones; if in the false direction, more will turn into dissonant than into blocked situations.

(4) *Pervasive* situations can change only in a false direction, but will turn more into conflictual than into dissonant or blocked situations, in that order.

Tables 10.2 and 10.3 show that these requirements are met in most of the test opportunities, both North and South. There are, altogether, 66 opportunities for change (three per four situations in three issue areas in two regions—3x4x3x2=72—but six altogether empty cells in the South, due to absence of cases in two situations, reduce the number to 66 change opportunities). As the parenthesized figures in Tables 10.2 and 10.3 indicate, there are eight errors of direction, i.e., an error ratio of 12%. Four of these errors are for cases moving in the right direction and four for cases moving in a false direction. The figures also show that the proportions of cases moving in the false direction are never more than 15% of all cases in the situation of origin. Of the errors in the right direction, three involve "jumps" of cases from blocked situations of origin.[12]

Turnover analysis lends considerable credence to the validity of the representational typology. There is relative stability of situation where it makes sense to expect most stability, and there is relative change where it makes sense to expect most change. Moreover, the changes are in theoretically viable directions and involve surprisingly few errors. There are deviations from what a perfect turnover structure might look like; but as we are dealing with empirical structures in six existentially very different circumstances involving three different issue areas quite differently experienced in two regions of the country, the results of the turnover analysis are highly supportive of the theoretical validity of the representational typology and of the four representational situations as such.

VALIDATION THROUGH DEPENDENT VARIABLE TEST

If representational situations are at all valid constructs of the political reality in which representatives orient themselves to action, they should be of predictive or explanatory use. In the Miller-Stokes model, Congressmen's ability or success in accurately perceiving their constituents' preferences served as a critical intervening variable mediating between constituency preferences and congressional roll call behavior. Because we do not include perceptual accuracy as a component property of representational situations, we can use it to test the validity of the representational typology.

Other things being equal, one should find more representatives with accurate perceptions in situations in which they vote *with* their constituencies—pervasive and dissonant—than in situations in which they vote *against* constituency preferences—conflictual and blocked. If this were not the case, if representatives were voting in accord with their constituents' preferences "blind," any relationship between constituency preferences and legislative conduct on issues would have to be considered a matter of pure chance. But it can be assumed that the structures emerging from linking various event-variables are not fortuitous occurrences. In particular, if representatives vote their constituencies' preferences, they presumably do so in reasonably accurate knowledge of what these preferences are. This would be especially compelling in the dissonant situation in which the representative votes with the constituency against his own preferences. Being willing to subordinate one's own preferences to those of constituents is something the representative would not want to do unless convinced that he has a fairly accurate understanding of what constituents' preferences really are.

By way of contrast, in conflictual situations in which the representative fails to vote with his constituency, the political stress involved, due to value conflicts, is likely to make for affective ambiguity and, as a result, for cognitive distortion. Misperception, in turn, inadvertently confirms the representative's belief that, by voting his own preferences, he is in fact voting those of his constituency. In this situation, then, inaccurate perceptions serve to make an otherwise politically difficult set of circumstances a viable alternative to the dissonant situation in which accurate perceptions incline the representative to sacrifice his own preferences.

It is difficult to speculate about the effect of blocked situations on the perception of constituency preferences. On the one hand, in these situations the representative presumably takes his cues from external actors or conditions; so it does not matter whether he perceives his constituency's preferences accurately or not. On the other hand, as his own preferences and those of the constituency are identical, yet he votes against both (see Diagram 4, Figure 10.3), he may well know what he is doing and have very accurate perceptions of constituency wishes. It is difficult to say, therefore, whether one should expect many or few representatives with accurate perceptions in the blocked situation. Unfortunately, an answer will remain empirically moot because an insufficient number of cases precludes analysis.

Table 10.4 presents the findings. In addition to whatever situational effects there may be, there are both issue-domain and regional effects. As the marginal totals show, in each region and in each period, the proportions of representatives

Table 10.4: Proportions of Representatives with Accurate Perceptions of Constituency Preferences, by Representational Situations, Issue Areas, Region and Period

	Per- vasive	Con- flictual	Disso- nant	Blocked	Total	Missing Cases
North, 1956-1958						
Civil rights	72% (714)	32% (373)	74% (227)	91% (42)	62% (1356)	114= 7%
Social welfare	59% (687)	25% (475)	15% (156)	54% (91)	43% (1409)	182=11%
Foreign involvement	40% (267)	11% (437)	56% (235)	0% (90)	28% (1029)	153=12%
North, 1958-1960						
Civil rights	63% (858)	39% (329)	69% (316)	0% (0)	59% (1503)	154= 9%
Social welfare	49% (676)	37% (624)	50% (144)	46% (24)	44% (1468)	232=13%
Foreign involvement	24% (443)	21% (384)	37% (204)	34% (94)	26% (1125)	148=13%
South, 1956-1958						
Civil rights	76% (475)	49% (78)	100% (23)	0% (0)	73% (576)	112=16%
Social welfare	18% (110)	0% (299)	0% (79)	0% (94)	4% (573)	150=20%
Foreign involvement	21% (96)	29% (260)	0% (0)	45% (115)	31% (471)	252=34%
South, 1958-1960						
Civil rights	93% (273)	58% (315)	100% (23)	0% (0)	75% (611)	44= 6%
Social welfare	0% (355)	17% (116)	0% (0)	0% (59)	4% (530)	82=13%
Foreign involvement	72% (153)	14% (255)	0% (9)	0% (54)	31% (471)	184=28%
Falsification ratio*	75%	83%	58%			

*Falsification ratio is, in pervasive and dissonant columns, the percentage of cells out of all cells in which proportions of representatives with accurate perceptions are **above** proportions recorded in corresponding cells of total column; in conflictual column, the ratio refers to cells where proportions are **below** proportions in corresponding cells of total column.

with accurate perceptions decreases systematically (with the exception of the welfare area in the South) from the civil rights through the social welfare to the foreign involvement areas. This result is what one would expect from knowledge about the salience of the three issue areas during the two periods and, as a bonus, confirms the validity of the accuracy measure (which is also confirmed by the ascending proportion of "missing cases" as one moves from civil rights to foreign involvement). The regional effect is most noticeable in the civil rights area where more Southern than Northern Congressmen have accurate perceptions, and in the social welfare area where Southern Congressmen, in contrast to their Northern colleagues, seem extraordinarily inept (in both periods) in appraising their constituents' preferences.[13] Finally, in the foreign involvement domain (where accuracy in perceptions is probably most difficult to come by), the proportions of Congressmen with accurate cognitions are strikingly similar in North and South.

What of the effect of the representational situations? Leaving out the blocked situations because of the small numerical bases for percentaging, the data generally confirm the hypotheses. In situations in which the representative votes with his constituents, the pervasive and dissonant, there are more accurate perceptions (see cells with double underlining in Table 10.4) than in conflictual situations where comparatively fewer accurate perceptions are found (see cells with single underlining). There is a slight tendency for the dissonant situations to produce more accurate perceptions than do the pervasive situations, as was anticipated. Of eleven possible comparisons, 63 percent show more representatives with accurate perceptions in the dissonant than in the pervasive situations, but the differences are often very small. However, the pervasive situations, with a falsification ratio (see Table 10.4 for explanation of ratio) of 75 percent, are evidently more conducive to accuracy in perceptions than the dissonant situations with a falsification ratio of only 58 percent. (But the latter ratio may not be fully reliable because of data limitations in the Southern sample.)

An additional test is possible by examining the relationship between representational situations and perceptual accuracy under conditions of stability and change. If our original hypothesis is correct, the proportions of accurate perceptions should remain relatively larger in stable pervasive and dissonant than in stable conflictual situations, while they might decline in changed circumstances. To examine this proposition, we use a turnover table for the representational situations in the North (but omit Northern blocked and all Southern data because of possible unreliability). As the cells in the main diagonal of Table 10.5 show, stable pervasive and dissonant situations continue to include more Congressmen with accurate perceptions than do the stable conflictual situations. But the table shows another interesting and serendipitous result. As representatives find themselves in circumstances where 1956-1958 pervasive situations have changed into conflictual ones in 1958-1960, more of them have accurate perceptions than those who have remained in stable conflictual situations; the proportional numbers of the latter remain about the same as they had been in the earlier period. The proportions

Table 10.5: Proportions of Congressmen in Stable and Changed
Representative Circumstances with Accurate Perceptions of
Constituency Preferences in Three Issue Areas, North

| | Situation 1958-1960 | | |
	Pervasive	Conflictual	Dissonant
Civil Rights, 1956-1958			
Pervasive	79% (588)	50% (96)[a]	0% (30)
Conflictual	31% (144)	33% (229)	—
Dissonant	0% (4)	— —	75% (223)
Social Welfare, 1956-1958			
Pervasive	59% (436)	59% (251)[a]	— —
Conflictual	33% (174)	20% (218)	24% (83)
Dissonant	— —	0% (99)	42% (57)
Foreign Involvement, 1956-1958			
Pervasive	25% (123)	52% (144)[a]	— —
Conflictual	14% (185)	12% (200)	— —
Dissonant	31% (82)	— —	68% (110)

of those with accurate perceptions whose situations changed from pervasive to
conflictual are considerably higher for all three issue areas, as follows:

| | *Accurate Perceivers in Conflictual Situations* | | |
	1956-1958	*1958-1960 Stables*	*1958-1960 Changers*
Civil rights	32%	33%	50%
Social welfare	25%	20%	59%
Foreign involvement	11%	12%	52%

Overall, then, the dependent variable test shows the representational typology
to have considerable predictive and explanatory potential in both synchronic and
diachronic treatment. It seems to measure with reasonable validity and reliability
outcomes of behavior at the microlevel in at least three of the four representational
situations. If the test has not validated the blocked situation, it is because of the
instability and possible unreliability of the data in this category of the representational typology.

APPENDIX

THE MILLER-STOKES
AMERICAN REPRESENTATION STUDY MEASURES

The dependent variables of the Miller-Stokes model were the roll call votes of Congressmen during the 85th (1957-1958) Congress in three issue areas designated as "civil rights," "social welfare," and "foreign involvement." These roll calls—six on civil rights issues, eight on social welfare issues, and ten on foreign involvement issues—were Guttman-scaled, with very high reproducibility coefficients. Similar scales of roll calls in the same three issue areas are available for the 86th (1959-1960) Congress. (For a description of the scale components and scale procedures, see ICPR: 1971: 619-624.)

The independent variables of the Miller-Stokes model were the attitudes on matters of civil rights, social welfare and foreign involvement of citizens obtained from interviews with a national probability sample conducted in connection with the 1958 congressional elections. Responses to particular questions were initially combined into indices, and scores were assigned to the individual respondents in the sample. However, in order to correlate the political attitudes of the respondents, in each congressional district where they were interviewed, with the attitudes and roll call votes of their respective Congressmen, the individual-level index scores were transformed into district attitude scores by way of aggregation—the district measure being the arithmetic mean of the individual-level scores. Similar district-level measures of citizen attitudes in the three issue areas are also available for the 1956 and 1960 national elections. Indeed, the bulk of the respondents for the three elections constitute a panel, and it is the panel data that are used in the present analysis. (For a full description of the mass-public attitudes and the procedures used in constructing the indices and aggregating the individual-level data, see ICPR, 1971: inserted note 8, dated January 21, 1972.)[14]

The intervening variables in the congruence model were, first, the Congressmen's own attitudes in the three issue areas of civil rights, social welfare and foreign involvement; and second, their perceptions of their constituents' attitudes in the same three areas. The attitude measures were derived from relevant items in the interviews with Congressmen and congressional candidates and constituted Guttman-type scales. (For a description of the scales, see ICPR, 1971: 611.) Congressmen's perceptions of constituent attitudes were elicited by the following question which was asked concerning each of the three issue areas: "How do the people in your district feel about . . . ? Would you say that: more of them are in favor; they are evenly divided or not much opinion on this in the district; or more of them oppose it." For detailed wording of the questions, see ICPR, 1971: 173-174).

In order to develop our own measure of perceptual accuracy, we crosstabulate Congressmen's perceptions of district opinions with the actual (aggregated) district attitudes in each of the three issue domains. As the perception variable was measured on a three-point scale, we also trichotomize the originally continuous district attitude scores by partitioning the range of the scores so that the pro, neutral and con categories of the trichotomized measure stand in a 2:1:2 relationship. Crosstabulation of the two trichotomized measures yields a nine-cell table. Cases falling into the main diagonal (pro-pro, neutral-neutral, con-con), are characterized as being "accurate"; all other combinations as "inaccurate."

To correspond to the two time periods, 1956-1958 and 1958-1960, and to be consistent with the arrangement of the Miller-Stokes data into preelection files and postelection files, we construct the accuracy measure for both 85th Congress incumbents and those elected to the 86th Congress (15% of the Congressmen in the "new" 86th Congress were themselves new members). In both cases 1958 constituency preferences serve as bases for determining the accuracy of representatives' perceptions. The 1958 (rather than 1956 or 1960) district preferences are used because they are temporally most proximate to representatives' perceptions and, therefore, probably provide the most reliable measure of accuracy.

NOTES

1. For critical treatment of the prevailing research traditions, see Eulau and Karps, 1977. Although many studies often cite Pitkin's work in a footnote, they do not follow her instructions. Neither do they adopt her definition of representation as responsiveness, nor do they raise analysis to the systemic level. Exceptions are Prewitt and Eulau (1969); Eulau and Prewitt (1973); Jennings and Zeigler (1971).

2. The main reason for the poverty of appropriate data in the study of representation has been the cost of data collection. Although Wahlke et al. (1962) had proposed interviewing both constituents and lobbyists as "significant others" in an original research design, they had to be satisfied with interviewing legislators alone because of the cost factor (but, perhaps, also because the sponsoring Political Behavior Committee of the Social Science Research Council did not, at the time—1955-1956—appreciate the importance of the proposal to interview representatives as well as represented). The Miller-Stokes 1958 data sets are therefore unique.

3. The data used in this research have been made available through the Inter-University Consortium for Political and Social Research.

4. For an introduction to the language of multilevel analysis, see Eulau, 1969; on data transformation across levels of observation and analysis, see Eulau, 1977.

5. Connoisseurs of social science terminology (which is not unrelated to one's thought processes and products) are probably aware of our indebtedness, in adopting the concepts of "event" and "emergence" as well as "process," to the political theories of Harold D. Lasswell. See, especially, Lasswell, 1948; and Lasswell and Kaplan, 1950: ix-xxiv; see also Eulau, 1968; and Marvick, ed. 1977.

6. Although "moment" is usually (and correctly) defined as a point or instant in time, it should be noted that it derives etymologically from the Latin verb *movere*, to move, which is at the base of the noun, *momentum*, movement. Just what a moment "is" depends, therefore, on the total time perspective in which it is calibrated. It may refer to a "stage" in historical development, that is, a relatively protracted period. The point to be made is that "moment" does not necessarily have the static implications that it seems to have in ordinary usage. It is an event in a series of moving events.

7. The concept of "situation" has not been given serious attention in political science or social science generally. The formulation presented here is indebted to a number of writers who, over the years, have influenced our thinking. But see, especially, Parsons, 1951; Volkart, ed., 1951.

8. It will be noted that we are not using 1958 constituency preferences in constructing the representational situations. We do not do so for two reasons: first, because the timing of the 1958 constituency preferences and representatives' preferences is coincidental—data concerning them being collected almost simultaneously; and second, because it would be impossible to properly sequence the roll calls, that is, it would make no sense to use the 1957-1958 roll calls which preceded the expression of preferences, but it would be difficult to use the 1958 constituency and representatives' preferences as not sequentially linked variables. Yet, our concept of situation requires clear sequencing of all the component event-variables.

9. There is another important reason for crude classification. Although the various measures of constituent preferences, Congressmen's preferences and their roll call scores in the three issue domains sought to achieve *conceptual* equivalence, there is much differentiation in the *empirical* data to caution against the impression that all three scales in a given issue area or across issue areas are identically calibrated. If one ignores this limitation in the data, one may place undue confidence into the more refined measures originally created. The procedure, though crude and yielding crude results, prevents one from misconceiving the nature of the original instruments and what they measure in reality.

10. We insert here this cautionary note because it should not be forgotten that we are dealing with weighted data. While the percentages for the Southern cases in Table 10.1 are based here on the full complement of the weighted data, it is evident that especially in some of the dissonant and blocked situations the percentages are quite small and, "in reality," stand for only one or two districts-cum-representative. In later tables the dissonant and blocked situations yield many "missing data" cells despite the fact that the weighted cases for the South are about 600. But it takes only one or two nonresponses to an interview question in the real world to drop the cases out of the cells of a crosstabulation.

11. Internal analysis of the data shows that in both the 85th and the 86th Congresses fully 100% of the Southern Congressmen in the weighted sample (N=655) voted *against* civil

rights. Of the 80% *Southern* pervasive-situation civil rights cases in 1957-1958, all (100%) were *against* civil rights (con-con-con). By way of contrast, of the 49% *Northern* pervasive-situation civil rights cases in the same period, 94% were *for* civil rights (pro-pro-pro) and only 6% were against (con-con-con). The fact of course is that, in the fifties, civil rights was a much more salient, constituency-based issue in the South than in the North.

12. One can express the error ratio obtained for the six turnover tables also in terms of the actual changes at the level of each unique case. There were, altogether, 2,771 changes over all issue areas in both regions; of these 437, or 15%, were in directions not meeting the stipulated requirements for change.

13. In fact, the proportions here are so much "out of line" that one must suspect the reliability of the data more than the perceptual ineptness of Southern Congressmen; our apologies in advance.

14. The aggregation of individual-level index scores at the district level has been criticized because, in the case of some districts, the responses of at best a handful of interviewees were used to obtain the district measure. As a result, one can entertain reservations about the reliability of the measures thus obtained. Miller and Stokes have defended the use of the aggregated data in terms of the weighting of the sample of districts into which the individual respondents were distributed (see Miller and Stokes, 1963: 46-47, note 3; see also ICPR, 1971: memorandum of January 21, 1972, p. 11). We are not in a position to assess the validity and reliability of the Miller-Stokes weighting procedures, but we are most cautious when, in using the weighted data, we encounter cells where the size of N strikes us as being so small as to make the distributions highly labile, even if we obtain acceptable confidence levels.

PART III.
Continuities

INTRODUCTORY NOTE

The pressures of teaching and research are great. Few scholars can find the time or make the effort to orient themselves in the ever-changing literary and investigative context of their work. The standard Ph.D. dissertation usually includes a "review of the literature," but much of active research proceeds without reference to the literature as a whole. A great deal of this literature may be obsolete, but the epistemological status of the social sciences is of a kind that warns against dogmatic foreclosure of what in past literature or research may or may not be salient.

This rather prudent principle is, in our own case, something of a passion. Years ago, when we readied ourselves for the research reported in *The Legislative System,* we undertook an exhaustive survey of the literature whose by-product was a comprehensive "reader" in theory and research (Wahlke and Eulau, 1959). A few years later, Wahlke (1962) prepared a critical essay on the then still sparse number of "behavioral analyses of representative bodies." The rapidity of research expansion in the early sixties is evident if one compares that essay with the extended review of the literature—for the period from 1961 to 1964 alone—prepared by Eulau and Hinckley (1966). Research on legislatures abroad had also grown enough by the late sixties for a review essay on "comparative legislative behavior" to be published by Patterson (1968b). Keeping up with the flow of the research literature in the study of legislatures and related topics is an almost impossible task if one wants to get on with research; yet, it is a task which must be continued, for without it one cannot appraise the continuities that promote research development and make for new lines of inquiry, and one cannot be aware of those discontinuities that make for proliferation and redundancy.

On the whole, as Wahlke shows in a recent reappraisal (Chapter 11), studies in the legislative field have been more cumulative than not, with continuities clearly outdistancing discontinuities. As he points out, "the knowledge we have is exceedingly incremental. What we know has grown by accretion of numerous bits and pieces; we can point to no striking 'breakthroughs' or major discoveries that increased or changed our understanding in dramatic or revolutionary fashion. Although there are obvious differences in quality and value among the many studies extant, few represent critical turning points or major landmarks." These lines must not be misunderstood. They are not meant to be critical. On the contrary, they suggest that, in the legislative field, there has been no breakdown of normal science as envisaged by those for whom Kuhn's (1962) "scientific revolution" has become gospel because they would welcome a breakdown. But this is also not to say that there are no difficulties or anomalies in the several prevailing research traditions. Some of these problems were noted especially in Chapters 2, 3 and 4, as well as elsewhere in previous chapters. However, resolution of these difficulties or anomalies does not require the grandiose "paradigm change" that critics of empirical research in political science seem to cherish.

This is so for an obvious reason: if research meets the standards of what Landau (1972) calls "due process of inquiry"—the criteria on which reasonable persons can agree as appropriate in scientific investigation—then the theoretical imagination can absorb and use accumulated and relevant knowledge in assessing the validity of alternative models of political behavior, processes and institutions. Dissatisfaction with prevalent research tendencies does not require colossal shifts in paradigms. Even Marxian economics is not a replacement of classical economics but an alternative model of the economic system. The nature of the social sciences is simply such that radical change in paradigms is extremely rare. Perhaps the replacement of the Aristotelian teleological approach by the modern scientific method was a paradigm change, but Aristotelianism still survives in the Catholic tradition of social thought. Perhaps the appearance of probabilistic thinking in the late eighteenth century had a paradigmatic effect on the social sciences. But, in general, what one encounters in the social sciences are competing models of some aspect of human behavior or action that, if research is reasonably intersubjective and disinterested, will draw on the same data bases for proof or disproof of derivative hypotheses.

In "Recent Research on Congress in a Democratic Perspective" (Chapter 12), Eulau and Abramowitz draw on the rich literature and research concerning the Congress of the United States to appraise their utility and relevance in the perspective of three competing models of democracy—the participatory, the competitive, and the representational. They find that research on Congress has been largely isolated from contemporary thinking about democracy (just as the theorists of democracy largely tend to ignore the empirical research on democratic processes and institutions). Of course, certain aspects of one or another model are often implicit in the research. In fact, Eulau and Abramowitz argue that the tensions among the three models, which they interpret as three different modes of aggregating individual into collective choices, go a long way in explaining why the Congress is as complex an institution as it is. Even if one mode of democratic aggregation is at times being submerged by another in a given subinstitutional setting, process or situation, each has the potential of being mobilized with changing conditions external to the legislative institution itself. The review shows that the best of knowledge about the Congress and its committees can be fruitfully organized and employed to affirm or rebut alternative conceptions of democracy that are more or less germane to the American legislative arena at the national level.

A very real weakness of research on Congress does not lie in theoretical limitations, however, but in its isolation from research on other domestic legislative bodies at the state and local level as well as on parliamentary institutions abroad. There is little intellectual traffic between students of Congress and the much more "comparatively oriented" scholars who work in the subnational and cross-national arenas. It is as if the American Congress were so unique an institution that comparing it with other legislative assemblies could yield only spurious results. For instance, in the only chapter on "Legislatures," prepared for the eight-volume *Handbook of Political Science* by one of its editors, himself an eminent student of Congress (Polsby, 1975), the bibliography of some 184 references include 70 references to Congress, or 34%; 34 references to foreign governments though not necessarily legislatures, or 18%; 25 references to England or Parliament, or 14%; another 25 references, or 14%, to what can be classified as comparative textbooks, essays or surveys; and 22 references, or 12%, best called "miscellaneous." Only five of the references concern American state legislatures and a mere three deal with American local councils, altogether 4 percent. Despite an effort to be comparative, this otherwise delightful essay is paradoxically provincial. It ignores significant works on subnational American legislative behavior and institutions as well as important works on Western and non-Western legislatures published abroad.

Some of the foreign literature is given its due in Patterson and Wahlke's "Trends and Prospects in Legislative Behavior Research" (Chapter 13). Although by no means exhaustive, the chapter is suggestive of the possibilities for comparative legislative research if scholars only pay attention to each other's work. There was a time, not too long ago, when it was believed that comparative analysis could proceed only *after* something called "structural-functional" theorizing had legitimated just what is to be compared. The resulting abstractions did not promote the comparative enterprise and, it seems, have been abandoned in favor of greater sensitivity to level-of-analysis problems and, as Patternson and Wahlke make clear, to such system properties as settings, contexts, capacity, consequences, and diffusion patterns. Their essay suggests that there are concepts of the middle range that can be applied more universally than had been thought possible even ten years ago, the proof not being a matter of structural-functional logic but of experience in actually operationalizing these concepts in cross-national empirical research. They note important work along role-analytic lines being done in several European democratic nations. A more comprehensive review would include studies being done in Africa, Asia and Latin American as well—at least in those countries where the rudiments of democracy are present and legislatures have some chance to exist.

The comparative treatment of legislative behavior, processes and institutions reminds us that, counter to political mythology, democracy as a form of governance does not emanate from the wrath of "the people" in revolt against despotism and tyranny, but that it is the outcome of evolutionary developments covering many centuries. In these developments, beginning in the Middle Ages in England, France and Spain, representational institutions have played a critical part. Their continuing study around the world is much needed to understand democracy and to give substance to democratic theories which are to be something more than ideological statements. We therefore conclude as we began almost twenty years ago when we wrote: "Of all political institutions, none is more vital to the process of linking governors and governed in relationships of authority, responsibility, and legitimacy, than the modern legislature. Without some understanding of its character and functioning one can have only a very partial understanding of the process of government and its place in society" (Wahlke and Eulau, 1959: 3).

Chapter 11

CONTEMPORARY PERSPECTIVES ON LEGISLATURES

JOHN C. WAHLKE

It is often said that the development of legislative study, as of political science generally, spans three "stages"—"institutional," "process-oriented," and "behavioral" (the "postbehavioral" revolution heralded by David Easton (1969) so far appears to have had little influence on legislative study). The statement is inaccurate as literal intellectual history, and its typology sometimes genrates as much polemical heat among political scientists as its sheds intellectual light on political phenomena. But it can help to highlight some of the differences among the various (but not necessarily contradictory or incompatible) legislative studies now available.

The most important points of difference commonly associated with the classical trichotomy include: (1) the principal concern of the research (i.e., the set of broad questions that particular research efforts are designed to answer); (2) the key political concepts and variables used to orient and formulate the questions for research; epistemological premises, including (3) the kinds of questions asked and (4) the kinds of evidence and reasoning processes used for accepting or rejecting the answers found; and (5) research design and methods (i.e., primarily broad research strategies and intellectual conceptions of the research process, rather than just specific tactics and techniques for collecting and manipulating data). Table 11.1 presents a very gross and simplistic picture of the different connotations most commonly suggested by the three constituent terms of the schema in question.[1]

As the table suggests, legislative study as a distinctive field of attention in American political science, where it first appeared as such, was for a time characteristically preoccupied with rather formalistic depiction and evaluation of the structure and function of legislative bodies. Attention was given mostly to enumerating such details as the number of chambers, the powers and duties of presiding officers, committee chairman, and other legislative officials, and methods of choosing them; the authority and "functions" of the legislature, in the sense of

Table 11.1: Some Frequent Connotations of a Familiar Typology of Legislative Research

Types of Legislative Studies	Main Object of Interest	Key Political Concepts	Main Kinds of Questions	Typical Modes of Reasoning, Kinds of Evidence	Characteristic Conceptions of Research
"Institutional studies"	Legislative Institution: Structure Function	Institution(?) Legislation	Descriptive Classificatory Evaluative, prescriptive	"Formal": Legal Logical (Definitional) Historical Subjective insight, judgment	Case study: U.S. Congress; British Parliament Literature, Lore Documents
"Process-oriented studies"	Legislative Process: Decision-making Functioning	Power, Influence Representation (?)	Factual ("realistic description") Explanatory (?)	Inductive Empirical	Case study: U.S., British Parliament Documents Aggregative Data (roll calls, biographies)
"Behavioral studies"	Legislators: Attitudes Behavior Legislative Decision	Representation Legislation Political System (Input, Output, etc.) (?)	Factual: Descriptive Relational Explanatory Theoretical (?)	Logico-empirical: Inductive and/or Deductive Empirical	Case study: U.S., other nations Cross-sectional, Comparative Study Aggregative data (roll calls, biographies) Survey data Electoral data

its legally assigned powers and duties; and constitutionally prescribed methods of choosing its members. It was usually taken for granted that the principal mission of a subject body was "legislation," which was taken to mean the formal business of proposing, debating, amending, resolving, and enacting. Hence legislative procedures were often minutely and painstakingly examined. "Representation" referred mainly to the formal provisions for choosing legislators—for example, the time and manner of electing them, the legal requirements and qualifications for election to office, the franchise governing such elections, and perhaps extrapolation from these data to such formal properties of the system of representation as the numerical ratio between enfranchised electors and legislators.

To study a legislature not uncommonly meant to describe and classify such formal properties of it, to judge the arrangment as more or less good or bad in the light of an a priori conception of the "good" or "right" way to organize such bodies, and perhaps to prescribe some changes in the relevant constitutional and legal provisions that might bring formal structure more into line with presumed proper or ideal structure. "Data" consisted mainly of constitutional and statutory documents, legislative records pertaining to structural and procedural characteristics (by-law, rules of procedure, etc.), and historical antecedents of these. The method of "proof" used to arrive at prescriptive and evaluative propositions was generally logical deduction from the a priori principles and logical extrapolation from the structure and functions formally described. In any case, there was characteristically scant systematic observation of day-to-day activities of legislators or voters, of the contents of bills, resolutions, or laws processed by them, or of any empirical, observable material other than the documents on which institutional description was mainly based.

Although some scholars did try to set down generic accounts of legislatures in approximately the terms just described, the more frequent form of legislative study was straightforward description/prescription with respect to a particular system, usually the Congress of the United States or the British Parliament (see Luce, 1924; Galloway, 1953; Young, 1943; Jennings, 1936, 1957). Besides the formal documentary data that provided the main grist for such studies, researchers commonly surveyed and summarized the assorted literature and lore of their predecessors. Their principal analytic tool was the subjective judgment, insight, and imagination of the individual analyst, usually applied in unsystematic and unreplicatable but nonetheless intelligent and sometimes brilliant fashion.

One must by no means infer from the foregoing sketch that all or more institutional studies of legislatures were false starts on wrong roads, of no value then or later. On the contrary, more often than not they were comprehensive, thorough, and highly informative. They provided not only interesting and useful information about the formal characteristics of specific legislative bodies, but also a sense of their historical development and of institutional continuity and stability, as well. Equally important, although not recognized for some time, they contained an implicit conception of the legislative institutional structure as a set of effective, channeling constraints that shape and pattern the behavior of legislators in important ways. Institutionally oriented scholars were generally interested not in the activity of legislators in the legislative arena, but in the shape and character of the arena itself. They therefore tended to ignore the behavioral implications of their descriptions of institutional structure. Indeed, they neglected what seems to be an obvious empirical question: to what extent and in what way do formal institutional properties and rules influence the behavior of role incumbents of the institutional group? If anything, they took it for granted that official behavior naturally or automatically conforms to formal rule and abstract description. Later reflection and study suggest that the "structure" of a legislature officially inheres not in the verbal abstractions of analysts or in the formal rules enacted to govern the behavior of the group's members, but in the dependably repetitive patterns of behavior displayed by almost every legislator involved. Apparently, these patterns are more or less responsive in part to the formal prescriptions, although they manifest also common informal rules and understandings about what constitutes appropriate institutional behavior.

Although the institutional outlook was chronologically prior and was clearly predominant throughout almost a half-century of legislative research, there is less chronological difference and more substantive overlap among studies representing the other two approaches. Process-oriented studies began to appear somewhat earlier and were the prevailing kind in the 1940s and 1950s. But behavioral studies emerged almost as early, even though their spread was not quite so rapid. Similarly, athough studies best characterized as behavioral are probably more numerous today than process-oriented ones, it would be wrong to suggest that the latter are now being superseded altogether.

In general, process-oriented researchers reverse the emphasis and concerns of institutionalists. Where the latter typically preoccupied themselves with institutional structure—the framework within which legislative action takes place—and were little interested in that action as such, process-oriented researchers take the institutional character of the legislature for granted and concentrate on the activity transpiring within its framework. Where "legislation" for institutionalists refers mainly to the presumed generic function of legislatures, it is for process-oriented researchers the central object of attention. Their aim is, in general, to discover what legislation emerges as the product of legislative activity, and how. Where institutionalists detailed the mechanics of legislative procedures and proceedings, succeeding researchers visualized a sequence of activities, above all decisional activities, constituting a legislative *process.* That process, moreover, is commonly described in terms of which protagonists win and which lose particular contests, and that, in turn, is taken to be a measure of the participants' relative power or influence (also key concepts in this genre of research). Not uncommonly, process-oriented investigators use "representation" of the public and its elements to refer to the relative power and influence over legislative decisions of those outside the law-making body.

"Process-oriented" research is generally less interested in the final product of the legislative process, except perhaps as that serves to index the overall power and influence of participants, than in the sequence of decisions and the application and results of power at various points and stages along the way. It usually seeks above all to observe and describe accurately what transpires throughout the process. The fruits of research, therefore, tend to be detailed and realistic accounts of events and activities, rather than generalizations or theoretical abstractions.

Given this essentially descriptive goal, it is only natural that the prevailing type of process-oriented research design is the case study. Some studies offer overall pictures of the legislative process in particular legislative systems; others follow one decisional strand or a related bundle of them, as particular instances of the working of the legislative process (see, f.i., McKean, 1938; Zeller, 1937; Gross, 1953; Schattschneider, 1935; Bailey and Samuel, (1952). Surprisingly few, however, extend their view beyond the supposedly archetypal Anglo-American systems; most indeed are exclusively concerned with the American Congress. By comparison with earlier institutional studies, process-oriented research is also characterized by more concern for explanation as well as more realistic description. "Explanation" in this case often takes the form of measuring the relative power or influence of major factors or contenders (party, constitutency, etc.) in collective decisions; sometimes it consists of cataloguing various properties and attributes thought to be sources or correlates of those contenders' power and influence. (For one of the earlier systematic, comprehensive studies, see Lowell, 1902; better known and equally illustrative is Turner, 1951.)

Documents are an important source of data for process-oriented and institu-tional studies, alike, but they are now searched more for traces of the legislative process than for descriptive evidence about legislative structure. Aggregative data about legislative decision makers (roll-call votes, legislators' biographies, etc.) and descriptive data about various extralegislative participants (size of member-ship, socioeconomic and other characteristics of groups, parties, administrators, etc.) are the common raw materials for this type of research. At the same time, process-oriented researchers often go beyond official and semiofficial documents to read the reports of political reporters and other external commentators as data sources. They also look at and listen to the process of legislation, purposefully consulting well-informed participants.

As is true of most case studies, very little process-oriented research starts by devising hypotheses from theories about legislative processes or institutions. As a rule, its generalizations are derived inductively post facto and do not extend beyond the case at hand. That is, the work rarely starts from theory and just as rarely aims at producing theoretical generalizations. Indeed, such investigations seldom even seek to generalize about case studies comparatively.[2]

Although realistic depiction of the day-to-day legislative process is the hallmark of process-oriented legislative research, these studies remain almost as formal and unrealistic as their institutionalist predecessors in the picture of legislators as persons that they implicitly paint. The behavior of legislators is no more the prime concern of process-oriented studies than it was of institutionalist research. Institutionalists found no reason to investigate the actions of legislators presumed to be rationally and individualistically judging the desirability of alternative proposals that seem to appear before them mainly through the operation of formal rules and procedure. On the other hand process-oriented research often appears to assume that legislators' behavior consists mainly of essentially passive, neutral reactions to demands, pressures, and influences put on them by such extrainstitutional actors as pressure groups, political party agencies, administrators, and executive agencies. Although process-oriented studies are concerned with questions about process dynamics that did not interest institutionalists, for one reason or another they generally look outside rather than inside the collective body of legislators for the moving forces, the dynamic elements of the process.

Of course the characteristic that chiefly distinguishes "behavioral" studies from both the other two varieties is that they focus attention on the persons and activities of legislators themselves. As often as not, the individual legislative actor is the unit of analysis; that is, research aims at explaining variations among those individuals' attitudes and behavior. Even when the unit of analysis is the legislative body or a subunit of it (chamber, committee, etc.), the individual legislator is the unit of observation, and the collectivity is analyzed in light of the properties emergent from the pattern of component individual actions and behaviors.[3]

Like many process-oriented studies, much behavioral work is concerned with explaining the decision-making activity of the legislature. But behavioral research in such questions focuses more on the individual choice-making behavior, the decisional premises of legislators and others, tending to view external pressures and influences through the perceptions of the legislative actors subjected to them. For example, whereas a common central question for process-oriented studies is the relative aggregate influence of party as compared with constituency pressures over the legislative product, behavioral research is more likely to investigate the factors that might make individual legislators respond differently to the influence of party, constituency, or pressure groups. Process-oriented studies provide demographic and socioeconomic background profiles of the legislature as a collective body, suggesting that these might operate as intervening variables affecting the influence of party, constituency, or pressure groups; but behavioral studies are more likely to investigate the conditions under which these profiles might operate as described, and why. Behaviorists are also concerned with how such actions vary among individual legislators. How, for example, do legislators' individual ideological views and biases, as related to party, constituency, or group pressure affect their voting behavior? (Kingdon, 1973; Jackson, 1974). How much, and how, does the relative safeness or competitiveness of legislators districts affect their responsiveness to party and other voting cues? (Fiorina, 1974). These are only the most common of a widening variety of questions addressed by behavioral research in pursuit of essentially the same knowledge sought by process-oriented research.

Another distinguishing characteristic of behavioral research, however, is its attention to questions that transcend matters directly affecting legislation, legislative decisions, or power and influence within the legislative process. For example, an early subject of behavioral research was the "institutional behavior" already mentioned. Quite apart from their voting decisions and directly related actions, legislators' behavior comprises varying degrees and modes of awareness of and conformity to both the formal descriptions of legislative and, equally important, various informal norms and rules-of-the-game that supplement and sometimes modify them (see Matthews, 1960; Wahlke et al., 1962; Barber, 1965). Likewise, underlying and helping to shape most legislative activities are members' role conceptions relative to legislative and subject-matter expertise, leadership office, and other positions and statuses, not to mention their interpersonal relationships with colleagues and other participants in the legislative process. The term "legislative behavior" thus comes to cover perceptions, attitudes, beliefs, habit patterns, and actions of a variety far greater than was originally suggested by the term. Increasingly, "legislative behavior" is used to refer not just to intracameral activities of legislators and the ideas and attitudes relating thereto, but to extracameral behavioral phenomena—being recruited and campaigning for legislative office, errand running for constituents, and many others.

In effect this expansion of meaning of the term "legislative behavior" reflects an important conceptual shift. It is the *representative* character and function of the representative body, not primarily its legislative function, which is increasingly the principal theoretical focus of investigation. This course is evident in the formulation of research questions about the relationship between legislators' voting behavior (policy decisions), their ideological and other personal views and biases on the issues they handle, the cues and clues from their party or from interest groups, and the policy views and demands of constituents and public (Miller and Stokes, 1963). In addition, however, there is increasing recognition of the possibility that the response and reaction of public and constituents to legislative events might be quite independent of legislative policy output simply conceived (Wahlke, 1971). In short, legislative research begins to recognize the importance of *legitimizing* government and governmental policies, and to investigate what part the legislature and legislators play in that process and function, as well as how they play it.

Despite much change from earlier approaches, behavioral legislative research has not made a substantial theoretical leap forward over the conceptualization and design of nonbehavioral research. The conceptual span of behavioral research covers a much wider territory than either institutional or process-oriented conceptions or both of them together, and perhaps it incipiently attacks problems tying them together. But behavioral research is rarely much more theoretical in the proper sense of that word than most other legislative research. Many studies, it is true, use the language of "political systems analysis"—the "inputs" of demands and support, the "outputs" of policies and other "authoritative allocations of value," the "feedback" of output to the input side of the system. But these terms serve more often as labels for filing and systematizing research findings than as basic concepts in theoretical generalizations from which researchable hypotheses are (or could be) deduced. One often encounters borrowings from middle-range psychological "theories" about cognitive dissonance (balance), role, reference group, and so on. But these, too, rarely serve as genuine sources of hypotheses to be tested; still more rarely do they benefit from the results of legislative behavior research.

Systematically collected survey data from samples or whole memberships of legislatures is perhaps the characteristic raw material for behavioral legislative research, which also sometimes utilizes legislative electoral data rarely exploited before. But there is still heavy reliance on roll-call, biographical, and other aggregative data long familiar in legislative research. Although the focused, cross-sectional study is increasingly more common than the more holistic depiction of legislative institutions and processes, the study of the single-case or the single-system research site still overwhelmingly outnumbers comparative investigations of even two systems or sites. Although more and more studies (institutional and process oriented, as well as behavioral) of European, non-European, and non-Western legislative systems are now appearing, it remains true that the favorite research sites for legislative study are American (both state and national) and, to a lesser extent, British and Western European (see Kornberg, 1972; Kornberg and Musolf, 1970).

LEGISLATIVE RESEARCH AND POLITICAL KNOWLEDGE

More directly germane to present purposes than the characteristics most commonly exhibited in legislative studies individually is the collective product they constitute. It would be egregiously presumptuous to attempt to synthesize or even systematically summarize here the substantive results of the four-score-or-so years of legislative research so rudely characterized in the previous section. But several observations can be offered without venturing quite that far.

First, the knowledge we have is exceedingly incremental. What we know has grown by accretion of numerous bits and pieces; we can point to no striking "breakthroughs" or major discoveries that have increased or changed our understanding in dramatic or revolutionary fashion. Although there are obvious differences of quality and value among the many studies extant, few represent critical turning points or major landmarks.

Some observers have viewed the changes in prevailing mood and conception from institutional to process-oriented and behavioral research as constituting something like significant landmarks. Insofar as that view implies an evolutionary progress from "lower" to "higher" forms of research, it is clearly wrong. At best that sequence of development is the simple reflection of the incremental process whereby today's research of necessity builds on whatever has gone before. To be sure, the terms "institutional," "process oriented," and "behavioral" describe bodies of research that differ in their objectives and their methods, as described. And up to a point there is a certain logical order of priority among the bodies of knowledge yielded by each one. That is, understanding of legislative processes rests on a fundamental grasp of the institutional framework—the stable political structures—that surround and organize the variable, dynamic activities of goal-pursuing legislators, enabling them to deal predictably with one another. Likewise, there is (for students of government and politics) no special reason to be interested in the behavior patterns of legislators in particular, and no basis for knowing which of their behavior patterns are interesting, except as curiosity is guided by more general concerns about political and social consequences of legislative institutions and processes. But more important than this kind of logical relationship among the three principal emphases historically represented in legislative study, we must stress that they are essentially different emphases, and not wholly alternative, contradictory approaches. They are complementary pieces of a larger whole. Their results are not competitive with one another but additive in the overall incremental body of knowledge.

A second observation, not really as critical or unkind as it may at first glance appear, is that the increments so far amassed tend mainly to answer questions about what, where, and how. That is, we have produced mostly descriptive information about legislative institutions, processes, and behavior, in particular times and places. Even the "explanations" offered by many process-oriented and most behavioral studies are essentially factual statements about observed correlations between one or another dependent variable in, again, particular cases. Insofar as we have similar information or correlations about several or many different political or-legislative systems, it might appear that we have comparative analysis pushing beyond mere description. But such cross-system data and findings seldom constitute synthesis or genuine comparative analysis but only the additive presentation of descriptive statements about the various individual systems and cases described. Above all, we rarely have answers to the question, why do the institutions and processes look and work the way they do in system A but not in systems B, C, and D? Why do legislators feel and think as they do and go about their business one way in system E, but another way in systems F and G?

At the same time it must be recognized that even our descriptive knowledge is far from comprehensive or complete. On the one hand, even in purely descriptive terms, our information about some political and legislative systems is meager or at best fragmentary and uncertain. This is most obviously the case with respect to representative bodies in newer nations and so-called developing societies. But it is also true of a number of American states, and the statement is still more applicable to our knowledge about city councils and other local representative bodies in the United States and elsewhere. Nor do we have a very clear picture, in a purely descriptive sense, of institutions, processes, or legislators' behavior in historic systems of the past.

By the same token, for any system about which we do have substantial descriptive information, there are always important categories of information missing, not just about legislators' attitudes and behavior as revealed by survey data, which is in some respects more difficult to amass on a broad front, but also about legislative institutions and processes that might be thought to be more readily susceptible to descriptive scrutiny. An obvious example is roll-call data, which are only now becoming truly abundant for that most studied legislative body, the Congress of the United States. Similarly, surprisingly little is known about the social backgrounds and demographic characteristics of legislators in more than a few sessions of any given legislature. Thus whatever research site a modern researcher chooses, and however abstract and theoretical his research objectives, he will probably feel the need for more complete descriptive characterization of the legislative situation—in institution, process, and behavioral respects—than is immediately available to him. Correlatively, legislative research that is purely descriptive in its objectives, so long as it provides "old-fashioned" information about systems for which such data were hitherto lacking or increases the dimensions of our information about even well-studied systems, is likely to contribute just as significantly to our knowledge as more ambitious and more sophisticated efforts.

A third observation relates to the other side of the theory-data or explanation-description coin, that is to the character of conceptual and theoretical problems in the field. To admit the necessity and value of further descriptive research is not to belie the importance of these problems. Obviously, some theoretical notions or conceptual orientations, however implicit or inchoate, are inevitably governing researchers' choices about what data to collect and how to organize and classify them. Just as obviously, therefore, an important task of legislative research is to make these guiding notions explicit and clear, and to explain their theoretical justification. It also seems obvious, at least in the abstract, that the results of even the most purely descriptive data collection and analysis can be interpreted and evaluated only in the light of a more general conception, a "theory," that identifies the logical relationship among the various topics and subjects of research and maps out other areas of knowledge and ignorance in relation to them. Bits and pieces of information do not "cumulate" into knowledge autonomously and automatically by simple accretion; they must be organized into logically ordered sets and hierarchies of generalizations by analytic and synthetic intelligence. There is perhaps nothing more characteristic of the field of legislative research as a whole than the absence of such theoretical integration (see Loewenberg, 1972).

This lack is sometimes taken to imply the need for high-priority efforts to formulate an overarching ideational structure, a "theory of legislatures," that would logically interrelate all the presently disparate pieces of our information and at the same time provide the stimulus, the organizing principles, and the theoretical objectives for future research.

The course and the fruits of past research, however, suggest that conceptual and theoretical problems might more profitably be tackled in somewhat different fashion. One most troublesome problem is the commonly ambiguous relation of legislative study to broader political study; indeed, some commentators have cited lack of clear relevance to more general concerns. The questions that most call for answering are not theoretical questions about why the facts of legislative life are what they are found to be, but questions about why it matters that we know what they are, and what difference it makes to anyone "politically" (using the term in its most generic sense) that they are that way. What is called for is not a "theory of legislatures" but a slightly more simple notion no less difficult to formulate: a coherent conception of the generic character of government as a basic social process in human society, surely including an idea of the place that legislative institutions and processes do, could, or might occupy in it, and of how variations in that state would affect social and political life.

LEGISLATURES, REPRESENTATION, AND SUPPORT

A number of recent legislative studies move in the direction just described. Current work puts less emphasis on explicit, self-conscious attempts at formal model following or theory building. It also differs from earlier efforts because the problems attacked have broader political science implications. Moreover, the newer studies design their research and report its results with more careful attention to what the data say about the bearing of the legislative institutions, processes, and behavior examined on the wider processes of government in the societies under investigation.

The changing research role and meanings of the concept of "representation" not only offer an excellent example of movement in the direction of more broadly based studies but bring us directly to the work at hand. Inasmuch as the terms "legislature" and "representative body" have long been used almost synonymously, one would think that this concept constituted a crucial, if not the most central theoretical focus of legislative research from the beginning. But as our discussion of changing research emphases may already have suggested, that is not quite the case. As a theoretical concept, the term "representation" clearly has reference to the linkage between the apparatus and activity of government on the one hand, and the general body of citizens—the public and its individual and various group components—on the other (Pitkin, 1967). Until very recently, however, legislative research—whether institutional, process oriented, or behavioral—generally has not asked questions and gathered data about that linkage itself but has simply made unquestioned assumptions about it and looked at some presumed part of it, usually on the legislative side. At the same time, political research in other fields that might have been seized on as shedding light on the problem likewise tended to take for granted the character of the linkage per se, proceeding to examine one or another facet of public and citizen attitudes and behavior through opinion surveys, voting studies, and so on. In both cases, the linkage was conceived of not primarily as a *process*, an actual connection to be empirically examined, but as a static comparative relationship between the two elements linked. And in both cases, both public and legislative side were conceived of fairly simply in terms of the conscious will and intent of the individual actors involved respecting the legislative (policy) decisions that the representative body might or might not make. Thus without ever being formally defined or even much discussed, "representation" for most legislative research was long unthinkingly viewed as having to do with how closely the results of actions by legislators (representatives) matched the wishes or desires (interests) of citizens.

From institutional studies we can learn something about the formal electoral relationship between legislators and the constituents who elect them, but not very much in actual fact about the correspondence between legislators' action and voters' thoughts, whose variation in consequence of varying electoral arrangements would seem to be the justification for studying the institutions in the first place. We can learn something, too, about the variations in the decision-making structure within the legislature. For example, Woodrow Wilson (1885), first professional scholar to study a legislature, described how the tyrannical powers of Congressional committees constitute a structure of decisional power different from and contradictory to what was constitutionally intended. The clear implication, which Wilson and later students well recognized, is that decisions reached by committee and imposed on the whole Congress might well differ from decisions that would have been reached by the whole body working differently. But it was many years before either Wilson or his successors investigated empirically the character of those putative differences or compared the policy decisions made by Congress' "little legislatures" with any observed desires, feelings, or thoughts of the public. Similarly, studies of legislative procedure, organization, staffing, and other institutional features as such, were seldom concerned with examining the effects of variations in such features on legislative performance in general, let alone their effects on anything more immediately touching the representative relationship.

One variety of process-oriented study narrowed its focus as just mentioned and suggested some possible connections between legislative performance and institutional structure. This is the set of studies tabulating and examining the number of bills, resolutions, and statutes in various subject-matter categories that are introduced, considered, and acted on in a given legislative time and place, exploring the amount of time spent on these instruments in various procedural activities (committee hearings, floor debates, etc.) and the kinds of final decision reached (see, f.i. Chamberlain, 1946). Such works add substantially to our picture of the overall shape and character of the legislative process, and the allocation of legislators' time, attention, and energy, yet they rarely compare or facilitate comparison of the product of legislative activity with anything outside the legislature, on the public side of the representational relationship. They mainly suggest how one or another variation in the institutional framework and the established ways of operating in a given legislative body might affect the overall efficiency or productivity of the legislative operation.

More directly pertinent to the subject of representational linkage are process-oriented case studies of particular policy decisions, since most of these not only describe the substantive policy content of particular legislative acts but usually point out explicitly how that product compares with the wishes of extralegislative interests and forces active in promoting and inhibiting enactment. We have already noted that such studies come close to defining representation in terms of the power and influence over the decisions of the beneficiaries and victims most immediately concerned. The studies do not, however, push actual observation beyond that kind of description. They offer no empirical data about how parts of the public other than the winners and losers in a given struggle might feel about the decisions, or what either they or the actors do about such feelings. Nor do they tell us much about how legislators are guided in making their decisions, and how the guidance received might affect legislators' relationship with active elements in the public.

Process-oriented studies, therefore, contain some useful and important information about the collective decision-making patterns of some legislatures, and even more about the connection observed in some particular cases between very specific legislative objectives of certain types of political actors, namely, organized political interest groups, and those legislative outputs of direct interest to the groups specified. Each kind of knowledge is valuable in itself, but none takes us very far toward understanding representation in its broader, more interesting connotations.

Many behavioral studies go considerably further in this direction. Most deal with the choice-making behavior of the individual legislator. Earlier behavioral studies especially approach this problem indirectly, by compiling profiles of the occupational and other socioeconomic and personal background characteristics of the memberships of various legislative bodies. The common conclusion of such investigations is that the legislature is highly "unrepresentative" of the people it is supposed to serve. Comparing the individual legislator with the average for people in his district, or comparing the average of a whole legislature with the averages of their total public, we find almost invariably that legislators are older, more often male than female, better educated, wealthier, of higher occupational status, and so on. The tacit assumption is that the choices made by a legislator or a legislature of one kind of background would differ from those made by another, but the character of the differences to be expected and the mechanism underlying the choices are rarely made precise or explicit. The conceptual inadequacy of merely comparing demographic characteristics of legislators and their publics without relating observed differences to expected or observed attitudes, actions, or behavior of either the public or the representatives is by now quite familiar.[4]

Many more recent behavioral studies expressly recognize this shortcoming and examine the relationship between representatives and represented more directly, not just to discover the effects of their respective socioeconomic and personal characteristics, but with a somewhat broader perspective. Current investigations tend to be conceived in terms of a Burkean typology of possible representational relationships. That is, they seek to learn whether, how far, and under what circumstances legislators know what their electors want, do what they think their electors want, or pursue their individual notions in the face of, at the expense of, or to the neglect of electors' desires. These studies not only widen the angle of vision that legislative research can take in both legislative and public sides of the representational relationship, they also begin to look into the character of some of political parties, legislators' actual contacts with constituents, and so on. Thus we are beginning to see genuine studies of representation, unlike most earlier projects of research.

Besides offering valuable knowledge of the previously enumerated aspects of the representational relationship, the findings of the more recent studies reveal some of the limitations of the prevailing conceptions of the problem of representation and suggest ways of correcting and improving it. For example, the prevailing concern has been with relationships between specific public-policy wishes and will of public, individuals, and groups, on the one hand, and legislators on the other. There is little doubt that a substantial portion of legislators' attitudes and activity can be realistically described in terms relating to such policy concerns, but recent research leaves even less doubt that they are applicable to only a fraction of the political behavior of only a part of the public. Similarly, the representational relationship is generally conceived of primarily as linking legislators with "constituents," rather than with "citizens" or "public," in more general terms. Again, research findings show that legislators are acutely aware of the special relationship between themselves and the voters who elect them, and that they are intensely concerned with what kind of judgment, primarily but not solely electoral, their constituents (not some general public) will pass on them and their actions. But again, research also clearly reveals that most people who constitute the public only occasionally see themselves as and act like "constituents," although more often and in other ways they may well be concerned with and react to government in general and legislative activity in particular.

In thinking about the linkage between legislators and citizens, therefore, it seems clearly desirable and necessary to look beyond the formal legislative policy decisions and the related choice-making activities of individual legislators, beyond voters' policy preferences (if any) and their electoral decisions for or against legislative candidates, and beyond the person-to-person relationships between representatives and their constituents (both face to face in capitol and constituency, and further removed) through the various media of mass communications. All these, to be sure, are important elements of the representative relationship, by no means to be overlooked or ignored. It is particularly worth investigating the extent to which and the conditions under which different legislators and different citizens entertain attitudes and engage in behavior appropriately described in terms of this instrumental, constituency-to-policy conception of representation. Equally useful would be a measure of what proportion of actual legislature-public relationships in a given case can be appropriately described in that fashion, and how far different political systems differ from one another with respect to that proportion.

To deal with such questions requires preliminary notions about what aspects of representative relationships exist other than the instrumental one. It is here that the concept of "support," originally introduced to political research in David Easton's (1953; 1965) conceptualization of "the political system," comes into play. The concept of support has reference, in the first instance, to the *effects* of citizens' attitudes and behavior on governmental officials, processes, and institutions. Anything people do or do not do, think or do not think, believe or do not believe, that has the consequence of promoting the continued existence and activity of a government, an institution or process, or an official career, is by definition supportive of that object; actions, ideas, and beliefs that work against it are by defition nonsupportive.

Easton's distinction between "specific" and "diffuse" support is particularly relevant to moving the conceptualization of representation beyond the long-prevalent instrumental version of it. In these terms, instrumental conceptions of representation logically lead to studies of "specific support" only—more often than not to specific support by constituents of their own representatives, not of legislative products or government more generally. Recognition of phenomena suggested by the term "diffuse support" and continuing efforts to distinguish that concept theoretically and empirically from "specific" support rapidly introduced a wide variety of new topics and problems into the domain of research on representation. For example, once this line of thinking is begun, it becomes apparent that people's perceptions of the response of the collective legislative body, the legislature as an institution, in terms of vaguely perceived and often casually evaluated general performance are as vital an element in the representational relationship between public and legislature as more self-conscious and specific judgments about particular policy actions of individual legislators or the legislature as a whole. And from that it becomes equally plain that people are as often responding to symbols and symbolized characteristics as to matter-of-fact observations of legislative activity or observable material consequences of legislative actions or overall performance.

What governs such symbolic and global responses by public and constituents? How much do the day-to-day decisions and actions of legislators individually, or of the legislature collectively, have to do with the mechanism(s) of control? How do such attitudes and actions on the part of public and constituents affect the attitudes and behavior of legislators? To such questions, legislative research to date provides no answers and few clues to where such answers may be sought, since they stem from conceptions of representation more complex than those of the investigators.

CONCLUSION

Recent research by Patterson and associates (1975) reflects concern for representation in the wider sense and offers at least tentative answers to some of the questions posed. Their findings help to broaden our conception of representation and present important additions to our knowledge about that relationship as more broadly conceived.

In the process, they also demonstrate that other quality described previously as conspicuously needed in modern legislative research—namely, relevance to more fundamental problems and questions of government in human affairs. For better understanding of the dynamics of support for legislators and legislatures will clearly add to our understanding of the working of representative democracy. Better knowledge of the distribution of support among population, and about the participation of various segments in granting, withholding, or being unconcerned about such support, adds an important dimension to our knowledge about the behavior of citizens in democracies. Still more generally, if more indirectly, findings about the symbolic bases of legislative support will relate directly to our efforts to answer broader questions about politics as symbolic behavior. And knowledge about differences in goals, perspectives, and modes of behavior between legislators and public, and between different categories and groups of each, will have relevance to more general questions about the character, causes, and consequences of different relationships between "elite" and "mass" in politics everywhere, not just in representative democracies.

The general conclusion from this survey of the course of legislative research, then, is reasonably optimistic: researchers today are generally better aware than were their predecessors of where they are going and what steps are appropriate to arrive at the destination. It would no doubt be a wild-eyed exaggeration to use that basis to say of legislative research what Condorcet said of mankind and society—that the Golden Age lies ahead of us, not behind us. But then, the aim of scientific research is less utopian than rapid entry into the Golden Age.

NOTES

1. The table and accompanying discussion obviously do not offer a comprehensive account of legislative research. There are no doubt important studies that fit poorly into the framework, and there are few that are fully described by any one category. The schema is offered as a set of "ideal types," a heuristic device to aid thinking about future research, not as a comprehensive classification of past studies. For more general and descriptive surveys see Eulau and Hinckley, 1966; Meller, 1960, 1965; and Wahlke, 1962.

2. A noteworthy exception is the pioneering work of Lowell, 1902.

3. The distinction is best illustrated by Eulau and Prewitt, 1973, which utilizes survey data about city councilmen's perceptions to investigate the decisional structures of the city councils in the San Francisco Bay Area.

4. In an early study, still one of the most thorough of its kind, Hyneman (1940) explicitly pointed out that there is no reason to examine such characteristics or make such profiles without looking for the behavioral consequences of the differences found.

Chapter 12

RECENT RESEARCH ON CONGRESS IN A DEMOCRATIC PERSPECTIVE

HEINZ EULAU
ALAN ABRAMOWITZ

The flowering of research on the Congress of the United States in the seventh decade of the twentieth century made for a curious paradox in the relationship between empirical knowledge and theoretical utilization of that knowledge for an understanding of democracy.[1] Although scholars had probed into the institutional mysteries of Congress, provided fresh perspectives on its political life, and corrected false impressions of its role in the governmental scheme of things, at the end of a decade unequalled in scientific attention it is doubtful that understanding of the Congress in a democratic perspective had measurably improved over what it was at the beginning of the decade. There seems to prevail much hesitancy to exploit the new knowledge about Congress for a realistic view of democracy, even among those who presumably have been exposed to the new knowledge. In a terse but insightful paragraph the late Morton Grodzins (1966: 3) summarized the common dilemma:

> Democratic government, in the abstract at least, should be simple government, if not simple in process at least structured simply enough to be easily comprehended by the citizenry. For simplicity maximizes fulfillment of an important democratic ideal: that citizens understand public institutions. Without this understanding the public cannot make intelligent judgments, especially cannot know how to reward at the polls those who have done well and penalize those who have done poorly. *But government in the United States is not simple, either in structure or process.*

If a thing is complex, it tends to call for specialization in knowledge-making. But specialization may have the effect of making the complex thing even less understood than it was before. In the scholarly community one sometimes hears the complaint that the expert knows more and more about less and less. The complaint is banal because it is an indictment that cannot be prosecuted, for the remedy implied is surely an absurdity. Who would be willing to argue that it is preferable to know less and less about more and more? The problem is not cutting back on specialized knowledge-making, although the word seems to be out from time to time that "we know enough about this particular thing, let's get on with something else."[2] Rather, the problem is to absorb the new and specialized knowledge into a comprehensive, but hopefully also more reliable and valid, understanding of the thing that the specialists have taken apart. This is the task of the theorist, and to be suggestive in this respect is the task we have set for ourselves in this look at some of the research on Congress in the sixties.

If the specialized literature on the Congress can be faulted, it can be faulted on the ground that it remains isolated from democratic theory. This is not to say that all of the research has been untheoretical, in the sense that no theory was brought to bear on it. On the contrary, some of the Congressional research made good use of the abundance of the theories now available in the social sciences, such as role theory, exchange theory, systems theory, organizational theory, conflict theory, institutionalization theory, and so on.[3] But rarely is the effort made to link this research to models that permit seeing the Congress in a democratic perspective. It is the fate of the Congress that it is all too often seen as a mere "debating society," a "rubber-stamp" of presidential initiative, or a pit of "pork barrel" politics. Whatever partial truths there may be in such skewed generalizations from empirical evidence, their very occurrence suggests the need for correct abstraction if a fantastically complex institution like the Congress and its place in the democratic scheme of things is to be understood.

It is perhaps too much to ask of Congressional scholars that they relate their work to some single, elegant and economic theory of democracy. For there is no such theory that would give the research on Congress democratic "relevance."[4] Moreover, the theory gap is by no means attributable to Congressional scholarship alone. If the literature on Congress remains isolated from democratic theory, the converse is also the case—political theory is isolated from empirical research, on Congress as on other aspects of politics. This is generally so in all of political science, although there are now a few political theorists who have come to absorb at least some empirical knowledge into their formulations, especially knowledge stemming from research on voting behavior, public opinion and legislative behavior.[5]

A look at the research on Congress in the sixties may well take as a focus, therefore, the contribution it can potentially make to democratic theory. The focus is admittedly congenial to us because, not being Congressional scholars, we lack the expertise for critical technical and substantive assessment. Fortunately, a very competent appraisal has been published recently by Robert L. Peabody, one of the most knowledgeable of Congressional scholars.[6]

We should make clear, however, what we have in mind. We do not propose to "test" propositions or models of democratic theory with the material now available on Congress. Nor is it our purpose to "build" or "revise" democratic theory with the research findings at hand. Rather, our intention is to see what "bearing" the research on Congres has for one or another aspect of democratic theory, what it can tell us about democratic theory. We wish to "exploit" empirical knowledge of Congress from a democratic perspective.

Two things are to be said about this enterprise. First, *we assume that "democracy" is not the only property* of the American commonwealth and that, therefore, only some kind of democratic theory can be used to explain the American "system." There are many aspects of American political life and, with it, of Congressional operations that have nothing to do with democracy (and whether they are democratic or undemocratic strikes us as a silly question, given the complexity of the system.) And, second, we realize that "using" the research on Congress in a democratic perspective is hazardous because empirical knowledge does not speak for itself and inferences from empirical findings may do violence to the data and to the theoretical meanings one gives them.[7] But this is a danger that can be corrected easily enough by minds more subtle or sophisticated than our own.

DEMOCRATIC MODELS OF AGGREGATION

That there is no single, comprehensive theory of democracy by which to look at Congressional research is a minor obstacle to proceeding in the way we have proposed. We shall be arbitrary and simply employ three models of democracy—the participatory, the competitive, and the representational. More bothersome in relating empirical research on Congress to democratic theory is a difficulty that stems from considerations not often articulated but invariably implied when the effort is made. This is the problem of making inferences from institutional behavior to a theory that is built on individualistic assumptions.

Congress is a social group that can be reduced, for the purposes of internal analysis, to the individual members who compose it, and much that can be validly said about it can be said by way of inference from the behavior of its members (or, for that matter, from the behavior of sub-units like committees or state delegations). But when it comes to saying something about the theoretical implications of research on Congress as an *institution,* as a body composed of individual members but also with a collective life of its own, one is faced with the ticklish problem of level of analysis (see Eulau, 1969; 1971). For received formulations of democracy are intrinsically individualistic.

Democracy means, if it means anything, that the worth and dignity of the individual are the end values of governance. Whatever the particular formulation, therefore, no theory of democracy (at least no theory Western-style) is readily willing to abandon the individual as the basic unit of analysis. This is sometimes disguised, in some formulations, by references to "the people," "the constituency," or "the electorate," but these are assumed to be shorthand expressions which do not invalidate the basic premise of the individual as the starting point of theory.

But there is another reason for methodological individualism. It is that no inter-subjectively communicable model of democracy is possible without such individualistic assumptions as that the citizen is motivated by self-interest and guided by rational choice. The individualistic premises, it is generally conceded, are not supported by the empirical evidence of citizen behavior.[8] Any one citizen may not know what his interest is; his conduct is not necessarily rational; and his choices may be serverely restricted. Yet, theory construction proceeds despite these falsifications (see Buchanan and Tullock, 1962; Downs, 1957).

All special theories of democracy, whether of the participatory, competitive or representational kind, share the assumptions of methodological individualism and differ only in the roles they assign to particular individual actors in the political process. In the participatory model a collective choice emerges from the direct involvement of all in the participatory process (see Pateman, 1970). In the competitive model a collective choice emerges out of the competition among alternatives (candidates for office or issues) for citizen votes (see Schumpeter, 1942). In the representational model collective choice emerges out of some link (such as shared personal attributes, partisan or ideological views, or assumed virtual identity of interests) between one citizen as the representative and another citizen as the represented (Pitkin, 1967; Pennock and Chapman, 1968). Whatever the particular model or mixture of models, individualistic theories of democracy assume that collective choice results from the aggregation of individual preferences, and they only differ with regard to the processes of governance that will accomplish it.

How, then, can empirical research on Congress as an eminently collective choice-making institution be brought to bear on a theory of democracy that proceeds from individualistic assumptions? We propose to relax the individualistic assumptions of democratic theory without, hopefully, doing violence to the meaning of democracy as the form of governance that aims to safeguard and promote the worth and dignity of the individual person.

To relax the individualistc assumptions, it may be useful to think of democracy as meaning that government has the *potential* for participation, competition, or representation. So conceived, participation, competition and representation are not properties of the individual actor but *emergent* systemic properties of democratic government. If only potential is assumed, the emergence of participation, competition and representation becomes both a matter of degree and empirical demonstration. For instance, rather than stipulating that *all* citizens *must* be involved in the participatory process for a genuine collective decision to be made, it need only be stipulated that there be the potential for participation. This would seem to be a more realistic requirement than the implicitly idealistic (and coercive)[9] assumption of the participatory model about universal participation as a necessary condition for genuinely collective choice. The relaxed model permits empirical observation of the surge and decline of citizen involvement as a criterion for assessing the *social unit's* participatory potential, without running the risk of falsifying a necessary assumption of theory about the behavior of individual actors.

While participatory potential is a necessary condition of democracy, it is not a sufficient condition. Even if the participatory potential of a polity were fully realized in that all eligible citizens participated in all decision affecting them, the quality of this participation would remain as a theoretical issue. A high level of citizen participation does not necessarily mean that the participatory process effectively aggregates individual preferences into a collective choice. It is stipulated, in the competitive model of democracy, that participants, be they few or many, must have a choice among alternatives. Choice among alternatives makes for a *social unit's* competitive potential as a group property that does not depend on the individual calculus. But competitive potential is also only a necessary, and not sufficient, condition of democrary.

The relationship between democracy's participatory potential and competitive potential is problematical and there seems to be an almost inevitable tension in the relationship. "Maximum feasible participation" and "maximum feasible competition" coexist in a precarious balance. An increase in participation not accompanied by an increase in competition may make the political agenda in-digestible and unmanageable, the familiar case of immobilism. For this reason, the democratic process is not something that can be left to self-correction. It requires political engineering. Such engineering is provided for in the representa-tional model of democracy.

Conceptions of democratic representation, and there are many, assume a two-stage decisional process, involving first the selection of representatives from the pool of eligible citizens and then their commissioning for choice-making among alternatives. All of the models also assume that the relationship involved in repre-sentation is one between individual representative and individual represented, although they differ a great deal on the nature of the relationship. Finally, probably all conceptions of representation agree on the primary existential reason for representation—namely, the sheer size of the citizenry in mass societies which makes "direct democracy" impossible.

To mediate the tension between democracy's participatory potential and competitive potential, a requisite model of representative democracy cannot rely on individualistic assumptions about the nature of representation but must view representation as a systemic property of democracy.

If representation is treated as a systemic property—that is, as somehting predi-cated on the existence of a network of multiple linkages rather than on a strictly inter-individual relationship, as something that is a property of the whole rather than of its parts, it can be and probably must be treated as an emergent phenome-non, as something that may or may not occur in the course of multiple interactions among multiple actors.[10] Moreover, if representation may but need not emerge as a collective property of democracy, it follows that it is best to speak of "representatinal potential" rather than representation. This formulation implies that the election of representatives is not enough for representation to emerge, that it is perhaps a necessary but not sufficient condition. Rather, it calls attention to other conditions of representation, notably the responsiveness of the representative assembly to citizen demands or needs, on the one hand, and the citizenry's ability to hold the assembly accountable, on the other hand.

The representational model has the capability of mediating the tension between democracy's participatory and competitive components. This is made possible, on the one hand, by the aggregation of multiple preferences and demands in the representative body, provided, of course, that all preferences and demands have access to the representative assembly. The condition satisfies the requirements of the participatory model. The citizenry, by referring a multiplicity of preferences and demands to the representative assembly for aggregation or integration, is freed from a task that it cannot perform itself because, under conditions of mass democracy, it does not have the means (like coming together in the *agora*) to do it.[11] The representative assembly, on the other hand, presents the electorate with relatively simple choices in periodically seeking its own renewal in the electoral process. If the assembly has performed its aggregative or integrative functions well, by reducing many alternatives to relatively few, the representational model is conducive to maximizing democracy's competitive potential.

We managed to discuss the three models of democracy without building in conventional notions about the role of political parties. This we did advisedly. For, it seems to us, parties are the effects and not the causes of success in the aggregation of multiple preferences. The more the representative assembly succeeds in giving access to, being responsive to, and aggregating multiple preferences, the greater is the likelihood that few rather than many parties emerge in a political system. In other words, the representational model makes parties dependent on intervening variables in the political process. Parties in the model are not the sources but the consequences of aggregation.[12] We cannot pursue this theme here, but it is pertinent to our interpretation of the research on the parties in the Congress of the United States.

PARTY AS FOCUS OF AGGREGATION

The Congressional parties are institutions within institutions.[13] This circumstance, perhaps more than anything else, explains many of the tensions that make the Congress so fascinating to those who watch and study it. If the parties controlled the House and Senate in some pervasive sense so that all Congressional behavior could be reduced to party behavior, much of the drama of Congressional politics would be lost, for what remained would be predictable behavior (and all too predictable behavior is usually unbearably dull). But the parties are controlling factors of Congressional life in only a very limited sense, and much of Congressional behavior is also shaped and constrained by other structures and norms of the House and Senate as autonomous institutions. What Congressional politics would look like if there were not parties is a titillating if idle question. Congressional scholars rightly do not ask it. If they did and answered it, they would probably conclude that Congressional politics would be very much the same, the difference being that what the parties are now doing would simply be more difficult to do.

All of this is to say that one must treat the Congressional parties with great caution, and one should never treat them in isolation from their institutional moorings in the House or the Senate. Yet, the danger of doing so always looms, for it is difficult to talk about everything at once, and the tendency of scholars to give specialized attention to this or that facet of party organization, leadership or behavior may easily have a distorting effect on perceptions of reality. It is to the great credit of recent Congressional scholarship that it has largely avoided over- or under-emphasis on partisanship. In part this has been due to much greater treatment in depth of whatever aspect of the party phenomenon was being investigated; in part it has been due to a much keener sense of the importance of change through time in Congressional politics generally. Both tendencies have had the effect of precluding easy generalizations from limited temporal and situational "cases" as well as stimulating a search for empirically viable categories of analysis.[14] As a result, too, party came to be treated as a variable which could take different values in different historical and political contexts.[15]

Party is most easily dealt with as a variable in the analysis of roll-call votes; but while roll-call votes are enormously important as the final declarations of Congressional policy, they are not necessarily the best indicators of party influence in Congressional decision-making. This is so even if the party factor is more or less isolated by controlling for other factors: notably the nature of the issues, socio-economic or political constituency characteristics, or state delegation activity (see Truman, 1959; Fiellin, 1962; Kessel, 1964). That party affiliation remains as the single most efficient predictor of Congressional roll-call voting, despite much technical progress in multivariate and regression analysis (see MacRae, 1970; Anderson et al., 1966), makes the conventional finding all the more deceptive. It is to be noted, therefore, that in addtion to much methodological refinement in roll-call analysis, there has been considerable increase in sophistication as to what one may infer from a finding that, from A. Lawrence Lowell's (1902) pioneering research of seventy years ago on, has been repeatedly confirmed. One need only compare Julius Turner's (1951; 1970) work of the early fifties, recently up-dated, with Shannon's (1968) work of the late sixties to appreciate this greater sensitivity to the problem of inference. As alternative methods are used, as new control variables are introduced, and different time series examined, the evidence becomes more confusing or contradictory than earlier and simpler analyses had indicated.

In general, then, there has been a trend away from reifying the party as a "political force" that somehow, along with other "forces," influences Congressional voting. Voting on roll-calls is no longer seen, as it was also seen for a long time in electoral voting, as an aggregation of individual preferences by mere counting of noses. Just as electoral voting research identified aggregative processes like the two-step flow of communication or reference group behavior, so Congressional voting research has become sensitive to alternative means of aggregation.[16] Formally, of course, voting under some decision rule is probably the only viable means for aggregating individual preferences when the collectivity is very large, as in modern mass electorates, because it is difficult to think of an alternative formal mode of aggregation. And this remains true even if the collectivity is relatively small, as it is in legislative bodies. But there is growing realization that the roll-call vote may be at best a summary indicator that, under democratic rules, legitimizes the aggregation of preferences accomplished elsewhere in the legislative process by other means.

What made this realization possible was, among other things an increasing attention to the organizational and leadership features of party behavior in the wake of interview research and participant observation that, prior to 1960, had been the exception in the study of Congress.[17] What stimulated the new type of research was the discovery that, technically proficient though roll-call analysis had become, it failed to explain the numerous exceptions and deviations from the kind of voting that different models would predict. This is not to say that the search for uniformities and regularities in Congressional behavior does not remain the goal of the new research into party organization and leadership. In fact, as interview research sought to locate its findings in long-term institutional transformations of the two houses that could be observed by inspection of documentary historical evidence, it provided more contextual flavor than roll-call analysis, usually restricted to short time series or perhaps only to a single Congress, had been able to provide. As a result, there is now a good deal of knowledge about party organization, party leadership and party policy-making that deals with party as a factor of Congressional life in both a broader historical and a richer contextual perspective (see Jones, 1964, 1970; Ripley, 1967, 1969).

There still remains, of course, the problem of generalization. If roll-call analysis did not reveal whether a party vote stemmed from organizational exertion by the party leadership, neither did organizational research directly reveal whether leadership success stemmed from leaders' pursuing a policy attractive to a majority of "interested" (in the constituency sense) Congressmen in the first place, with "indifferent" party members going along. If such is the case, one may conclude that the leaders have in fact done their homework. This is by no means easy. The majority party leadership's interstitial position between the White House and the Congressional membership complicates its task of mobilizing support. Much does obviously depend on the strength and composition of the majority and minority parties in the houses.

As one reads the literature on Congressional party organization and leadership, what remains impressive is the long list of conditions and contingencies that intervene between the "party factor," however it is operationalized, and the policy outcomes that it is supposed to explain. There is clearly no easy street from idiographic to nomothetic explanation. If, on the whole, the research on the place of party in the two houses of Congress has been singularly free from commitment to conceptual schemes or models, this has been a wise strategy of Congressional scholarship.[18] But it also represents a continuing challenge to research on the party factor in Congress.

If, as the evidence would seem to show, the parties are not effective institutional means of aggregating preferences, whether one thinks of the party as a cue-giving reference group or as a political organization, how can one account for partisan cleavages when they do occur? The representation of constituency interests by the parties may produce this result on some issues, but even the earlier finding that the Congressional party may be simply a coalition of constituencies needs qualification.[19]

On a limited number of issues, party leaders, and in almost all cases this involves the President, may invest sufficient political resources to forge a partisan coalition behind their preferred alternative (Manley, 1970). More commonly, some combination of the two processes—representation of constituency interests and party leadership—facilitates political aggregation so that a winning coalition can be mobilized behind one policy alternative (see Jewell, 1962).

From the perspective of democracy's competitive potential, present modes of aggregation in Congress by way of the party mechanism are not promising. This is hardly news. It has been the empirical starting point of those who have advocated what they call "responsible party government" or a "more responsible two-party system."[20] There is no need here to review the demise of this particular aberration from both good political science and good policy science (see Kirkpatrick, 1971). Suffice it to say that by compulsively identifying democracy with a competitive two-party system and only so identifying it, without regard to either the participatory or representational potentials of democracy this model ignores the fact that on most issues aggregation along partisan lines could occur only by an inordinate investment of presidential resources, and at the expense of reducing democracy's representational potential. For the President and Congress represent different constituencies and interests.

Even though the parties as such are not effective mechanisms of aggregation, they may serve as *foci* of aggregation through the mechanism of electoral accountability. The critical theoretical issue here is how competition and representation blend into each other. This depends a great deal on the transactional aspect of the representational relationship. Representational potential is maximized not only if the representative assembly is responsive to the represented, but also if the represented react to the representative body. Unfortunately, there is little literature that directly links Congressional action to electorate behavior, and the evidence is difficult to interpret. What is one to make of the findings that the great proportion of incumbents are reelected every two years (see Cummings, 1966; Jones, 1967; Hinckley, 1970); that the rate of Congressional turnover has steadily declined over time; that mid-term elections continue the main lines of party voting from the previous presidential-year election (Hinckley, 1970); or that safe seats are both increasing in number and are more widely dispersed through the nation? (Wolfinger and Heifetz, 1965). Given the fact that electorates have exceptionally low levels of information about their Congressmen or the particular policy stands they have taken (Stokes and Miller, 1962; Eldersveld, 1965; Erickson, 1971), does it mean that representational potential is served?

In the perspective of the responsible two-party model, with its individualistic assumptions of rationl voting behavior, the answer would probably be negative; in the view of representation as a systemic property of a relationship between the Congress as a collectivity and its multiple electorates as collectivities, the answer may be positive. Electorates, in the latter perspective, do in fact react, not necessarily to a particular piece of legislation or to a particular Congressman, but to the over-all political climate or mood of the Congress. There is, in the absence of direct research at the appropriate level of analysis, some risk involved in the systemic interpretation. For it is assumed that the mood of the Congress or its over-all performance are comprehensible in terms of the party labels that provide electorates with clues on how to respond.

It is equally difficult to appraise the consequences of the relationship between Congress and its electorates for the competitive potential of democracy. On the one hand, the data would seem to suggest that, paradoxically, maximization of representation implies minimization of competition. If the probability of incumbents to be reelected and of challengers to be defeated is so high, the competitive potential seems to be reduced. But before this conclusion is reached, it is essential to examine the function that partisan challengers do perform, a task only recently begun (see Fishel, 1969; Leuthold, 1968), and to analyze in more detail what effect the stabilization of opposition in Congress (prescisely because minority party members are as likely to be reelected as majority party members) has on the competitive potential over the long run. These are clearly problems still on the agenda of research.

AGGREGATION THROUGH REPRESENTATION

The Congress is a representative *assembly* whose most significant product—legislation—is a property of the whole rather than a property of individual Congressmen. Yet, when the question of representation is raised, it is usually asked "how and whom or what does the Congressman represent" in the legislative process and not "how and whom or what does the Congress represent?" The two questions relate to different levels of representation, but most work on representation does not distinguish between representation *in* the Congress (micro-level approach) and representation *by* the Congress (macro-level approach).

The level of analysis problem is confounded by the fact that research on representation is conducted with different, more or less (and more often less than more) explicit models of the representational process. As a result, the bulk of the work on representation in or by the Congress is rather inconclusive, for most findings are neither comparable nor cumulative. This is so even when the investigator seeks to test a theoretically derived hypothesis rather than practice *post-facto* interpretation.

Even though one's over-all impression is one of randomness in the Congressional representational process, the search has been for classes of variables that, on theoretical grounds, may be helpful in discovering some orderliness and regularity. Depending on what model is used, variables to explain representation have ranged from Congressmen's personal characteristics, private preferences and perceptions, or role orientations (all micro-variables) to the socio-economic or political characteristics of Congressional districts, dominant pressure groups or articulate elites in the districts, or the "objective interests" of districts (all macro-variables) (see Froman, 1963; Turner, 1951; MacRae, 1958; Truman, 1959; Rieselbach, 1966). Policy issues have proved to be powerful constraints on generalizations about representation. Roll-call behavior usually serves as the dependent variable, even though it is agreed to be a poor indicator of political life in the Congress. Not surprisingly, dubious inferences are made about the sources of Congressional representation and the performance of the Congress as a representative body. This is so not only because, given the multiplicity of independent variables that remain uncontrolled, it is impossible to tell what correlations are spurious; but also because too much is taken for granted about the independent variables as indicators of Congressmen's own or citizen preferences. The tendency to be implicit rather than explicit about the model of representation involved in correlational analysis further aggravates the problem of inference. Most of the correlational roll-call studies assume that the condition of representation is met when the Congressman's policy positions, whether derived from interviews, votes or other documentary evidence, correlate with presumed or actually identified constituency preferences or interests. But the correlations are sufficiently low to shake one's confidence in the "mirror model or "pressure model," whichever, that may underlie these investigations (see Miller and Stokes, 1963). None of these studies seems to doubt that the district as a whole constituency, or some sub-constituency or some individuals in the district, are in fact meaningfully represented.

What gives credence to this view is the fact that Congressmen do interact with individuals or groups in their district in a variety of ways. Even a Congressman from a solid one-party district may maintain a "home office," though it is only the telephone number of a second cousin; he will periodically "go home," especially at primary time, even though he has actually lived in Washington for twenty years; and he will, in person or through his staff, attend to a multitude of requests for help from his constituents, usually involving his intercession with an administrative agency—something that has come to be called his "case load" (see Tacheron and Udall, 1970). These contacts and communications do give the impression that he is serving as a representative whose "happiness and glory," in Burke's famous words, is "to live in the strictest union, the closest correspondence, and the most unreserved communication with his constituents. Their wishes ought to have great weight with him; their opinion high respect, their business unremitted attention." This is not all Burke said about representation, of course, and it gives an altogether erroneous impression of what really was on his mind (see Eulau, 1967; this volume Chapter 2). But the notion is not uncommon that because the Congressman, whatever his reasons, does special favors or services for constituent individuals or groups, he is performing a representative function. Similarly, if he is successful in securing federal grants or contracts for his district, or at least in giving the impression of having been influential in this regard, his performance is interpreted as representational in nature. Of course, errand-boy and benefactor are politically interesting roles, for electoral survival may depend on them. At least this is assumed (an assumption, it seems, that derives from competitors' allegations to this effect) (see Clapp, 1964). But these linkages, in themselves, are neither necessary nor sufficient conditions of representation.

A Congressman is invariably linked with some interested persons or groups—interested in the sense that they may wish him to do something that he would not otherwise do. These persons or groups may be "constituents" in the geographic meaning of the term, or they may be functional "clienteles" of a regional or national scope. What is one to make of these linkages from the standpoint of representation? If the Congressman's response seems compliant in that he will do something that he would not otherwise do, the tendency is to refer to the stimulus as "pressure" and to suspect the response as not being genuinely representational. It is difficult to see why this should be so. It is in practice almost impossible to determine whether what a Congressman does in response to pressure, so-called, is not something he would not have done anyway. To call pressured response non-representational and a non-pressured response representational would seem to be quite arbitrary. In general, the newer literature on pressure politics, interest-group politics or lobbying suggests that the Congressman pretty much controls what he wants to hear and do by selective attention,[21] and that lobbyists are much less effective (Milbrath, 1963; Eulau, 1964; Scott and Hunt, 1966) than the older literature on interest group representation before Congress had concluded (Herring, 1929; Schattschneider, 1935). Indeed, the Congressman himself may generate the "pressure" to which he then responds.

It is for this reason that the "classical" formulations of representation, usually associated with the name of Edmund Burke, and the ensuing controversy over whether representation implies "delegation" and "mandate" on the one hand, or "trusteeship" and "free judgment," on the other hand, do no longer seem particularly germane to contemporary conditions. Quite apart from the methodological individualism involved in these formulations, there is reason to suspect that pertinent hypotheses cannot be falsified because, paradoxically, it is just the multiplicity of demands made on him ("mandate uncertainty") that gives the Congressman considerable latitude in his actual behavior. Research on representational role orientations suggests that modern legislators may still define themselves in terms of the classical formulation, and the roles of trustee, delegate or "politico" may have some behavioral consequences (see Davidson, 1969). But there are serious difficulties in interpreting these findings. In the first place, generalized role orientations do not inform about the focus of representation—that is, they are mute on what interests within his geographical district or elsewhere, the Congressmen will "speak for" in one representational style or another. Second, the representational role actually taken may vary from issue to issue. And third, what stand the Congressman finally takes on an issue may depend less on his conception of his representational role or, in fact, on externally generated considerations at all, and more on the constraints imposed on his conduct by the complexity of the Congress' internal organization and procedures as well as by its norms of appropriate conduct in committee and on the floor.

All this is not to say that role formulations are unhelpful in analyzing and explaining representational behavior and other forms of political conduct at the individual level of analysis. There always remains the task of demonstrating and explaining how specific onduct in the performance of a role, like that of the "insider" or "outsider," of the "leader" or of the "maverick," has an impact on the group, and it is for this reason that role analysis at the level of the individual is important.[22]

The Congressman's "significant others" in the representational relationship are often not only other individuals but also collectivities (districts, organizations, interest groups, and so on). Moreover, their own "institutionalization" has made the houses of Congress and the Congress as a whole "real actors." For this reason, representation, if and when it emerges, is properly conceived as a property of the Congress as a whole, its houses or committees. The difficulty in relating Congress as a representative institution to the represented stems, of course, from the fact that it is in many respects a unique institution that one cannot systematically compare with other legislative institutions, say state legislatures or foreign legislatures. In the absence of meaningful comparisions, therefore, it is difficult to specify the conditions under which collective representation emerges or does not emerge in the Congress. Because the houses of Congress generally act on the recommendations of their committees, and the Congress as a whole on the recom-

mendations of their committees, and the Congress as a whole on the recommendations of its conference committees, it may ultimately be possible to say something
significant about the emergence of representation in the Congress as a whole
from comparison of committee behavior in response to external demands. But this
type of analysis is still in its infancy.

Representation emerges if the Congress can be shown to be responsive to its
multiple constituencies and clienteles. To answer the question, "how does it
represent and to whom is it (or is it not) responsive?", it is critical to keep in mind
that it functions in a federal system and pluralistic universe. Few, if any, students
of Congress have given sufficient attention to this circumstance in treating it as a
representative institution.[23] In fact, insofar as the federal and pluralistic
character of the Congress is taken into (mostly implicit) consideration, it is
deplored as a source of weakness. More often than not, the "localism" of Congressional orientations is unfavorably compared with the President's "national"
orientation.[24] But these are judgments based on political predilection rather than
empirical evidence. They ignore, on the one hand, Congressmen's relative latitude
in responding to pressure. And on the other hand, they ignore the aggregative
and integrative functions that Congress performs through its complex internal
processes and modes of conduct. From this perspective, a measure of the
responsiveness of Congress and a criterion for assessing its representational
potential would seem to be its success in harnessing diverse demands into national
compromises. These compromises variously benefit some constituencies or
interests more than others, and they may not benefit some interests at all because,
like the poor, they do not have the resources to make their voices felt. But it does
not follow that the Congressional "system," if system it can be called, is devoid
of what we consider a necessary condition of democracy, namely, a representational potential. Rather, it means that because of the unequal distribution of
resources in the society, the representational potential has not yielded sufficient
responsiveness to all conceivable interests and needs. In this sense, failure of
representation to emerge weakens democracy's participatory potential which, in
turn, may have an effect on the degree to which representation is subject to accountability.

The difficulty with accountability at the individual level stems from the evident
failure of *particular* electoral districts to hold *particular* Congressmen accountable
for their conduct. This failure is due, in part, to the electorate's disinterest in or
ignorance of Congressional affairs.[25] But even if there were an electorate as
interested and informed as prescriptive democratic theory would wish it to be, it
is doubtful that, in a federal system, this particular electorate could hold a
particular Congressman to account. For representation, as something that emerges
from the representative assembly as a whole, can not be "enforced" in a system of
geographical constituencies by holding an individual member of the assembly
accountable. The evidence to this effect is overwhelming. Although there is some

turnover in the membership of Congress caused by defeat in primaries or general elections, the vast proportion of incumbents is reelected. This does not mean that the individual Congressman has been invariably responsive to his constituents, for he probably has not been on all issues of constituency concern. It can mean, however, that in general performance of the Congress as a whole has satisfied most constituencies. The fact that incumbents of both parties are reelected regardless of the positions they have taken on controversial issues or regardless of the compromises they have accepted as necessary, suggests that constituencies react to some general feeling of how things are going in the country rather than to the particular conduct of their Congressmen. What the election results suggest, in turn, is that through its multiple channels of access and information the Congress is sensitive to what is and what is not acceptable to most people. It does not so much respond to electoral sanctions as to its own anticipated reactions to the feelings of the many electorates that constitute the Congressional quilt of constitutencies. If representation is an emergent property that can be identified by Congressional responsiveness to the demands made on it, from whatever source, this responsiveness seems to be rooted in a healthy respect for what is and what is not acceptable policy in most constituencies. In this way legislative responsiveness maximizes democracy's participatory potential.

AGGREGATION THROUGH ORGANIZATION

Institutionalization transforms individual behavior into organizational behavior. Organization, as Schattschneider (1960: 71) once put it, "is the mobilization of bias. Some issues are organized into politics while others are organized out." Issues are cystallized, clarified and resolved by the Congress through its organizational structures and processes. Some of these processes and structures are formal, others are informal. Organization, in this sense, is another means of aggregating individual preferences into social choices. The processes and structures of organization are thus genuinely independent variables that define what will and what will not be on the agenda of politics. By organizing some issues into politics and other issues out of it, the Congress greatly influences the participatory, competitive and representational potentials of democracy. Congress is not a neutral register of wins and losses in aggregation; it introduces its own particular biases into collective choice.

Floor votes in the Congress are often perfunctory exercises serving mainly to record and legitimate agreements reached elsewhere. This was one factor that, in the sixties, led scholars to investigate with great care Congressional sub-structures and processes. Another was the recognition that the rational ordering of preferences in a deliberative body stumbled over the insoluble transitivity problem posed by the "paradox of voting" (see Riker, 1958). Perhaps, too, the biases inherent in Congressional organization deserved more unbiased treatment than they had been hitherto given in the literature on Congressional reform. Perhaps these biases were conducive to the successful aggregation of preferences and, as a consequence, of instrumental value from the perspective of democracy's competitive potential. Not that these concerns were necessarily articulated openly; but they seem to have been there nonetheless.

What had been known intuitively before, namely, that a great many techniques were available to aggregate competing preferences into a manageable number of alternatives, came to be demonstrated in a variety of structured settings, notably committees and subcommittees. Although "bargaining" is the general heading under which these techniques are usually treated in the literature (see Froman, 1967), they encompass such practices as compromise, exchange, log-rolling, reciprocity, persuasion, side payments and even "twisting an arm" (which is a polite form of threat or coercion) or, at the other end, apathy.

Unlike voting outcomes that can be reduced to individual votes, the results of these political processes of aggregation cannot be reduced to the level of individual actors. There is a fundamentally interactive aspect to such processes that is lacking in the case of voting. Congress and/or its committees had to be seen and analyzed as *social* systems if the interactive nature of preference aggregation was to be understood, and group-level concepts like "integration" would be employed to deal with the aggregative aspects of Congressional decision-making.[26]

Attention to the Congress or one of its houses as a group required understanding of the value premises underpinning structural and behavioral manifestations. These would be expressed in the operating norms that prescribe what is acceptable and unacceptable conduct for members of the group. If the decade of research on Congressional internalities began, auspiciously, with Matthews' (1960: 92) discovery that "the Senate of the United States, just as any other group of human beings, has its unwritten rules of the game, its norms of conduct, its approved manner of behavior," it ended, ten years later, with a frank analysis of the biases inherent in the norm of seniority (see Hinckley, 1971). What became clear in much of the work of the intervening years was that for most Congressmen, at most times, the internal expectations seemed to be more salient and pressing than the cues received from reference groups outside the chambers. Declining competition for many Congressional seats and the resulting stability of membership in the House and the Senate suggest that the ratio of salient internal to external cues may be increasing (Hinckley, 1971). As a socializing agency, Congress routinizes relations among its members. The individual member is not an isolated, rationally calculating actor, for he is deeply involved in a complex network of social relationships: "The complexity of the organization and procedures of Congress reduces the effect of external voices on it. Its social organization exerts constraints on what any single congressman can do. It also enables him to confuse the issue as to what he has in fact done" (Bauer et al., 1963: 432). Perhaps it is more correct to state that the complexity of the organization and procedures of Congress mediates the effect of the external pressures on it. In other words, institutionalization and routinization do not necessarily imply less responsiveness to the environment, but they may imply that the quality of responsiveness of the Congress as a whole is affected through the mobilization of internal biases. Unfortunately, research has not really concerned itself with the consequences of internal institutionlization on the routinization of external relations. But if the hypothesis of simultaneous internal and external routinization is correct, rapid changes in the political environment may lead to a disjunction between the Congress' representational potential and the demands made on it by newly mobilized constituencies.

It is in this light that internal Congressional processes by which alternatives are clarified through political aggregation may be examined. Congressional committees, because of their relatively small size, have proved excellent sites for studying the processes of "no-count" aggregation. Fenno's forthcoming comparative study of six House committees as they functioned from 1955 to 1966 will undoubtedly supersede the work on individual committees done in the sixties; yet some of this work will remain of permanent value (see Fenno, 1973). In any case, given the common agreement on committee dominance in Congressional decision-making one would expect that, to the extent that political aggregation takes place within the Congress (rather than in the executive branch or the electorate) prior to roll-call voting, it takes place within the committees.[27] This is not to say that the committee itself is the only institutional means for aggregation; it is to say that it is the forum in which aggregation takes place by way of different techniques for aggregation.

Although no single pattern of aggregation ever appears in pure form, three distinctive patterns seem to be characteristic of Congressional committees. We shall refer to them as bargained, commissioned, and partisan types.[28] They are most readily distinguished by their emergent decisional structures—unipolar, non-polar, and bipolar, respectively.[29] But the ultimate structuring of alternatives can only be understood in relation to the process of aggregation preceding it. Of interest, then, are the conditions under which different ways of aggregating preferences obtain in Congressional committees and the implications of these ways for the participatory, competitive and representational potentials of democracy.

Unanimous or near-unanimous agreement is quite common in committees, as is the case on the floors of the House and Senate. What this tells about the process of aggregation in committee is, however, by no means clear. In some cases, unanimity may be achieved without the necessity of any prior clarification of alternatives. Leaving aside trivial issues, unanimity may reflect the existence of alternative aggregating mechanisms outside of a committee or the Congress.[30] But in other cases unanimity may be bargained, as in the House Appropriations Committee where subject matter, composition and stability of membership, and internal cohesion facilitate position and stability of membership, and internal cohesion facilitate aggregation through bargaining (see Fenno, 1966; Pressman, 1966). But the impact of these predisposing factors appears to be mediated by the committee's "strategic premises," especially the distributive formula by means of which budgetary increments are allocated. As Wildavsky (1964: 136-137) has pointed out, agreement "comes much more readily when the item in dispute can be treated as differences in dollars instead of basic differences in policy. Calculating budgets in monetary increments facilitates bargaining and logrolling." As a result, it is unnecessary to consider possibly competitive policy alternatives. The bias mobilized and institutionalized through the internal decision-making structure and operating norms is incrementalism.[31] Bargaining on the distribution of budgetary increments eliminates, or at least reduces, the competitive struggle for a piece of the pie among interested constituencies.

Where a permanent bargaining formula cannot be agreed on, a committee is less likely to serve as the institutional means by which preferences are aggregated. If committee members see themselves and act as commissioned by conflicting interests and clienteles on the outside, as was the case with the House Labor and Education Committee in the fifties and early sixties in regard to federal aid to education, the only way to aggregate preferences is to form coalitions. But, in this case no durable coalition could be forged behind any single alternative. Temporary alliances were not enough to make for legislative success at the various decision points of the legislative process. The Committee's internal dissension undermined its effectiveness on the floor of the House of Representatives. Either it could not bring a bill out at all, or if it did its recommendations would be blocked by the Rules Committee (see Robinson, 1963), or defeated on the floor. The proliferation of issues in the Committee correspond to the multiplicity of conflicts outside. As Munger and Fenno (1962: 173) suggested, proponents of federal aid not only had to overcome resistance to a novel idea, they also had to "eliminate these multiple controversies so that legislators [might] ultimately be led to line up for or against some single identifiable program." While commissioned aggregation, insofar as it is successful, maximizes democracy's participatory potential, it reduces its competitive and representational potential. Although the Education and Labor Committee had many clients, indeed because of it, it could not be responsive to their demands; its internal fragmentation prevented it from presenting clear-cut alternatives.

Bargained unanimity, on the one hand, and fragmented coalition-building, on the other hand, represent extremes of preference aggregation in committees. Not enough committees have been studied intensively to know much about the distribution of these types of aggregation in the Congress as a whole and, for that matter, about the type of partisan aggregation that seemed to be characteristic of the House Committee on Agriculture analyzed by Jones (1961) in the early sixties. The Committee's membership came from Congressional districts with significant interests in farm policy. The organization of bias in the committee resulted in a correspondence of commodity interests and party allegiance, so that different commodity interests were ordinarily favored when different parties controlled the House. Members were generally assigned to sub-committees on the basis of their district interests, but party considerations would bring some members on sub-committees that were of no concern to them. Partisan cleavage was avoided by an informal norm—members from districts with no stake in the sub-committee's work "are expected either to remain silent during hearings or not to attend." The partisan structure was conducive to political compromise because interests were clearly identifiable and politically adjustable. Evidently, even if district and party interests overlap, aggregation may be possible by partisan mutual adjustment.

Partisan considerations of a strategic as well as policy sort seem to guide the processing of conflicts by the House Ways and Means Committee described by Manley (1970). A committee concerned with a wide range of policy issues, Ways and Means yet places a great emphasis on technical expertise that tempers its partisan stance and is at times conducive to accommodations of policy differences. Because the House as a whole is greatly dependent on the committee's recommendations, its influence is predicated on a sense of responsibility to the party leadership whose support bolsters the committee's own independence. A bill that cannot pass the House is unthinkable; it is, therefore, the anticipated reaction of the House that serves as a strategic guide and makes for a partisan form of bargained aggregation.

Committee organization, procedures and decision rules are, of course, not the only means by which bias is mobilized in the Congress. Although there seemed to be less emphasis in the research of the sixties on recruitment as a source of bias (see Matthews, 1960; Snowiss, 1966), increasing routinization of leadership selection procedures within the Congress, as evidenced by growing reliance on the seniority criterion, introduces bias of one kind or another, probably facilitating bargained or partisan aggregation in a conservative direction. The mobilization of bias notwithstanding, the distinctive representational capabilities of the Congress, rooted as they are in geographical but also certain functional constituencies, have positive implications for democracy's participatory potential. Institutional impediments to progressive action within the Congress are serious and have often been emphasized. What is less widely recognized are the institutional channels within the Congress by means of which interests not aggregated elsewhere may receive expression and compete for recognition and support. As Sundquist (1968) has shown, the political groundwork for the legislative programs of the Kennedy and Johnson administrations was laid by an activist bloc within the Congress before presidential intervention made partisan aggregation possible.[32]

And Congress, through its committees, is the most important institutional means by which bargained aggregation of one kind or another is accomplished. While the "irrationality" of political aggregative processes through incremental or partisan mutual adjustments is sometimes deplored (Horn, 1970), the implications of these modes of aggregation for the competitive potential of democracy should be recognized. By means of compromise, bargaining, and other techniques, the preferences of widely divergent interests can be transformed into competitive alternatives. What critics ignore is the problem of how different interests can be otherwise weighted and adjusted. It is precisely for this reason that in evaluating the outcomes of bargained aggregation it is important to know what sort of distributive bias or biases are involved in the institutionalized processes of the Congress. But one should expect that bargained aggregation will result in a considerable time lag in Constitutional responses to the demands of newly mobilized constituencies, possibly reducing democracy's representational potential.

PRESIDENTIAL ENCOUNTER

Intuitively, and there is much to be said in this connection for the use of intuition, the most significant feature of the Congress of the United States seems to be the sometimes all too visible, sometimes all too invisible presence of the President of the United States. This is widely recognized, but while there is much writing on Congressional-Presidential relationships under all kinds of political conditions and on all kinds of issues, there is surprisingly little systematic research. Much of the research on Congress proceeds, and perhaps must proceed, as if the President did not exist—as if the President were some sort of incarnation of *ceteris paribus*. This is a risky affair because not even the most empirical researchers of Congress are immune to a wide range of assumptions about the relationship between President and Congress spawned by a variety of normative models *au courant* at one time or another.[33]

There are now books on "The President *and* Congress" or with similar titles that include a chapter or two on the relationship *between* the two institutions, but many more chapters are devoted to each institution separately (see Koenig, 1965; Polsby, 1964). This probably reflects quite accurately the current stage of research development. The day may come when someone will do research on the *President-in-Congress*, but at this time the revolutionary theoretical implication of this notion is only a glimmer in the creator's eyes. One must still go to case studies of legislation to gain insight into the relationship between President and Congress, as Sundquist did in order to develop a conception of the "dual legislative process." But the case studies treat President and Congress as independent actors, as perhaps they should, although their interdependence is such that the conception of the national government implied by the term "President-in-Congress" is not far-fetched by any means.[34]

Case studies tend to deal with spectacular incidents of conflict or cooperation between the President and Congress or one of its houses. Even though the situations they describe may have farreaching consequences and numerous side-effects for the course of political events and even the long-range prospects of the American system of government, they are evidently too idiographic to permit valid inferences, even in a single issue domain;[35] and they are even more difficult to use in a democratic theoretical perspective. Insofar as theory is involved, discussion turns on the doctrine of the separation of powers, which is of admittedly great interest to constitutional lawyers, but rarely turns on the democratic aspects of the relationship.

In the perspective of the doctrine of the separation of powers, the focus is on the swing of the power pendulum between the two branches of government. Most of the inferences made are impressionistic, even if supported by "box scores" of the President's success in having his proposals approved by Congress.[36] If one finds that the median of Presidential success lies well below the 50 per cent mark, what theoretically meaningful inference is one to make? The two branches might be seen in a stand-off position vis-a-vis each other, and their institutional relationship might be interpreted as a form of "antagnonistic cooperation" or its converse, "friendly competition." If one were then to introduce competitive potential to interpret the relationship, one would have to conclude that the closer the box score is to the fifty-fifty mark, the more democratic is the system—an obviously absurd inference.

Similar inferential difficulties occur if one introduces some hierarchial preconceptions about the place of either the Congress or the President in American politics. If one assumes that the Congress is the "first branch" of government (De Grazia, 1967), or if one assumes that the President, being elected by the national electorate, is the true spokesman of the people, the answer one gives is totally dependent on the assumptions one makes. The ascendancy of one branch over the other will be variously interpreted as being more or less conducive to democracy. The debate, dependent as it necessarily is on opposed axioms, can go on forever without a conclusion ever being reached. In general, therefore, most scholars have shied away from making such prejudgments that elude empirical testing.

The question as to which of the two branches—Congress or Presidency—is "dominant" at any one time or in any one issue area is not really germane to the perspective of democratic theory. The notion that democracy is predicated on a separation as well as a balance of power between two formally equal branches is not theoretically viable, for it is falsified by the parliamentary system, such as England's, which is built on the fusion of powers. And no one has been found to argue that, from the constitutional standpoint, one or the other system is "more democratic." Empirical research on the swing of the power pendulum between Congress and Presidency may tell us a great deal about the validity of the theory of the separation of powers, therefore, but it cannot tell us anything about the workings of democracy, unless one assumes that the separation of powers is a necessary condition of democracy. But this it is not. Of course, there is always the extreme possibility of total usurpation of power by either branch (under foreseeable conditions more probably by the President), in which case the emergence of dictatorship would mean the end of democracy as we commonly understand it, even if it were called a "people's democracy" or some such. Yet, this prospect is so remote that, even as a "developmental construct," it could hardly be deduced from current tendencies.

It is not the competitive potential but the representational potential in the relationship that seems to make for the kind of antagonistic cooperation between the two branches. Their *mutual* difficulties—and we emphasize mutual to avoid being apologists for one or the other institution—are evidently grounded, in part at least, in the different constituencies from which they derive. As Polsby (1964: 102) has neatly put it, "the germ of conflict over policy is contained in the very rules by which congressmen, senators, and Presidents are elected and sustained in office." But these rules have two sets of consequences. One set refers to the peculiar internal control mechanisms which are quite different in the two institutions; the other relates to inter-institutional controls. By these we do not mean the kind of controls of interest to the constitutional lawyers, but the controls that stem from the ebb and flow of electoral tides that engulf both institutions. The historicity of these tides is such that the conventional ecological-demographic analyses of the different constituencies are themselves subject to recurring changes in the moods of particular electorates. But the varying representational potentials of the Congress and the President, rooted as they are in different constituencies, are only part of the picture. At least equally important in defining the shape of Congressional politics are the Presidential strategies that are employed to mobilize support for Presidential programs. But Presidential strategies, in turn, depend on the size of the majority coalitions that can be put together, and these vary a good deal over time (see Patterson, 1967; Silbey, 1967; Holt, 1967).

If one introduces electoral politics into the equation, the problem of Congressional reform, traditionally perceived as requisite to improved Presidential-Congressional relations, assumes a new dimension. One trouble with Congressional reform proposals is that, if they are enacted, their enactment is usually too little and comes too late (for the Congress is an intrinsically leisurely institution). By the time a reform is introduced, the electoral situation may have radically changed. Who would be willing to predict at this moment what consequences the apparent revival of an ethnic politics at the national level will have for the relationship between Congress and President? How will an excessive ethnic pluralism redefine the relationship between the two institutions?

Perhaps the shape of things to come, if they should come, had some mysterious anticipatory effect on the proposals for Congressional reform that emerged in the sixties. The earlier reform literature had tended to proceed from a view of the Congress as an obstreperous institution that whimsically thwarted vigorous action in the public interest by the President who, as a tribune elected by the whole people, was seen as the embodiment of the nation's democratic will (see Galloway, 1946). "Streamlining Congress" meant making the Congress "more efficient" in supporting Presidential initiatives and programs. In the sixties some of these proposals—concerning seniority, filibuster, committee chairman power, and so on —were sometimes warmed up and regurgitated, mainly in the name of internal democracy rather than efficiency (see Clark, 1964; Bolling, 1965); but another approach to reform had as its purpose less to strengthen the influence of the President than to make the Congress itself a more viable governing institution by expanding and improving its staff operations (Kofmehl, 1962), its information gathering and processing capabilities (see Chartrand et al., 1968), or its oversight functions vis-a-vis the federal bureaucracy (see Wallace, 1960; Kirst, 1969; Henderson, 1970; Harris, 1964). Such reforms would tend to maximize the representational potential of the Congress and to facilitate its own responsiveness rather than to further steps to bring it more effectively under the presumed "democratic control" of the President.[37] If anything, control would be the other way round. No wonder that, in the sixties too, executive liaison officers appeared in Congress in numbers perhaps outmatching the traditional private lobbyists. What this development suggests is that executive-legislative relationships, at least at the second echelon level, may become more consultative and less antagonistic than they have been in the past.

Because marginal or more drastic changes in Congressional-Presidential relations may strengthen Congressional influence on legislation or serve to put brakes on executive action, this need not mean that thereby democracy's participatory potential is maximized. It is only if the public, and especially the attentive public, are able to form appropriate judgments and bring these judgments to bear on public policy that the participatory potential of American democracy can come closer to fulfillment.

CONCLUSION

On the face of things, it is not easy to reconcile the discrepancy between the three received models of democracy—the participatory, the competitive and the representational—and the mediating, negotiating, bargaining and compromising methods by which Congress aggregates individual and group preferences and thereby resolves societal conflicts. Yet, if the research of the sixties shows anything of theoretical importance, it is that the intervention of Congress in the political process has an autonomous effect on the working of democracy as variously stipulated in the received models. Insofar as democracy-in-operation approximates the conditions for the aggregation of preferences on which the models are premised or, put differently, insofar as the participatory, competitive and representational potentials of democracy are maximized, Congress seems to play a critical role.

To expect that all Congressional behavior will at all times conform to one or another model, or to all three models simultaneously, or that it should so conform, is quite unrealisitc. It is equally unrealistic to suppose that mere affirmation of one or another model will bring about the conditions necessary for that model to function, if such conditions can even be imagined. It is precisely because Congressional operations and performance do not conform to the requirements of the received models in their pristine purity, that what would otherwise seem to be mutually exclusive ways of aggregating preferences are integrated in the truly hybrid form of democracy encountered in reality. In this form, any one of the received models loses much of its theoretical exclusivity, but the interdependence of all three models would seem to be confirmed. Each of the models yields its own criteria for assessing the quality of democratic politics, but none alone satisfies all of the conditions of democracy. Under some conditions all three potentials—the participatory, competitive and representational—may be maximized; under other conditions all three potentials may be reduced. But under most conditions of real-world politics as played out in the Congress, it is more likely that one potential is maximized only at the expense of another.

NOTES

1. This essay pursues a theme and is not intended to be an exhaustive review of research and writing on the Congress of the United States in the sixties. Excluded, on the one hand, are general works, usually of a textbook character; included, on the other hand, are a number of outstanding articles reporting research on topics not treated in book form. We should, however, mention three "readers" that contain a number of important research articles: Patterson (ed.), 1968; Peabody and Polsby (eds.), 1969; Wolfinger (ed.), 1970.

2. This seems to be all too often the attitude of the foundations on which modern social science research increasingly depends. There is no doubt in our minds that the flowering of research on the Congress in the sixties was greatly influenced by a generous grant to the American Political Science Association from the Carnegie Foundation for what came to be known as the "Study of Congress." But how sustained is the Foundation's interest? Because successful research invariably suggests new areas for research, will the Foundation remunerate the success by a new grant to follow up? Will any other foundation, and on a scale that is commensurate with research needs? Although the Association's Congressional Fellowship program did not have research as its primary goal, the program also had an identifiable effect on the flowering of research. What is the future of the program? For an appraisal of the research needs of political science and recommendations for sustained support, see Eulau and March, 1969.

3. But the complaints about lack of theory continue. Here are two typical comments culled from recent book reviews. In order not to step on anyone's toes by giving the impression that we necessarily agree with the reviewers, we shall give the location of the quotations but not the titles of the books reviewed or the names of the reviewers. One writes: "The lack of a theoretical framework for comparative committee analysis, the few insights offered into the highly variable internal dynamics (as opposed to structural arrangements) of committees,

the absence of typologies for the exploration of such questions as differing patterns of committee leadership, the relatively small emphasis on coalitions as basic explanatory units of legislative strategy—all of these limit the utility of this book for those seeking help on questions not readily asked from a traditional perspective." Another writes: "The contribution is merely additive, however. The study offers no theoretical framework for analysis. It is not concerned with possible interrelations among the committee variables that are described, and it is not concerned with comparison." There is, on the other hand, a healthy reaction to the phony use of some fashionable theory, as in this comment: "Why worry about whether Congress and the executive are political systems or not? By starting with that assumption . . . one faces having to generalize at a very high level. That can be most frustrating as you try to accommodate the endless number of exceptions. And maybe, just maybe, they aren't systems. Why assume it in advance? Isn't that something to be demonstrated? Those who write about systems do offer a set of criteria to be met. I have yet to see these criteria really applied to both institutions, however, or even made very operational for research purposes."

4. We are using the word "relevance" most reluctantly, given its fashionable misuse in recent years. That is, we are using it strictly as a syntactical term that has no immanent meaning or referent. In particular, we do not mean that if something does not relate to democracy, it is therefore not relevant.

5. An example of a political theorist who has no hang-up in moving back and forth between inherited theory and new empirical research is Thompson, 1970. See also Pitkin, 1967, who, at least in footnotes, gives reluctant, if all too scant, attention to some empirical studies.

6. Peabody, 1969: 3-73. For an earlier survey that also covered the literature on state legislatures, see Eulau and Hinckley, 1966.

7. We have in mind here the inferences about the relationship between citizen apathy and system stability made (from their own data) by Berelson et al., 1954, Chapter 14.

8. There are, however, some dissents from the floor. See Key, 1966; RePass, 1971.

9. Although some nations have made voting in elections obligatory, on the individualistic assumption that each citizen has both a right and duty to participate, involuntary participation deprives the individual from one possibly rational choice—to abstain and do so freely and openly. See Olson, 1965.

10. For an empirical test of the notion of representation as an emergent and systemic property of governance, see Prewitt and Eulau, 1969; this volume, Chapter 7.

11. We also assume that referenda are not feasible means of governance in modern societies for reasons other than the size of the electorate.

12. This has the virtue of avoiding unnecessary and arbitrary statements about whether a two-party system, for instance, is "better" than a multi-party system, a question that can only be answered by asking "better for what?" Translated into empirical terms, one would have to ask "what functions" does a two-party system perform that a multi-party system does not; or "what effects" do two-party as against multi-party systems have? Our formulation, in making party the dependent variable, explains why two- or more-party systems emerge. The independent variable is success in the aggregation of preferences. A totally successful and non-coercive aggregation pattern is difficult to imagine, but if it did occur one would predict a one-party system.

13. Although Polsby does not deal with the "party factor" as such, his work on institutionalization is most important in this connection because it clearly shows that an institution

is not simply a pattern of behavior but a *changing* pattern that follows its own laws of development (Polsby, 1968). There is much linearity in Polsby's data over time. Party behavior may be more cyclical or, perhaps, spiral, and therefore eludes equally systematic analysis.

14. Examples are Peabody's "types of intra-party leadership change" or Jones' "minority party strategies." See Peabody, 1967; Jones, 1968.

15. By all odds the most impressive work of a truly contextual genre is Young, 1966. See also Rothman, 1966.

16. The possible importance of "communication" is demonstrated, if by way of simulation, in Cherryholmes and Shapiro, 1969.

17. The most remarkable of these studies is Bailey, 1950. Although heavily relying on roll-call votes, Truman also used interviews to round out his interpretation; see Truman, 1959.

18. What happens when a theoretically and operationally difficult concept like "power" is used to deal with institutional complexity and change is illustrated by Ripley, 1969. The analysis simply does not ring true.

19. See Mayhew, 1966. This is by far the most sophisticated, from a theoretical point of view, of all roll call studies. The Democrats emerge as the party of "inclusive" and the Republicans of "exclusive" compromise.

20. See Committee on Political Parties, 1950. The main proponent of this view today is Burns, 1963. See also Bailey, 1966.

21. The outstanding work of the sixties on Congressional rsponse to interest group pressures and a source of numerous new insights is Bauer et al., 1963. See also Engler, 1961; and note Dexter, 1969.

22. No Congressional scholar has shown this better than Huitt in his pioneering articles of Congressional committees and leaders now available in book form. See Huitt and Peabody, 1969.

23. An exception is, of course, Grodzins, 1966, but he was not a specialist on Congress; see his Chapter 8, "Local Strength in the American System: Patterns of Representation." For an excellent case study of how representation and federalistic arrangements intersect, see Farkas, 1971.

24. This point of view was articulated by Huntington, 1965: 17: "Particular territorial interests are represented in Congress; particular functional interests in the administration; and the national interest is represented territorially and functionally in the Presidency." For another assessment, see Saloma, 1969: 61-70. See also Price, 1965: 51, who concludes that both houses of Congress, despite their federalistic origins, "have developed into complex institutions whose internal norms and procedures are often of as much importance as outside influences."

25. On constituency ignorance of Congressional behavior, see Key, 1961, Chapter 19, "Representation." That even "party" is a weak link between Congressman and constituency is the conclusion reached by Stokes and Miller, 1962.

26. The most influential work in this respect was Fenno, 1962.

27. In addition to the committee studies more specifically mentioned below, the following should be mentioned: Morrow, 1969; Goodwin, 1970; Farnsworth, 1961; Riddle, 1964.

28. We are using here the concept "bargained" to encompass the wide range of practices discussed previously; "commissioned" in this connection means that committee members see themselves as agents of outside interests, regardless of whether they were actually instructed or not in taking positions.

29. The same three basic types of structure were identified in a study of 82 city councils; see Eulau and Prewitt, 1973.

30. This appears to be the case with reciprocal trade legislation, for instance, where most aggregation now takes place within the executive branch.

31. The House Armed Services Committee appears to operate in a similar fashion. See Dexter, 1963.

32. Sundquist's is, in some respects, the most magisterial work on the problem. Its particular normative presuppositions, however, are not well grounded theoretically and are therefore likely to deprive it of the influence on research it might otherwise have.

33. Its title notwithstanding, Saloma, 1969, is very suggestive in this respect because, unlike most works on Congress, the author's sensitivity to various normative formulations prevents myopic concentration on one when he deals with the empirical phenomenon that interests him.

34. See, in particular, Green and Rosenthal, 1963, a subtle description and interpretation of legislative-executive relations in a policy arena whose substantive novelty also made for novel governmental processes.

35. The most significant work of this genre is Robinson, 1967, which relied, in addition to the author's own case study of the Monroney Resolution of 1958, on 22 cases prepared by different authors, from the neutrality legislation of the thirties to the Cuban Decision of 1961. Robinson valiantly struggled with the problem of generalization and theoretical inference.

36. As Polsby, 1964: 101, points out, box scores of Presidential success "are somewhat unrealistic in that they are usually weighted heavily toward presidential priorities and toward newly proposed legislation. Renewals of old programs, although they may occupy much congressional time and effort, rarely appear in the accounts, nor does noncontroversial legislation."

37. Davidson et al., 1966, is a skillful introduction to the problem of Congressional reform that brings the new empirical knowlege to bear on assessment of relevant proposals. See also Saloma, 1969, who stresses the impact of the computer revolution on the future of Congress.

Chapter 13

TRENDS AND PROSPECTS IN LEGISLATIVE BEHAVIOR RESEARCH

SAMUEL C. PATTERSON
JOHN C. WAHLKE

There is general informal agreement among scholars that the techniques and technology of research on legislative behavior, processes and institutions are now as advanced and sophisticated as are found in use in any area of political research today. Indeed, we can hardly begin to illustrate the many different methods of data collection and data analysis now in common use among legislative behavior researchers. There also is widespread consensus on what uses are appropriate and what are inappropriate for most of these methods, even the newest, most complex, and most innovative.

The point to be made however, and one upon which there is also general agreement, is the lack of a common framework, common focus, and common agreement upon what problems are important, and what questions most need answering. Time and again questions are raised, not about the validity or the intrinsic merits or interest of any given contribution or research finding, but about the bearing of findings in one area upon findings and questions in others. In short, as has often been recognized in other contexts, the greatest needs are not methodological but theoretical and conceptual.

The need is not so much for "the" theory, or even "a" theory of legislative behavior, although should genuine theory in the usual, scientific sense of that term be available it would no doubt represent landmark progress. It is necessary to settle for something considerably less at the present stage of research on legislative behavior and institutions, but it is possible to make considerable progress even with something less. What would seem, under the circumstances, to be attainable as well as useful is a conceptual map that would relate the various concerns to one another, thereby helping us to see more clearly where the investment of research energy is most needed and where it is most likely to yield substantial payoffs.

While there has been considerable theoretical and conceptual progress in the global mapping of research on mass political behavior, there has been no comparable schematicization which could bring some paradigmatic order to scientific analysis of political institutions such as the legislature. To pursue the metaphor, despite an impressive amount of legislative research, mostly about legislatures in the United States and much of it characterized by considerable conceptual and methodological sophistication, we really do not know where we are on the map in comparative, analytic terms (but see Patterson, 1968b). Indeed, we have hardly begun the research-mapping operation that would give us the map on which to try to locate the corpus of extant legislative research.

It could be argued that attempts at global mapping for legislative research, at constructing a paradigm for systematic, comparative investigation, are unnecessary or premature (see LaPalombara, 1970). Gaps in knowledge about legislative institutions and behavior are enormous. For many countries, even elementary information about legislative organization, procedures, political powers, or legitimate authority is not available in a substantial or meaningfully comparable form. Even for highly developed political systems alone, the scope of existential statements available about legislative structures and processes is narrow, and the availability of systematic evidence is remarkably uneven. It could reasonably be contended that the major preoccupation for comparative legislative research, at least as a first step, should be to develop a monographic literature at the level of sophisticated descriptive, institutional analysis. We could, without resolving conceptual problems about what constitutes a legislature or how to assemble conceptually equivalent cross-national (or even comparative subcultural) evidence, simply pursue descriptive studies so that, hopefully for a wide range of systems, we would answer such questions as: "How is the institution called *legislature* organized in Country X? What formal and informal powers does it have? What tasks does it have to perform? How does it process its work? Who are the people who constitute it and run it?"

We could be ahead of the "knowledge game" if we had this kind of primitive, existential information about a wide range of operating legislative institutions. It seems clear that progress in legislative research is more likely to be made by mounting a range of descriptive studies of legislatures in countries where it is reasonably easy to identify such an institution than to proceed by the more circuitous and conceptually ambiguous strategy of attempting a precursory definition of legislative *functions* to be followed by potentially quixotic cross-national inventories of how and where these functions are performed. Little lessons about functional sensitivity need not be lost even though we may reject the field research imperatives of functional analysis.

Loewenberg's (1967) seminal work on the West German Bundestag could be taken as a model for the proliferation of monographic studies which is critically needed in legislative research. Loewenberg adroitly sets the lower house of the

German parliament into its historical and political setting, pointing to the relevant factors of institutionalization which have affected the viability of the institution in the post-World War II period and isolating the main constraints affecting the linkages between the German legislator and his constituents. His analysis elucidates the context of the parliament, showing the principal characteristics of legislative recruitment and the socioeconomic status of the Bundestag membership. He is able to suggest how the *status distinctiveness* of the German legislator both facilitates and inhibits political representation through the parliamentary institution in that political system (see Eulau, 1967). His thorough description of the structural context in which the German legislator operates consciously attempts to relate the main structural features of the institution to its performance as a legislative body. He then analyzes the performance of the Bundestag with respect to its role in cabinet formation, lawmaking, and representation of constituents by carefully examining the instrumental and symbolic behavior of members, the activities of parliamentary committees, and the character of party cleavages and party leadership within the legislature. If a study of this caliber were available for a large number of political systems, theorizing, or at least empirically grounded mapping of comparative analysis, could proceed much more effectively.[1]

But the urge to look beyond an array of descriptive, institutional analyses is compelling if, however gropingly, we are to hope that we will have built the foundations for deductive theory in the comparative analysis of legislative systems. Some progress in the direction of operational mapping for comparative legislative research may be made if we attempt specification of three identifiable analytical problems: levels of analysis, system properties, and analysis of individual behavior.[2]

FOCUS OF
COMPARATIVE LEGISLATIVE RESEARCH

Levels of analysis problems are endemic to comparative political research in general, although they may have much greater complexity in institutional analysis than in research on mass political behavior. There, the main problems involve territorial considerations, concern with appropriate research strategies for analysis of electoral or other mass political behavior in different kinds of territorial units, or the methodological considerations involved in making reciprocal inferences between aggregate and individual data. In legislative research, there is great temptation to generalize from research at one territorial level of analysis to another, even though it cannot be said that conceptual, institutional, methodological, or other difficulties in generalizations across territorial levels of analysis have been much taken into account or even speculated about. In the United States experience, we simply have not dealt with the question of the idiosyncrasy of legislative institutions operating for different territorial units. Some persist in hoping for an analytic level-specific theory, such as a "theory of congressional behavior" (see, f.e., Peabody,

1969: 3-73). Much of the so-called behavioral research about legislative politics in the United States is grounded in studies of the state legislature, often as if no analytical difficulties attend inferring to a national parliament from research on the representative institution in one or more of its territorial subunits.

Quite apart from territorial levels of analysis, comparative legislative research will want to deal with different levels of analysis within the system of legislative behavior in whatever territorial unit (see Eulau, 1969: 1-19). The legislative system should be operationally defined so as to encompass not only the official legislative assembly, but also the components of political interest groups, the executive in his role as legislative leader, the bureaucracy when it seeks legislative representation or is supervised by legislative elites, extra-parliamentary party orgnaizations, and so forth. The legislative system is a constellation of relevant components, and we may wish to investigate the structure and process of interest group legislative representation, as has been attempted across the United States (Zeigler and Baer, 1969). The focus of research may, therefore, be on the legislative system as a whole, on one or more of its subsystems, or on the individual participant in legislative politics. Here, some algorithm of the ecological fallacy may plague legislative research if we are not careful in making inferences about individual behavior from analyses of aggregate subsystem behavior. In the United States context, for instance, there has been difficulty for a long time in inferring about the behavior of lobbyists from the behavior of pressure groups (see Milbrath, 1963).

Again, insofar as comparative legislative research will want to focus heavily upon the legislative assembly itself, we can within it break out commonplace differences in analytical levels. The legislature is a nesting of these levels. We may focus on the parliament as a whole, on its separate houses in bicameral cases, on its party or fraction structure, on its committees or commissions, on friendship or subterritory delegation cliques, on pairs of legislatures, or on the individual representative. Our understanding of a given legislative institution may depend upon how well we can account for the way in which these components are assembled, and our facility in comparative analysis will certainly depend upon working out ways to test the linkages among components of the parliamentary institution and to make comparisons across legislatures in terms of the organizational constraints which may be differentially operating at different levels of the institution.

LEGISLATIVE SYSTEM PROPERTIES

System or group properties are those attributes that, while they affect the behavior of individuals in the system, either characterize the system as a whole in such a way that they cannot be inferred from individual behavior, or are aggregates of individual properties to the system level. A high priority in comparative legislative research is to develop system-level indicators which can be used as variables in cross-national or comparative subnational research. A tentative inventory of the kinds of system properties relevant to comparative legislative research would include *settings, contexts, capacity, consequences,*and *diffusion patterns.*

Settings

Settings are made up of properties of the legislative system itself; they constitute major aspects of the institutional environment in which legislators and other participants in the legislative system behave. The environmental mapping necessary for comparative legislative research certainly would include such properties as the historical setting, the institutional matrix, external linkages, the behavioral environment, and the physical setting or ecology of legislative life. Each of these properties has been explored to some extent in some legislative system, although very little work is comparative. Polsby's (1968, 1969) work on the institutionalization of the United States House of Representatives illustrates the possibilities for comparative research on the historical settings of legislative institutions. Probably the best analysis of the institutional matrix of a legislature is the work of Richard Fenno (1966) on the budgetary committees of the U.S. Congress. External linkages have been examined in research on legislative apportionment and electoral laws (see Cotteret et al., 1960; Rae, 1967). In addition, some work has been done in the United States on support for legislatures in mass publics and among political elites (see Boynton et al., 1968, 1969; see Patterson et al., 1969, 1973). The behavioral settings for legislatures are indicated in research on party cleavages, and especially inventive in this connection has been the work of Mogens Pedersen (1967; see also MacRae, 1958; Finer et al., 1961; MacRae, 1967; Nyholm, 1961; Aydelotte, 1963). Similarly, the research of Eulau and Prewitt (1973) on the emergent decision-making properties of small legislative groups has been an important contribution. While little has been done with the physical setting in which legislative behavior occurs, some analyses have made reference to the importance of this property (as in Patterson, 1959).

Contexts

We may take the term contexts to refer to the aggregated attributes or properties of individuals behaving in the legislative system. Individual legislative behavior may vary in terms of the contextual climate of the legislative institution—the preponderance of lawyers, men of high status, adherents to a particular religious sect, working-class representatives, or members of particular political party can be expected to have an influence on the behavior of legislators. Dominant patterns of value or role expectations may constitute significant contextual effects. In legislative research, we do have a fairly extensive literature on the composition of legislative bodies, and particularly on the social background characteristics of members. The work of Canton (1966) in Argentina, Sartori (1963) in Italy, Hellevik (1969) in Norway, Daalder (1970) in The Netherlands, Dogan (1967) in France, Noponen (1964) in Finland, or Matthews (1960) in the United States illustrate the extent of work in individual countries on the social composition of legislative elites.

Studies of legislators' role orientations, while they have not satisfactorily provided explanatory variables from which to account for the roll-call voting behavior of representatives, have greatly enriched our knowledge about the legislative context, and role analyses may ultimately serve as important providers of contextual variables in comparative analysis (but see Jewell, 1970). The original major work was done by Wahlke and his associates (1962), whose research focused on four of the United States. Stemming from his work, Kornberg (1967) was able to use role analysis to reinterpret the context of the Canadian Parliament. Similar work has been done by Gerlich (1969), who worked with the Vienna Diet, and by Debuyst (1966), who studied the Belgian House of Representatives.

Capacity

Analysis of the capacity of legislative systems involves developing ways to gather evidence about the capabilities the legislative system has to perform effectively. Legislative tasks, goals, and functions vary in importance and emphasis across legislative systems, and ultimately, it will be necessary to delineate the varying statuses and functions of legislative systems in different polities. However, at least for the rather large subset of legislative systems in which the legislature has some political power—some role to play in substantive political decision-making—we could begin to make comparative estimates of legislative capacity by analysis of such components as (Fried, 1966; 28-43):

(1) The *intelligence* capability of the legislature. Is substantial information relevant to substantive policy decisions available to legislators, and do legislators have sufficient expertise and expert staff support to use information effectively?

(2) The *status* of legislators. Are legislators sufficiently prestigious in popular imagery and do they occupy adequate status within the political elite to play a viable role as influencers and makers of public policy?

(3) *Support* for the legislature. Is the legislative institution supported in the critical constituency; does it enjoy substantial social power, popularity, and legitimacy?

(4) Legislative *leadership*. Is the leadership structure of the legislature well organized and sufficiently powerful to provide the steering for the legislature so that it can perform effectively within its terms of reference?

(5) The *organization* of the legislature. Is the legislative institution organized so that it enjoys relative organizational autonomy and is characterized by procedural and structural complexity responsive to its tasks, functions, and goals?

(6) The *formal power* of the legislative branch. Does the legislature have formal, legal power commensurate with its expected role in the polity?

(7) The relative *importance* of the legislature as a policy-making entity. Does the legislative role in the polity carry substantial weight?

As Blondel (1969-1970) has said, the *viscosity* of the legislature in the processes of government varies among political systems. What are the dimensions of these variations? How are these variations affected by the structural location of the legislative body in the polity—whether the legislature is largely part of the input machinery transmitting demands to policy-makers, whether the legislature is mainly involved in supervision of rule implementation, or whether the legislature is the principal rule-making agency in the governmental process?

Consequences

Hopefully, it will not seem irrelevant to assert that legislative systems have consequences. Their existence and their activities produce effects. In the case of highly-institutionalized, policy-making legislatures like that of the U.S. Congress, the tendency in research has been to take the consequences of legislative activity as self-evident. As a result, United States political scientists have not paid much attention to the policy or systemic impacts of legislative activity, especially beyond the point of accounting for the shape of legislative policy outputs. In a comparative framework, the saliency of analysis of the consequences of legislative activity ought to be clear. At the level of immediate legislative consequences, we would want comparative data on the differential outputs of legislative systems—the relative role of policy outputs, symbolic outputs, and services in different kinds of systems. We would want evidence about the relative short-run consequences of these differential outputs on social, political, or economic change in different kinds of polities. Packenham (1970) has tried to open the discussion of these kinds of effects in underdeveloped countries. And we would want data about the longer-run consequences of legislative activity on the flow of demand inputs and support for the legislature (feedback effects). Loewenberg (1971) has begun to probe these long run consequences in his analysis of the effects of legislative behavior on regime stability.

Diffusion Patterns

While it involves a general problem of comparative social research, analysis of patterns of diffusion of political structures or values may be especially critical in comparative research on highly institutionalized behavior such as we would expect to find exhibited in legislative settings.[3] It seems highly likely, for example, that research findings about role expectations held by legislators or about specialized legislative structures may not indicate functional relationships to other individual attributes or system properties, but rather emerge because legislative conceptions and practices are often spread by diffusion. Little explicit research in political science has been given to the diffusion process (but see Walker, 1969). Nonetheless, it does seem clear that, let us say, British and United States legislative models have been widely copied. Thus, the Indian Lok Sabha is patterned in many respects after the British House of Commons (Singhvi, 1970); the Philippine

Congress bears many resemblances to the United States Congress (Stauffer, 1970); United States forms and practices very much influenced the development of the Congress of Micronesia (Meller, 1969). In our analysis of functional linkages among variables or attributes in comparative legislative behavior research, we must be alert to the extent to which correlations may be largely artifacts of diffusional processes. If we were to discover, for instance, that 60 percent of the national legislators in Cambodia articulated Burkean expectations about their legislative role and that there was a high correlation between trustee role orientations and the marginality of elections in legislative constituencies in that political system, we may not be talking about a functional linkage at all. Anglo-American conceptions about what a legislator ought to do may be articulated widely in Third World settings without their having much meaning at all (see Hopkius, 1970) At the same time, patterns of diffusion may be of great interest in their own right. Intrinsically, mapping the diffusion of legislative structures and values on a cross-national basis may greatly illuminate the processes of institutionalization of legislative bodies, and provide an analytical device for plumbing in greater depth modes of cultural adaptation to innovations in institutions.

INDIVIDUAL LEGISLATIVE BEHAVIOR

Although the individual behavior of representatives has been conceptualized and measured in a variety of ways, the predominant interest in such behavior has been focused upon two kinds of dependent variables: role orientations and policy or issue attitudes. The study of legislators' conceptions of their jobs as representatives was opened by the seminal research of Wahlke, Eulau, Buchanan, and Ferguson and pursued by a host of investigators, including Gerlich, Debuyst, Kornberg, Barber (1965), and Davidson (1969). Substantial research effort has been invested in identifying both the congeries of role orientations extant in different legislative bodies and the independent variables which help to account for variations in role conceptions held by legislators. Because of the interest of United States investigators in the representational linkages between legislators and their constituents clustered in territorial districts, much of the research in the United States has been concentrated on so-called "representational" roles; research outside the United States, in systems in which the impact of political parties appears to have *prima facie*, the profoundest effect upon the perspectives of elected representatives, has given more attention to party-related role orientations. Although a large number of independent variables have been constructed to account for variations among legislators in their role orientations, most common have been those of legislators' social background characteristics, and attributes of the milieu from which legislators have been elected. In making an assessment of the outcomes of a number of these investigations, Jewell (1970: 483) concluded that

The evidence concerning possible sources of legislative roles is fragmentary and sometimes contradictory. For these reasons it would be hazardous to draw any firm conclusions about the sources of roles. The evidence does suggest that no single variable offers an adequate causal explanation and that characteristics of districts as well as personal qualities and experiences of legislators are associated with differences in roles. The fact that so many variables appear to have some effect on roles enhances the value of role as an analytical concept. It is doubtful that we could ever measure with great accuracy the impact that a combination of personal and district variables has on the attitudes and perceptions of an entire legislative body. Role provides a shortcut, a way of summarizing the total effect that these various forces have on legislators. An examination of the sources of role is useful because it can make us aware of the complexity of causal factors and point out those which are most likely to be important.

Analysis of the individual policy or issue attitudes of legislators has largely taken place where the roll-call voting behavior of representatives could provide the data necessary to construct a metric indicating legislators' relative location in regard to some issue domain (e.g. welfare support, internationalism, support for civil rights), or some generalized dimension of attitude (e.g. liberalism to conservatism). The methodological strategies and problems associated with constructing the appropriate dependent variable from roll-call voting data have been worked over pretty thoroughly (see MacRae, 1970; Anderson et al., 1966). Among the independent variables which have been investigated are those of political party, constituency factors, regionalism, legislators' personal predispositions and background characteristics, factors of legislative structure such as clique, committee or delegation, and legislative norms.[4] A finding of general importance has been that, even in the fluid partisan structure of United States legislatures, political party differentiation provides the independent variable of greatest importance in accounting for variations in the policy attitudes of representatives. Comparisons of different houses of bicameral legislatures, examination of different policy dimensions, analysis of voting dimensions over time, and analysis of voting behavior in multiparty legislatures have made it possible to specify the conditions under which party and constituency influences on roll-call voting have differential impacts on representatives (see Clausen and Cheney, 1970; MacRae, 1967; Rosenthal, 1969). The now-classic Miller-Stokes (1963) analysis illustrates the analytical potential of combining legislative roll-call data and data from systematic interviews with legislators and samples of legislators' constituents so as to make it possible to introduce as independent variables legislators' own perceptions of constituents' opinions, legislators' policy orientations measured independently from their voting behavior, and constituents' issue opinions. Unfortunately, this very imaginatively designed analysis was based upon very small constituency samples and has not been replicated for elections beyond that of the 1959 congressional election in the United States (but see Cnudde and McCrone, 1966).

Ingenious attempts to construct dependent variables for legislators' policy attitudes where roll-call votes do not, in general, provide the basis for scaling nuances in issue attitudes have been made in research on the British House of Commons. The most imaginative effort of this kind has been that of Finer, Berrington, and Bartholomew (1961), who analysed so-called "early day" motions in the House of Commons to array Labour and Conservative MPs on a number of issues dealing with foreign affairs, social welfare policy, civil liberties, European unity, and penal policy. Variations in attitudinal positions within British parliamentary parties were investigated in terms of the independent variable of occupational background, education, trade union sponsorship, age, and type of constituency. In addition, attempts have been made at the analysis of the individual behavior of backbenchers in the House of Commons by selecting out for detailed analysis divisions on which significant rebellions occurred within one or both of the two major parliamentary parties, and this type of analysis is well-illustrated by the work of Jackson (1968). Finally, Richards (1970: 179-196) has analyzed a fairly large number of "free votes," on which MPs voted without the benefit of party whips. Richards' analysis involved an effort to assess the effects of occupation, education, age, religion, and region on voting on bills dealing with capital punishment, homosexuality, abortion, divorce, and Sunday entertainment. While his analysis is unnecessarily inconclusive, it does represent an illustration of the possibilities of analyzing the joint effects of party, constituency, and personal factors in legislators' policy attitudes, even in legislative institutions where most issues are decided purely along party lines.

The general task of mapping comparative legislative research strategy will require the time and effort of a large number of scholars in various countries who can refine and elaborate conceptual and strategic research problems and who can add bricks to the construction of comparative-based theory by persistent empirical research.

NOTES

1. For a synthesis of work on legislative behavior in the United States, see Jewell and Patterson, 1973.

2. These problems are, of course, matters of general discussion in comparative politics. See, for example, Przeworski and Teune, 1970.

3. This is a problem of considerable complexity which cannot be elucidated here in any detail. It has been discussed most thoroughly in cultural anthropology, and especially by Naroll, 1968.

4. An excellent summary and bibliography can be found in Cherryholmes and Shapiro, 1969. Major American studies would include Truman, 1959; Mayhew, 1966; Shannon, 1968; MacRae, 1958; Turner, 1970; Rieselbach, 1966.

BIBLIOGRAPHY

ABRAMS, M. (1962) "Social trends and electoral behavior." *Brit. J. Soc.* 13: 228-242.

ALMOND, G. A. (1965) "A developmental approach to political systems." *World Politics* 17: 183-214.

——— and VERBA, S. (1963) *The Civic Culture.* Princeton, NJ: Princeton U. Press.

ANDERSON, L. F., WATTS, M. W. Jr., and WILCOX, A. R. (1966) *Legislative Roll-Call Analysis.* Evanston, IL: Northwestern U. Press.

ANTON, T. J. (1967) "Roles and symbols in the determination of state expenditures." *Midw. J. of Pol. Sci.* 11: 27-43.

ARISTOTLE (1943) *Politics.* New York: Modern Library.

AXELROD, R. (1967) "The structure of public opinion on policy issues." *Publ. Op. Q.* 31: 51-60.

AYDELOTTE, W. O. (1963) "Voting patterns in the British House of Commons in the 1840's." *Studies in Society and History* 5: 134-163.

BACHRACH, P. (1967) *The Theory of Democratic Elitism.* Boston: Little, Brown.

BAILEY, S. K. (1966) *The New Congress.* New York: St. Martin's.

——— and SAMUEL, H. D. (1952) *Congress at Work.* New York: Holt.

BARBER, J. D. (1965) *The Lawmakers.* New Haven, CT: Yale U. Press.

BARKER, E. (1945) "Burke and his Bristol constituency, 1774-1780," in *Essays on Government.* Fair Lawn, NJ: Oxford U. Press.

BAUER, R. A., de SOLA POOL, I., and DEXTER, L. A. (1963) *American Business and Public Policy: The Politics of Foreign Trade.* New York: Atherton.

BEARD, C. A. and LEWIS, J. D. (1932) "Representative government in evolution." *Amer. Pol. Sci. Rev.* 26: 223-240.

BEER, S. H. (1957) "The representation of interests in British government." *Amer. Pol. Sci. Rev.* 51: 613-650.

——— (1966) "The British legislature and the problem of mobilizing consent," in E. Frank (ed.) *Lawmakers in a Changing World.* Englewood Cliffs, NJ: Prentice-Hall.

BELOFF, M. [ed.] (1948) *The Federalist or, The New Constitution.* Oxford: Blackwell.

BERELSON, B., LAZARSFELD, P. J. and McPHEE, W. (1954) *Voting.* Chicago: U. of Chicago Press.

BIRCH, A. H. (1964) *Representative and Responsible Government.* Toronto: U. of Toronto Press.

——— (1971) *Representation.* London: St. Martin's.

BLAKE, D. H. (1967) "Leadership succession and its effects on foreign policy as observed in the general assembly." Mimeo. Annual Meeting of Midwest Conference of Political Scientists, Indiana.

BLONDEL, J. (1969-1970) "Legislative behavior: some steps towards a cross-national measurement." *Government and Oppostion* 5: 67-85.

BLOOM, A. (1963) "Jean-Jacques Rousseau," in L. Strauss and J. Cropsey (eds.) *History of Political Philosophy.* Chicago: Rand McNally.

BLUHM, W. T. (1965) *Theories of the Political System.* Englewood Cliffs, NJ: Prentice-Hall.

BOLLING, R. (1965) *House Out of Order.* New York: Dutton.

BOYNTON, G. R., PATTERSON, S. C. and HEDLUND, R. D. (1968) "The structure of public support for legislative institutions." *Midw. J. of Pol. Sci.* 12: 163-180.

——— (1969) "The missing links in legislative politics: attentive constituents." *J. of Pol.* 31: 700-721.

BOYNTON, G. R., PATTERSON, S. C., and WAHLKE, J. C. (1972) "Dimensions of support in legislative systems," in A. Kornberg (ed.) *Legislatures in Comparative Perspective.* New York: McKay.

BRAILSFORD, H. N. (1961) *The Levellers and the English Revolution.* Stanford, CA: Stanford U. Press.

BRYCE, J. (1921-1924) *Modern Democracies.* New York: Macmillan.

BUCHANAN, J. M. and TULLOCK, G. (1962) *The Calculus of Consent: Logical Foundations of Constitutional Democracy.* Ann Arbor: U. of Michigan Press.

BUCHANAN, W. (1965) "An inquiry into purposive voting." *J. of Pol.* 18: 281-296.

BURKE, E. (1774) "Speech to the electors of Bristol." *Works.* London: S. & C. Rivington.

BURNS, J. M. (1963) *The Deadlock of Democracy: Four-Party Politics in America.* Englewood Cliffs, NJ: Prentice-Hall.

CAMPBELL, A., CONVERSE, P. E., MILLER, W. E., and STOKES, D. E. (1960) *The American Voter.* New York: John Wiley.

——— (1966) *Elections and the Political Order.* New York: John Wiley.

CANTON, D. (1966) *El Parlemento Argentino en Epocas de Cambio: 1890, 1916 y 1946.* Buenos Aires.

CANTRIL, H. and STRUNK, M. (1951) *Public Opinion 1935-46.* Princeton, NJ: Princeton U. Press.

——— (1965) *The Patterns of Human Concerns.* New Brunswick, NJ: Rutgers U. Press.

CHAMBERLAIN, L. H. (1946) *The President, Congress and Legislation.* New York: Columbia U. Press.

CHARTRAND, R. L., JANDA, K., and HUGO, M. [eds.] (1968) *Information Support, Program Budgeting, and the Congress.* New York: Spartan Books.

CHERRYHOLMES, C. H. AND SHAPIRO, M. J. (1969) *Representatives and Roll Calls: A Computer-Simulation of Voting in the Eighty-Eighth Congress.* Indianapolis: Bobbs-Merrill.

CLAPP, C. (1963) *The Congressman: His Job as He Sees It.* Washington, D.C.: Brookings Institution.

CLARK, J. S. (1964) *Congress: The Sapless Branch.* New York: Harper and Row.

CLAUSEN, A. R. (1973) *How Congressmen Decide.* New York: St. Martin's.

CNUDDE, C. F. and McCRONE, D. J. (1966) "The linkage between constituency attitudes and congressional voting: a causal model." *Amer. Pol. Sci. Rev.* 60: 66-72.

COHEN, M. R. (1931) *Reason and Nature.* New York: Harcourt, Brace.

――― (1933) *Law and the Social Order.* New York: Harcourt, Brace.

――― (1949) *Studies in Philosophy and Science.* New York: Holt.

COMMITTEE ON POLITICAL PARTIES OF THE AMERICAN POLITICAL SCI― ENCE ASSOCIATION (1950) "Toward a more responsible two-party system." *Amer. Pol. Sci. Rev.* 44, Supplement.

CONVERSE, P. E. (1964) "The nature of belief systems in mass publics," in D. E. Apter (ed.) *Ideology and Discontent.* New York: Free Press.

――― and DUPEUX, G. (1962) "Politicization of the electorate in France and the United States." *Publ. Opinion Q.* 26: 1-23; reprinted in Campbell et al., *Elections and the Political Order,* 1966: 269-291.

COTTERET, J. M., EMERI, C., and LALUMIERE, P. (1960) *Lois Electorales et Inegalites de Representation en France, 1936-1960.* Paris.

CUMMINGS, M. C., Jr. (1966) *Congressmen and the Electorate: Elections for the U.S. House and the President, 1920-1964.* New York: Free Press.

CUTRIGHT, P. (1965) "Political structure, economic development, and national security programs." *Amer. J. Soc.* 70: 537-548.

DAALDER, H. and HUBEE-BOONZAAIJER, S. (1970) "Sociale herkomst en politieke recrutering van Nederlandse kamerleden in 1968." *Acta Politica* 5: 292-333.

DAHL, R. A. (1956) *A Preface to Democratic Theory.* Chicago: U. of Chicago Press.

――― (1961) *Who Governs?* New Haven, CT: Yale U. Press.

――― (1966) "Further reflections on 'the elitist theory of democracy.'" *Amer. Pol. Sci. Rev.* 60: 296-304.

――― and LINDBLOM, C. E. (1953) *Politics, Economics and Welfare.* New York: Harper and Row.

DAVIDSON, R. H. (1969) *The Role of the Congressman.* New York: Pegasus.

――― KOVENOCK, D. M., and O'LEARY, M. K. (1966) *Congress in Crisis: Politics and Congressional Reform.* Belmont, CA: Wadsworth.

DAWSON, R. E. and ROBINSON, J. A. (1963) "Inter-party competition, economic variables and welfare policies in the American States." *J. of Pol.* 25: 265-289.

DEBUYST, F. (1966) *La Fonction Parlementaire en Belgique: Mecanismes d'Acces et Images.* Brussels.

DeGRAZIA, A. (1951) *Public and Republic-Political Representation in America.* New York: Knopf.

――― (1967) *Congress: The First Branch of Government.* Garden City, NY: Doubleday Anchor.

DE JOUVENEL, B. (1961) "On the nature of political science." *Amer. Pol. Sci. Rev.* 55: 773-779.

DE MONTESQUIEU, B. (1962) *The Spirit of the Laws.* New York: Hafner.

DEXTER, L. A. (1963) "Congressmen and the making of military policy," in R. L. Peabody and N. W. Polsby (eds.) *New Perspectives on the House of Representatives.* Chicago: Rand McNally.

――― (1969) *The Sociology and Politics of Congress.* Chicago: Rand McNally.

DEWEY, J. (1938) *Logic: The Theory of Inquiry.* New York: Holt.

DOGAN, M. (1967) "Les filieres de la carriere politique en France." *Revue Francaise de Sociologie* 8: 468-492.

DOWNS, A. (1957) *An Economic Theory of Democracy.* New York: Harper and Row.

DYE, T. R. (1966) *Politics, Economics and the Public: Policy Outcomes in the American States.* Chicago: Rand McNally.

EASTON, D. (1953) *The Political System.* New York: Knopf.

———— (1965) *A Framework for Political Analysis.* Englewood Cliffs, NJ: Prentice-Hall.

———— (1966) *A Systems Analysis of Political Life.* New York John Wiley.

EDELMAN, M. (1964) *The Symbolic Uses of Politics.* Urbana: U. of Illinois Press.

———— (1971) *Politics as Symbolic Action.* Chicago: Markham.

EHRENBERG, V. (1957) *Der Staat der Griechen I. Teil: Der Helenische Staat.* Leipzig: Teubner.

ELAZAR, D. J. (1962) *The American Partnership.* Chicago: U. of Chicago Press.

———— (1966) *American Federalism: A View from the States.* New York: Thomas Y. Crowell.

ELDERSVELD, S. J. (1964) Political Parties: A Behavioral Analysis. Chicago: Rand McNally.

ENGLER, R. (1961) The Politics of Oil. New York: Macmillan.

EPSTEIN, L. D. (1964) "Electoral Decision and Policy Mandate: An Empirical Example." Publ. Op. Q. 28: 564-472.

ERIKSON, R. S. (1971) "The electoral impact of congressional role call voting." *Amer. Pol. Sci. Rev.* 65: 1018-1032.

EULAU, H. (1941) "Theories of federalism under the Holy Roman Empire." *Amer. Pol. Sci. Rev.* 35: 643-664.

———— (1957) "The ecological basis of party systems: the case of Ohio." *Midw. J. of Pol. Sci.* 1: 125-135.

———— (1962) "Comparative political analysis: a methodological note: *Midw. J. of Pol. Sci.* 6: 397-407.

———— (1964a) "Lobbyists: the wasted profession." *Publ. Opinion Q.* 28: 27-38.

———— (1964b) "Logics of rationality in unanimous decision-making," in C. J. Friedrich (ed.) *Rationality.* New York: Atherton.

———— (1967) "Changing views of representation," in I. de Sola Pool (ed.) *Contemporary Political Science: Toward Empirical Theory.* New York: McGraw-Hill.

———— (1968) "The maddening methods of Harold D. Lasswell: some philosophical underpinnings." *J. of Pol.* 30: 3-24.

———— (1969) "On units and levels of analysis," in H. Eulau, *Micro-Macro Political Analysis: Accents of Inquiry.* Chicago: Aldine.

———— (1971) "The legislative system and after: on closing the micro-macro gap," in O. Walter (ed.) *Political Scientists at Work.* Belmont, MA.: Duxbury.

———— (1977) "Multilevel methods in comparative politics." *Amer. Behavioral Scientist* 21: 37-59.

———— and EYESTONE, R. (1968) "Policy maps of city councils and policy outcomes: a developmental analysis." *Amer. Pol. Sci. Rev.* 62: 124-143.

EULAU, H. and HINCKLEY, K. (1966) "Legislative institutions and processes," in J. A. Robinson (ed.) *Political Science Annual I.* Indianapolis: Bobbs-Merrill.

EULAU, H. and KARPS, P. D. (1977) "The puzzle of representation: specifying components of responsiveness." *Legisl. Studies Q.* 2: 233-254.

EULAU, H. and MARCH, J. G. (1969) *Political Science.* Englewood Cliffs, NJ: Prentice-Hall.

EULAU, H. and PREWITT, K. (1973) *Labyrinths of Democracy: Adaptations, Linkages, Representation, and Policies in Urban Politics.* Indianapolis: Bobbs-Merrill.

EULAU, H., WAHLKE, J. C., BUCHANAN, W. and FERGUSON, L. C. (1959) "The role of the representative: some empirical observations on the theory of Edmund Burke." *Amer. Pol. Sci. Rev.* 53: 742-756.

EYESTONE, R. and EULAU, H. (1968) "City councils and policy outcomes: developmental profiles." in J. Q. Wilson (ed.) *City Politics and Public Policy.* New York: John Wiley.

FAIRLIE, J. A. (1940) "The nature of political representation." *Amer. Pol. Sci. Rev.* 34: 236-248; 456-466.

FARKAS, S. (1971) *Urban Lobbying: Mayors in the Federal Arena.* New York: New York U. Press.

FARNSWORTH, D. N. (1961) *The Senate Committee On Foreign Relations.* Urbana: U. of Illinois Press.

FARRINGTON, B. (1963) *Greek Science.* Baltimore: Penguin.

FENNO, R. F. (1962) "The House Appropriations Committee as a political system: the problem of integration." *Amer. Pol. Sci. Rev.* 56: 301-324.

――― (1966) *The Power of the Purse: Appropriations Politics in Congress.* Boston: Little, Brown.

――― (1973) *Congressmen in Committees.* Boston: Little, Brown.

――― (1977) "U.S. House members in their constituencies: an exploration." *Amer. Pol. Sci. Rev.* 71: 883-917.

FIELLIN, A. (1962) "The functions of informal groups in legislative institutions." *J. of Politics* 24: 79-91.

FINER, H. (1949) *The Theory and Practice of Modern Government.* New York: Holt.

FINER, S. E., BERRINGTON, H. B. and BARTHOLOMEW, D. J. (1961) *Backbench Opinion in the House of Commons, 1955-1959.* Oxford.

FIORINA, M. P. (1974) *Representatives, Roll Calls, and Constituencies.* Lexington, MA: D. C. Heath.

――― (1977) "The case of the vanishing marginals: the bureaucracy did it." *Amer. Pol. Sci. Rev.* 71: 177-181.

FISHEL, J. (1969) "Party, ideology and the congressional challenge." *Amer. Pol. Sci. Rev.* 63: 1213-1232.

FISHER, R. A. (1937) *The Design of Experiments.* Edinburgh: Oliver and Boyd.

FRANCIS, W. L. (1967) *Legislative Issues in the Fifty States.* Chicago: Rand McNally.

FRIED, R. C. (1966) *Comparative Political Institutions.* New York: Macmillan.

FRIEDRICH, C. J. (1946-1950) *Constitutional Government and Democracy.* Boston: Ginn and Company.

FROMAN, L. A., Jr (1963) *Congressmen and Their Constituencies.* Chicago: Rand McNally.

――― (1967) "An analysis of public policies in cities." *J. of Politics.* 29: 94-108.

――― (1967) *The Congressional Process: Strategies, Rules and Procedures.* Boston: Little, Brown.

GALLOWAY, G. (1946) *Congress at the Crossroads.* New York: Thomas Y. Crowell.

――― (1953) *The Legislative Process in Congress.* New York: Thomas Y. Crowell.

GALTUNG, J. (1969) *Theory and Methods of Social Research.* New York: Columbia U. Press.

GARCEAU, O. (1951) "Research in the political process." *Amer. Pol. Sci. Rev.* 45: 69-85.

GERLICH, P. and KRAMER, H. (1969) *Abgeordnete in der Parteiendemokratie.* Vienna: Verlag fur Geschichte und Politik.

GERWITH, A. (1956) *Marsilius of Padua: The Defender of Peace.* New York: Columbia U. Press.

GOODWIN, G., Jr. (1970) *The Little Legislatures: Committees in Congress.* Amherst: U. of Massachusetts Press.

GOSNELL, H. F. (1948) *Democracy: The Threshold of Freedom.* New York: Ronald.

GREEN, H. P. and ROSENTHAL, A. (1963) *Government of the Atom: The Integration of Powers.* New York: Atherton.

GRODZINS, M. (1966) *The American System: A New View of Government in the United States.* Chicago: Rand McNally.

GROSS, B. D. (1953) *The Legislative Struggle.* New York: McGraw-Hill.

HADDEN, J. K. and BORGATTA, E. F. (1965) *American Cities: Their Social Characteristics.* Chicago: Rand McNally.

HARRIS, J. P. (1964) *Congressional Control of Administration.* Washington, D.C.: Brookings.

HELLEVIK, O. (1969) *Stortinget: En Social Elite?* Oslo.

HENDERSON, T. A. (1970) *Congressional Oversight of Executive Agencies: A Study of the House Committee on Governmental Operations.* Gainsville: U. of Florida Press.

HERRING, E. P. (1929) *Group Representation Before Congress.* Baltimore: Johns Hopkins.

HINCKLEY, B. (1967) "Interpreting house midterm elections: toward a measurement of the in-party's 'expected' loss of seats." *Amer. Pol. Sci. Rev.* 61: 694-700.

——— (1970) "Incumbency and the presidential vote in senate elections: defining parameters of subpresidential voting." *Amer. Pol. Sci. Rev.* 64: 836-842.

——— (1971a) *The Seniority System in Congress.* Bloomington: U. of Indiana Press.

——— (1971b) *Stability and Change in Congress.* New York: Harper and Row.

HOFFERBERT, R. I. (1966) "The relationship between public policy and some structural and environmental variables in the American states." *Amer. Pol. Sci. Rev. 60:* 73-82.

HOLDEN, A. M. (1930) "The imperative mandate in the Spanish Cortes of the middle ages." *Amer. Pol. Sci. Rev.* 24: 886-912.

HOLT, J. (1967) *Congressional Insurgents and the Party system, 1909-1916.* Cambridge, MA: Harvard U. Press.

HOLTZMAN, A. (1970) *Legislative Liaison: Executive Leadership in Congress.* Chicago: Rand McNally.

HOPKINS, R. F. (1970) "The role of the M.P. in Tanzania." *Amer. Pol. Sci. Rev.* 64: 754-771.

HORN, S. (1970) *Unused Power: The Work of the Senate Committee on Appropriations.* Washington, D.C.: Brookings.

HUITT, R. K. and PEABODY, R. L. (1969) *Congress: Two Decades of Analysis.* New York: Harper and Row.

HUNTER, F. (1953) *Community Power Structure.* Chapel Hill, NC: U. of North Carolina Press.

HUNTINGTON, S. (1965) "Congressional responses to the twentieth century," in D. B. Truman (ed.) *The Congress and America's Future.* Englewood Cliffs, NJ: Prentice-Hall.

HYNEMAN, C. S. (1938) "Tenure and turnover of legislative personnel." *Annals of the Amer. Acad. of Pol. and Soc. Sci.* 195: 21-31.

——— (1940) "Who makes our laws?" *Pol. Sci. Q.* 55: 556-581.

INTER-UNIVERSITY CONSORTIUM FOR POLITICAL RESEARCH (1971) "The 1958 American representation study: congressmen and constituents (SRC 433)." Ann Arbor: ICPR.

JACKSON, J. E. (1974) *Constituencies and Leaders in Congress.* Cambridge, MA: Harvard U. Press.

JACKSON, R. J. (1968) *Rebels and Whips: An Analysis of Disension, Discipline, and Cohesion in British Political Parties.* London.

JACOB, H. and LIPSKY, M. (1968) "Outputs, structure and power: an assessment of changes in the study of state and local politics," in M. D. Irish (ed.) *Political Science: Advance of the Discipline."* Englewood Cliffs, NJ: Prentice-Hall.

JACOB, H. and VINES, K. N., [eds.] (1965) *Politics in the American States.* Boston: Little, Brown.

JANDA, K. (1961) *Democratic Theory and Legislative Behavior: A Study of Legislator-Constituency Relationships.* Unpubl. Ph.D. thesis, Bloomington: Indiana University.

JENNINGS, I. (1936) *Cabinet Government.* Cambridge, MA: Cambridge U. Press.

——— (1957) *Parliament.* Cambridge, MA: Cambridge U. Press.

JENNINGS, M. K. and ZEIGLER, H. (1971) "Response styles and politics: the case of school boards." *Midw. J. of Pol. Sci.* 15: 290-321.

JEWELL, M. E. (1962) *Senatorial Politics and Foreign Policy.* Lexington: U. of Kentucky Press.

——— (1970) "Attitudinal determinants of legislative behavior: the utility of role analysis," in A. Kornberg and L. Musolf (eds.) *Legislatures in Developmental Perspective.* Durham, NC: Duke U. Press.

——— and PATTERSON, S. C. (1966) *The Legislative Process in the United States.* New York: Random House.

JONES, C. O. (1961) "Representation in Congress: the case of the House Agriculture Committee." *Amer. Pol. Sci. Rev.* 55: 358-367.

——— (1964) *Party and Policy-Making: The House Republican Policy Committee."* New Brunswick: Rutgers U. Press.

——— (1967) *Every Second Year: Congressional Behavior and the Two-Year Term.* Washington, D.C.: Brookings.

——— (1968) "The minority party and policy-making in the House of Representatives." *Amer. Pol. Sci. Rev.* 62: 481-493.

——— (1970) *Minority Party Leadership in Congress.* Boston: Little, Brown.

KESSEL, J. H. (1964) "The Washington congressional delegation." *Midw. J. of Pol. Sci.* 8: 1-21.

KEY, V. O., Jr. (1961) *Public Opinion and American Democracy.* New York: Knopf.

——— (1966) *The Responsible Electorate: Rationality in Presidential Voting, 1936-1960.* Cambridge, MA: Harvard U. Press.

KINGDON, J. W. (1967) "Politicians' beliefs about voters." *Amer. Pol. Sci. Rev.* 61: 137-145.

——— (1973) *Congressmen's Voting Decisions.* New York: Harper and Row.

KIRKPATRICK, E. M. (1971) "Toward a more responsible two-party system: political science, policy science, or pseudo-science?" *Amer. Pol. Sci. Rev.* 65: 965-990.

KIRST, M. W. (1969) *Government Without Passing Laws: Congress' Nonstatutory Techniques for Appropriations Control.* Chapel Hill: U. of Carolina Press.

KOENIG, L. W. (1965) *Congress and the President.* Chicago: Scott, Foresman.

KOFMEHL, K. (1962) *Professional Staffs of Congress.* West Lafayette, IN: Purdue U. Studies.

KORNBERG, A. (1967) *Canadian Legislative Beahvior: A Study of the 25th Parliament.* New York: Holt, Rinehart and Winston.

——— (1972) *Legislatures in Comparative Perspective.* New York: McKay.

——— and MUSOLF, L. D., [eds.] (1970) *Legislatures in Developmental Perspective.* Durham, NC: Duke U. Press.

KUHN, T. S. (1962) *The Structure of Scientific Revolutions.* Chicago: U. of Chicago Press.

LANDAU, M. (1972) *Political Theory and Political Science.* New York: Macmillan.

LaPALOMBARA, J. (1970) "Parsimony and empiricism in comparative politics: an antischolastic view," in R. T. Holt and J. E. Turner (eds.) *The Methodology of Comparative Research.* New York: Free Press.

LARSEN, J.A.O. (1955) *Representative Government in Greek and Roman History.* Berkeley: U. of California Press.

LASKI, H. J. (1939) "The obsolescence of federalism." *The New Republic.* Pp. 367-369.

LASSWELL, H. D. (1948) "General framework: person, personality, group, culture," in *The Analysis of Political Behavior.* New York: Oxford U. Press.

——— and KAPLAN, A. (1950) *Power and Society.* New Haven, CT: Yale U. Press.

LASSWELL, H. D., MERRIAM, C. E. and SMITH, T. V. (1950) *A Study of Power.* Glencoe, IL: Free Press.

LATHAM, E. (1952) *The Group Basis of Politics.* Ithaca, NY: Cornell U. Press.

LAZARSFELD, P. F., BERELSON, B. and GAUDET, H. (1944, 1948) *The People's Choice.* New York: Columbia U. Press.

LEUTHOLD, D. E. (1968) *Electioneering in a Democracy.* New York: John Wiley.

LEWIN, K. (1935) "The conflict between Aristolelian and Galileian modes of thought in contemporary psychology," in K. Lewin, *A Dynamic Theory of Personality.* New York: McGraw-Hill.

LINDBERG, L. (1966) "The role of the European parliament in an emerging European Community," in E. Frank (ed.) *Lawmakers in a Changing World.* Englewood Cliffs, NJ: Prentice-Hall.

LINDBLOM, C. E. (1965) *The Intelligence of Democracy.* New York: Free Press.

——— and BRAYBROOKE, D. (1963) *A Strategy of Decision.* Glencoe, IL: Free Press.

LIPPMANN, W. (1946) *Public Opinion.* New York: Penguin.

LOEWENBERG, G. (1967) *Parliament in the German Political System.* Ithaca, NY: Cornell U. Press.

——— (1971) "The influence of parliamentary behavior on regime stability." *Comparative Politics* 3: 177-200.

——— (1972) "Comparative legislative research," in S. C. Patterson and J. C. Wahlke (eds.) *Comparative Legislative Behavior: Frontiers of Research.* New York: John Wiley.

LOEWENSTEIN, K. (1957) *Political Power and the Governmental Process.* Chicago: U. of Chicago Press.

LOWELL, L. (1902) "The influence of party upon legislation in England and America." *Annual Report of the American Historical Association for 1901.* Vol. 1: 321-542.

LOWI, T. J. (1964) "American business, public policy, case studies and political theory." *World Politics* 16: 677-715.

LUCE, R. (1924) *Legislative Assemblies.* Boston: Houghton Mifflin.

MACIVER, R. M. (1947) *The Web of Government.* New York: Macmillan.

MACRAE, D., Jr. (1958) *Dimensions of Congressional Voting.* Berkeley: U. of California Press.

——— (1967) *Parliament, Parties, and Society in France, 1946-1958.* New York: St. Martin's.

——— (1970) *Issues and Parties in Legislative Voting: Methods of Statistical Analysis.* New York: Harper and Row.

MACRIDIS, R. C. and BROWN, B. E. (1960) *The de Gaulle Republic.* Homewood, IL: Dorsey.

MANLEY, J. F. (1970) *The Politics of Finance: The House Committee on Ways and Means.* Boston: Little, Brown.

MARVICK, D., [ed.] (1961) Political Decision-Makers. Glencoe, IL: Free Press.

———[ed.] (1977) *Harold D. Lasswell on Political Sociology.* Chicago: U. of Chicago Press.

MATTHEWS, D. R. (1954) *The Social Background of Political Decision-Makers.* Garden City, NY: Doubleday.

——— (1960) *U.S. Senators and their World. Chapel Hill, NC: U. of North Carolina Press.*

——— and STIMSON, J. A. *(1975) Yeas and Nays: Normal Decision-Making in the U.S. House of Representatives.* New York: John Wiley.

MAYHEW, D. R. (1966) *Party Loyalty Among Congressmen.* Cambridge, MA: Harvard U. Press.

McPHEE, W. N. and GLASER, W. E. (1962) *Public Opinion and Congressional Elections.* New York: Free Press.

MEEHAN, E. J. (1967) *Contemporary Political Thought.* Homewood, IL: Dorsey.

McCLOSKY, H. (1964) "Consensus and ideology in American politics." *Amer. Pol. Sci. Rev.* 58: 361-382.

McKEAN, D. D. (1938) *Pressures on the Legislature of New Jersey.* New York: Columbia U. Press.

MELLER, N. (1960) "Legislative behavior research." *West. Pol. Q.* 13: 131-153.

——— (1965) "Legislative behavior research." *West. Pol. Q.* 18: 776-793.

——— (1969) *The Congress of Micronesia.* Honolulu: U. of Hawaii Press.

MERZ, J. T. (1896) *A History of European Thought in the Nineteenth Century.* Edinburgh.

MILL, J. (1937) *An Essay on Government.* New York: Cambridge U. Press.

MILNE, R. S. and MACKENZIE, H. C. (1955) "The floating vote." *Pol. Studies* 3: 65-68, in R. Rose (ed.) *Studies in British Politics.* New York: St. Martin's.

MILBRATH, L. W. (1963) *The Washington Lobbyists.* Chicago: Rand McNally.

MILLER, W. E. (1964) "Majority rule and the representative system of government," in E. Allardt and Y. Littunen, *Cleavages, Ideologies and Party Systems.* Transactions of the Westermarck Society, Helsinki.

——— (1977) "Private communication." June 14, 1977.

——— and STOKES, D. E. (1963) "Constituency influence in Congress." *Amer. Pol. Sci. Rev.* 57: 45-56; reprinted in Campbell et al., *Elections and the Political Order,* 1966: 351-372.

MORROW, W. L. (1969) *Congressional Committees.* New York: Charles Scribner's.

MULLER, E. N. (1970) "The representation of citizens by political authorities: consequences for regime support." *Amer. Pol. Sci. Rev.* 64: 1149-1166.

MUNGER, F. J. and FENNO, R. F., Jr. (1962) *National Politics and Federal Aid to Education.* Syracuse: Syracuse U. Press.

NADEL, S. F. (1957) *The Theory of Social Structure.* Glencoe, IL: Free Press.

NAROLL, R. (1968) "Some thoughts on comparative method in cultural anthropology," in H. M. Blalock,Jr. and A. B. Blalock (eds.) *Methodology in Social Research.* New York: McGraw-Hill.

NOELLE, E. and NEUMANN, E. P. (1958-1964) *Jahrbuch für Offentliche Meinung*. Allensbach and Bonn: Verlag für Demoskopie.

NOPONEN, M. (1964) *Kansanedustajien Sosiaalinen Tausta Suomessa*. Helinski.

NORTHROP, F.S.C. (1947) *The Logic of the Sciences and the Humanities*. New York: Macmillan.

NYHOLM, P. (1961) *Suomen Eduskuntaryhmien Koheesio*. Helsinki.

OLSON, M.,Jr. (1965) *The Logic of Collective Action*. Cambridge, MA: Harvard U. Press.

PACKENHAM, R. A. (1970) "Legislatures and political development," in A. Kornberg and L. Musolf (eds.) *Legislatures in Developmental Perspective*. Durham, NC: Duke U. Press.

PARSONS, T. (1951) *The Social System*. New York: Free Press.

PATEMAN, C. (1970) *Participation and Democratic Theory*. Cambridge, MA: Cambridge, U. Press.

PATTERSON, J. T. (1967) *Congressional Conservatism and the New Deal: The Growth of the Conservative Coalition in Congress, 1933-1939*. Lexington: University of Kentucky Press.

PATTERSON, S. C. (1959) "Patterns of interpersonal relations in a state legislative group: the Wisconsin assembly." *Pub. Opinion Q.* 23: 101-109.

——— (1967) *Midwest Legislative Politics*. Iowa City: Institute of Public Affairs, U. of Iowa.

——— (1968a) *American Legislative Behavior*. Princeton, NJ: Van Nostrand.

——— (1968b) "Comparative legislative behavior: a review essay." *Midw. J. of Pol. Sci.* 12: 599-616.

——— BOYNTON, G. R. and HEDLUND, R. D. (1969) "Perceptions and expectations of the legislative and support for it." *Amer. J. of Sociol.* 75: 62-76.

PATTERSON, S. C., HEDLUND, R. D. and BOYNTON, G. R. (1975) *Representatives and Represented: Bases of Public Support for the American Legislatures*. New York: John Wiley.

PEABODY R. L. (1967) "Party leadership change in the United States House of Representatives." *Amer. Pol. Sci. Rev.* 61: 675-693.

——— (1969) "Research on Congress: a coming of age," in R. K. Huitt and R. L. Peabody (eds.) *Congress: Two Decades of Analysis*. New York: Harper and Row.

PEABODY, R. L. and POLSBY, N. W. [ed.] (1969) *New Perspectives on the House of Representatives*. Chicago: Rand McNally.

PEDERSEN, M. N. (1967) "Consensus and conflict in the Danish Folketing, 1945-1965." *Scandinavian Political Studies* 2: 143-166.

PENNOCK, J. R. (1968) "Political representation: an overview," in J. R. Pennock and J. W. Chapman (eds.) *Representation*. New York: Atherton.

——— and CHAPMAN, J. W. [eds.] (1968) *Representation*. New York: Atherton.

PETERSON, P. E. (1970) "Forms of representation: participation of the poor in the community action program." *Amer. Pol. Sci. Rev.* 64: 491-507.

PITKIN, H. F. (1967) *The Concept of Representation*. Berkeley: U. of California Press.

——— (1961) *The Theory of Representation*. Ph.D. dissertation, University of California, Berkeley.

PLAMENATZ, J. (1958) "Electoral studies and democratic theory: I. a British view." *Political Studies* 6: 1-15.

POLSBY, N. W. (1964) *Congress and the Presidency*. Englewood Cliffs, NJ: Prentice-Hall.

——— (1968) "The institutionalization of the U.S. House of Representatives." *Amer. Pol. Sci. Rev.* 62: 144-168.

———— (1975) "Legislatures," in F. I. Greenstein and N. W. Polsby (eds.) *Handbook of Political Science,* Vol. 5. Reading, MA: Addison-Wesley Publishing Company.

————, GALLAHER, M. and RUNDQUIST, B. S. (1969) "The growth of the seniority system in the U.S. House of Representatives." *Amer. Pol. Sci. Rev.* 63: 787-807.

POPPER, K. R. (1945) *The Open Society and its Enemies.* London: Routledge and Kegan Paul.

PRESSMAN, J. L. (1966) *House vs. Senate: Conflict in the Appropriations Process.* New Haven, CT: Yale U. Press.

PREWITT, K. (1965) "Political socialization and leadership selection." *Annals of the Amer. Acad. of Pol. and Soc. Sci.* 361: 96-111.

———— (1970) *The Citizen-Politician: A Study of Leadership Selection.* Indianapolis: Bobbs-Merrill.

———— and EULAU, H. (1969) "Political matrix and political representation: prolegomenon to a new departure from an old problem." *Amer. Pol. Sci. Rev.* 63: 427-441.

PROTHO, J. W. and GRIGG, C. M. (1960) "Fundamental principles of democracy: bases of agreement and disagreement." *J. of Politics* 22: 276-294.

PRZEWORSKI, A. and TEUNE, H. (1970) *The Logic of Comparative Social Inquiry.* New York: John Wiley.

PYE, L. W. (1966) *Aspects of Political Development.* Boston: Little, Brown.

RAE, D. (1967) *The Political Consequences of Electoral Laws.* New Haven, CT: Yale U. Press.

REPASS, D. E. (1971) "Issue salience and party choice." *Amer. Pol. Sci. Rev.* 65: 389-400.

RICE, S. A. (1925) "The behavior of legislative groups." *Pol. Sci. Q.* 40: 60-72.

RICHARDS, P. G. (1970) *Parliament and Conscience.* London.

RIDDLE, D. H. (1964) *The Truman Committee: A Study in Congressional Responsibility.* New Bruswick: Rutgers U. Press.

RIESELBACH, L. N. (1966) *The Roots of Isolationism.* Indianapolis: Bobbs-Merrill.

RIKER, W. H. (1958) "The paradox of voting and congressional rules for voting on amendments." *Amer. Pol. Sci. Rev.* 52: 349-366.

———— (1959) "A method for determining the significance of roll-call votes in voting bodies," in J. C. Wahlke and H. Eulau (eds.) *Legislative Behavior.* Glencoe, IL: Free Press.

RIPLEY, R. B. (1967) *Party Leaders in the House of Representatives.* Washington, D.C.: Brookings.

———— (1969a) *Power in the Senate.* New York: St. Martin's.

———— (1969b) *Majority Party Leadership in Congress.* Boston: Little, Brown.

ROBINSON, J. A. (1963) *The House Rules Committee.* Indianapolis: Bobbs-Merrill.

———— (1967) *Congress and Foreign Policy-Making.* Homewood, IL: Dorsey.

ROSENBERG, M. (1968) *The Logic of Survey Research.* New York: Basic Books.

ROSENTHAL, H. (1969) "The electoral politics of Gaullists in the fourth French Republic: ideology or constituency interest?" *Amer. Pol. Sci. Rev.* 63: 476-487.

ROTHMAN, D. J. (1966) *Politics and Power: The United States Senate, 1869-1901.* Cambridge, MA: Harvard U. Press.

SABINE, G. H. (1937) A History of Political Theory. New York: Holt.

SAIT, E. M. (1938) *Political Institutions: A Preface.* New York: Appleton-Century-Crofts.

SALISBURY, R. H. (1968) "The analysis of public policy: a search for theories and roles," in A. Ranney (ed.) *Political Science and Public Policy.* Chicago: Markham.

SALOMA, J. S., III (1969) *Congress and the New Politics.* Boston: Little, Brown.

SARTORI, G. (1958) "Electoral studies and democratic theory: II. a continental view." *Pol. Stud.* 6: 1-15.

SARTORI, G. (1963) *Il Parlemento Italiano, 1946-1963.* Naples: Edizioni Scientifiche Italiano.

SCHATTSCHNEIDER, E. E. (1935) *Politics, Pressures and the Tariff.* New York: Prentice-Hall.

——— (1960) The Semisovereign People. New York: Holt, Rinehart and Winston.

SCHLESINGER, J. (1966) *Ambition and Politics.* Chicago: Rand McNally.

SCHUMPETER, J. A. (1942) *Caplitalism, Socialism, and Democracy.* New York: Harper and Brothers.

SCOTT, A. M. and HUNT, M. A. (1966) *Congress and Lobbies: Image and Reality.* Chapel Hill: U. of North Carolina Press.

SHANNON, W. W. (1968) *Party, Constituency and Congressional Voting: A Study of Legislative Behavior in the United States House of Representatives.* Baton Rouge, LA: Louisiana State U. Press.

SHARKANSKY, I. (1969) *The Politics of Taxing and Spending.* Indianapolis: Bobbs-Merrill.

SHOWELL, M. (1953) "Political consciousness and attitudes in the State of Washington." *Publ. Opinion Q.* 17: 394-400.

SIGMUND, P. E. (1963) *Nicholas of Cusa and Medieval Political Thought.* Cambridge, MA: Harvard U. Press.

SILBEY, J. H. (1967) *The Shrine of the Party: Congressional Voting Behavior, 1841-1852.* Pittsburgh: U. of Pittsburgh Press.

SIMON, H. A. (1957) *Models of Man.* New York: John Wiley.

SINGHVI, L. M. (1970) "Parliament in the Indian political system," in A. Kornberg and L.D. Musolf (eds.), *Legislatures in Developmental Perspective.* Durham, NC: Duke U. Press.

SMITH, T. V. (1938) "Two functions of the American state legislator." *Ann. Am. Acad. Pol. Sci.* 195: 183-188.

SNOWISS, L. M. (1966) "Congressional recruitment and representation." *Amer. Pol. Sci. Rev.* 60: 627-639.

SORAUF, F. J. (1963) *Party and Representation.* Englewood Cliffs, NJ: Prentice-Hall.

STAUFFER, R. B. (1970) "Congress in the Philippine political system," in A. Kornberg and L. D. Musolf (eds.), *Legislatures in Developmental Perspective.* Durham, NC: Duke U. Press.

STOKES, D. E. (1963) "Spatial models of party competition." *Amer. Pol. Sci. Rev.* 57: 368-377.

STOKES, D. E. and MILLER, W. E. (1962) "Party government and the saliency of Congress." *Public Opinion Q.* 26: 531-546; Reprinted in Campbell et al., 1966: 194-211.

STONE, W. J. (1976) *Representation in the United States House of Representatives.* Unpublished Ph.D. dissertation, University of Michigan.

STOUFFER, S. A. (1962) "Some observations on study design," in S. A. Stouffer *Social Research to Test Ideas.* New York: Free Press.

SUNDQUIST, J. L. (1968) *Politics and Policy: The Eisenhower, Kennedy, and Johnson Years.* Washington, D.C.: Brookings.

——— (1969) *Making Federalism Work: A Study of Program Coordination at the Community Level.* Washington, D.C.: Brookings.

TACHERON, D. G. and UDALL, M. K. (1970) *The Job of the Congressman.* Indianapolis: Bobbs-Merrill.

TEGGART, F. J. (1960) *Theory and Processes of History.* Berkeley: U. of California Press.

THOMPSON, D. F. (1970) *The Democratic Citizen: Social Science and Democratic Theory in the Twentieth Century.* Cambridge, MA: Cambridge U. Press.

TRUMAN, D. (1959) *The Congressional Party: A Case Study.* New York: John Wiley.

TRUMAN, D. B. (1966) "The representative function in Western systems," in E. H. Buehrig (ed.) *Essays in Political Science.* Bloomington: Indiana U. Press.

TURNER, J. (1951) *Party and Constituency: Pressures on Congress.* Baltimore: Johns Hopkins.

——— and SCHNEIER, E. V., Jr. (1970) *Party and Constituency.* Baltimore: Johns Hopkins.

VERBA, S. et al. (1967) "Public opinion and the war in Vietnam." *Amer. Pol. Sci. Rev.* 61: 317-333.

——— and NIE, N. H. (1972) *Participation in America: Political Democracy and Social Equality.* New York: Harper and Row.

VOEGELIN, E. (1952) *The New Science of Politics.* Chicago: U. of Chicago Press.

VOLKART, E. [ed.] (1951) *Social Behavior and Personality: Contributions of W. I. Thomas to Theory and Social Research.* New York: Social Science Research Council.

VON GIERKE, O. (1939) *The Development of Political Theory.* New York: Norton.

VON RANKE, L. (1877) *Sammtliche Werke.* Leipzig.

WAHLKE, J. C. (1962) "Behavioral analysis of representative bodies," in A. Ranney (ed.) *Essays on the Behavioral Study of Politics.* Urbana, IL: 173-190.

——— (1971) "Policy demands and system support: the role of the represented." *Brit. J. of Pol. Sci.* 1: 271-290.

——— and EULAU, H., [eds.] (1959) *Legislative Behavior: A Reader in Theory and Research.* Glencoe, IL: Free Press.

——— BUCHANAN, W. and FERGUSON, L. C. (1961) "The annals of research: a case of collaboration in comparative study of legislative behavior." *Amer. Behavioral Scientist* 4 (May): 3-9.

——— (1962) *The Legislative System: Explorations in Legislative Behavior.* New York: John Wiley.

WALKER, J. L. (1966) "A critique of the elitist theory of democracy," *Amer. Pol. Sci. Rev.* 60: 285-295.

——— (1969) "The diffusion of innovations among the American states." *Amer. Pol. Sci. Rev.* 63: 880-899.

WALLACE, R. A. (1960) *Congressional Control of Federal Spending.* Detroit: Wayne State U. Press.

WILDAVSKY, A. (1964) *The Politics of the Budgetary Process.* Boston: Little, Brown.

WILSON, W. (1885) *Congressional Government.* Boston: Houghton Mifflin.

WOLFINGER, R. E. [ed.] (1970) *Readings on Congress.* Englewood Cliffs, NJ: Prentice-Hall.

——— and HEIFETZ, J. (1965) "Safe seats, seniority, and power in Congress." *Amer. Pol. Sci. Rev.* 59: 337-349.

WOODWARD, J. L. and ROPER, E. (1950) "The political activity of American citizens." Amer. Pol. Sci. Rev. 44: 872-885.

YOUNG, J. (1966) *The Washington Community, 1800-1828.* New York: Columbia U. Press.

YOUNG, R. (1936) *This is Congress.* New York: Knopf.

ZELLER, B. (1937) *Pressure Politics in New York.* New York: Prentice-Hall.

ZEIGLER, H. and BAER, M. (1969) *Lobbying: Interaction and Influence in American State Legislatures.* Belmont, CA: Wadsworth.

ZEIGLER, L. H. and JENNINGS, M. K. (1974) *Governing American Schools,* No. Scituate, MA: Duxbury.

ZOLNHOFER, W. (1965) "Parteiidentifizierung in der Bundesrepublik und den Vereinigten Staaten," in E. K. Scheuch and R. Wildenman (eds.) *Zur Soziologie der Wahl.* Koln: Westdeutscher Verlag.

INDICES

Name Index

Subject Index

ABOUT THE AUTHORS

HEINZ EULAU holds the endowed William Bennett Munro professorship of political science and is a senior fellow of the Hoover Institution at Stanford University. He received his Ph.D. at the University of California (Berkeley) in 1941. After serving in wartime Washington he was an editor of *The New Republic* and taught at Antioch College. He has been a fellow of the Social Science Research Council and of the Center for Advanced Study in the Behavioral Sciences. In 1972 he was elected fellow of the Academy of Arts and Sciences. A past president of the American Political Science Association, he is now chairperson of the Board of Overseers of the National Election Studies at the Center for Political Studies, University of Michigan, and an associate director of the Inter-University Consortium for Political and Social Research. Professor Eulau has served as the associate editor for political science of the *International Encylcopaedia of the Social Sciences* and general editor of the *International Yearbook for Political Behavior Research.* He is a member of the editorial boards of the *American Journal of Political Science, American Politics Quarterly, Legislative Studies Quarterly,* and *Experimental Study of Politics.* Professor Eulau is the author of *The Legislative System,* with Wahlke, Buchanan and Ferguson (1962), *Class and Party in the Eisenhower Years* (1962), *The Behavioral Persuasion in Politics* (1963), *Journeys in Politics* (1963), *Lawyers in Politics,* with J.C. Sprague (1964), *Micro-Macro Political Analysis* (1969), *State Officials and Higher Education,* with H. Quinley (1970), *Labyrinths of Democracy,* with K. Prewitt (1973), and *Technology and Civility* (1977). His edited books include *Political Behavior,* with Eldersveld and Janowitz (1956), *Legislative Behavior,* with Wahlke (1959), *Political Behavior in America* (1966), and *Behavioralism in Political Science* (1969). He also edited, with James G. March, *Political Science* (1969), the report of the Political Science Panel of the Behavioral and Social Sciences Survey, National Research Council.

JOHN C. WAHLKE is professor of political science at the University of Iowa. He received his Ph.D. from Harvard University in 1952. He has taught at Amherst College, Vanderbilt University and the State University of New York at Buffalo and at Stony Brook. He has also been visiting legislative research professor at the University of California (Berkeley), a resident fellow at the Netherlands Institute for Advanced Study in the Humanities and Social Sciences, and a lecturer in the Nice Seminar in Political and Social Science. He has been chairperson of the Council of the Inter-University Consortium for Political and Social Research and president of the Midwest Political Science Association. During 1977-1978 he served as president of the American Political Science Association. He is a member of the editorial board of the *American Journal of Political Science*. Dr. Wahlke's previous publications include *The Causes of the American Revolution* (1950, 1962, 1973), *Loyalty in a Democratic State* (1952), *The Legislative System*, with H. Eulau, W. Buchanan, and L. C. Ferguson (1962), *Legislative Behavior*, edited with Eulau (1959), *Government and Politics: An Introduction to Political Science*, with A. N. Dragnich (1966, 1971), *The American Political System*, edited with B. E. Brown (1967, 1971), and *Comparative Legislative Behavior*, edited with S. C. Patterson (1972).